VISIBLE CITIES,
GLOBAL COMICS

VISIBLE CITIES, GLOBAL COMICS

URBAN IMAGES AND SPATIAL FORM

BENJAMIN FRASER

University Press of Mississippi • Jackson

The University Press of Mississippi is the scholarly publishing agency of
the Mississippi Institutions of Higher Learning: Alcorn State University,
Delta State University, Jackson State University, Mississippi State University,
Mississippi University for Women, Mississippi Valley State University,
University of Mississippi, and University of Southern Mississippi.

www.upress.state.ms.us

Designed by Peter D. Halverson

The University Press of Mississippi is a member of
the Association of University Presses.

First printing 2019
∞

Library of Congress Cataloging-in-Publication Data

Names: Fraser, Benjamin. author.
Title: Visible cities, global comics: urban images and spatial form /
    Benjamin Fraser.
Description: Jackson: University Press of Mississippi, [2019] | "First
    printing 2019." | Includes bibliographical references and index. |
    Identifiers: LCCN 2019011953 (print) | LCCN 2019020239 (ebook) | ISBN
    9781496825056 (epub single) | ISBN 9781496825063 (epub institutional) |
    ISBN 9781496825070 (pdf single) | ISBN 9781496825025 (pdf institutional)
    | ISBN 9781496825032 (cloth) | ISBN 9781496825049 (pbk.)
Subjects: LCSH: Comic books, strips, etc.—History and criticism. | Graphic
    novels—History and criticism. | Cities and towns in literature. | Public
    spaces in literature.
Classification: LCC PN6714 (ebook) | LCC PN6714 .F74 2019 (print) | DDC
    741.5/358209732—dc23
LC record available at https://lccn.loc.gov/2019011953

British Library Cataloging-in-Publication Data available

CONTENTS

ACKNOWLEDGMENTS

Visible Cities represents an unusual situation for me as an author. This was the first time that I received a contract for a single-authored manuscript without having first delivered a draft of the complete manuscript to a publisher. For this unexpected result, I am indebted to Vijay Shah, acquisitions editor for comics studies at the University Press of Mississippi. I thank him for questions and suggestions that pushed me toward realizing the book's current approach. At the time of submitting the proposal for this monograph, I had been working for over a decade on themes of urban cultural studies. Yet the idea that I would have something to say about urban comics in particular was a more recent notion. I was more sure in this case than I had been with any other book that a contract would prove elusive. I believed that much of the difficulty would come from crossing the disciplinary boundary of Hispanic studies. Another factor was the matter of my being a relative newcomer to studying the ninth art. I first published an article on comics in 2012. As I write this in 2018, I do not feel any less like a beginner. I continue to be fascinated by what comics artists are able to do on the page. This book was an opportunity to continue searching for adequate theories and words to explain this fascination.

Having a contract in hand was unusual for me, and I approached research and writing in a new way. I wrote about one comics artist while researching the next. The table of contents changed many times as I thought about new ways to organize the book. Along the way I confirmed certain suspicions. One was the idea that existing research into the work of global comics artists frequently lags behind the translation of their work into English. Even when artists have been familiar to English readers for decades—as in the cases of Joost Swarte and Mark Beyer, for instance—extended reflections of their works by comics scholars can still prove to be particularly scarce. Where academic criticism in English is less than plentiful regarding a certain artist or their work,

I sometimes turn to criticism published in Spanish, French, Portuguese and Catalan or, to the degree possible, other languages. I rely also on interviews or book reviews where possible and relevant. I draw on existing close analyses of comics texts where they can be found, supplying my own interpretations wherever possible. Because I am specifically concerned with an urban analysis of the comics under study in this book, I sometimes present existing analyses in a descriptive or historical mode before advancing my original interpretations. At other times, I cite and adapt previous analyses to square with my own, and to better highlight a given theoretical insight drawn from the interdisciplinary field of urban studies.

The material in this book represents completely new writing. That said, part of chapter 5 returns to and cites material originally published in Spanish as Benjamin Fraser and Claudia Méndez, "Espacio, tiempo y ciudad: La representación de Buenos Aires en *El Eternauta*," *Revista Iberoamericana* 78.238–39: 57–72. Similarly, part of chapter 4 returns to and cites material originally published as Benjamin Fraser, "Comics Art, Urban Cultural Studies Method and Chris Ware's *Building Stories* (2012)." *Journal of Urban Cultural Studies* 3.3: 291–99.

In all of my work on comics I am indebted primarily to scholars from Hispanic studies who have offered pioneering studies on the ninth art in article- or book-length form: David William Foster, Howard Fraser, Anne Magnussen, Ana Merino, Joanna Page, Pedro Pérez del Solar, Charles Tatum, Steven Torres, and Teresa Vilarós. I thank my colleagues at the University of Arizona for welcoming me into the Department of Spanish and Portuguese and the College of Humanities. I would not have finished this project without the material support of COH Dean Alain-Philippe Durand. Thanks as always go to Malcolm Compitello, Susan Larson, Araceli Masterson-Algar, Steven Spalding, and Stephen Vilaseca for modeling superb interdisciplinary scholarship dedicated to the urban humanities. In addition, Eugenia Afinoguénova, Agustín Cuadrado, Rebecca Haidt, Sheri Spaine Long, Mark Del Mastro, Bill Nichols, Randolph Pope, and Michael Ugarte have provided me with encouragement and support, in ways great and small, for which I am extremely grateful.

FOR ABBY

VISIBLE CITIES, GLOBAL COMICS

INTRODUCTION

Visible Cities, Global Comics: Urban Images and Spatial Form explores representations of the city in a selection of comics from across the globe. This research monograph accomplishes two interrelated goals. First, it brings insights from urban theory to bear on specific comics texts, and second, it uses comics texts to elucidate themes of urbanism, architecture, planning, and the cultures of cities. In the process, each chapter introduces readers to specific comics artists and texts and investigates a range of matters pertaining to the medium's spatial form, stylistic variation, and cultural prominence.

Following an urban cultural studies approach to the medium of comics, the chapters in this book give equal weight to what cultural studies pioneer Raymond Williams once called "the project" (or, art) and "the formation" (or, society).[1] Adapting this premise to study the culture(s) of cities, comics are approached here as an artistic form to be understood in the context of an urbanizing society. At the same time, however, each chapter emphasizes the artistry of the comics medium, paying close attention to structural and spatial elements of the form, such as panel composition and transitions, word and thought balloons, page layouts, and other formal aspects or elements of graphic style. The point is not to suggest that global comics generally deal with the urban in the same way. In fact, comics may deal with the city as an idea, a historical fact, a social construction, a concrete built environment, a shared space forged from the collective imagination, or a social arena navigated according to one's personal desire. The organization of the book into thematic units allows for implicit and explicit points of comparison to emerge within and across its five chapters.

Visible Cities is best seen as an urban contribution to an interdisciplinary phase in comics studies. Much work has already been directed toward establishing the basis for the study of comics and graphic novels as an autonomous field, as can be seen in the publication of *A Comics Studies Reader* (2009), edited by Jeet Heer and Kent Worchester. A number of scholars, however, assert the relevance of comics to a range of interdisciplinary formations and topics pertinent to critical theory. Recent books, for example, connect comics with themes of gender studies, autobiographical narrative, disability studies, and black identity: *Straight from the Heart: Gender, Intimacy, and the Cultural Production of Shojo Manga* (2011), by Jennifer Sally Prough; *Autobiographical Comics: Life Writing in Pictures* (2012), by Elisabeth El Refaie; *Death, Disability and the Superhero: The Silver Age and Beyond* (2014), by José Alaniz; and *The Blacker the Ink: Constructions of Black Identity in Comics and Sequential Art* (2015), by Frances Gatewood and John Jennings. Importantly, there is also growing recognition of global traditions, as evidenced by scholarly books on Latino, Italian, French, Japanese, and Russian comics—all available from the publishing line of the University Press of Mississippi. As an urban contribution to this interdisciplinary and global rethinking of comics traditions, the present book is interested in a wide range of thematic concerns: activism, architecture, alienation, city planning, colonialism, consumerism, crime, disease transmission, everyday life, flânerie, gender, gentrification, the human senses, humor, industrialization, magical realism, memory, the monumental city, the mystery story, the occult, science fiction, sexual orientation, suburbanization, tactility, tenement housing, traffic, and working-class labor. It is significant that all of these themes are interrogated by way of their connections with the modern urban form.

Because of its varied subject matter, a book like this needs to strike a balance between descriptive, historical, analytical, and theoretical modes. Few readers will have knowledge of the full range of comics artists discussed in this volume. Area scholars with interests in a given linguistic or national context may know very little about cultural production outside of their chosen subdiscipline. Specialist scholars of the ninth art may be familiar with comics theory, but less so with urban theory. Those who are interested in urban themes may know very little about comics form. Different sets of readers may thus have very different expectations. Because this book is so interdisciplinary in its conception, I attempt to deliver a bit of what each reader may be hoping to find. There is an episodic quality to the way in which new comics texts are introduced in the chapters that follow. I generally begin with concise descriptions of global comics artists and their oeuvre, layer in some artistic background and relevant history, fold in a bit of close analysis, and add a dash or two of theory. This approach ensures that the majority of readers are never too far from something that will interest them.

It is important to address potential objections to this approach from the outset. Some readers will undoubtedly find the pace of this book's argumentation to be too brisk. This brisk pace, however, is necessary if we are to sustain a focus on broader trends in the urban representations of comics. Others may find the sheer quantity of information and the range of thematic variations presented here to be overwhelming. I insist, however, that the city is a necessarily broad topic, one that cannot be narrowed without sacrificing its essential trait of multiplicity. I suppose that those readers who are more curious about some comics artists than others could also jump to the sections of the book that interest them most. I see no harm in treating this book as a compendium of sorts. Still other readers may rightly point out that the material in this book is far from realizing an exhaustive treatment of the city in comics. I would respond to this objection with equal skepticism—one can never, in my view, exhaust the meanings of the urban experience. In each of the potential reactions I have just listed there is something justifiable. More curious, however, they can also be understood as echoes of urban discourse. That is, the pace of urban life has appreciably quickened in our modern cities. The density of the urban social form itself has historically overstimulated the human senses. Cities also bring into being forms of social complexity that ultimately prove difficult for the individual to grasp through narrow categorizations. In the end, this book is not meant to be exhaustive or encyclopedic. Instead, it seeks to contextualize, globalize, and theorize that subset of comics that delve deeply into the vastness of the urban experience.

THEORIZING URBAN COMICS

As a contribution to contemporary traditions of urban cultural studies research, this book emphasizes the importance of geography for comics studies and underscores the value of the cultural turn in urban research. In essence, I seek to connect two contemporary turns in spatial research that have unfolded in the second decade of the twenty-first century. Geographers have been turning more and more toward the humanities, as indicated by texts such as *GeoHumanities: Art, History, Text at the Edge of Place* (2011) and *Envisioning Landscapes, Making Worlds: Geography and the Humanities* (2011).[2] In the same way, scholars in the humanities have been increasingly adopting spatial and geographical methods, as evidenced by volumes such as *The Spatial Humanities: GIS and the Future of Scholarship* (2010) and *Deep Maps and Spatial Narratives* (2015).[3] Moreover, academic journals created in the second decade of the twenty-first century, such as the *Journal of Urban Cultural Studies* (2014–) and *Geo-Humanities* (2015–), have provided new publication venues for this type of discipline-crossing scholarship on art, space, landscape, and cities. The study of cities in all their complexity increasingly requires that scholars blend methods from the social sciences and the humanities.

In theoretical terms, this book builds on increasing general interest in the urban and spatial aspects of comics. The recent publication of scholarly edited volumes such as *Comic Book Geographies* (2014) by Jason Dittmer and *Comics and the City* (2010) by Jörn Ahrens and Arno Meteling indicates that a move is under way to forge stronger connections between comics and spatial theory.[4] These texts assert the value of geographical perspectives for the ninth art. In essence, they build upon a remark by a noted comics theorist. In an article published in the journal *European Comic Art* in 2008, Thierry Groensteen wrote that "semiotics, history and sociology are, it seems, the three major academic disciplines brought into play by the study of comics."[5] Along with semiotics, history, and sociology, however, the discipline of urban geography must also be seen as crucial for the development of comics studies. Acknowledging the importance of matters of space/place for artistic forms—including the spatial medium of comics and graphic novels—fosters further contributions to the interdisciplinary field of urban studies.

This book invokes a somewhat cohesive tradition of urban thinkers in order to explore how cities are represented in comics. Spatial thinkers who are concerned with the contradictions of urban form constitute the main axis of this tradition: Raymond Williams, David Harvey, Andy Merrifield, Jane Jacobs, Georg Simmel, Walter Benjamin, Lewis Mumford, for example, and perhaps most of all, Henri Lefebvre. A common thread running through this volume is urban theorist Lefebvre's question: Who has *the right to the city?* Lefebvre's oft-cited refrain from *Le droit à la ville* (*The Right to the City*) (1968) underscores that the urban is a collective project. As such, the implication is that the city should belong to those who inhabit it. Globally speaking, this is very seldom the case. As explored by the French thinker in works such as *La Révolution urbaine* (*The Urban Revolution*) (1970), the reproduction of modern city form is governed disproportionately by a special class of urban planners, speculators, and capitalists. Significantly, Lefebvre's theory of the urban phenomenon drew from the thought of Jane Jacobs and heavily influenced David Harvey's work, arguing that aesthetic matters deserved more attention, and that the cultures of cities were far more than mere superstructural concerns for the strategies of modern capitalist urbanization. It comes as no surprise that readers of global comics must continuously confront the spatial and social inequity that drives production of the urban form. Whether individual comics deal with city referents that are real or fictional, they nonetheless use representational, artistic, and narrative strategies to comment on the nature of modern urban life. In doing so these comics are implicated in the wider urban imagination of a global society that fashions concrete spaces of the city in response to certain power dynamics. Using the tools pertinent to the ninth art, comics artists necessarily comment on the way social power drives the structure of the city, resulting in the exclusion of certain groups and certain ideas. In the right hands, the visual structure of the comics page thus becomes a way of exposing, questioning, critiquing and perhaps even correcting this systematic urban imbalance.

Though this is the first scholarly monograph on global urban representations in the ninth art, I am greatly indebted to previous book publications that have paved the way. The two edited volumes mentioned above are crucial for understanding the interconnection of space, cities, and comics. In *Comic Book Geographies*, Jason Dittmer acknowledges that space has been explored somewhat thoroughly in comics by thinkers such as McCloud, Groensteen, Charles Hatfield, and Douglas Wolk, a list to which one must certainly add Pascal Lefèvre. In truth, theorizations of panel space, page space, spatial relationships between nonadjacent images, and the like are the bedrock of contemporary comics studies. In the introduction to *Comics and the City*, Ahrens and Meteling write, "From an historical point of view and against the backdrop of the modern age, comics are inseparably tied to the notion of the 'city.'"[6] They intend this, in part, as an affirmation that the contemporary comic was an expression of an urbanized consciousness, though they do not use this term explicitly. This idea is important, but it is not necessarily new. Already the authors of *A History of the Comic Strip* (1968) had written definitively, "The world of the comics [. . .] is an urban world."[7] In their chosen visual medium, comics artists have long been thinking through what it means to live in urban modernity. Similarly, scholarship has long recognized the urban backdrop of comics, at least implicitly. What is new, however, is the push—initiated by Ahrens, Meteling, Dittmer, and the contributors to their respective edited volumes—to explore this idea explicitly and thoroughly, and moreover, by invoking the breadth and depth of urban studies scholarship. *Visible Cities* is conceived as a further contribution to this trend.

There are three aspects of the connection between cities and comics that deserve mention in this introduction: subject matter, artistic form, and method of production. First, the city becomes a privileged subject of comics. Second, the panel-and-gutter structure of comic strips, in particular, reflects the way in which art was impacted by tropes of linearity and rational planning that were themselves synonymous with the urban form. Third, the mass production of comics showcases its links with forms of industrialization that are urban in origin. Initially, it is necessary to present each of these as if it were discrete from the others, though in the chapters of this book all three become entangled as we undertake a journey that will carry us through a range of global urban comics.

Subject matter seems a relatively straightforward consideration. On the drawn comics page, the city becomes an iconic expression of modernity in comics. In this sense, the development of the ninth art parallels what happens in various other forms of visual media. One can make the argument that painting was famously impacted by the modern urban form, for example, as seen in the depiction of city scenes in work by the Impressionists. When the cinema appeared at the dawn of the twentieth century, works by many of its most revered practitioners revealed a similar urban influence, for example, as seen in the scenes of everyday urban life captured by the Lumière brothers in Paris or Fructuós Gelabert in Barcelona. As the first two chapters of *Visible Cities* explore, the fascination of contemporary comics with the city as an image can be traced back to eighteenth-century engravings, nineteenth-century drawings in sequence, and twentieth-century woodcut novels. Comics artists from these periods brought the shifting urban world they saw all around them to life on the page. It is important to recognize that the timing of these developments is no coincidence. As the chapters of this book bear out, it is precisely during this time that the modern discourse of urbanism took root.

This book's focus on visual representations of the city in comics must be seen in both of two ways: from an urban cultural studies perspective and from a comics studies perspective. Following from the concise examples of painting and cinema given above, an urban cultural studies perspective understands the fascination of comics with the city as part of the modern urban form's broader impact on social and artistic trends. Yet this focus on the iconic properties of the ninth art is simultaneously important from the perspective of comics studies. There is growing support among comics theorists that the role of the image should be prioritized in our understanding of comics narration. This argument returns to cartoonist Rodolphe Töpffer's 1830s definition of the "comics album as 'a book that, addressed directly to the eyes, expresses itself through representation and not through narration.'"[8] Inspired by prioritization of the visual field expressed through Töpffer's definition, a whole tradition of contemporary comics theory is reasserting the primacy of the image.[9] This counteracts, to some degree, the assertion that comics are best defined as text-image combinations, as made by prominent comics scholars such as Scott McCloud (1993) and Will Eisner (2008). Thus, for some contemporary critics, comics are primarily a visual art form, and not necessarily a dual (text-image) art form.

Approaching the ninth art in this way is particularly revealing when it comes to the significance of city images. Urban comics foreground iconic signifiers that are already linked with contradictory social meaning. The city can be viewed as a triumphant expression of the values of modern society and thus as a sort of monument to the powerful social strata that construct it. It can be seen as an aestheticized object of beauty or a functional agglomeration of services. It is both the backdrop of the individual or social experience, and a privileged contributor to that experience. The goal of this book is to decipher how these various meanings inform a given comic. All of this rests, however, on the primacy of the image in the ninth art. Prioritizing the visual aspect of the comics medium makes it possible to underscore two points important for *Visible Cities* as a whole. First is the fact that the iconic representation—of, for example, city architecture, identifiable buildings, entire skylines and blocks, as well as the residue of specific urban plans—provides visual links with global urban environments. Every chapter in this volume emphasizes the significance of iconic urban comics representations, whether imagined or real, or some mix of the two, as is revealed in chapter 5. The second point is that comics can, through the representation of images alone, communicate and even narrate the urban experience. This point is most pronounced in chapter 2's exploration of the wordless novel tradition but is relevant also to investigations conducted in other chapters.

Artistic form is another important consideration that nonetheless tends to be undervalued in critical explorations of comics and space. As Dittmer's volume shows, there are multiple considerations implied in a spatial approach to comics. In his introduction Dittmer applies a media typology fashioned by Paul Adams to trace connections among space, place, and the comics medium.[10] Accordingly, there are four conceptual quadrants to consider: "space in comics," "place in comics," "comics in space," and "comics in place." Geographical space is an underappreciated but important consideration for understanding the work of comics artists. Yet geographical space is not the same thing as urban space. Urban space is, perhaps, a more specific beast. The artistic form of comics—or at least the form of comics most ingrained in the popular imagination, the strip—is not unrelated to social shifts driving increased urbanization. City images and the linearity of empaneled comics structure were interrelated expressions of an increasingly regularized and urbanized world. As discussed further in chapters 1 and 3, the rationalizing logic of urban planners manipulated the structure of cities to both constrain and make possible certain social interactions. Modern city plans created open spaces that served a dual function. They encouraged new forms of publicity through the design of wide boulevards and open squares. Yet such large-scale design also ensured that a modern police force could better quell uprisings and control dissent. At the same time, comics structure was developing into a linear form. Distilled from the more open format of the comics broadsheet tradition, the modern comic strip emphasized a rationalized and mechanical linear narrative structure. Typical examples would consist of three or four panels with a climax and resolution.

The drive toward regularization is thus common to both the construction of modern city blocks and comics panels. Common to both enterprises was a distinctly modern spatiality. Within the circuits of planning and design, a new conception of space arose. Space was a tool rather than an end in itself. Planners envisioned and produced a form of space that could be infinitely measured, partitioned, and designed to suit the needs of an ascendant social class. The notion that space could be a use-value for city dwellers was, histori-cally speaking, subjugated to the notion that space could serve the accumula-tion of power and control. These tensions are most visible in discussions carried out in chapters 2 and 3. Overall, *Visible Cities* approaches the city as a social form that enjoys an uneven geographical development. This means that there is no one approach to understanding the production and experience of city space that can be universally applied across the entire globe. The relationships between urbanites and their built environments vary substantially over time and space. Yet even so—to the degree that the social and material form of the city is increasingly subjected to planning, and to the degree that city planners in one urban area learn of and seek to replicate perceived successes from other urban areas—there are themes that emerge in global planning. As the chapters in this book suggest, nineteenth-century plans for Paris, carried out by Baron Haussmann, and twentieth-century plans for New York, carried out by Robert Moses and contested by Jane Jacobs, are paradigmatic examples that convey the brute power and key limitations of contemporary urban planning as a global social activity.

In the end, urban form is visible in comics not merely in the layout and punctuated beats of the regularized, linear strip format, but in a variety of other ways. As explored most directly in chapter 4 of this book, selected artists replicate aspects of urban form in the architectural organization of the comics page or the comics multiframe. Comics artists also use panel size and shape to replicate the urban form's role as a tool for shaping our experience of the city. As underscored in chapters 2 and 3, panel form can mimic urbanism in one of two ways. The panel frame sometimes represents the constraints placed upon the lives of city dwellers and their social alienation from one another, as in the case in some of Julie Doucet's work. Dispensing with the panel frame, however, can offer an ephemeral sense of freedom, as in some of Will Eisner's layouts. As explored throughout this book, other representational strategies pertinent to comics are equally important for artists who wish to convey insights into the key aspects of modern urban living. Simply put, artistic form is just as important as content in an urban reading of comics.

Perhaps most important, the urban as a theme does not merely offer iconic modern content or suggest innovations in artistic form on the page. The city is not solely an image or a layout strategy. Urban environments have also played a key role in fostering the circulation, growth, and reception of the ninth art. Embedded in urban circuits of cultural production, comics were, in many ways, the logical and representative cultural form of the modern city. A key assertion made in Ahrens and Meteling's edited volume is that the density and industry inherent in the modern city allowed newly organized forms of cultural production to emerge. As André Suhr's contribution to *Comics and the City* makes clear:

> When early "comics" appeared in newspapers for the first time, this coincided with the pinnacle of cultural modernity in the late nineteenth/early twentieth century, a time which finds its paradigmatic locus within the modern city. The parallel evolution of the modern city and comics is not a purely spatio-temporal coincidence—newspapers and thus comics were in fact a medium primarily located in cities.[11]

As explored in chapter 1 of *Visible Cities*, the incursion of comics into the Sunday pages of newspapers in New York was an important milestone in the development of the art form. Comics gained an expanded urban circulation through this exposure, and the content of comics even began to incorporate this burgeoning form of urban literacy in its represented content.[12]

The planned city was the product of a bourgeois modernity, which sought to rationalize the urban environment and maximize industrial productivity in the process. The attention given through planning to patterns of industrialized production also brought greater awareness of class issues. As noted later in this book, Will Eisner was himself known for pioneering an artist-owned version of the comics workshop, one that nevertheless could not fully expurgate the same forms of worker exploitation present in other mass-produced industrial processes. Modern comics artists have frequently been forced to work within what one critic calls "the constraints of a deeply commodified industry."[13] Perhaps most interesting, it is not at all uncommon for the ninth art to reference the collaborative forms of work that drove industrialized comics production in the first half of the twentieth century. In terms of the organization of labor involved, the production of comics sometimes mirrored patterns from other industries. It was not unusual for there to be a conveyer-belt style of production where the contributions of multiple roles would be integrated into a single process: for example, a writer, an artist, an inker, a colorist, and so on. Visual representations of such comics workshops are discussed in passing in chapters 2 and 4.

GLOBAL COMICS, GLOBAL READERSHIP

As a point of departure, I ask readers to accept that comics are a global phenomenon. This insight is supported by a wave of contemporary scholarship situating popular culture and the ninth art specifically within transnational flows of creation, distribution, and consumption.[14] As comics scholar John Lent points out in his foreword to *Transnational Perspectives on Graphic Narratives: Comics at the Crossroads* (2014), edited by Shane Denson, Christina Meyer, and Daniel Stein, it is useful to recognize many comics creators as transnational agents. The contents of many comics can be seen as representations of transnationalism, and many comics titles and characters are themselves transnational.[15] Describing the experience he had connecting with American superhero comics while surrounded by *bandes dessinées* in Paris, Derek Johnson reflects on "the privilege of being able to move about the globe and have my comic book culture physically move with me through a complex global network of distribution."[16] It is possible, as Katherine Kelp-Stebbins does in a 2018 publication, not only to interrogate comparisons between the work of Zeina Abirached, focused on life in Beirut, Lebanon, and Marjane Satrapi, depicting Tehran, Iran, but also to explore the reception of the artists' comics in Europe and the United States. Kelp-Stebbins underscores that comics themselves do not merely reflect but also can be seen to actively imagine the world.[17] And as Wonho Jang and Jung Eun Song (2017) cover in the case of Korean webtoons, comics themselves have become a crucial ingredient in forging new forms of glocal (global-local) culture. The present book owes much to the global and transnational insights of such previous comics criticism, which I adapt here to an urban mode. Rather than contribute to the theorization of "global comics" per se, as have others, I am interested in the possibilities such theorists have opened up for comics scholarship in a general sense.

There is value in applying the insights made by Ahrens, Meteling, and Dittmer to a greater range of global contexts, as each chapter of this book does and as future scholarship may also bear out. In line with contributions to those previous volumes, I adopt a similarly interdisciplinary approach to urban culture. Rather than investigate the global urban social spaces in which comics traditions have been forged themselves, this book is most concerned with the discourse of comics art. Nevertheless, this artistic discourse, of course, can never be fully separated from the social, cultural, political, and economic dimensions of global urban life. Urban cultural studies method thus informs the way I approach links between the social sciences and the humanities. It is important to understand that artistic representation is always tied to the material world in which we live. Most often, comics cities represented in the texts chosen for the chapters that follow are connected in some way with specific real cities. Readers will encounter representations of Barcelona (Catalonia, Spain), Buenos Aires (Argentina), Geneva (Switzerland), London (England), Lyon (France), Madrid (Spain), Montevideo (Uruguay), Montreal (Canada), New York (USA), Paris (France), and São Paolo (Brazil), for example. At other times, urban centers such as Oslo (Norway) and Tokyo (Japan) are implied in fictionalized cities that go unnamed in the individual comics text.[18] Moreover, artist Daishu Ma depicts what might seem to be a city from her native China to explore a more universal tension between urban industry and organic life. The verve with which Canadian comics artist Seth imagines the fictional town of Dominion in both visual and tactile dimensions allows us to consider the more systematic way in which the human imagination becomes material in the creation of the built environment of the city. While this book's global coverage is nowhere near total, focusing on these texts and places has allowed me to address a more coherent set of urban concerns.

There are undoubtedly geographic gaps in this enterprise. To highlight one glaring example: comics from Africa. While both strong and emerging African comics traditions are already in existence, their investigation by critics has often lagged behind production, which can pose real obstacles for interdisciplinary scholars.[19] The work of some of these creators no doubt will be interesting from an urban perspective. One such example would be the work of Adérito Wetela (Mozambique, 1978) who studied architecture before turning to comics. More broadly, increased research into African comics traditions will also provide scholars in general with a greater understanding of how comics are always in dialogue with global flows.[20] In Nigeria there is YouNeek Studios, founded by Roye Okupe, who is also the creator of "E.X.O.—The Legend of Wale Williams," a superhero narrative that unfolds in fictional Lagoon City.[21] The Comic Republic company, also in Nigeria, specializes in superheroes such as Guardian Prime and from the outset has offered free downloads of its comics via the web (see thecomicrepublic.com). Moreover, there are collectives and associations of African cartoonists and comics artists that deserve close attention, for example, Mada-BD (Madagascar), Acria (DRC), Tache d'encre (Côte d'Ivoire), MAC BD (Cameroon), Bénin Dessin (Benin), and Association Farafin'c (Burkina Faso).[22] Some African comics have already received significant critical attention, such as the graphic novel series *Aya of Yop City* by Marguerite Abouet (Côte d'Ivoire), who is "the first African comics artist to be awarded a prize at the Festival International de la Bande Dessinée d'Angoulême."[23] There are of course comics conventions that draw large crowds in Nigeria (Lagos Comic Con) and Zimbabwe (Comexposed Harare), and the pan-African comic book database Kugali was formed in 2016.[24] My hope is that authors of future studies will bring greater breadth and depth to the urban approach to global comics carried out here, giving close attention to African cities and other urban areas across the globe that I have not been able to address in this book.

The chronological range of the texts discussed in the chapters that follow is worthy of note. As scholars of the art form have shown, comics draw on a number of preexisting artistic traditions. Perhaps most important among these are traditions of visual representation and visual narrative. Any attempt at defining the origins of an art form so rooted in images necessarily risks establishing a starting point that is somewhat arbitrary. Accounts of the modern comic have tended to assert its origin with nineteenth-century figures such as the Swiss artist Rodolphe Töpffer or the French-born illustrator Gustave Doré. Newer perspectives, however, have pushed further into the eighteenth century to assert the important role of English engraver and painter William Hogarth in defining elements of a modern comics tradition.[25] With only a few exceptions, this book tends to concentrate on widely circulated contemporary texts or on more recent reprints of earlier publications. These are the texts that should be more readily available to interested readers eager to confirm, contest, or continue to develop this book's ideas. While the first two chapters focus on the development of an urban comics legacy in the eighteenth, nineteenth, and early twentieth centuries, overall there is a pronounced emphasis on the period spanning from the 1950s to the present-day. Though there are chronological elements to chapters 1 and 2 in the need to establishing the legacy of urban comics, I admit that I have not set out to write yet another history of comics. In this sense, I regard it as particularly significant that each chapter includes commentary on at least one work from the twenty-first century, if not a few such contemporary comics.

This book emphasizes works that have already been translated into English. There are only two exceptions.[26] These exceptions are consistent with my goal, writing as scholar whose disciplinary home is in the field of Hispanic studies, of exposing Anglophone readers to a range of Spanish-language comics in particular. I believe that the fact that the vast majority of the material discussed in *Visible Cities* is already available in English translation will prove to be of interest to Anglophone scholars. By this I do not mean to include merely comics scholars but also those interested in urban geography, sociology, anthropology, philosophy, art history, world literature, and more. It is a sign of the increasing cultural attention comics enjoy that there have already been film adaptations made corresponding to a handful of the texts studied. These include: *From Hell* (Moore and Campbell), *Chuecatown* (Martínez Castellanos), *The Extraordinary Adventures of Adèle Blanc-Sec* (Tardi), and *Seth's Dominion* (Seth). It should be beneficial that the vast majority of titles analyzed in this volume are incredibly well known, even if they have not yet been studied from an urban cultural studies perspective.

It is intentional that the chapters of this book show a clear preference for alternative and independent small-press comics artists over more mainstream traditions of superhero comics and popular franchises. One cannot deny that the theme of the urban environment is certainly very closely connected with superhero comics traditions. To confirm this, it is sufficient merely to consider Batman's Gotham City and the connections between the Marvel Universe and New York City.[27] My exclusion of superhero comics from this book should not be taken as comment on the value of studying that genre. Instead, it is an affirmation that the urban environments of such traditions deserve exploration on their own terms. This thematic limitation notwithstanding, *Visible Cities* covers considerable ground in formal terms. Included are engravings, woodcuts, early newspaper comics, single-panel work, the serialized comic strip, digital comics, comics series, full graphic novels, manga, trading cards, and ambitious boxed comics sets. It must be acknowledged from the outset that not all comics artists in the world comment meaningfully on the urban experience. Thus, in selecting works of comics art to discuss in this volume, I have left out many well-known and lesser-known artists whose work may be less directly urban, and as a consequence beyond of the scope of this research.[28] Not all comics works that depict cities are addressed in this book. I might have chosen a number of other represented cities for the analyses that follow, Adrian Tomine's Los Angeles in *Killing and Dying*, Marjane Satrapi's Tehran in *Persepolis*, or Guy Delisle's representations in *Jerusalem, Shenzhen*, and *Pyongyang*, for instance. By selecting some comics whose themes are arguably more representative of key urban issues, I admit that I have necessarily neglected others.

Still, those comics artists who receive extended consideration here represent an incredible array of contributors to the medium. This includes some of the most notable international figures as well as lesser-known artists of significance whose reputations continue to grow: Mark Beyer, Pierre Christin and Olivier Balez, Raquel Córcoles Moncusí, Julie Doucet, Will Eisner, William Hogarth, Ben Katchor, Rafael Martínez Castellanos, Daishu Ma, Frans Masereel, Marc-Antoine Mathieu, Winsor McCay, Fábio Moon and Gabriela Bá, Alan Moore and Eddie Campbell, Tsutomu Nihei, Héctor Germán Oesterheld and Francisco Solano López, Richard F. Outcault, Benoît Peeters and François Schuiten, Hariton Pushwagner (Terje Brofos), Rodolfo Santullo and Matías Bergara, Seth (Gregory Gallant), Joost Swarte, Jacques Tardi, Rodolphe Töpffer, El Torres and Jesús Alonso Iglesias, Chris Ware, and Sophie Yanow. These comics artists themselves are connected with a range of global locations, including cities in Argentina, Belgium, Brazil, Canada, China, England, France, Holland, Japan, Norway, Spain, Switzerland, the United States, and Uruguay.[29]

CHAPTER SUMMARIES

Visible Cities: Urban Images and Spatial Form in Global Comics is divided into five chapters that explore overlapping themes of urbanism, urban life and the representation of global cities. The first two chapters deal with the urban legacy of early comics. The next two chapters deal with urbanism and the built environment. The final chapter of the book explores selected global cities that have been tied with danger, disease, and death in the graphic comics imagination. These chapters are written in a way that presumes no previous knowledge of either urban theory or the ninth art on the part of readers. Each centers on a more-or-less defined topic and explores a handful of comics texts of importance. These thematic explorations are driven by insights from urban theory and/or comics form. Along the way, readers are introduced to names, places, historical events, urban thinkers, and formal elements of the comics medium with which they may not be familiar. Extensive endnotes provide further elaboration and references to additional source material for those readers who specialize in either urban or comics theory. One image per comic discussed in depth appears in each chapter in order to support detailed analysis of the artistic aspects of comics form.[30]

Chapter 1, "The Modern City Streets," explores the way in which early comics established a legacy emphasizing urban street life. It begins by detailing the connection of comics with urban environments, themes and circulation patterns in eighteenth-, nineteenth- and twentieth-century London, England, Geneva, Switzerland, and New York. For this discussion, *A Harlot's Progress* (1732) by William Hogarth (1697–1764), the caricature and urban themes of Rodolphe Töpffer (1799–1846, including *Histoire d'Albert* 1845), and Richard F. Outcault's *The Yellow Kid* and *Hogan's Alley* (1895), serve as paradigmatic examples. Attention then turns to Winsor McCay's vibrant Sunday-page, color *Little Nemo* comics, which harnessed suburban dreams at the dawn of the twentieth century. Finally, an example from the twenty-first century demonstrates how these earlier themes are important for understanding the continuing legacy of urban comics. Canadian artist Sophie Yanow's *War of Streets and Houses* (2014) recalls the graphic and stylistic innovation and spatio-historical context of Töpffer's comics production. Yet in bridging urban themes from that French colonial conflict with the 2012 activist movement of the Maple Spring (*le printemps érable*) in the province of Quebec, Canada, the creator's focus on queer identity and contemporary urban activism also sets up themes to be explored in subsequent chapters of this book.

Chapter 2, "The Passions of Everyday Urban Life," continues to explore the comics depiction of life on the modern city streets. This time, however, discussion concentrates on the twentieth and twenty-first centuries, and is carried out through the lens of the human passions. Here the urban themes of these comics are just as significant as their aesthetic form and composition. First, the wordless novels by Belgian artist Frans Masereel serve as yet another paradigmatic example of the urban legacy of early comics. *The Passion of Man* (1918), *Passionate Journey* (1919), and *The City* (1925) exalt the sensuous nature of the urban experience against the dehumanizing forces of industrialized and planned modernity. Will Eisner's trilogy *A Contract with God* (1978), *A Life Force* (1988), and *Dropsie Avenue* (1995) use tenement life as a stage for the Jewish American urban experience of New York. The emphasis he places on the details of facial expression—against hazy backdrops and thinly outlined architectural form—codes his graphic novels as urban theaters of the human senses. *My New York Diary* (1993–1998) by Julie Doucet blends the artist's feminist commitment with themes of urban alienation and entrapment. As her autobiographical persona struggles for a place of her own, she is confined by her relationships with men and at once by the panel frames of the comics page. In twenty-first-century Madrid, Spain, Raquel Córcoles Moncusí a.k.a. "Moderna de pueblo" (*I'm a Small-Town Girl*, 2011; *Dickheads Don't Give You Flowers*, 2013) and Rafael Martínez Castellanos (*Chuecatown*, 2002) explore romantic and sexual passions as they line up with the social identities of women and gay urbanites. Finally, Daishu Ma's *Leaf* (2015) returns to hallmark aspects of Frans Masereel's style nearly one hundred years later. Taking place in a nameless but highly archetypal city, the Chinese-born artist's graphic novel opposes the sensuous qualities of urban life to the persisting machine logic of the industrial age.

Chapter 3, "Urban Planning, Built Environment, and the Structure of Cities," analyzes a group of comics in which the large-scale machinations of urban planning culture have negatively impacted the lives of city dwellers. Norwegian artist Hariton Pushwagner's *Soft City* (1969) indulges in the social alienation that results from the linear monotony of the metropolis. In his oversized page-spanning images, city dwellers sacrifice their identities to urban routine, as rendered graphically in the city's overwhelming traffic and the meaningless commute to towering but nondescript office buildings. The tyranny of urban planning is dramatized in *Samaris* (1983) by Belgian creators Benoît Peeters and François Schuiten. Here the dehumanization of the urbanite through a built environment that suits only the needs of the powerful is carried to an extreme as a fantastic city alienates and even feeds off of its inhabitants. *Dead Memory* (2003) by French creator Marc-Antoine Mathieu takes the spontaneous appearance of walls in the city as an impetus to play with themes of spatial form, memory, and language loss. Two final comics juxtapose the top-down method of urban planning with the experience of the city's built environment at the scale of the individual. *Robert Moses: The Master Builder of New York City* (2014) by French author and illustrator Pierre Christin and Olivier Balez depicts and questions the legacy of an influential planning figure, while American Ben Katchor's collection *Cheap Novelties: The Pleasures of Urban Decay* (1991) traces a real-estate-photographer-turned-flâneur throughout the streets of the modern city.

Chapter 4, "Architecture, Materiality and the Tactile City," continues to explore the built environment of the city but does so at a more personal scale. Architecture proves a way of linking the comics page with the tactile urban world beyond the panel border. In a cover titled "The Comix Factory" designed for the comics magazine *Raw*, Dutch artist Joost Swarte employs the formal depth of comics to suggest their connection to tactile qualities of urban life in three dimensions. American Chris Ware's ambitious boxed anthology *Building Stories* (2012) invites a tactile reading experience and pushes the architectural form of the comics multiframe to its limits. Also hailing from America, Mark Beyer's transposition of his popular Amy and Jordan comic to the format of "City of Terror Trading Cards" uses tactility to implicate comics in city circulation patterns. Canadian artist Seth, known as the creator of *Palookaville* (1991–) and *It's a Good Life, if You Don't Weaken* (1996), has also been building tactile models of buildings in Dominion, his fictional setting for many of his comics. Models of the town's iconic locations have been displayed in galleries in Phoenix, Arizona, and in Regina, Saskatchewan, complementing the photographic and hand-drawn images of Dominion readers can find in his comics texts. And in *The Ghost of Gaudí* (2017), created by El Torres and Jesús Alonso Iglesias, key architectural sites in the Catalonian capital of Barcelona, Spain, appeal to global readers through recognizable representations of the Park Güell, the La Sagrada Familia, and the tactile dimension of Antoni Gaudí's *trencadis* mosaic-tile technique.

Chapter 5, "Danger, Disease, and Death in the Graphic Urban Imagination," demonstrates how genre comics reflect the urban fears that have shaped the social environment of the modern city. The examples explored here show how even storytelling modes as diverse as science fiction, the occult and mystery tale, dystopian fiction, true crime narrative, and magical realism invoke the modern discourses of urban threat—danger, disease, and death—that circulated among urbanites since the nineteenth century. *The Eternaut* (1957–1959), created by writer Héctor Germán Oesterheld and illustrator Francisco Solano López, stages an alien invasion in the city of Buenos Aires, Argentina. *Dengue* (2012), by Rodolfo Santullo and Matías Bergara, follows suit, echoing aspects of *El Eternaut* in telling a story of invasion and disease transmission in the Uruguayan capital of Montevideo. Urban detective literature and the mystery/occult story are fused in Jacques Tardi's *The Extraordinary Adventures of Adèle Blanc-Sec* (1976), whose action unfolds in Paris. Created by Japanese manga artist Tsutomu Nihei, *Blame!* (1998–) fictionalizes the vertical architecture and immense scale associated with Tokyo in a visual dystopian tale. Adapting a now-discredited theory on the Jack the Ripper serial killings, Alan Moore and Eddie Campbell's graphic novel *From Hell* (1989–1996) links the slums, architecture, and patriarchal violence of Victorian London. Finally, Fábio Moon and Gabriel Bá's *Daytripper* (2011) treads fearlessly into serial confrontations with mortality in and beyond the context of São Paolo, Brazil.

CHAPTER 1

THE MODERN CITY STREETS

Comics frequently invite us to navigate the streets of the modern city. Early comics represented street scenes, sought urban readers, found urbanized circulation patterns, and reflected the hallmark traits of the modern city in their aesthetic composition. In exploring these aspects of early comics, this chapter moves from what Thierry Smolderen calls a "prephotographic tradition of illustration" toward the incursion of comics into twentieth-century print journalism.[1] Also considered here, in a striking example from the twenty-first century, is the continuing legacy of early urban comics.

The aesthetic properties and formal innovations readers encounter in early comics are themselves connected to the modern city environment. The canonical early comics discussed here are decidedly urban in orientation. This idea is not necessarily novel. What *is* new, however, is the way in which each subsection of this first chapter prioritizes an urban perspective as a way of revisiting key moments that figure into the history of the ninth art. These are distillations of insights from previous comics research where the role of the urban may have been rather subdued or peripheral to a main argument. Also novel in this chapter are the connecting threads that run through each of a series of concise discussions of urban comics. One thread is constituted by passing references to hallmark urban thinkers and spatial theorists. These include Charles Baudelaire, Walter Benjamin, Michel de Certeau, Jürgen Habermas, David Harvey, Jane Jacobs, Henri Lefebvre, Jacob A. Riis, Richard Sennett, and Georg Simmel. The other thread connects comics artists to the legacies of those who have preceded them. Whether these connections are intentional, acknowledged, or merely implicit, it is important for contemporary readers to understand the debt owed by twentieth- and twenty-first-century global comics artists to early comics creators. References to contemporary comics criticism and theory provide support along the way.

EARLY URBAN COMICS: HOGARTH, TÖPFFER, OUTCAULT

Emerging scholarship is pushing back the origins of the modern comic to the nineteenth and eighteenth centuries. A prominent article by Thierry Groensteen (1998), together with book-length studies by David Kunzle (1973, 2007) and Thierry Smolderen (2014), have established Rodolphe Töpffer (1799–1846) and now even William Hogarth (1697–1764) as crucial figures for understanding the development of comics as an art form in general.[2] Yet in addition, Hogarth's eighteenth-century London and Töpffer's nineteenth-century Geneva are themselves quite important for understanding the development of the comic as a specifically urban art form. In turn, the influence of both Hogarth and Töpffer is evident in the work of Richard F. Outcault (1863–1928). Outcault sustains an interest in visual depictions of the new public spaces associated with bourgeois urban modernity, this time in the context of New York. Tracing the rise of the modern urban comic in this way, from London to Geneva to New York, provides an opportunity to assess the significant impact of the cultures of cities on the ninth art. The content, form, and themes of these early comics are as urban as their readership and semiotic layering.

William Hogarth's Eighteenth-Century London

William Hogarth (1697–1764) was a caricaturist, painter, and printmaker in eighteenth-century London. He is most well known as the creator of four key works—*A Harlot's Progress, A Rake's Progress, Marriage A-la-Mode*, and *Industry and Idleness*—the first three of which were conceived as depictions of what he called "Modern Moral Subjects."[3] Certainly, Hogarth was known as a satirist. The objects of his satire were quite varied, and his work was often seen through contradictory lenses.[4] It is possible, as David Kunzle does, to paint a detailed picture of the artist without specifically prioritizing the theme of the city.[5] Yet it is clear enough that the city and the urban experience are essential for a thorough understanding of Hogarth's contributions to comics. It should not be downplayed that what Hogarth was known for satirizing might otherwise be called modern *urban* life. Hogarth's city dwellers represent stereotypical urban types. In the *Penguin Book of Comics*, George Perry and Alan Aldrige describe his work in terms that contrast upper-class drawing-rooms to the London slums.[6] In *Hogarth and His Times*, David Bindman suggests that the artist's work demonstrates a confluence of classical and modern, even urban, concerns. Thus, in the two works known as the "Progresses," he writes, there is a "precise delineation of place: almost every image is set within an identifiable location, itself imbued with symbolic meaning."[7] A central preoccupation of his images, in one scholar's view, is the fact that "the city is a place of meetings."[8]

The modern city is essential not merely to the topics and themes of Hogarth's work but also to his artistic method. The significance of the urban is palpable in his theoretical work *The Analysis of Beauty* (1753). Considered by some to be a significant contribution to the theory of art, this text nudged artists away from classical references and pointed to the life of the London streets as a privileged source for artistic inspiration.[9] One should not interpret this as a suggestion that artists turn their backs on existing literary and pictorial traditions, however. It is important to recognize that classical reflections—such as those on the vulgarity of city life made by Horace and Juvenal—nonetheless exercised an influence on Hogarth.[10] As mentioned below, he was well versed in many traditions of visual composition. Yet it cannot be ignored that the streets of England's capital city stimulated his artistic imagination. To wit, comics scholar Thierry Smolderen notes that Hogarth was a keen observer of street life.[11] In works such as *The Four Times of Day* (*Morning, Noon* . . . all from 1738), and *Beer Street* and *Gin Lane* (both from 1751) the artist depicted the social behaviors and inequities that became synonymous with modern urban culture.[12]

Beyond being a theme of artistic representation, the urban environment was also important for the production and circulation of his creations. As Bindman puts it, "Hogarth was assiduous in making his studio part of the urban spectacle."[13] That is, those interested could wander in to view painted versions of the prints in the studio and then subscribe to the series, receiving their order upon delivery of payment. His most successful work was arguably *A Harlot's Progress* (1732), which consisted of six engravings and famously sold to some 1,240 subscribers.[14] Moreover, the work was so popular that its theme continued to inspire musical compositions and the design of craft objects over the years.[15] Its narrative action begins outside on a city street. The first of six plates displays "a confrontation between rural and urban cultures,"[16] as a future harlot known as Molly Hackabout arrives in London.[17] In this scene the protagonist meets a madam, is ignored by a religious man, and falls under the gaze of a lecherous man (plate 1).[18] The remaining five scenes are all interiors. While supported by a rich merchant, the harlot also takes a younger lover (plate 2), is arrested by a judge (plate 3), is sentenced to prison labor (plate 4), has a child and later agonizes with syphilis (plate 5), and finally ends up dead in a coffin (plate 6). Throughout, the artist crafts extremely dense, detailed, highly symbolic and even allegorical scenes in a fashion typical of his style. As Smolderen has noted, Hogarth also dialogues with preexisting pictorial traditions by adapting an earlier story in pictures from Venice to a contemporary London milieu.[19]

Analyzed as an important work of visual art over centuries, the place of *A Harlot's Progress* in contemporary comics scholarship is a matter of somewhat more debate. Aaron Meskin and Roy T. Cook's introduction to *The Art of Comics* notes that opinions differ regarding whether Hogarth's prints should be classified as comics.[20] It is perhaps more easily accepted that eighteenth-century traditions of cartooning and caricature are a significant precursor of modern comics.[21] In this light, Hogarth's significance for the historical study of comics is generally acknowledged. Scott McCloud easily admits that "Hogarth is pre-comics."[22] Moreover, as the intersection between comics and art receives more attention, it should come as no surprise that Hogarth is one of the names "trotted out" in comparison in order to ground twentieth-century American underground comics pioneer Robert Crumb's works within a broader history of art.[23] Yet with the matter of Hogarth's generalized influence assured, the more specific question of whether his works are themselves actually comics has tended to divide scholars into two camps.

For example, Dominic McIver Lopes strongly believes that Hogarth's *A Rake's Progress* is a comic, while David Carrier is unequivocal that it is not.[24] The reasons Carrier gives have to do with the fact that the temporal gaps between one plate and the next are too great to form "one continuous story," an insight that would apply equally well to *A Harlot's Progress*. Nevertheless, however reasonable this judgment may seem to be, it implicitly affirms the definition of comics as "sequential art," a definition that, it should be noted, is still much disputed.[25] While this phrase "'sequential art" was made canonical for a time through the work of McCloud, who drew on an earlier formulation of comics as a sequential art by Will Eisner (see ch. 2), there have been many recent attempts to broaden this definition. In the twenty-first century, critics are more willing to allow for variations in narrative temporality across panels, intriguing non-panel constructions, new spatial innovations on the page, and, overall, greater play with the conventions of the ninth art by comics artists. There is increasing understanding that neither the panel nor the speech balloon is itself a requisite element of comics.[26] There is even support for the possibility that a single-panel comic can narrate through internal juxtaposition.[27] This newfound appreciation for the breadth and variation of comics traditions makes it possible to take renewed stock of Hogarth's relevance to the field.

In Smolderen's book *The Origins of Comics: From William Hogarth to Winsor McCay* (2014), the focus on Hogarth displaces for the first time the primacy given Töpffer in more-conventional histories of the ninth art.[28] Smolderen includes the Londoner's name in the title of his book, begins with discussions of his work, and invites a refreshing and innovative perspective on the history of comics. The critic's argument portrays the eighteenth-century artist as a definitive point of origin. Thus readers are made aware that Hogarth's work influences not only Töpffer but also later Richard F. Outcault, and Winsor McCay.[29] Somewhat defiantly, Smolderen even writes, "Despite its brevity, *A Harlot's Progress* (1732) must be regarded as a genuine novel in pictures."[30] Furthermore, the attention he gives to the intricate reading paths prompted by the work's detailed plates is true to the spirit of new directions in comics research.[31] Of course, if these arguments are not enough to convince traditionally minded scholars that Hogarth deserves a place at the table of comics scholarship, there is always the possibility of taking a slightly different approach. That is, there is always the intriguing detail noted by David Kunzle: *A Harlot's Progress* was arguably the first work to take the form of a newspaper comic strip when it appeared in sequence in 1828 in the print publication *Bell's Life in London and Sporting Guide*.[32] Beyond these disciplinary debates, however, Hogarth unequivocally remains a foundational figure for the interdisciplinary study of the connections between visual art and the urban environment.

While the modern city is significant for understanding the artist's topics, themes, method, and context, Bindman goes even further than this in his study. The scholar draws on Jürgen Habermas's theorizations of the public sphere to elucidate the connection between these elements of the artist's activity. Not only is it true that "the London of Hogarth's period was precisely the locus of the emergence of this public sphere," he writes, but also "printmaking of the kind practiced by Hogarth was in that sense the quintessential bourgeois art form. It was by definition urban and commercial."[33] One can make the argument that the bourgeois art form in which Hogarth engaged was made possible by the density and urban culture of the bourgeois city. Art and commerce were enjoying greater connections in a specifically urban modernity.

The essential dimensions of this urban modernity can be seen as dualistic, paradoxical, and contradictory. In Hogarth's time, the pictorial art of caricature, in particular, drew attention precisely to these dimensions of modern life. The artist's own interest in caricature can be seen in the work *Characters and Caricaturas* (1743).[34] No less an urban commentator than Charles Baudelaire wrote essays on the subject of caricature that can aid contemporary readers in thinking through issues associated with the visual representation of modern city life.[35] Baudelaire refers to Hogarth only briefly in his essays, but he does specifically praise *A Rake's Progress* and *Gin Lane*, among other compositions.[36] This requires us to shift momentarily from the discussion of comics to the discussion of the comic, that is, that which makes us laugh. Lest readers think this is too much of a detour, the gestational relationship between comics and the comic should be kept in mind.[37]

Although Michele Hannoosh's book *Baudelaire and Caricature: From the Comic to an Art of Modernity* (1992) is concerned with 'the comic' in the sense of humor, laughter, and social critique, the critic nonetheless identifies the modern city as a very appropriate setting for its visual representation. The street scenes composed by satirical artists such as Hogarth, she writes, tend to equate the urban and the modern, which becomes the very "locus of the comic."[38] Thus, one can speak in an urban key, as Hannoosh does, of "the comic aspect (in the Baudelairean sense) of modernist subjects and aesthetic values—the ugly, transitory, urban, banal, artificial, grotesque, ironic, multiple, and paradoxical."[39] These subjects and values were rendered visible by the social environment of the modern city. As a quintessentially disinterested city stroller, the nineteenth-century figure of the urban flâneur is immersed in the interplay of these modern subjects and aesthetic values. The flâneur is "both subject and object, observer and observed," and thus occupies a paradoxical position that is replicated also in the contradictions of the modern comic artist.[40]

In this context, Hogarth's satirical, urban, and comic legacy—not to mention also his comics legacy—occupies an important position in the development of caricature. Urban social relationships and comic art both rely on dualistic thinking.[41] Caricature rendered social relationships in visible terms, drawing out the dualistic, paradoxical, and contradictory aspects of modern urban life.[42] In addition, it was to be important in the stylistic transformation of the broadsheet. Caricature gradually became "a weapon in the political and social struggle" as well as "a new commercial commodity."[43] In due course it was intricately woven into the development of an "urban consumer society."[44] In the twentieth-century comic, caricature reappears in precisely this context in Hariton Pushwagner's *Soft City*, and for that matter the practice of flânerie takes center stage in Ben Katchor's *Cheap Novelties* (both in ch. 3). Yet while Hogarth's efforts resulted in a lasting tradition of urban caricature, it can be argued that the work of Töpffer forged an urban comics tradition.[45]

Rodolphe Töpffer's Nineteenth-Century Geneva

Swiss artist Rodolphe Töpffer (1799–1846) has been conventionally seen as the inventor of modern comics.[46] Nevertheless, the rise of interest in Hogarth and the scholarship on early comics in general has caused many to reassess and revise this commonplace. Among those in this group are Laurence Grove, Mark McKinney, and Ann Miller.[47] Santiago García distances himself from the matter, suggesting that perceptions of Töpffer's role are likely either exaggerated or irrelevant.[48] David Kunzle has written that if Töpffer is still the father of comics, then Hogarth is the grandfather of the ninth art.[49] Töpffer was certainly aware of and influenced by Hogarth, and his earliest stories appeared a century after the Londoner's *A Harlot's Progress*.[50] In the interim, artists such as Thomas Rowlandson and George Cruikshank in England and Jean Baptiste Greuze in France continued to captivate the public imagination. Yet by the 1820s, European caricature on the whole had become somewhat bland; in France, specifically, caricature was a largely anonymous art.[51] It was in this context that a Genevan teacher was to renew caricature and experiment with the comics form.[52] It is interesting to consider that someone who today is largely heralded as one of the greatest comics innovators would have been derided in his time for engaging in such a low genre of art as caricature.[53] Kunzle makes use of the artist's own declarations to assert that Töpffer's invention of comics occurred in the classroom.[54] There he made sketches quickly, and his "manuscript albums of comic picture-stories" were "eagerly devoured by the children of his school and his inner circle of friends."[55]

It is significant that in the 1830s Töpffer made strong contributions to both comics and comics studies.[56] If a six-plate sequence by Hogarth can be considered "a genuine novel in pictures," then perhaps Töpffer's works deserve to be seen as "graphic novels."[57] Kunzle uses the term "graphic novel" intentionally to characterize the textimage combinations that the artist saw as a secondary interest.[58] One should understand, however, that Töpffer's production overall was extensive. This mere hobby amounted to an impressive "total of eight stories (one not quite complete) and 1,523 drawings."[59] His work was also important from a theoretical point of view. The artist raised broader "concerns about modernization, industrialization, and mechanization" in texts such as *Essai de physiognomie* (Essay on Physiognomy) (1845) and *Essai d'autographie* (Essay on Autography) (1842).[60] There is reason to view these texts, along with his comics themselves, as the basis for what Smolderen refers to as an implicit theory of comics.[61] Jeet Heer and Kent Worchester remind us that Töpffer thought and wrote quite a bit about the nature of sequential images.[62]

As it was with his predecessor Hogarth, Töpffer's urban setting was crucial for understanding his work and legacy. In the simple sense, there is no doubt that he brought great artistic notoriety to his hometown of Geneva, which was already an "intellectual crossroads of Europe."[63] Perhaps because there may have been little need to go searching for cultural enrichment elsewhere, he seldom traveled outside of the city. The exceptions to this were relatively few, amounting to only a brief time spent in Paris as a youth and trips to Genoa, Venice, and Milan.[64] In *Father of the Comic Strip: Rodolphe Töpffer* (2007), Kunzle specifically seeks to portray the comics artist as "essentially a Genevan, to localize him in the great, small, and very cosmopolitan town in which he lived all his truncated life, and of which he was so proud."[65] Yet the urban must not be seen merely as a container, that is, the material place where Töpffer lived and worked. Instead, modern city life influenced his work at multiple levels, in terms of method, content, theme, narrative, and distribution or readership.

As if he were following Hogarth's suggestion in *The Analysis of Beauty*, the city streets were also the primary inspiration for Töpffer's art. Below I consider the artist's *Histoire d'Albert* as an intriguing example of the Genevan capturing on paper what was going on in the streets of the city he called home. Yet overall, at the level of content, one can see the results of this method in his works' thematic emphasis on urban life and their focus on city-dwelling protagonists.

Töpffer preferred to represent "basic social and satirical types: upstart, lover, educator, scientist, artist, bureaucrat, politician [. . .] thief."[66] At the level of narrative composition, the hustle and bustle of city life was reflected in the urban atmosphere and the pacing of Töpffer's picture-stories. Though not the first one he drew, *Histoire de Monsieur Jabot* was the first comics album to be shared publicly.[67] He distributed it himself and kept it out of the bookstores.[68] Following in due course were the titles *Monsieur Crépin, Histoire de M. Vieux Bois, Monsieur Pencil, Histoire d'Albert, Histoire de Monsieur Cryptogame, Tric-trac,* and *Le Docteur Festus*.[69] His comics of the 1830s can be seen as a sort of long-form social caricature that appealed to an urban-dwelling upper-class readership, with some middle-class readers.[70] In addition to "the bumbling, pretentious social climber (Jabot)" there were also "the limited but common-sensical father (Crépin); the flighty naturalist (Vieux Bois); the domineering fiancée (Elvire); [and] the prodigal son and revolutionary (Albert)."[71]

In terms of comics form, criticism has highlighted the advances in the graphic treatment of temporality made by Töpffer. For instance, if some have argued that the time gaps between Hogarth's plates are too great to be sequential art, it is significant that the Genevan's approach has not received the same complaint.[72] Moreover, if Romantic attitudes and "notions of caprice, change, instinct and the unconscious" found their way into Töpffer's prose, it is important that these were effectively associated with his characters' navigation, in pictures, of the modern urban environment.[73] In this respect Kunzle makes a comparison that is quite apt, writing of the Genevan that he shared with Baudelaire "the aesthetic of negligence, of spontaneity—and particularly of flânerie, which may be translated, in Töpfferian terms, as casual mental zigzagging around."[74] As readers explore urban spaces in his comics, they thus arguably adopt the dispassionate and meandering style of the urban flâneur.

There is also the matter of urban social attitudes to consider. Töpffer's feelings toward the rural peasantry were complex, but his works can be said to accept the primacy of the town over the rural environment.[75] As Kunzle explores, the artist's urban protagonists who venture into the countryside "are not prepared psychologically or physically for rural conditions."[76] The encounter between rural and urban forms of life is frequently mobilized to comic effect in his works. Yet the city itself is also a site of difference and even conflict. Initially, Töpffer seems to have navigated the urban conflicts around him with some trepidation. In general, the artist was selective about the topics he chose for criticism and was somewhat hesitant to carry that criticism too far.[77]

Toward the end of his life, he would even become more directly involved in the city's political turmoil. Significantly, in the 1840s, Geneva became one of many cities where the sparks of European revolution took flame. One must note, however, that the Genevan Revolution, "consummated in 1846 shortly after

Töpffer's death, was relatively bloodless," a detail that is particularly important when compared against the profiles of the 1848 revolutions that swept across Europe.[78] Espousing conservative perspectives on issues of the day, Töpffer had in fact exploited family connections to the educated elites in order to rise from the lower middle class.[79] The artist was angered enough by the radical escalations he saw around him that he edited the newspaper *Courrier de Genève* in the wake of the 1841 revolution.[80] These efforts in publication did not turn the tables of the ideological conflict, and it is easy to conclude that he was gradually frustrated and turned toward action.[81] In the end, he was not content merely to engage in combat through the medium of print, and he eventually made the decision to join in the fight against the radicals in 1845.[82]

Töpffer's late work *Histoire d'Albert*, first published in 1845, must be seen in light of these experiences. The comic depicts a young man who founds a fictional newspaper in the midst of radical activities. Originally titled *The Story of Jacques*, its protagonist was also partly modeled on Genevan radical James Fazy—filtered, of course, through the social lens of Töpffer's anti-radical perspective.[83] Notably, this picture story had a great cultural impact. It was widely circulated in Europe both before and after 1848.[84] In one sequence mentioned in Mark Traugott's historical book *The Insurgent Barricade* (2010), citizens sing the Marseillaise in the streets, and subsequent panels chart out the growing social discord ending in the construction of a barricade. Traugott continues, quoting the text beneath each of Töpffer's paneled images:

> Panel 2: "Issue Number 80 [of the fictional newspaper that Töpffer's protagonist, Albert, has founded] implores the authorities to grant the people's just demands." Panel 3: "Issue Number 90 implores the people to remain calm, as the authorities won't be able to deny the people's just demands much longer." Panel 4: "However, inasmuch as the people have begun to understand one another and to make themselves understood, citizens are shouting at one another, the Constitution has been overthrown, the town is in mourning, and business is ruined."[85]

One should note that urban conflict figures prominently in other albums by the artist. For instance: in *Mr. Vieux Bois,* where the protagonist chases his beloved and causes a general chaos amongst citizens and the national guard; in *Crépin* when a mini-riot erupts in the street; in *Pencil* when the national guard disperses an urban mob; and in *Cryptogame*, which is based on an urban fire that occurred in 1830s Algeria.[86] But the street fighting that breaks out in *Histoire d'Albert* hits a bit closer to home.[87]

Kunzle writes that "the purpose of *Albert* is to vilify the character of the revolutionary."[88] The notation that the people "have begun to understand one another" has clear political and revolutionary overtones. Specifically, this phrasing denotes the consciousness-raising activities and class fellowship that the density of the urban form made possible. In this comic Töpffer links the construction of the barricade to what he saw as the ills of revolutionary society, one that he tried in vain to prevent. It should not be lost on readers that fashioning a barricade in the city was a symbolic rewriting of its streets by radicals of the time. From this acknowledgement an interesting contradiction arises. It is possible for contemporary readers to see a contradiction inherent in Töpffer's art; that is, while he disparages radical social impulses and the barricade specifically, he nonetheless does so through one of the most democratic if not also populist visual art forms in history. One might conclude that ultimately Töpffer was unable to see the connections between his own creative activity—his innovative, flowing style and his free-form doodling on the comics page—and the creative expressions of radicals whose collective goal was to reclaim the street. This chapter returns to the theme of urbanites who take over the city streets in later discussions of Sophie Yanow's *War of Streets and Houses*, which can be seen to echo Töpffer's comic in significant ways. First, however, the city streets are represented as the site constructed through class differences in the work of two American comics artists.

Richard F. Outcault's Twentieth-Century New York

For those who approach the medium of comics from the perspective of mass culture, the contemporary American newspaper comic is a particularly important landmark.[89] Though Jörn Ahrens and Arno Meteling mention Hogarth and Töpffer in passing in their introduction to *Comics and the City*, the focus of the volume's essays is more clearly on twentieth-century urban representations. While discussions in their book range across both American and European contexts, many deal with New York, specifically, and it is no surprise that both of the first two chapters reference the work of Richard Felton Outcault (1863–1928). Even though it might be debated whether Outcault was in fact the creator of the "first true American comic," mention of his name has nevertheless tended to bring up an association with pioneering innovation.[90] Jens Balzer's essay frames Outcault as a point of origin for the ninth art by including the phrase "the Invention of Comics in New York City, 1895" in its very title, and Ole Frahm's contribution similarly emphasizes the legacy of his comics creations as continued by George B. Luks.[91]

In 1863 Outcault was born in Lancaster, Ohio. He studied art in Cincinnati—and later Paris, sent there by none other than Thomas Edison. At one time he was, in fact, the Edison lab's official illustrator.[92] He contributed to important publications like *Life* and *Judge*, as well as small-circulation magazines, went on to draw *Pore Li'l Mose* and *Buster Brown*, and achieved high levels of recognition for the impact he had on the comics form.[93] Eventually, he retreated from comics and ran an advertising agency in Chicago.[94] Exploration of Outcault's career is necessarily tied into the market for print journalism established by two late nineteenth-century newspaper giants. He was, in fact, a central figure in the ongoing competition between Joseph Pulitzer's *New York World* and William Randolph Hearst's *New York Journal.* Coulton Waugh's claim "Comics, therefore, owe their start to a newspaper war" is perhaps exaggerated, but it speaks nonetheless to Outcault's significance as an artist.[95] Undoubtedly, many print publications of the time turned to comics as a way of expanding their readership and increasing their sales. Outcault's success is what arguably spurred on the development of the "funny papers" in Sunday supplements by both publications.[96] Interestingly, he started out publishing in the Sunday supplement of the *World*, was soon hired away to Hearst's *Journal*, and then returned to Pulitzer's publication in 1898.[97] During this time the iconic character he created appeared in both venues.[98]

Though the figure had been published before 1896, many accounts privilege the publication of his Yellow Kid in vibrant color in the *World*'s Sunday edition in February of that year.[99] Clothed in a characteristic bright yellow dressing gown, he surfaced in a three-quarter-page cartoon called *The Great Dog Show in M'Googan Avenue.*[100] Intriguingly, this particular cartoon is often referenced by scholars interested in the visual technology of color printing. At the time the introduction of the color yellow to newspaper publishing was only a recent development, owing to successful experimentation with a tallow-based component carried out at the *New York World*.[101] This spectacular use of color, which was unusually striking in terms of the era's norms, was also arguably used to boost sales. While doubts have been expressed about whether *The Yellow Kid* itself actually led to increased circulation,[102] there can be no doubt that in the highly commercialized print market of the late nineteenth century, publishers were eager to do anything they could to expand readership in the city. This penchant for experimentation has caused many to link the new spectacular color with the sensationalist form of "yellow journalism" that sought readers at any cost.[103]

The urban environment was crucial to Outcault's efforts at the levels of represented content, readership, and formal aesthetics. In his so-called slum saga, the artist depicted "immigrant ragamuffins" in the working-class neighborhood of Hogan's Alley.[104] Its star urbanite was the Yellow Kid—described as a "roughneck character" or a "slum urchin"—in any case a boy who "appeared to have passed through the major experiences of life in the first six months."[105] The character proved to be somewhat threatening for some readers, perhaps a reminder of fears pervasive at the time regarding juvenile crime.[106] Outcault treated his subjects from a perspective blending satire, humor, and pathos, yet not all were comfortable with seeing images of slum life or street cruelty.[107] Some readers wrote letters asking for Outcault's cartoons to be taken out of the paper.[108] A number of teachers, educators, and public libraries found them to be objectionable.[109]

While Outcault's cartoons were seen as provocative and unsettling, they were simultaneously a way of dealing with urban social issues of the day through the medium of art. Perhaps the most pervasive of these urban social issues in his work was the subject of tenement housing. Existing criticism has suggested not only that Outcault's work represented urban life and themes, but also that readers of *Hogan's Alley* were themselves "slum dwellers."[110] The artist's preference for representing children living in slums at events of those with high social and class status led to a form of urban humor that was not without an implicit critique of class disparities.[111] One must appreciate, as Richard Marschall does in *America's Great Comic-Strip Artists* (1989), the links between the Yellow Kid's visual world and the cramped conditions of New York's tenements as documented by Danish immigrant Jacob A. Riis.[112] Riis famously captured the lives of the urban underclass of New York's Lower East Side in the photojournalistic masterpiece *How the Other Half Lives* (1890). According to Riis, tenement residents suffered cramped housing, and unhygienic or even dangerous conditions, frequently lacked heat and water, and lived in an area whose density rivaled that of Calcutta, India.[113] In their content, the Yellow Kid cartoons thus brought widespread attention to the everyday realities of tenement living.

Whether in Hearst's publication or Pulitzer's, Outcault's iconic character graphically disrupted the urban fabric, sowing discord and leading or symbolically prompting waves of street vengeance. For example, in the comic titled "The Yellow Kid Treats the Crowd to a Horseless Carriage Ride" (*New York Journal*, 17 October 1897), Outcault's character causes chaos on Uneasy Street, acting as a clear force of disruption.[114] In "The Great Bull Fight in Hogan's Alley" (*New York World*, 24 August 1896), a goat substitutes for the bull while the Yellow Kid and other street urchins find camaraderie in a popular form of street celebration.[115] Many look on from atop a fence, a power line pole, and the obligatory fire escape of a tenement building.[116] In "What They Did to the Dog-Catcher in Hogan's Alley" (*New York World*, 20 September 1896), throngs of neighborhood children surround the dog-catcher, who lies on the ground. He is beaten with sticks and bitten by dogs, and he covers his face with his arm to protect against thrown rocks and an empty soup can.[117] This image, argues Smolderen, functions as an inverse of plate 1 of Hogarth's *The Four Stages of Cruelty* (1751), which depicted a depraved scene of men, boys, and onlookers harming animals on an urban street.[118] This comparison is not at all casual if one understands that Hogarth's earlier images in fact influenced many nineteenth-century visual artists.[119]

Like Hogarth's images, Outcault's cartoons are consistently described as teeming with detail.[120] They are crowded with people, flooded with movement, and filled with signage. Smolderen writes of "the swarming effect" of Outcault's images.[121] Yet in Outcault's images these qualities—variety, intricacy, and above all else, visual density—are pushed even further to link up with hallmark characteristics of the modern urban environment. Balzer's essay in the *Comics and the City* volume synthesizes comments on urban perception by Walter Benjamin and Jonathan Crary in an analysis of the *Hogan's Alley* images. Key to his argument is the way in which the city encourages a wandering gaze. The constant movement of the urban environment gives rise to the figure of the flâneur. Perception becomes ambulatory.[122] The density of the city's visual stimulation induces distraction and doubt. In urban modernity, the singular attention of contemplation is definitively replaced by the distracted attention of an ever-moving thought. In this context, Outcault's "teeming" images refine and carry forward patterns of reading already present in the eighteenth and mid-nineteenth centuries. Smolderen emphasizes the "zigzagging circulation of the reader's gaze" in Hogarth, and Kunzle insists on Töpffer's predilection for "casual mental zigzagging around," a trait shared with Baudelaire.[123] Similarly, in reading images of the Yellow Kid's antics, viewers are somewhat more challenged to find a foothold amidst the overwhelming overstimulation and overcrowding of the modern city.

Outcault's carefully staged urban scenes constitute a "space of the distracted gaze" and even "demand the distracted gaze of the *flâneur* in the city."[124] Here it is important to discuss how the artist's formal innovations contribute to an urban aesthetic of the distracted gaze. Many commentators have credited Outcault with the creation of the word balloon in comics.[125] Even though these accounts may be somewhat inflated, the artist's images are certainly rife with words.[126] Balzer underscores how words become graphic objects in Outcault's work. They appear inside balloons (or not), inscribed on walls or signs, floating in mid-air, and quite prominently on the Yellow Kid's nightshirt.[127] Rather than separating text from images with a panel bar as Töpffer had done, the *Hogan's Alley* comics integrate words and pictures seamlessly.[128] Though perhaps intentionally distracting, this invasion of the image plane by text is tied to the rise of print in the modern urban experience.[129]

Perhaps due to the overall chaos represented in Outcault's urban scenes, criticism has largely underplayed the foreground–background relationship of his images. Of course, it has been noted that the Yellow Kid stands out graphically on account of the vibrant color in which he is printed. Also important is his prominent positioning, often in the center or right-foreground of the frame.[130] Yet the relationship between the Kid and the other details of the scene deserve further reflection in light of an urban approach to Outcault's comics. Due to his intentional foregrounding, vibrant coloring, and dual service as both character and signage, he demands the reader's contemplation in a way that other aspects of the image do not. Readers who shift their gaze from the Yellow Kid to other urbanites and situations in the frame experience a visual shock. In this movement from foreground to background, contemplation cedes to distraction. What emerges is the threat of being lost in the crowd or even con- sumed by the city. Behind the iconic figure lie the teeming urban slums, which readers either identified with or perhaps feared. Scholars may have overstated Outcault's artistic innovations or his role in high-profile newspaper circulation wars, but in the story of urban comics, there is no doubt of his significance.[131]

WINSOR MCCAY'S EARLY TWENTIETH-CENTURY (SUB)UR-BAN DREAMSCAPES

Because some details have been somewhat cloudy, scholarship has not tradi- tionally agreed on the circumstances and upbringing of the artist who was born in the US state of Michigan as Zenas Winsor McCay (1867–1934).[132] That said, critics do overwhelmingly agree on the significance of his work. McCay is of indisputable importance in histories of comics. He influenced a number of esteemed artists from Charles Schulz to Robert Crumb, Art Spiegelman, and Chris Ware (ch. 4).[133] Scholar Jeet Heer writes of the early twentieth-century artist, "If not the greatest of cartoonists, [Winsor] has a uniquely pivotal role in the history of the form."[134]

Like many comics artists, in his youth Winsor McCay could not be prevented from drawing. He carried this passion for visual art with him later even as he became a student at Cleary's Business College in Ypsilanti, Michigan. In fact, instead of attending classes, he snuck off to Detroit to draw visitor portraits at a local dime museum called Sackett & Wiggins's Wonderland and Eden Mu- sée.[135] In 1889 he moved for two years to Chicago, where he would apprentice at the National Printing and Engraving Company. In 1891 he moved from Chicago to Cincinnati to work at Kohl and Middleton's Dime Museum, where he designed sets for what were generally referred to as exotic curiosities or freak show acts.[136] He then worked as a newspaper illustrator at the *Cincinnati Commercial Tribune* and later became the head of the art department at the *Cincinnati Enquirer*. In 1903 he ventured to New York and began drawing strips for the *New York Herald*, run by a competitor of Hearst and Pulitzer.[137] Though his work on *Rarebit Fiend* was clearly more mountainous than *Little Nemo*,[138] it was the latter comic that has become synonymous with his reputation. Its success at the *New York Herald* contributed to his move, in 1911, to work for Hearst's paper, where he would become the magnate's chief editorial cartoonist. Leaving the title *Little Nemo in Slumberland* behind, he continued to publish the strip under the name *In the Land of Wonderful Dreams*.[139]

One perspective on comics artists of the early twentieth century distinguishes the entertainers from the thinkers. The authors of *A History of the Comic Strip* place McCay in the latter category of artists. These thinkers were a group whose members "wished to 'intellectualize' the comics, and attempt to explore all their possibilities, both formal and narrative."[140] The comics for which McCay is most well known—*Little Sammy Sneeze* (1904), *The Dream of the Rarebit Fiend* (1904), *Hungry Henrietta* (1905), and *Little Nemo in Slumberland* (1905)[141]—are true to that characterization. Full of formal innovations, they played with and even broke narrative conventions. Perhaps the most famous example of this penchant for the unconventionally self-reflexive is a single six-panel strip of the *Little Sammy Sneeze* series. In the iteration of the comic published on September 24, 1905, the title character's sneeze is so powerful that it causes the panel frame to collapse around him. This self-reflexive act breaks through from the diegetic plane of the comic as Sammy and his story merge with the world of the reader. Overall, as this example illustrates, McCay's success came from knowing how to contrast "the sterile rhetoric of automation and fixed formulas with the verve of a lively thought"—a quality that Smolderen has used to compare the artist with Hogarth and Töpffer.[142]

Among McCay's innovations, including advances in color and design, perhaps none is as important as his contribution to panel framing.[143] This constitutes, as Katherine Roeder notes, a further connection with Töpffer, who had played with panel size to great effect to convey different ideas of time in *Histoire d'Albert*.[144] McCay's panels are panoramic, and of variable size.[145] The artist harnessed such spatial innovation in support of his narrative, resulting in a unique page composition.[146] The result was a unique page composition.[147] The fact that *Little Nemo*, for example, took up a full newspaper page (of sixteen by twenty-one inches) in the *Herald*'s color comics Sunday supplement only gave the artist a bigger canvas to fill using his intricate graphic detail and bold formal innovation.[148] His ability to integrate the strip into a page format while preserving its own logic and rhythm is notable and has attracted the attention of scholars such as Thierry Groensteen and Benoît Peeters.[149]

Influenced by European illustration traditions on one hand, and on the other by visual spectacles such as the Chicago World's Columbian Exhibition of 1893 and Coney Island, McCay sought to reach a relatively sophisticated group of readers.[150] His general themes reflect the aesthetics of the dime museums and circuses that captured the public imagination in the early twentieth century.[151]

He was as captivated as anyone by these popular forms of entertainment and was clearly drawn to appreciate their spectacular dimensions.[152] Beyond comics, he was also known for his vaudeville acts and experimental animated films.[153] He frequently appeared on the same vaudeville bill as the Three Keatons (the most famous of the three being Buster Keaton) and would screen his animated masterpiece *Gertie the Dinosaur* (1914) in such a way that he appeared to interact with and even tame the beast on screen.[154] He also made a number of other animated films—*How a Mosquito Operates* (1912), *Little Nemo* (1913), and *The Sinking of the Lusitania* (1918), for example—each of which required the creation of somewhere between four thousand and twenty-five thousand hand-drawn images.[155] In light of the routine distance that so often obtains between studies of comics and studies of animated films, McCay's comics and his animated film aesthetics suggest important and intriguing links between the two art forms.[156]

The urban aspects of strips like *Little Nemo* and *Rarebit Fiend* are unavoidable. Interestingly enough, Catherine Labio begins a broadly conceived article titled "The Architecture of Comics" with a remark on McCay's work.[157] Fascinated by architecture, the artist's comics carefully represented public places linked with a burgeoning consumer society, such as department stores and amusement parks. Yet he also depicts elevated train lines and other urban and architectural hallmarks of the modern city.[158] While panel architecture and city architecture are both unavoidable topics when discussing McCay, however, existing criticism has usually stopped short of acknowledging how pervasive and important the theme of the urban is to understanding his oeuvre. A prime exception is Katherine Roeder's *Wide Awake in Slumberland: Fantasy, Mass Culture, and Modernism in the Art of Winsor McCay* (2014). Roeder explores the urban themes and architectural qualities of selected *Rarebit* episodes in depth. One example includes an episode where a dreamer becomes a giant destroying New York City, complete with aerial views and iconic representations of the Flatiron Building, the Brooklyn Bridge, and the Statue of Liberty.[159] More generally, she argues, the strip depicted and even poked fun at its urban readers, critiquing the fast pace of urban living and expressing urban anxieties.[160]

McCay's masterpiece, *Little Nemo*, was no less a vehicle for urban critique. The strip ran from 1905 to 1914 and was briefly revived between 1924 and 1927.[161] Its first appearance was October 15, 1905. As Roeder puts it, "*Nemo* is a truly baroque labyrinthine voyage, filled with serpentine lines, kaleidoscopic effects, perforated panels, and flamboyant architecture."[162] In every episode of the comic, the title six-year-old protagonist seamlessly enters a dreamscape or a nightmare, only to end up in the comfort of his bed in the last panel of the page. Considering selected examples from this comic in depth allows readers to see how thoroughly McCay's work was immersed in the context of urban modernity.[163]

The mixture of fantasy and reality in the *Little Nemo* strips is inextricable from its urban context.[164] It is important to keep in mind Richard Marschall's general observation that McCay relied heavily on skyscrapers and dragons.[165] Slumberland is at once a fantasy realm and a realistic space associated with the development of the modern city. Many, but not all, of Nemo's fantasies are specifically urban dreams or urban nightmares. The recurring fantasy characters in the series—King Morpheus, a beautiful princess, and others such as Impy, Dr. Pill, and Flip—demonstrate an ambivalent connection with urban class narratives of the time. On one hand, the world of fairy tales can be seen to function as an ideological veil, one linked to the consumerist escapism upon which twentieth-century America began to capitalize. New patterns of consumption connected urbanites to an economy of spectacle wherein culture could be seen simplistically as a relatively autonomous area of modern urban living. Yet, on the other hand, fantasy stories also functioned as critique. They quite often underscored the ills of an increasingly industrialized, mechanized, and commoditized contemporary world.[166]

To assess this ambivalence in relation to McCay's high-profile comic, one merely need start with an iconic example. The *Little Nemo* page published July 26, 1908, in the *New York Herald* famously uses the trope of fantasy adventure to highlight the spatial distance and cultural contrast between urban downtowns and suburban living in early twentieth-century America. The class associations of its two protagonists, Nemo and Flip, are crucial to this contrast. The strip's title character, Nemo, is clearly "a middle-class child of the suburbs," and the opening and closing panels of this episode characteristically reinforce this in the depiction of an equally middle-class bedroom.[167] While Nemo represents the privileged white suburban middle class, however, Flip is graphically othered in line with the fantastical premise. His appearance and his actions are drastically different from Nemo's. He has been described as both "the green grimacing dwarf who involves [Nemo] in increasingly dangerous escapades" and "a cigar-smoking leprechaun type who appeared as a menacing figure but eventually became a disruptive associate."[16] As his name seems to reflect, Flip is the flip-side or other-side to Nemo, just as the world he inhabits is the fantasy escape from the modern urban world. Yet, as it is with all fantasy narratives, this dualism has its complement in urban reality. It is not surprising that Flip has been compared to the Yellow Kid from Hogan's Alley, who as we saw earlier embodied and symbolized the urban underclass of New York's Lower East Side.[169] Juxtaposed with Nemo, who "carries the mantle of respectable, middle class boyhood," Flip is then a "reckless yet engaging agent propelling the narrative forward."[170] Slumberland is in this sense not just a fantasy narrative but also a visual text through which one can reread the class dimensions of the modern American metropolis.

A second example shows how the space of the city is implicated in *Little Nemo*'s class-inflected narrative. A nod to the routine established in McCay's continuity strip,[171] the July 26, 1908, example begins in Nemo's middle-class suburban bedroom. The six-year-old's bed grows stilted legs, carrying both him and Flip from the suburbs into an urban downtown. They soon tower above even the tallest buildings. The verticality of the adventure emphasizes the height of the modern city—its tall buildings and its even taller skyscrapers. Formally, McCay connects the notion of verticality with urban anxiety by slowly increasing the height of the panels over the course of three rows. Of course, this progressive increase also visually recapitulates the gradual landscape shift experienced by those venturing into the city. Row by row, the panels stretch in height to reflect the transition from fenced single-family homes to buildings of five to seven stories and finally thirteen stories and taller. The stilted bed-legs tangle around an ornate cupola and threaten disaster.[172] McCay then uses the notion of falling as a bridge between the fantasy narrative and the middle-class routine of its protagonist. In the final panel, Nemo wakes up on the ground in his bedroom, having fallen out of his bed. It is important that this last panel of the final triple-height row is split in two. A top panel takes up two-thirds of the total height, while the bottom panel returns to the original height of the comic's first row. While the telescoping vertical shift carried out through the first two rows of the comic reflects an increasingly urban scale of experience (and the urban anxiety associated with it), the gradual collapse of the panel dimensions at the end of the third row reflects a return to the ordinary, that is, middle-class, suburban scale.[173] Because it is depicted as neither sudden nor harmful, this gradual panel collapse is itself carried out in a way that evokes the care and comfort demonstrated perhaps by a parent carefully and gently laying a child down in his or her bed. Emotionally, then, the comic begins and ends with images of the comfort and security that readers would also associate with life in the suburbs.

Throughout, McCay's comic normalizes the suburban experience and spectacularizes urban density. His paradigmatic innovation in the panel frame allows for height to connote anxiety and fear of the urb's vertical towers. If the progressive, stretched verticality of panels is purposely disorienting to readers, the last images enunciate a return to the horizontality of the initial panels—metonymically, then, to the reduced vertical dimension of suburban living. If the vertical disorients, it is due to the connections of urban downtowns with the working class and immigrant populations made famous in *Hogan's Alley*—also reflected indirectly through Flip's class associations. If the flattened horizontal dimension connotes safety and stability in this particular strip, it is in response to the seeming threat posed by those same urban populations to the construction of middle-class comfort. It should not be ignored that the class dimensions of the modern city are addressed in this example at a certain distance. Once again the comparison with the Yellow Kid can be instructive. One must keep in mind who the readers of *Little Nemo* may have been. Whereas "Outcault's *Hogan's Alley* was soon deemed too unsavory for the new middle class," McCay's intellectualized strips appealed to readers who might identify with Nemo's circumstances, specifically his rootedness in the suburban life of "a rather prosperous and certainly pedestrian urban couple."[174] From a class perspective, such readers engaged with the material conditions faced by the urban underclass only at a remove.

While readers may consider the material conditions of urban life to be merely implicit in the previous example, other comics by McCay deal with class more directly, even if still through the lens of the fantasy narrative. The aptly titled "Shanty Town" sequence of *Little Nemo*, which ran from March 22 through April 26, 1908, provides a glimpse into the lives of the urban poor as mediated by a suburban middle-class perspective. In one of the sequence's episodes, Nemo wanders through a desolate urban area. Dressed up as a combination of bourgeois prince and urban dandy, he takes stock of what he sees and exclaims, in the first panel, "This is the worst town I was ever in: Everything is a wreck!"[175] Initially, not a single person can be seen on the sidewalks. The windows of buildings are cracked, and a streetlight leans to one side, badly in need of repair. Miraculously, in the second panel, a sort of angel descends into the frame and hands Nemo a magic wand that will turn his wishes into reality. The fact that this scene unfolds against a black background implies that its action takes place in another plane of existence. Nemo then wanders around town, meeting the urban poor and, to put it bluntly, wishing them into class privilege with the powers of his magic wand. He gives a man new clothes, summons a fancy stroller for a woman's child, and conjures a new leg for an amputee. By the penultimate panel, a throng of urbanites crowds the streets, following Nemo as if he were the pied piper. "I'm Little Nemo!" he shouts. "Follow me and you'll all be happy!!! I will turn this place into a paradise!"

In its form and content, this full-page comic reproduces both the spirit and ideology of nineteenth- and early twentieth-century urban reform. On one hand, it communicates in a rather straightforward fashion the concerns of prominent reformers such as Jacob A. Riis, who had documented the deplorable conditions of the urban poor. On the other hand, it also replicates the limitations of an urban reform focused on symptoms rather than root cause. As urban theory has explored in great depth and historical breadth, the desire to ameliorate certain conditions of urban life was often articulated without a desire to introduce a fundamental change to the class structure of contemporary urban society. Thus, Henri Lefebvre was able to write extensively of nineteenth-century city planning and its legacy as a class project of urban modernity. Undoubtedly, McCay expresses a concern for the conditions of the residents of Shanty Town. Yet the fusion of a fantasy narrative with a form of social realism here is characteristically ambivalent in the sense already described above. The visual depiction of a hero who wishes the poor into the image of a middle-class, able-bodied consumer is a well-intentioned reformist's ideal, yet one that expresses also the limitations of a reformist's critique of social institutions.

Selected aspects of the image can be taken as politically progressive. It is important in this comic that the image of a vibrant community hinges on the movement of that community from their homes into common areas of the city, specifically the streets. The blackened doorways that run down the left and right sides of the page emphasize a large-scale collective movement of the community into the streets. The visual repetition of these empty spaces communicates the social power of such disalienating urban action. By connotation, the residents who constitute Shanty Town move en masse from their isolated private lives toward the cohabitation of shared public spaces. As Shanty Town collectively claims the right to the city, the comic underscores the potential of community action.

Nevertheless, there are subtle indications in McCay's page that complicate its presentation of the reformist's ideal. As Marschall mentions, this sequence is quite uncharacteristic, due to the way in which the artist "invested the usually passive Nemo with active powers."[176] The middle-class six-year-old's central role in what unfolds is more marked than it would otherwise be, and thus it deserves further scrutiny. In effect, the ex nihilo gifting of the magic wand to Nemo reinforces the centrality of a privileged class in resolving social problems. At the level of the page, this centrality in the reform process is supported by his positioning toward the center of each row. Interestingly, the urban underclass faces him from the page's left and right extremes, thus symbolically still located at the margins of social transformation. A visual relationship is established between the black-background panel in the first row of the page, in which Nemo receives the wand, and the landscape panel in the final row, in which he displays the wand proudly as he leads a throng of well-dressed urban poor triumphantly toward the reader. His position toward the center of each row belies the page's vertical organization and portrays the protagonist as central to both visual page and represented society. The fact that Nemo has been chosen by a higher power imbues his role with a sense of privilege that one might also associate with class interests. This privilege tends to naturalize and authenticate his leadership of the magical urban reforms that follow. In the end, the form and content of this image reflect not merely the dream of urban reform but also its key limitation, namely, a refusal to directly combat the ideology that preserved structural class interests even as reformers sought better living conditions for the urban poor.

Another comic in this Shanty Town sequence reveals how McCay prompts considerations not merely of urban reform but also the voyeuristic spectacularity of urban class tourism and the bourgeois science of city planning, specifically. In an installment published on April 5, 1908, Nemo uses his magic wand to turn an eviction cart into a sightseeing tour wagon whose side paneling is inscribed with the words "Seeing Shanty Town." The bright yellow color of the multitiered wagon is a striking reminder of the way that this color became associated with an urban underclass in Outcault's Yellow Kid comics. Here, however, the striking effect of the color yellow is reappropriated for the more privileged classes. It is not difficult to connect this comic's content to the way in which new voyeuristic forms of urban class tourism emerged in the twentieth century. Roeder reminds us in her analysis of this image, "Slum tours, which enabled well-heeled voyeurs the opportunity to survey the living conditions of those less fortunate, was a sanctioned form of entertainment at the turn-of-the-century."[177] A familiar ambivalence arises from the fact that the comic replicates in artistic form the visual conditions of the slum tour. Privileged readers are able to visually consume McCay's comics spaces as tourist-voyeurs visually consumed scenes of urban poverty. Both on and off the page, the social vision of reformers is thus flattened to its most simplistic and spectacularized form. In this same comic, McCay ties the theme of urban restructuring to nineteenth-century planning traditions. As the tour winds through a dilapidated urban block, Nemo uses his wand to create a broad modern avenue and an austere neoclassical building with marble columns. Driving by a large mud pit, the children on the cart exclaim that "it makes us sick when we play here," to which Nemo responds, "It won't make you sick anymore for I'm going to make it a park! My this is fun!" The penultimate image of the comic is a landscape panel containing a magnificent park with central plaza and ornate fountain. In the closing panel, Nemo's mother calls to him to get out of bed, and he responds, "I'm getting up as fast as I can, Mamma dear!" as if speaking on behalf of a city that wants to "modernize" as quickly as possible.

Here McCay manages to reference both the contemporary reformist support for the parks movement and the tradition of modern urban planning pioneered by Baron Georges von Haussmann in nineteenth-century Paris. In Roeder's words, "as Nemo plays the tour guide he becomes a little Baron Haussmann, explaining to his captive audience how he intends to transform the crooked streets and abandoned houses into wide boulevards and formal gardens, all with a wave of his 'wonderful wish stick.'"[178] In urban geographer David Harvey's phrasing, Haussmann famously "bludgeoned the city [of Paris] into modernity," destroying the old fabric of the city and constructing modern avenues on a geometrical grid.[179] The French planner also exemplifies Lefebvre's account of how the bourgeois science of city planning reinforced the class interests of a specialized group of "capitalist speculators, builders and technicians."[180] As with Nemo's approach in this comic, the tradition of modern city planning inaugurated by Haussmann in Paris and replicated by Ildefons Cerdà in Barcelona sought the solution to urban social problems in the reorganization of the city's geometrical form. Haussmann's own magic wand was none other than what Richard Sennett calls the "visual technology of power" that alienated planners from the lived city.[181]

It is tempting to see the Shanty Town sequence and its engagement with social issues as a unique moment in *Little Nemo*, as does Tim Blackmore.[182] Yet as suggested above, the comic is consistently in dialogue with the class dimensions of urban society. This dialogue, of course, tends to oscillate between complicity and critique regarding class narratives deeply embedded in the experience of the modern city. A final example illustrates how critical McCay could be in addressing the class relationships underlying the production of a modern urban society. In a comic from April 24, 1910, Nemo, Impy, and Flip travel to Mars. Even from outer space, the team can see evidence of the capitalist colonization of urban space. McCay covers the planet in signage that recalls Outcault's innovative use of text in the *Hogan's Alley* panels. From reading an excessive amount of repetitive wording, it becomes clear that a company called B. Gosh and Co. owns all the real estate on Mars. The plot action culminates in a later panel where the team learns that even the breathable air on the planet must be purchased. As Heer writes of this sequence, Mars is "the ultimate corporate dystopia."[183] In line with Lefebvre's account, whether on other planets or on familiar suburban and urban locations of Earth, capitalism has preserved itself "producing space, by occupying a space."[184]

As these examples show, Winsor McCay used the culturally urban form of comics to depict the modern city as multidimensional space. In his vibrant color pages, fantasy is joined with commerce, while urban anxiety and poverty contrast with suburban comfort and security.[185] Whether one regards the ambivalent attitudes of *Little Nemo* overall as a critique or a celebration of urbanism, however, it cannot be denied that the city is a spectacle throughout. Perhaps most important, readers of these Sunday pages were wrapped up in the same circuits of urban exchange as McCay's characters. On and off the page, the modern city was a chaotic visual splendor. Amidst the hustle and bustle of the city streets and the burgeoning forms of twentieth-century consumerism captured so well in his comics, the deeper conflicts of urban life are somewhat anesthetized. However, this is not the case with the next example of an urban comic, in which such conflicts are clearly in the foreground.

A CONTINUING URBAN LEGACY: SOPHIE YANOW'S *WAR OF STREETS AND HOUSES* (2014)

The final artist discussed in this chapter constitutes a stark contrast with Mc-Cay's fantastical approach but links with early urban comics in other important ways. Born in California, Sophie Yanow (1987–) moved to Montreal, Canada, where she experienced and took part in the Maple Spring of 2012. As of 2017 she was teaching at the Center for Cartoon Studies in White River Junction, Vermont.[186] Yanow breaks with the tempered social critique that characterized McCay's earlier comics, in a defiant critique of capitalist urban control. Her work provides an illustration of how the fascination of early comics with modern city street scenes continues in the twenty-first century. As discussed below, however, in both formal terms and historical content her style recalls that of Töpffer. Her black-and-white images are drawn with fluid lines and appear to be composed somewhat rapidly, giving them the outward appearance of a rough sketch.[187] This outward appearance, however, belies a much greater emphasis on narrative density and the construction of comics with explicitly political or accumulating symbolic meanings. For example, another work by Yanow, titled *What Is a Glacier?* (2017), weaves global warming, carbon footprints, and the leisure-tourism economy together along with an introspective consideration of the protagonist's interpersonal relationships. The comic explored here, *War of Streets and Houses* (Uncivilized Books, 2014), is a deeply urban text that similarly showcases Yanow's ability to combine the personal and the political.

Originally published as *La guerre des rues et des maisons* (La mauvaise tête, 2013), *War of Streets and Houses* appeared in English translation one year after its French publication. Nominated for the Ignatz Award for Outstanding Graphic Novel and the Doug Wright Spotlight Award, it won *La prix Henri-full-fluo-Lefebvre* from *l'Académie de la vie littéraire,* an organization housed in Quebec. As explored further below, the title of this prize is significant—Yanow's comics text resonates with the spatial thinking outlined by Henri Lefebvre himself. It also connects with the spatial strategies espoused by Guy Debord and the Situationists and what Michel de Certeau calls urban tactics. Yanow's own deep involvement with urban spatial politics necessarily feeds into her comic's impact. As her text documents, she was a participant in the Montreal protests of the Quebec Maple Spring. The essay "Psychoprotest: Dérives of the Quebec Maple Spring" by Marc James Léger and Cayley Sorochan (2014) brings the struggles of those same committed activists into clear relief. As the scholars note, 2012 saw record numbers of protestors from across Quebec gather to march in Montreal. The purpose of the protests was to draw attention to threats posed to democracy. Among these threats were the continuation of neoliberal practices and the criminalization of dissent, as well as persisting issues of access, affordability and the commodification of education. The Maple Spring was an important node—one among many—in a global wave of anticapitalist urban protests that included the Arab Spring, the Indignados in Spain, and Occupy Wall Street in the US. The spirit of these protests can be felt in Yanow's stylistics: one reviewer writes that "despite the sketchiness of her line, one never feels cheated in terms of visual impact" and is exposed to "the adrenaline and fear she experienced."[188]

The artist herself is aware of a fundamental duality of urban living, one that is a hallmark aspect of Marxist thinking on the city from Henri Lefebvre through Jane Jacobs. The city's density and its open public spaces make new forms of communitarian solidarity possible. Yet these same qualities also allow for the entrenchment of individualist attitudes and in some ways facilitate the control of urban populations by modern policing. In an interview Yanow has affirmed the role of open urban spaces and walkable cities in promoting social change.[189] It makes sense that the comics artist's own perspective emphasizes the promise and potential of urban density, that is, that prizing heterogeneity and difference in public space can lead to consciousness-raising. Yet this relative freedom is in some ways counterbalanced by urban control, as she also acknowledges in the interview: "In the city, there's the freedom to find other folks like me (queer folks, artists), and to establish various communities. There are enough different types of people that we can live without constant scrutiny from people that have known us since childhood, or from people that disapprove of our lifestyles. However, public life in the city is scrutinized, and people are policed and surveilled."[190]

Unsurprisingly, the comic's treatment of urban space has begun to attract the attention of critics. Anna Giaufret writes that "cartes géographiques, plongées, contre-plongées, représentations, de la casbah d'Alger et de celle de Casablanca, du skyline et des ruelles de Montréal, des centres commerciaux, des carrefours, la géographie de Montréal et la perception de l'espace la hantent entièrement dans cette BD" [geographical maps, high- and low-angled perspectives, representations of the Casbah of Algiers and Casablanca, of the skyline and streets of Montreal, shopping centers, intersections, the geography of Montreal and the perception of space haunt the entirety of this comic].[191] Yet it is not just the depiction of city space and urban conflict as content that matters in the case of this comic. Instead it is the way that this content is represented in the artist's innovative page arrangements. Yanow's text envisions contemporary urbanism to be a violence performed upon urban forms of living, and specifically upon the forms of community, heterogeneity, and difference that invigorate city life. The appropriate response to this violence, as *War of Streets and Houses* communicates it, is to identify the spatial logic that structures the urban form—and through it urban society—and to resist and subvert that logic through a commitment to emancipatory spatial thinking and spatial practice.

The artist's page design is crucial to this endeavor. She deftly varies her compositional strategies to foreground the regularity of spatial norms and, even more importantly, offers them up to critical scrutiny. The comic's first page introduces a six-panel motif that will repeat, with variation and rupture, throughout *War of Streets and Houses*. Only a thin black-line frame separates three rows of two panels apiece. The fact that there is no gutter separating these six panels adds to the general intensity of Yanow's sketch-drawings of figures and places and arguably accelerates the act of reading. Yet the artist also plays with this intimate framing in various ways. At times the two panels of each row are rendered a single, wider panel instead. At other times, Yanow uses spatial raccords across vertical and/or horizontal panel divisions to great effect (e.g., 2014: 25, 28, 42, 43, 52, 53, 56, 62, 63). The six-panel framing is sometimes absent, yielding to the creation of a single page-spanning image (e.g., 2014: 14, 19). Whether actors are inside a building or out on the streets, drawn backgrounds are minimal, and there is a tendency to white out the background entirely. This encapsulates Yanow's images in a stark relief she often employs so as to emphasize the protagonist's internal thoughts or the intimacy of a conversation (e.g., 2014: 16–19, 36–37). In one two-page sequence, pure abstraction predominates as Yanow represents the directional energy and explosive power of the strike in points, lines, and vectors, with the only representational drawing being that of a single figure who stands alone against a background of white (2014: 26–27).[192] The preceding page politicizes this exercise by explicitly opposing abstraction to embodied subjectivity: "Thinking about space / abstracting / in order to understand / might be one way to deal. / I am trying to remove myself from the picture but it is impossible," she notes in the text annotation (2014: 25).

Carrying out a critical urban reading of the comic as a whole involves interrogating Yanow's page aesthetics. The way that her structuring lines and rough-sketch images vie for the reader's attention is crucial to understanding the relationship between the critical urban content of her work and its emphasis on radical spatial politics. The beginning of *War of Streets and Houses* uses the regularity of the six-panel motif to convey the demands of Maple Spring protestors concerning the right to education and the right to demonstrate in the city (2014: 8–9). Textual annotations are used throughout the work as a narration over drawn events. These are reflections on childhood, on the personal, social, and legal nuances of demonstrations, and on the nature of space and relationships. Yanow also occasionally relies on dialogue, however. Intercalated in the comic are intellectual thoughts and conversations among student activists that can also resonate with and even educate readers. These cover many topics:

the relationship between architecture and control (2014: 15), the nature and use of kettling as a strategy used by urban police (2014: 31), the way that race and immigration status impact dissent (2014: 32–33), the countryside as both an escape from the city and a retreat from challenging spatial power (2014: 7, 19, 51, 57–59, 62), and the urban politics of films like *La Haine* and *The Battle of Algiers* (2014: 52–55).[193] A particularly significant set of pages explores the commonality between two planners separated in time and space but united by a common scalar approach to modernizing the urban form: Haussmann in nineteenth-century Paris, and Robert Moses (ch. 3) in twentieth-century New York (2014: 44–45).

Arguably the most important sequence of all appears a bit over halfway through *War of Streets and Houses* and concerns the historical figure who has inspired the title of the comic. Thomas Robert Bugeaud (1784–1849) was a French general who in the 1840s famously tore apart the urban fabric of the city of Algiers during a colonial war. Frequently considered a tactical genius, he cut his teeth fighting for Napoleon in Spain and was present for the notorious uprising against the French occupation of Madrid on May 2, 1808, as well as the urban conflict in Saragossa in 1809.[194] He was particularly inspired by the guerrilla tactics he saw in Catalonia.[195] From his time in Spain, Bugeaud gained the reputation of "an expert at 'war of the streets.'"[196] *War of Streets and Houses* is thus also the title purportedly given to a manual he wrote on urban warfare and urban guerrilla tactics in 1847 or 1848. One scholar has written that it was less of a manual and more of a pamphlet, and the notes section at the end of Yanow's comic dares to assert that it was never even published.[197]

Doubts surrounding the status of the manual notwithstanding, Bugeaud's tactics became somewhat legendary and had a notable impact on military urban warfare. The enclosed spaces, curved streets, tight dimensions, and nooks and crannies of the city provided easy shelter and made it possible for small groups to hold off much larger forces. By modifying the urban fabric and clearing wide-open areas through systematic building demolition, however, an invading army could more easily control the battlefield. The restructuring of urban space was not just a strategy used by invading generals, however. Urban resistance fighters, for example, also saw the value of spatial tactics. This is reflected in an important work by Louis Auguste Blanqui, for example, an important figure connected to the Paris Commune.[198] As Yanow captures so well, in the twenty-first century both dissenting protestors and militarized police forces each seek to utilize the urban form to their own advantage in echo of ruminations by Bugeaud and Blanqui. Collectively, the movements and tactics used by these opposed groups inscribe the city with narrative of class conflict that mirrors what took place in Algiers in the 1840s under circumstances of colonial oppression.[199]

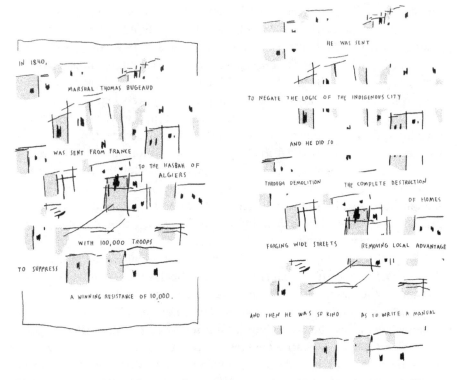

Figure 1.1—Yanow, *War of Streets and Houses* (Minneapolis: Uncivilized Books, 2014: 38–39)

The comic *War of Streets and Houses* returns to this heavily mythologized colonial war as an explicit intertext for contemporary struggles, including the Maple Spring. As the textual annotations on two unpaneled pages make clear:

> In 1840, / Marshal Thomas Bugeaud / was sent from France / to the Kasbah of Algiers / with 100,000 troops / to suppress / a winning resistance of 10,000. / He was sent / to negate the logic of the indigenous city / and he did so / through demolition / the complete destruction of homes forging wide streets / removing local advantage / and then he was so kind / as to write a manual. (2014: 38–39)[200]

As can be observed in figure 1.1, Yanow's drawings fashion a graphic representation of the Casbah in Algiers that is purposely fragmented and incomplete. The text is broken up over the space of the page rather than grouped together, reflecting the dispersion of small groups of fighters battling a colonial army. On the whole, empty space predominates, and the architectural connections between buildings are implied rather than depicted. The artist uses only dots for shading individual pieces of walls, amorphous shading to indicate doors and windows, and black lines for selected planes of buildings (roofs, facades, sides). From the verso to the recto page, these half-drawings expand to take up more of the total space of the image plane. In the process, they supplement the text's introduction of Bugeaud by crafting a visual representation that works at various levels. The density of the building structure is evident on both pages through the presence of lines and further implied through their absence. The gaps in the drawings convey the way that the nuanced architecture of the Casbah served both as a material challenge to French colonizing forces and also more symbolically as a more immaterial challenge to a totalizing military and cultural knowledge of the enemy. On subsequent pages (2014: 40–41), Yanow then includes text presumably taken from Bugeaud's manual concerning the practice of house-to-house demolition and the construction of urban barricades from the very architecture of buildings.

The intermittent rupture of the six-panel comics structure established over the pages of *War of Streets and Houses* recalls the destructive clearing of large sections in the Casbah by General Bugeaud. That is, the departure from the six-panel form on the pages introducing the general and his manual effects a shift in scale that can be tied to Bugeaud's military actions and that anticipates the large-scale planning carried out by figures such as Haussmann and Moses. Modern urban planning indeed owes much to military destruction.[201] In fact, scholars commonly assert a direct link between the French general Bugeaud and the French urban planner Haussmann. Eyal Weizman writes that the planner was directly inspired by a reading of the Marshal's manual, and that he used urban design to quell social resistance.[202] In *Cities under Siege* (2011), Stephen Graham counts Haussmann as an "avid reader" of Bugeaud's text.[203] Yanow herself renders Bugeaud's connection with Haussmann explicit in her comic, echoing Graham's language in portraying the urban planner as "an avid fan" of the Marshal's military strategies (2014: 42).[204]

> Some 20 years after Bugeaud takes Algiers / Haussmann, an avid fan, is hired to overhaul Paris / wartime need not be an excuse-/ slice through the tiny streets! / the Banalisation of the gutting of a city / Haussmann "modernized" until the money ran out. / Later / when the people of Paris barricade their streets (even the new wide boulevards)-/ and temporarily form a self-governing commune, Haussmann will lament, the story goes, / that if his work had been completed, the communards could never have taken the city. (though they were eventually slaughtered). (2014: 42–43)

On these pages, Yanow's style hints a return to the six-panel form but does not fully adopt it. The use of spatial *raccords* and double-wide panels on each page helps to foreground the fundamental duality of the line on the comics page. Conceived as a border, the line at once separates and also connects panels. The lack of an interpanel gutter lends a certain density to the hyperframe, as panel contents are pushed up against one another with little breathing room. Further, in fashioning images that span multiple panel borders, Yanow's use of spatial *raccords* challenges the solidity of the line. In formal terms, the artist subverts the strict structure of the panel form, making use of it as it suits her. Unlike the previous example (2014: 38–39), where the six-panel structure was cleared entirely resulting in a full-page image, here the panel structure informs but does not determine the layout of the sequence.

This subversion or appropriation of structure at the level of comics form has a clear complement in the social practice that subverts or appropriates urban form in the street protest. For the artist-activist, space is thus malleable in two senses. There is the physical or material malleability of space, the physical form of the city as constructed in the interests of empire, planners, builders, developers, and capital. Yet there is also the malleability of what Eyal Weizman calls the "political plastic" of architecture. Weizman notes, "The term architecture should be understood as a 'political plastic,' where political forces are reconfiguring the organization of matter."[205] The malleability of space simultaneously applies to urban form comics form. The duality of the line on the page—as a border that separates and connects —has its complement in the city street conceived as a line of urban form. On the page the structure of the comics grid shapes but does not determine its impact. Similarly, in the city the structure of urban streets shapes but does not determine social action.

As Yanow makes clear in a two-page spread (2014: 60–61), *War of Streets and Houses* is able to underscore the malleability of space by fusing these two considerations: urban form and comics form. A six-panel grid appears on each of the two pages. Against the pervasive white background, an agglomeration of buildings stands alone on each page. As if formed by separate smaller buildings drawn together by a magnetic force, the buildings have coalesced into one solid if convoluted structure. The use of spatial *raccords* by the artist represents the images as if floating in space across multiple panels. One corner of each agglomeration obscures the panel frames underneath it. The textual annotation is spread equally over each of the panel spaces:

In Casablanca / there are these buildings / hardly uniform / thoroughly lived in / you would never know / that balconies were closed in that floors were added that these were once modernist spaces / We can do with space whatever we like / dilute "the purity of the form" / uphold it / scale may play a role / in the end it's a question of ownership / but it's a pretty big question. (2014: 60–61)

As Henri Lefebvre asserted so carefully in his extensive publications, the urban form of the city is a social space that reflects the values of the society that produced and continues to reproduce it.[206] Lefebvre would agree that we "can do with space whatever we like," with the understanding that not all have an equal ability to shape space in their own interests. His oft-repeated call for urbanites to exercise "the right to the city" dovetails with the activist call for direct action and entertains the same goal: to understand the production of space as an inherently undemocratic enterprise co-opted and obscured by capitalist ideology.

Particularly because *War of Streets and Houses* won *La prix Henri-full-fluo-Lefebvre,* it is necessary to linger for a moment on the work's connection with Lefebvre's urban theory. Yanow's focus on Algiers is interesting in that it prompts a consideration of how advanced capitalism turned its accumulation strategies inward. This was a theme at the core of Lefebvre's three-volume *Critique of Everyday Life.* As McKenzie Wark notes: "Lefebvre starts from the observation that the leading strategists of advanced capitalism recognized the futility of clinging to colonies such as Algeria, and advanced instead a strategy of colonizing everyday life."[207] Yet even more important, the comic offers a valuable meditation on a key distinction of urban theory. Lefebvrian thought differentiates between the city and what is called the urban.[208] While the city is a practico-material fact, the urban is a less tangible set of relationships. Going beyond the simple materiality of the city, Lefebvre theorized the urban as defined by encounters and thus as a site defined by struggle. In *The Survival of Capitalism*, he wrote:

> It is worth remembering that the urban has no worse enemy than urban planning and "urbanism," which is capitalism's and the state's strategic instrument for the manipulation of fragmented urban reality and the production of controlled space. [. . .] The urban, defined as assemblies and encounters, is therefore the simultaneity (or centrality) of all that exists socially.[209]

While the city is an object or a relatively static set of structures, the urban is a dynamic relationship that is constantly being shaped and reshaped through practice.[210] The city is conceived as a form, while the urban necessarily resists and overflows that form. The conceptions of space imagined into being by developers, capitalists, and speculators engage the geometrical, static spatial vision that has for hundreds of years been the fundamental building block of modern urban planning, from Haussmann to Moses. Yet urban life is not always contained by space so conceived, and the distance between urban design and urban practice speaks to the conflict that is inherent to all urban space. Struggles over space, as Lefebvre asserts, are struggles that at once involve the whole of social life.

The philosophical through-line of Yanow's comic is rooted in Lefebvre's hallmark opposition between the city and the urban. Its pages return again and again to the distinction between spatialized urban control and the spontaneity of urban life, between ubiquitous surveillance and exceptionalized dissent. The use-value of the streets, their potential value for urbanites, is contrasted with the exchange-value of the city, or rather the notion that the city is a bourgeois space preserved by the state as a site for consumption and capitalist accumulation. While apparent in its macro theme of Maple Spring activism, this idea resonates even in the comic's most concise statements. To see an example, one need merely take note of a word balloon that reads, "I just can't hear one more person call a broken window 'violence'" (2014: 56). In comics form, *War of Streets and Houses* juxtaposes the coherence and the integrity of the image against the divisive logic of the line. As the final pages of the book demonstrate so well (2014: 62–63), the straight line cannot contain the unplanned and unplannable vibrancy of urban life.

The form of Yanow's comic links Bugeaud's military tactics with urban planning, architecture, and contemporary neoliberal urban control. Her pages relate urbanism's lengthy and nuanced history. She encapsulates the ongoing urban struggle from colonial Algiers through Haussmann, Moses, and the Maple Spring. In this way the comic becomes a vehicle for challenging the solidity of urban form and denouncing the spatial logic of neoliberal capitalism. Yanow's spontaneous and even Töpffer-esque style brings to the comics page an ephemeral energy, one that, importantly, reflects the ephemeral energy of the protest and the spontaneity of urban life more generally. Moreover, Yanow's fascination with radical protest needs to be understood as a specific contemporary variation on the obsession that early comics held for the streets of the modern city.

In conclusion, this chapter has traced the significance of the city streets for the early comic and its legacy from the eighteenth to the twenty-first century. Individual artists have served as representative examples of connections between the development of comics and the development of the urban form. Recent work by Thierry Smolderen prompted us to reconsider the origins of modern comics and specifically to recognize the early contributions of William Hogarth to an urban mode of the ninth art.[211] Rodolphe Töpffer's fluid, spontaneous line, his deep thinking and comics innovation must be seen in relationship to his urban themes—most of all, the country–city opposition, and the historical reality of armed urban conflict. Richard F. Outcault's comics representations of tenement life in *The Yellow Kid* and *Hogan's Alley* portrayed the modern city in terms of both population and semiotic density. Winsor McCay's work showcased the class character of consumer practices and city planning as well as the potential of fantasy to both provide escape from and at once comment on urban life. Finally, Sophie Yanow's work brought together many hallmarks of these varied legacies: Hogarth's urban mode, Töpffer's fluid line and theme of urban conflict, and the distance between the class character of Outcault's and McCay's urban representations. The remaining chapters of this book build on these themes, showing that the urban legacy of early comics continues to be reshaped and reimagined by contemporary artists. In chapter 2, "The Passions of Everyday Urban Life," this lengthy chronological journey is repeated, but in a different key. It begins with Belgian creator Frans Masereel's wordless comics in the early twentieth century and ends with Chinese-born artist Daishu Ma's wordless urban tale in the twenty-first.

CHAPTER 2

THE PASSIONS OF
EVERYDAY URBAN LIFE

This chapter traces the representation of a variety of human passions through urban comics. These are passions related to hedonistic pursuits, leisure time, religious belief, sorrow, familial bonds, sexuality, and romance. Also considered are the spontaneity of everyday life and consumerism—the latter understood as a leisure passion whereby spontaneity is co-opted by the logic of urbanized capital. This journey starts in 1919 and ends almost one hundred years later, in 2015. Along the way we travel from Belgium, to New York and its South Bronx, to Spain, and finally to China. Throughout, the role of the human senses in the passionate life of the city is underscored. This emphasis on the human senses is consistent with a Marxian approach to urban everyday life. From a Marxian perspective, the act of turning toward the full richness of the interior lives of urbanites can be understood as a reaction to the dehumanizing forces that pervade the modern city. The end goal of this process is to recuperate the use-value of the human senses. Such a move potentially connects readers and city dwellers alike with radical forms of modern subjectivity.

It is important to historicize and urbanize the notion of passion as it is employed in this chapter. Historically speaking, there were two important shifts underlying the cultural moment of the modern city's formation. The first concerned a distinctly modern form of urban planning that had crystallized during the nineteenth century and that continued into the twentieth. As mentioned in passing in the previous chapter, Baron Haussmann's demolition and reconstruction of central Paris was predicated on the desire to fashion a city whose streets could facilitate the march of a modern police force. Haussmann himself took lessons on urban destruction from Marshal Bugeaud's military urbanism in colonial Algiers. This form of modern urban planning was destructive even in the best of cases. That said, it was sometimes inflected by legitimate concerns for the well-being of the working class. Such is the case with Ildefons Cerdà's plans for reconfiguring nineteenth-century Barcelona, or alternately the views of urban reformers such as Jacob Riis in late nineteenth- and early twentieth-century New York. In neither case, however, did these concerns for the working class change the root nature of urban planning. Broadly considered, the structure of the modern planned city had become the product of a specialized class of thinkers. The bourgeois science of urban design was leveraged against the spontaneity of urban life in a way that suited the needs of the powerful.

The second shift of note has to do with the increased industrialization and technological mechanization that became synonymous with modern city life. Lewis Mumford's classic text *The Culture of Cities* (1938) explores how a mechanistic logic took root in society through processes of industrialization and was applied to the process of city growth.[1] The extension of the railroad from the mines to industrial centers was a historical-material fact that both signaled and drove this machine logic.[2] Factories changed the very structure of cities just as they changed forms of urban living. They brought about new forms of oppression, along with new forms of solidarity. Long hours and the repetitive labor performed on the factory floor threatened to reduce human workers to the status of mere machines. Time was splintered as the hours of the working day became a tool leveraged by capitalist power to exploit labor and increase production. Yet this capitalist exploitation also created the opportunity for labor to organize and articulate a collective interest in defined spaces of the city. Necessarily, the tension between work time and leisure time began to drive everyday life. Roy Rosenzweig's classic text *Eight Hours for What We Will* (1983) is the book that perhaps best expresses this tension.[3] The passions of urban life thus take on a highly pertinent role in a city context defined by both the geometrical structure of urban space and the mechanized subdivision of the working day.

In line with these historical concerns, this chapter relies on an urban cultural studies framework to analyze individual comics centering on human passions. This framework acknowledges the primacy of urban alienation. Moreover, it also emphasizes the potential for urban disalienation. By this I intend to reference the recuperation of the human senses as a way of resisting the linear structure of modern urban planning and the drudgery of mechanized industrialization. Put another way, a return to the sensuous nature of the urban experience is one of the keys to combatting alienation. Significantly, Karl Marx's oft-ignored and frequently undervalued early writings—specifically the *Economic and Philosophical Manuscripts of 1844*—emphasize that "the transcendence of private property is therefore the complete *emancipation* of all human senses and qualities."⁴ The essential insight to keep in mind, as Andy Merrifield explains, quoting from Marx, is this:

> "The positive supersession of private property," Marx writes, "means the *sensuous* appropriation of the human essence and human life." Human essence doesn't just revolve around possession, around simply having or owning: people, according to Marx, appropriate their integral essence in an integral way, as "total people." Thus, "human relations to the world—seeing, hearing, smelling, tasting, feeling, thinking, contemplating, sensing, wanting, acting, loving—in short, all the organs of his individuality . . . are in their *objective* approach or in their approach to the object, the appropriation of the object."⁵

The human senses must be emancipated: to some, this may seem like a deviation from radical social critique. Yet those who approach Marx in the narrowest of senses—merely as an economic thinker rather than a philosopher of the totality of modern life—are seeing only part of the picture. As outlined in *The Economic and Philosophical Manuscripts*, from which Merrifield cites here, returning to the sensuous nature of experience is an important response to the alienation that for Marx was synonymous with modernity. Modern people are alienated from the product of their labor, alienated from themselves, and alienated from others. Based on these insights, an entire tradition of urban Marxist research has elaborated upon the importance of a sensuous approach to the modern city. Directly or indirectly, one encounters this tradition in the writings of Guy Debord and the Situationists, Michel de Certeau, David Harvey, Jane Jacobs, and Henri Lefebvre, as well as a host of more specialized academic works.

As theorists have noted, Henri Lefebvre is particularly responsible for transposing Marx's exploration of alienation into an urban key.⁶ He did this by fashioning an extensive *Critique of Everyday Life* that appeared in three volumes during his lifetime (1947, 1961, 1981), and whose fourth volume was published posthumously as *Rhythmanalysis* (1992). The forms of exploitation that for Marx expressed themselves in the class character of nineteenth-century life and that were visible on the factory floor took on new forms in the twentieth century. Lefebvre's work emphasized contemporary dimensions of alienation that Marx had not theorized as extensively. The multidimensionality of this continued Marxian critique relies on the Lefebvrian insight that daily life has been colonized. Thus "capitalist leaders treat daily life as they once treated the colonized territories: massive trading posts (supermarkets and shopping centers); absolute predominance of exchange over use; dual exploitation of the dominated in their capacity as producers and consumers."⁷ Alienation for the French spatial theorist was at once economic, social, political, ideological and philosophical.[8] Furthermore, this take privileged the urban field, as Lefebvre makes clear in *The Urban Revolution* where he writes, "Urban alienation contains and perpetuates all other forms of alienation."[9] Everyday urban life in the city was then a battleground. It was a realm where two opposing forces confronted each other in perpetual tension. As Merrifield explains, everyday life became "colonized by the commodity," but precisely for that reason it became a "primal site for meaningful social resistance."[10]

Over the second half of the twentieth century, the shift Lefebvre identifies in the everyday life of the European postwar extends across a range of global spaces. The simple consumerism of the early twentieth-century city, as reflected in the comics work of Winsor McCay (ch. 1), for example, soon fed into systematic exploitation of what Marx had called the tertiary circuits of capital. According to Lefebvre, capitalism survived throughout the twentieth century by producing space in its image.[11] David Harvey—who was inspired consistently by Lefebvre's ideas, from his early book *Social Justice and the City* (1973) through *Rebel Cities* (2012)—has theorized this shift in terms of capitalist strategies of flexible accumulation. Attention to this shift by Marxian spatial theorists such as Neil Smith (1984) has underscored the importance of the uneven geographical development of capitalism.[12] In certain locations, then—those places where conditions were conducive to this shift—industrial capitalism was eclipsed by the more flexible dynamics of post-industrialization. The exploitation of labor remains crucial to capitalist accumulation strategies under the paradigm of postindustrial production, but the service economy begins to displace the factory as a key node in the struggle between labor and capital. While direct action of the sort represented in the first chapter's investigation of *War of Streets and Houses* by Sophie Yanow is indispensable for those seeking social change, it is thus also important to reveal the many ways in which alienation figures into the urban environment at the level of everyday experience.[13]

This chapter relies on insights from the Marxian critique of urban alienation outlined above in its analyses. Yet instead of fleshing out the theoretical nuances just introduced, it engages with specific global comics texts. It moves from the social milieu associated with factory life in the early twentieth century to address the pervasive colonization of everyday life spanning the postwar period through the early twenty-first century. It focuses above all else on the role of the human senses in challenging the alienation and estrangement of modern urban life. Foregrounding a sensuous engagement with the urban experience in the analyses of these comics is a way of humanizing the city. Returning to the human senses potentially recuperates the city from circuits of exchange-value to assert the use-value its spaces hold for individual urbanites. The depiction of everyday urban life in these comics thus functions as a way of exposing the nature of the city as a battleground. Daily life in the city is a site of conflict.

Concerted control from above is met with everyday resistance from below. The comics discussed here address this tension by asserting the vitality of passions against the dehumanizing forces that pervade the modern city. The human senses and the passionate life of the modern city potentially disalienate urbanites from a pervasive individualism. The human passions connect city dwellers with others, with something outside of themselves, and they reconnect urbanites with the use-value of urban space against the exchange-value of the city. Each of the comics artists and individual texts selected for this chapter provides a different perspective on this universal human struggle to carve out a space within the modern city for passionate life. Yet what they all share is a concern with a conflict embedded in urban life. The key question is whether the city is imagined as a space for urbanites to use and enjoy, or whether it is a mere tool in cycles of capitalist reproduction and profit.

FRANS MASEREEL'S WORDLESS CITY WINDOWS

Born in Blankenberge, Belgium, Frans Masereel (1889–1972) lived in Ghent, Geneva, Berlin, London, and Paris. While younger than Winsor McCay, both urban comics artists were active in the first third of the twentieth century. Precisely because their styles are so strikingly distinct, it is interesting to pause and consider the distance between them. While McCay brought (sub)urban fantasy to life in narrative strips integrated to form full-page color spreads, Masereel strung together single-panel, black-and-white woodcut images to make novels in pictures. While the American employed a child protagonist and tended toward fantasy adventure themes, the Flemish artist preferred social realism and depicted adult struggles. Masereel was just as entranced by the urban experience as was McCay, but he adopted an explicitly working-class perspective on life in the modern city. McCay tended toward representations of middle-class comfort and spectacular consumerism. His comics imagination was filtered through the trope of the department store window, and it foregrounded the exchange-value of the city. Masereel, on the other hand, tended toward the comparatively coarse life of the streets. His perspective was filtered through the toils of factory life, and he exalted the city streets as a use-value for the urban dweller to enjoy.

Masereel worked as a political cartoonist, illustrated the books of others, and created over fifty wordless books of his own.[14] Drawn to depictions of the machine age and the disasters and aftermath of war, he is known for "his embrace of the larger themes of love and rejection, desire and despair, as well as his repeated attempts to create work depicting the struggle to find a meaningful political and social role in a hostile and demeaning world."[15] By the 1920s the artist had earned an international reputation, and prominent exhibitions were dedicated to him in New York (1923), Moscow (1926), and Mannheim (1929).[16] On the whole, his works are "dramas of class struggle, of the degradation and the thrill of urban life."[17] His leftist commitment led to his books being banned in Nazi Germany.[18] After 1933 he moved to London and later Paris. When France fell under German occupation, he lived in hiding with his wife, escaping only in 1945, and later returning to Nice in 1949.[19]

One could argue that the global rise of the woodcut novel owes to the quality of Masereel's compelling picture stories. More broadly speaking, as Florian Groß notes, wordless comics in general—whether woodcut novels or not—are a genre with a "transnational lineage" traceable to the Belgian-born comics artist.[20] Masereel sparked imaginations in Germany, Czechoslovakia, Hungary, Canada, and the United States. He prompted a parody titled *He Done Her Wrong* (1930), created by American Milt Gross (1895–1953), and inspired a great number of early twentieth-century artists and more contemporary graphic novelists. This lengthy list includes Adolphe Willette, Wilhelm Busch, William Gropper, Adrezej Klimoski, James Reid, Otto Pankok, Charles Turzak, Helena Bochorákavá-Dittrichová, Giacomo Patri, Laurence Hyde, Peter Kuper, Eric Drooker, George A. Walker, and even Will Eisner (below, ch. 2), Seth (ch. 4), and Jason Lutes.[21] The last section of this chapter also presents the opportunity to consider Masereel's influence on Chinese artists in general, and on the work of Daishu Ma in particular.

The American artist Lynd Ward, a relative contemporary of Masereel's, is a particularly interesting figure to consider in parallel to the Belgian artist. Ward studied graphic arts in Germany and, while there, discovered Masereel's works.[22] Because the latter were not widely distributed in the United States, as David Beronä notes, Ward's own woodcut novel *Gods' Man* (1929) was able to attract high levels of public attention, much as his forerunner had done in Europe.[23] As it was with Masereel, one of Ward's central concerns was also social injustice.[24] Yet there are certainly noticeable differences between the styles of the two woodcut artists. For example, Santiago García distinguishes the "rounded simplicity of Masereel and the sophisticated lines of Ward."[25] Beronä writes that Ward was "less explicit in his portrayal of sex than Masereel."[26] An additional consideration here would have to be the relatively prudish attitudes of American publishers. To wit, it is interesting to note, as Beronä does, that the publisher of the American edition of Masereel's *Passionate Journey* dropped two plates from the work, as if anticipating the likelihood of adverse reactions by readers: one where the male protagonist urinates from atop a tall building onto those walking below, and another depicting sexual intercourse.[27]

The wordless comics format immediately recalls Hogarth's eighteenth-century sequential engravings in England (ch. 1). It also raises—and in my view dispenses with—the same doubts identified by Thierry Smolderen about whether an image can narrate on its own terms without text. Yet, as a product of the early twentieth century, wordless comics also merit comparison with another visual technology of the time. Comics scholars have been tempted to see the success that both Ward and Maereel had with readers as relating to the existing viewership of silent movies.[28] The authors of wordless novels arguably shared with filmmakers of the moment a "fascination and dread in the face of the velocity and violence of contemporary life."[29] They also focused on the city as an emblematic site where the fast pace and rhythms of modern life could be observed. Santiago García goes on to state that films such as Walther Ruttmann's *Berlin: Symphony of a Great City* (1927) served as complements to the novels in pictures developed by visual artists of the time period.[30] It is important to note the deceptive simplicity of the format of wordless novels. Peter Kuper, a comics artist indebted to Masereel, has written that the lack of words in such novels requires "the reader to decipher what has taken place, then connect the dots from one image to the next. Though these stories can be quickly scanned and comprehended, what they offer grows with repeated viewing."[31] Likewise, scholars who study the form tend to emphasize that wordless comics are a genre with greater narrative demands.[32]

Among Masereel's many titles are *The Passion of Man* (1918), *My Book of Hours* (1919), *The Sun* (1919), *Story without Words* (1920), *The Idea* (1920), and *The City* (1925).[33] These works consistently portray the divisions between powerful industrialists and the working underclass in urban areas. The factory looms large in his images, paralleling cinematic depictions of the industrialized city that would later gain mass exposure through Fritz Lang's *Metropolis* (1927) and Charlie Chaplin's *Modern Times* (1936). Momentarily freed from the drudgery of their working hours, Masereel's protagonists passionately embrace the hedonistic life offered up by the city streets. His workers oscillate between systematic structure, order, and confinement, on one side, and ephemeral thrills, fleeting freedoms, and passionate movements, on the other. This tension is a fundamental theme of Masereel's oeuvre dating from his early work *The Passion of Man*. Beronä writes of this work that its backdrop is that of "an industrialized city—constrained and unfeeling—that overshadows human beings. The lines of buildings and machines are vertical and bold while those of the hero blend with rhythm and rise with motion."[34] While comparatively brief at only twenty-five panels, *The Passion of Man* establishes the hallmark stylistic conceit of his art that will be continued over the course of Masereel's career. Its storyline follows "a worker's life from cradle to grave."[35] As an adult, the man becomes a factory laborer, finds solidarity among his fellow workers, and enjoys hedonistic pursuits involving alcohol and sex. His rising class consciousness pushes him in search of knowledge and prompts him to lead others in revolt. In the end, he is arrested, put on trial and sentenced to execution, the sacrificial victim of an exploitative capitalist system.

In general, the artist's wordless panels function much as window scenes for readers to contemplate. Because there is only one image per page, the reader is in this sense more of a viewer. These viewers must engage in a visual scanning of the page, an act that foregrounds the interaction between individual elements contained within the image. In this way, Masereel's comics windows recall the way in which the artistic craft of painting had, for centuries, already allowed for narrative to exist in purely visual terms. The simple geometrical form of the panel and the lack of textual explanation suggest the view of street life that would be familiar to residents of an urban tenement. These are comics windows into everyday urban scenes whose rich textures evoke the contrasts of the modern city: the gap between working-class labor and upper-class opulence, between the social oppressions of state power and religion and the collective desire for leisure and escape, and between the industrial and the passionate views of the human being. The human body was tied to industrialization and regarded as a productive machine by capitalists, yet the human senses, stifled during the drudgery of the working day, were reserved a privileged place after hours. On the whole, Masereel's woodcut novels from the early twentieth century tend to focus on working-class life. This commitment forms the ground from which the artist pursues a pointed critique of the power inequities implicit in the modern city.

Passionate Journey (1919) was Masereel's most popular work and is still in print today. Not to be confused with *The Passion of Man* (1918), it was originally titled *Mon livre d'heures* and was published in the United States in 1922 under the English title *My Book of Hours*.[36] The book consists of over 160 woodcuts and is arranged with one 3 1/2 x 2 3/4-inch panel to each page. *The City* (1925) is similarly extensive in composition, also remains in print today, and is another one of his more popular works. In these two visual texts, Masereel's representation of his urban heroes corresponds to three pictorial scales. Some woodcuts show them as a minuscule speck, in others they are towering larger-than-life figures, and still others depict the human figure in harmony with its surroundings. These views correspond loosely to three perspectives on the relationship between the individual and the modern urban environment. Each of these perspectives deserves consideration.

When depicted as a small figure, Masereel's hero is revealed to be a relatively insignificant part of the larger industrial urban machine or the spectacular city. This perspective is frequently exaggerated by the figure's location at the margins of the panel edge or at the bottom of the woodcut. Towering city buildings frequently loom over individuals and signal their lack of agency against the social forces that dehumanize urban dwellers. At times a lone human figure scurries along the city streets as if a rat. At other times, it is easy to lose sight of the human figure, as in an image from *Passionate Journey* wherein a man stares out at an expansive cityscape, his figure enveloped by the textured urban fabric. One pair of images from *The City* portrays the human figure in ways that stress the insignificance of the individual. On the verso page, viewers delight in a fireworks display that erupts above darkened buildings and what seems to be a packed public square in the distance. The lone woman who leans out of a window resting her right arm on the windowsill to take in the festivities is hardly noticeable. She is cut into the wood in such a way that her figure blends in with the building rather than standing out in her own right. On the recto page, a solitary woman hurries home. She treads a brick pavement beneath intermittent streetlamps that cast shadows as often as they illuminate her path. Because of the way her arms are holding her head as she moves, it seems she is emotionally upset or even in tears. The overwhelming verticality of the modern city rises up behind her, indifferent to her concerns. Both of these images are in truth two sides of the same coin, for they express the tremendous magnificence and the extraordinary loneliness that can inform the urban experience.

When Masereel's human figures are represented as oversized or larger than life, however, they instead loom over their surroundings. Such is the case with the scene from *Passionate Journey* where the protagonist urinates on city dwellers below, with one foot atop each of two large buildings. A similarly composed image from *The City* shows a solitary man with a pickaxe atop a tall building. The man is depicted in relief against the surrounding cityscape and is located at the center of the image (see figure 2.1). The effect is as if he were a living statue raised in tribute to the working class, upon whose backs the modern city has been built. Another oversized image of the human figure appearing in *The City* portrays a man and a woman floating in the center of the panel against an urban background. A cloudlike border surrounds them, marking their separation from the urban environment and giving the couple's emotional intimacy an oneiric quality. This manner of presentation gives the impression that the notion of human intimacy is a powerful if idealized and fleeting notion. The sequential location of this image within the larger storyline only makes the aforementioned idealization more extraordinary by contrast. That cloudlike idealization appears after a panel depicting a rich man who pays for sex in a brothel, and before two images portraying the crowded spectacle of an urban nightclub and a solitary man who has hanged himself. In these examples, the spectacular city and its dehumanizing consequences are never far from the reader's thoughts.

Between each of these perspectives, the midscale comics representation of the human figure is perhaps more common in Masereel's works. The relative frequency of this view does not mean, however, that its meaning is unremarkable.

Figure 2.1—Masereel, *The City* (Mineola, NY: Dover 2006[1925]: no pag.)

In one image from *Passionate Journey*, the artist depicts his protagonist as being of equal size to a large factory gear. There is thus a certain harmony established in visual terms. The image evokes a correspondence between the human being and the machine. This visual correspondence is, of course, crucial to the developing theme of the protagonist's burgeoning class consciousness. Without needing text, the artist's decision to depict such proportionality or visual equivalency reinforces the theme of political equilibrium, that is, the potential for factories to be owned and controlled by the proletariat, directed by and in harmony with the interests of the working class. Elsewhere, the protagonist is sized to blend in with his factory colleagues as a formal expression of working-class solidarity or is depicted with urbanites who are enjoying the use-value of the city streets. This theme of urban community is essential to Masereel's art. The epigraph chosen by the Belgian artist to begin *The City* asserts this theme via a quotation from Walt Whitman: "This is the city and I am one of its citizens, Whatever interests the rest interests me."[37] Though the city may not always belong to its inhabitants, the Belgian artist is insistent that it is ideally understood as a collective project.

Masereel's urbanites negotiate what Florian Groß has called "a chaotic geography of anonymity and alienation,"[38] but they nevertheless find fleeting solace in the human connections that urban density makes possible. Alongside another quotation by Whitman, a quotation from the work of Romain Rolland serves as a second epigraph for *Passionate Journey* and underscores the sensuous nature of human experience: "Pleasures and pains, cutting remarks, experiments and follies, straw and hay, figs and grapes, unripe fruit, sweet fruit, roses and rose hips, things one has seen and read and known and had—lived through!" The senses are crucial components in the construction of these human relationships and play a key role in the process of combatting urban alienation. Readers should keep in mind that *Passionate Journey* was "the first of these adult novels in pictures that explored many facets of human nature including sexuality in an open and direct manner."[39] Also important is the fact that "Masereel presents the act of sexual intercourse between two adults in a pleasant, light-hearted atmosphere and not with the traditional immoral dark overtones."[40] In particular, as Beronä has explored, Masereel employs a "progressive display of human sexuality"—this display uses sexuality not as "titillating, pornographic material," but instead as a part of the sensuous experience of urban life.[41]

Beronä writes this of the protagonist at the end of *Passionate Journey*: "His love for all humankind is genuine and his revolt against commercialism and inequity eventually leads him away from the city into nature where he dies. He rises into the heavens and stomps on his heart before he walks serendipitously off into the cosmos."[42] As this ending reveals, and as Masereel's work consistently emphasizes, life is human passion, and the end of this human passion is death. The Belgian artist's persistent interest in the human passions—whether the passions of sexuality, romantic love, or the passionate desire for community building and justice—presents the city as a space defined by human action and human agency. The emotional states expressed in *Passionate Journey* run the gamut: desire, love, hate, regret, sadness, despair, grief, loneliness, commitment, exhilaration, the tedium of work, the value of work, the innocence of play, and the passion of ecstatic zeal. The representation of this full range of states of consciousness is significant. It constitutes an attempt by the artist to free the human senses from their alienation and to open up the full potential of the urban experience. As Lefebvre expresses well, the human being must respond to the alienation heaped upon us in the modern age: "The many forms of alienation are experienced obscurely and provoke muffled and profound anxiety. This is the source of the surge of spontaneity."[43] Only a spontaneous human response—that is, action freed from the constraints of mechanized routine, industrialization and the exchange of commodities, action that only begins with the dis-alienation of the senses—can emancipate the senses and lay claim to what Marx called the "total person." Ultimately it is the "*sensuous* appropriation of the human essence and human life" that leads to change in the material conditions that govern modern urban life. The comics that follow in this chapter continue to explore the significance of the human senses for urban life in echo of Frans Masereel's concerns.

WILL EISNER'S TENEMENT PASSIONS: FAITH, AGONY, LOVE, AND LOSS

Born to Jewish immigrants on March 6, 1917, Will Eisner began work as a child selling comics and cartoon books at a stand on Wall Street.[44] He ended his career as one of the most accomplished and widely recognized comics artists in the United States. Along the way, he worked for his high school newspaper, cleaned printing presses, and was employed at various publishing companies.[45] He founded his own comics company with his friend Jerry Iger, created the American Visuals Corporation, which produced comics for educational and commercial customers, including even the US Army, and later taught cartooning at Sheridan College and still later the School of Visual Arts in New York.[46] The insights he delivered in his class lectures found their way into two important publications: *Comics and Sequential Art* (1985) and *Graphic Storytelling and Visual Narrative* (1996).[47] The first of these, in particular, was seen as a groundbreaking theoretical work, and it had a significant impact on Scott McCloud's own theoretical presentation of comics as sequential art in

Understanding Comics (1993).[48] Will Eisner, many readers will already know, has comics prizes named after him. Along with the Harvey Award, named after Harvey Kurtzman, the Eisner Awards are the most important awards to recognize cartooning in the US. Since 1988 these awards have been inducting artists into what is recognized as a veritable comics hall of fame.[49]

Eisner's reputation has only grown since his death in 2005. Charles Hatfield refers to him as a "venerable comic book pioneer," and Greg M. Smith emphasizes how the artist "became an emblem for creator-driven quality comics."[50] Perhaps the most noteworthy period of his career in this respect is his partnership with Jerry Iger. In what is commonly referred to as the Eisner-Iger Studio, the pair were known for producing comics rapidly and in large quantities for pulp publishers.[51] Santiago García explains the larger context of comics workshops:

> The comic book business inherited many of the features of the pulps business: the publishers were outsiders and of dubious background, and their only objective was to produce material rapidly and to recuperate their investment as quickly as possible. There emerged a production system organized in "shops," studios or "workshops" that functioned like real assembly lines where entire comic books were produced for the publisher that commissioned them.[52]

One can argue that the value of Eisner and Iger's studio was somewhat ambivalent. On one hand, it was a success for the two owners, who occupied a position few other artists were able to enjoy in the industry. "Will Eisner owned everything he did, and reaped the rewards," Roger Sabin writes, adding that "the more common story is one of exploitation and disillusion."[53] Nevertheless, Eisner and Iger also perpetuated an industrialized form of artistic production that was all too common of comics publishers of the day. While their studio offered up a challenge to standard production hierarchies in the sense that it was owned by creators, it also continued the relegation of artists to secondary roles. Owners perpetuated the industrialized logic of the comics assembly line through publication pressures that limited the creativity of artists—tight deadlines and predetermined panel layouts, for example.[54]

The assembly-line production of print publications was pervasive in the early twentieth century. An image from Frans Masereel's *The City* illustrates this factory-style method of print production. It depicts a room housing a team of what seem to be either writers or possibly even illustrators. None of their faces are visible, such that they stand in for the generalized figure of the dehumanized worker. They sit at individual desks that are neatly organized into rows; each person is an isolated solitary node contributing to a larger production process. The inclusion of a window in Masereel's interior scene allows a glimpse of the urban environment outside. Importantly, this glimpse conveys an understanding of the larger context in which the finished print work will be viewed and circulated, bought and sold. A single-image cartoon titled *Comix Factory* designed by Joost Swarte for the cover of *Raw* magazine in 1980 returns to this motif (ch. 4). Yet Swarte's image restages the drudgery of production in a much more theatrical and even cinematic context. Interestingly, Eisner's own autobiographical comic *The Dreamer* explores his real-life experiences with such comics workshops, although with the use of pseudonyms.[55]

Largely because of the success of the studio he founded with Iger, Eisner was hired away from his own company by Busy Arnold (Quality Comics Group) to create sixteen-page comic inserts for newspapers. The continuity strip he titled *The Spirit*, which ran from 1940 to 1952, was the lead contribution of these inserts.[56] Bart Beaty writes of *The Spirit* that it is "the first of the comic books."[57] It was also highly successful, appearing "in 20 papers with a total circulation of 5 million."[58] *The Spirit* centered on "the hardboiled adventures of a mysterious masked crime-fighter and his black sidekick 'Ebony White.'"[59] The protagonist's real identity was "Denny Colt, a detective whose presumed death provided a cover for him" to investigate crime in Central City, a fictional stand-in for New York.[60] The urban dimension of this early success was palpable, as Stefan Helgesson draws out in a 2015 article: "The physical cityscape of *Spirit* is labyrinthine, cramped and poorly lit. In the final analysis, the cramped and threatening spaces of Central City are to an equal degree 'intimate,' an indication of Eisner's enduring faith in the capacity of people to inhabit their urban space as autonomous subjects. The city becomes its inhabitants."[61] Eisner's interest in the everyday lives of city dwellers is clear in this earlier action series, but the subsequent urban comics work that cemented his reputation is somewhat more introspective in character.

A Contract with God (1978) is the first of three interconnected long-form works by the artist that explore the everyday struggles of urban residents living on or near the fictitious Dropsie Avenue, located in the Bronx. Intentionally branded as a "graphic novel," *A Contract with God* brought a new level of attention to Eisner's oeuvre and was followed by two books that completed the trilogy: *A Life Force* (1988) and *Dropsie Avenue* (1995). It is common to read that the artist is "the patriarch of American comics" and even that he is "the father of the modern graphic novel."[62] While such attention itself may be indeed warranted, it is misleading to say that Eisner invented the graphic novel. The work of David Kunzle and David A. Beronä on comics of the nineteenth and early twentieth century illustrates that novels narrated through images were far from new when Eisner caught the public's eye in the seventies. The use of the specific term "graphic novel" in the twentieth century dates from at least the mid-sixties, though Eisner claims not to have known this at the time.[63]

Notwithstanding, it is quite reasonable to think that he was instrumental in popularizing the term.[64] At the time, Eisner was looking to develop comics that appealed to adult readers who were twenty-five or thirty years old.[65] In hopes of expanding his readership, he sought to "break into bookstores, not comics shops," and the explicit marketing of A Contract with God as a graphic novel was a crucial part of this strategy.[66] Eisner's explicit aim to bring comics into the literary market, however, has been increasingly viewed with skepticism, as scholars have struggled to distinguish the ninth art from literature and cinema and bring attention to the specific formal properties of comics.[67]

Urban passions are a crucial part of Eisner's later work. These are evident at the level of content in his trilogy's treatment of sexuality as well as its focus on the interior lives and the daily struggles of his protagonists. Notably, Eisner employed sexuality in A Contract with God to further the impact of his urban themes. The graphic novel was actually a collection of four shorter narratives, and as Beronä writes, "Eisner deals with human sexuality in three of the four stories in this collection. His portraits make us question appearances and stereotypes, predominantly in the movies, [that tend to portray] only glamorous figures [as] involved in sexual activity."[68] "The Street Singer" depicts a man who roams the city streets and sings to captive audiences living in its tall apartment buildings. These audiences respond by dropping coins from their windows and fire escapes. While the singer takes advantage of the density of the urban form to make a living, he is in turn taken advantage of by an older female singer who promises to advance his career. Intriguingly, once he finally decides to throw his lot in with hers, he can no longer remember the location of her building within the vast urban labyrinth. "Super Wanted" narrates the story of a young girl who manipulates a lonely building super. She plays into his sexual desire and manages to steal his moneybox for her family. "Cookalein" recounts a young city boy's first sexual experience at a rural summer camp in what Eisner has called "an honest account of my coming of age."[69] Overall, Beronä notes that "Will Eisner's skillful approach to the sexual themes in his first graphic novel was another progressive step in further opening the doors of pictorial realism to an adult audience."[70] Yet he also suggests that Eisner, together with underground comics artists, crafted a legacy of sexualized representation that catered to "a male-dominated audience of readers."[71] As later sections of this chapter make clear, subsequent artists have been able to refashion the relationship between sexuality and urban space in comics in a way that presents an implicit challenge to this limitation of Eisner's work.

The emotional core of A Contract with God is a tenement-dwelling father's experience of grief following the death of his child. This story itself reveals its author's autobiographical motivation, as Eisner himself lost his sixteen-year-old daughter Alice to leukemia in 1970.[72] In the graphic novel, an anonymous mother leaves an infant girl outside Frimme Hersh's apartment door (2006: 20).[73] The protagonist adopts Rachele as a young child and cares for her deeply, but she is stricken ill and dies quite suddenly. The plot emphasizes his grief, agony, and feelings of having been betrayed by God, who let his daughter die so young. The first pages of the narrative introduce us to Frimme without yet naming the cause of his anguish. What defines these pages is Eisner's characteristic use of rain to establish mood.[74] There is so much rain that the tenement at 55 Dropsie Avenue seems at risk of floating away (2006: 5–6). Because of the way that the rain saturates everything it touches, Eisner's drawings suggest that the water carries a heavy emotional weight. On the page, it covers the streets, overflows the sewers, and soaks Frimme. The density of the rain's moisture even impacts the font of the text, such that the print of certain words seems to bleed down the page. Such is the case, appropriately enough, with the phrase "Only the tears of ten thousand weeping angels could cause such a deluge" (2006: 6).[75]

While Eisner also depicts Frimme's earlier life in a shtetl named Piske prior to moving to New York (2006: 14–18), it is the urban environment of the South Bronx that is crucial to Eisner's telling of this tragic story. The plotline even becomes increasingly entangled with the urban form. After Rachele's death, Frimme's disillusion prompts him to become "a Bronx slum lord of economic means and power."[76] He shaves his beard, purchases the tenement building, raises the rents, and soon has enough to also buy the property next door. With all his newfound material success, and a shikse girlfriend to boot, he asks the elders of the synagogue to prepare him another contract with God. This they do. Upon reading it, he has a heart attack and dies. The last pages of the graphic novel depict a lightning bolt striking the city and "an angry wind" swirling around its tenement buildings (2006: 52–53).

When considering the artist's representation of urban passions, more important than the level of content is the level of comics form. Eisner's exploitation of the full expanse of the comics page, as opposed to the reliance on carefully framed sequential panels, may very well have been inspired by the single-panel work of Otto Nückel, Lynd Ward, and Frans Masereel, all of whom are mentioned specifically by the artist as influences.[77] This unrestricted approach allows Eisner's images to come alive and breathe on the page. In the preface to *A Contract with God and Other Tenement Stories*, he reflected at length on this stylistic aspect of his work:

> I set aside two basic working constructions that so often inhibit this medium—space and format. Accordingly, each story was written without regard to space and each was allowed to develop its format from itself; that is, to evolve from the narration. The normal frames (or panels) associated with sequential (comic book) art are allowed to take on their integrity. For example,

in many cases an entire page is set out as a panel. The text and the balloons are interlocked with the art. I see all these as threads of a single fabric and exploit them as a language.[78]

Appropriately enough, analyses of the artist's later work by Thierry Groensteen and Barbara Postema have emphasized the unique aspects of Eisner's full-page composition.[79] The scholars note that he eschews traditional gutters, relies on frameless panels, and alternates between black and white backgrounds to differentiate scenes on the page. In addition—anticipating the more conceptual work of comics artists such as Chris Ware (ch. 4)—Eisner uses architectural elements such as doors and windows to bring a structural form to his full-page layouts.[80]

Eisner's comics aesthetic immerses the reader in a city that is at once a theatrical stage for his character's inner experiences. As the "son of an immigrant painter who sometimes worked for the Yiddish theater in New York City," the artist found the theater very important to him.[81] Eisner strongly identified as a city dweller and once even remarked, "The city, to me, is a big theater."[82] His graphic novels in particular were intentionally influenced by plays, and his love for popular theater reveals itself in his characters and dramatic situations.[83] One critic who has underscored vaudeville's influence on Eisner writes, "This popular theatrical form not only provides characters and dramatic structures for his stories, but it also ties Eisner to the modern urban landscape. Melodrama is a response to the changing face of the city, and Eisner's obsession with making the city speak in his comics leads him to his formal experiments."[84] In formal terms, Dropsie Avenue is not merely a drawn neighborhood but also a theatrical space of urban appearance.

The title story included in *A Contract with God* offers the opportunity to explore how Eisner foregrounds the inner lives of his urbanites through a theatrical focus on facial expression and body composition. Eisner's aesthetic places the emotional lives of residents in the spotlight, sometimes even quite literally. The archetypal depiction of Frimme Hersh from this comic (2006: 23) is a full-page image.[85] The character's twisted hands are raised upward in anguish; one of them holds a Bible. He is captured in light and framed by shadow on account of the rectangular spotlight cast by an open doorway. Bent backward so that his eyes are not visible to readers, he shouts to the heavens, "No! Not to me . . . You can't do this . . . We have a contract!!" The word balloon containing this text is only half-drawn, as if his agony cannot be contained by this mere comics convention, or as if the words, sopping wet with emotion, have eaten through the bottom of their presumed container. All other pictorial details are whited out at the margins of the full-page panel. This use of white-out is a strategy that appears again and again throughout the trilogy as Eisner visually distinguishes selected images from their surrounding urban environment as a matter of emphasis. This strategy prioritizes the inner emotional life of his protagonists but does not intend to do away with the city per se. The reader's sense is more that the "expressive action" of Eisner's protagonists deserves attention in its own right.[86] This decision to focus on a character's emotional state at the expense of the exterior world can be seen as what Smith calls "a frozen moment of emotional tension."[87] Similar moments appear throughout the trilogy, for example, in *A Life Force,* Jacob contemplates a divorce from Rifka in a scene that recalls Hersh's agony (1988: 92); and in *Dropsie Avenue,* Abie and Marie talk on a stoop illuminated by a clearly defined spotlight cast by a nearby streetlamp (1995: 76).[88]

Greg M. Smith explores the link Eisner's work makes between melodrama and the urban context in a way that recalls the work of Georg Simmel. In this reading, the dramatic events experienced by the residents of Dropsie Avenue represent the "intense sensations" and the "series of shocks" that become synonymous with modern city life.[89] Eisner's graphic novels break the rigid sequential form imposed upon comics by the logic of industrialization and allow images to flood the page. These pages intentionally fuse melodrama and urban modernity. Whenever the passions of urban life become visible, the city is always there to give them greater meaning. Overall, Derek Parker Royal writes that *A Contract with God* has a "sense of urban centeredness," and the critic draws attention to the correspondence between urban content and form on the page: "In his introductory set up of the neighborhood, Eisner visually underscores the close nature of tenement living—words tumble down the relatively thin vertical margins of the page like the dirt that is shaken out of a neighbor's rug—while at the same time demonstrating the interlinked narrative 'apartments' that will follow."[90] Eisner aims to give readers a street-level view of the city. He has said: "The sewers, the fire hydrants, the stoops, the grilles, the grates, the fire escapes. *That's* what the city people who live in the city see all day."[91] For his urbanites, the fragmented architecture of the city suggests containment and isolation.[92] His characters are all trapped in one sense or another. His melodramatic spotlight on their emotion is sometimes expressed through an iconic representation of a streetlight, as a way of suggesting the shrunken spaces of their social world.[93] By turn, the city's open spaces suggest not freedom but rather loneliness and alienation. In Jeremy Dauber's words, while depicting urban density and crowding, Eisner dissolves panel structure and foregrounds large open space "to accentuate feelings of alienation and unease rather than a sense of possibility."[94]

Eisner's comics style distills the urban experience itself to a feeling. In order to emphasize feeling and inner experience over the strict geometry of the streets, he eschews the notion of "accuracy."[95] Instead, it is autobiographical intimacy that he seeks.[96] As comics artist Denny O'Neil explains with implications for the trilogy as a whole, "The Bronx of *A Contract with God* is much less precisely rendered than the Central City of *The Spirit*, and that is surely a conscious decision of a thinking artist intent on introducing us to his most private, interior experience instead of reproducing the world as most of us see it."[97] If Eisner "sketches in the merest outline of the cityscape" in the trilogy by comparison with *The Spirit*, he does so not to downplay the urban environment, but rather to underscore "the inescapable influence of urban modernity on the petty melodramatic narratives" of those who live in the city.[98] In sum, Eisner's graphic trilogy conveys the notion that our urban passions are shaped by the textures of the city's built environment.

It is the built environment of the South Bronx that is given greater attention throughout the trilogy. This is an area that for Eisner is deeply connected with a particular form of modern subjectivity shaped by the urban environment. Dauber writes that Eisner's work has been seen as a metaphor of American Jewish existence and, along with that, of "tenement life as a place of dreams often denied, promises broken, and pain, suffering, and poverty triumphant."[99] The artist's choice of the Bronx as the setting for his tenement building, which bears the fictional address of 55 Dropsie Avenue, is significant. As Joel Lewis puts it, "For Jews of the '20s, living in the Bronx was the announcement of hav- ing attained a somewhat higher station in the world than their relatives and landsleit still on the Lower East Side or in older Brooklyn neighborhoods like Brownsville."[100] The cultural space of the Bronx constitutes the narrative heart of *A Contract with God*. This emphasis continues even throughout the second and third books of the trilogy—*A Life Force* and *Dropsie Avenue*—as Eisner's story "is projected onto a much broader canvas, [that of] American ethnoracial relations as a whole and the process of urban assimilation."[101]

As if to announce the broader scale of the third volume in the trilogy, Eisner himself writes, "Neighborhoods have life spans. They begin, evolve, mature, and die. But while this evolution is displayed by the decline of its buildings, it seems to me that the lives of the inhabitants are the internal force which generates the decay. People, not buildings, are the heart of the matter" (1995: ix). This latter insight on "people, not buildings" recalls the emphasis made by Jane Jacobs (ch. 3) in her book *The Death and Life of Great American Cities* (1961), where she asserted the determining role of people and wider social relationships in sustaining a city. Eisner goes on to specifically reference the decline of the South Bronx in the 1960s, the reporting of sixty-eight thousand fires in the area in the 1970s, and the increase in abandoned buildings and blight. While the connection between melodrama and urban modernity continues to be a concern, as it was in the previous volumes, *Dropsie Avenue* gravitates more to- ward themes of a larger scale. There are many instances where the artist's drawn images "zoom out" from the "stoops, doorways, drain grates, windows, alleys

Figure 2.2—Eisner, *Dropsie Avenue* (New York: W. W. Norton, 2006[1995]: 159)

and so on" to depict a bird's-eye view. The graphic novel begins with images of the farmland that in 1870 was still not yet the quintessentially modern urban Bronx (1995: 2–3); it ends with a new form of working-class suburbanization (1995: 170–74). The climax depicts the fires, urban blight, and creative destruction of the 1970s. One image highlighted by Royal is particularly striking (1995: 159). It can be divided visually into three tiers (see figure 2.2). At the bottom is a demolished grid of the Bronx with no buildings, only rubble. Streetlights still stand on the curbs, and the elevated frames the left margin. In the distance to the north one can see the tall buildings of the city, in gray and white and meant to stand as background, communicating merely a feeling of urban density. The middle third is a cloud of dense smoke arising from a residential area. It takes the form of a mushroom cloud, as if in echoing events of World War II, an era kept alive in the continuing memory of the Jewish diaspora. In the top tier of the image, the head of the mushroom cloud is substituted by the last building to be demolished in the Bronx. Captured in the moment of its explosion, its supporting structures break and give way as its own weight pulls it down and raises another dust cloud.[102] This page expresses the explosive way in which collective urban dreams and their ruination can shape the architectural and social spaces of urban areas.

Throughout Eisner's trilogy the artist plays with framing, panel borders, and the power that architecture and planning have to structure both the built environment and the urban experience. In this way he emphasizes the passions of everyday life are shaped and given meaning, but also restricted and constrained by their urban context.[103] As the rest of this chapter bears out, the themes and graphic style of *A Contract with God*, *A Life Force*, and *Dropsie Avenue* are a necessary touchstone for later comics artists. In representing the struggle to find human connection and a place for everyday passions in the modern city, such artists continue Eisner's legacy but also reshape it in significant ways by moving away from his male-dominated perspective to catalog other urban experiences.[104]

URBAN CONFINEMENT: *MY NEW YORK DIARY* (1993–1998) BY JULIE DOUCET

Born in Saint-Lambert, a suburb of Montreal, Canada, Julie Doucet (1965–) occupies a curious position in scholarship on the ninth art. She is one of the most internationally known comics artists and yet quite inexplicably has largely escaped sustained scholarly attention. In the 1980s she self-published works created while studying at CÉGEP du Vieux Montréal and the Université du Québec à Montréal.[105] These appeared in photocopied form as pamphlets or zines, which she either distributed herself or asked independent bookstores to sell for her.[106] In these early years, "Doucet drew from the aesthetics and ideological impetus of do-it-yourself zine culture."[107] Notably, this form of comics production marked a sharp turn from the comics workshop that, for example, had brought Will Eisner success. Individual artists embracing zine aesthetics were willing to sacrifice the potential of financial rewards if it meant they retained "some measure of creative control."[108] Doucet's comics later appeared in local magazines and, eventually, also in *Weirdo*, the famed anthology magazine created by Robert Crumb, and later edited by Peter Bagge, and then by Aline Kominsky-Crumb.[109]

In the 1990s the artist moved around quite a bit: from Montreal to New York, then Seattle, Berlin, and finally back to Montreal.[110] During this time, she was "one of the first signature authors for Drawn & Quarterly, one of the most influential comics publishers in Canada."[111] The twelve issues of Doucet's minicomic *Dirty Plotte* (1988–1989) prompted an eponymous long-running series published with Drawn & Quarterly (1991–1998). In the same year that series began, she won the Harvey Award for Best New Talent (1991). Throughout the decade her collections appeared in Montreal's Drawn & Quarterly and also L'Association in Paris, making her a staple of both the North American and European markets.[112] Among the works she published during this time are *Dirty Plotte* (Drawn & Quarterly, 1991–1998), *Lève ta jambe, mon poisson est mort!* (*Lift Your Leg, My Fish Is Dead!*) (Drawn & Quarterly, 1993), *My Most Secret Desire: A Collection of Dream Stories* (Drawn & Quarterly, 1995), *Ciboire de Criss!* (L'Association, 1996), and *Changements d'adresse* (L'Association, 1998). Though a native speaker of French, she started publishing in English and only later switched back to French, sometimes translating her own work.[113] Her comics were featured in important fanzines and professional publications beyond North America. Two such examples are *La Monstreuse* in France, and *Stripburger*, created in 1992 in Slovenia by the Stripcore collective, both of which were winners of the Alph-Art Fanzine award for a comics anthology.[114] Doucet in fact has been a key artist of the "small-press comics explosion since the 1990s" in Europe, and her work has appeared in translation in other languages, including Spanish and Finnish.[115]

For all these reasons, the lack of sustained critical attention she has received can be perplexing. In *The Great Women Cartoonists* (2001), Trina Robbins mentions Doucet only in passing.[116] Charles Hatfield's *Alternative Comics: An Emerging Literature* (2005) mentions the artist on a few pages, but overall the scholar gives her short shrift.[117] Hillary L. Chute notably expressed explicit regret that she was unable to include Doucet in her book *Outside the Box: Interviews with Contemporary Cartoonists* (2014).[118] A handful of articles in French and in English have explored her work, however, and from these and recent examples of thesis and dissertation work by a new generation of scholars, it is possible to construct a concise artist's portrait.[119] Doucet's reputation as a feminist comics creator stems from her insistence on "challenging patriarchal logic," "work[ing] against the visual order of the phallocentric and heteronormative," and focusing on "the micro-politics of the body."[120] The way that these elements of her work gain force within her depiction of everyday urban environments is particularly compelling.

Understanding Doucet's position relative to the wider comics field is crucial to advancing an urban reading of *My New York Diary*. It must be understood that alongside the male-centered tradition of underground comics of the 1960s and '70s, which is often associated with R. Crumb, there existed another tradition of comics drawn by female artists. The Wimmen's Comix tradition was "pioneered by artists like Mary Fleener, Diane Noomin, Aline Kominsky, Roberta Gregory, Trina Robbins, Lynda Barry, Jessica Abel, Debbie Dreschler, and Phoebe Gloeckner, who, according to Ana Merino, 'over the course of several decades have tried to include and create dialogue over their differences in the predominantly masculine universe of comics.'"[121] As Merino notes, those artists contributing to the first volume of *Wimmen's Comix* in 1972 "offered their readers a feminist and quite radical agenda."[122] Since then, the range of artists engaged in what Alisia Chase calls "the difficult feminist art agenda of transforming women's circumstances into artistic subject matter" has expanded considerably.[123] Even in the twenty-first century, however, research into comics by women creators has been insufficient at best. Thus, even in planning the 2013 University of Florida's Conference on Comics and Graphic Novels, for example, Jeffrey A. Brown and Melissa Loucks still "hoped to bring women in comics to the forefront of scholarly discussion."[124]

That Doucet's work occupies a privileged position within this tradition of comics by women creators is arguably due to several circumstances.[125] First among these is the serendipitous timing of her output. It is significant that her early comics appeared in the late 1980s in zine form and further gained traction with international audiences in the '90s. This meant that she was necessarily in a position to benefit from the fact that other artists, as highlighted by Merino, had already carved out an alternative space in comics publishing for works by women creators. At the same time, a more general stylistic shift from underground to alternative comics was taking place. This shift brought widespread public attention to comics, and the growing prestige of comics as an art form was further reflected in the establishment, in 1988, of both the Harvey Award and the Eisner Awards. While the timing of Doucet's emergence onto the international comics scene was favorable in these senses, however, this should not be read as taking away from the strength of her accomplishments in the medium.

Second in this regard, it is important to note her contribution to the development of autobiographical comics work in particular. In Elisabeth El Rafaie's assessment, along with their general impact on the ninth art, "female commix creators also had a big influence on the early development of the graphic memoir."[126] Doucet excelled at reinterpreting the themes of underground comics (sexuality, transgressive behaviors, drinking, drug use) from a feminist perspective, incorporating what El Rafaie in *Autobiographical Comics* (2012) calls "explicit, shameless representations of bodily functions such as menstruation, sexual intercourse, and miscarriage."[127] Yet the artist did this in a way that expresses the hallmark aspects of autobiographical comics more generally. The situations offered up in her narratives appear to be highly personalized. As a consequence, García associates her with cartoonists who followed the "road of abject revelation" in their comics, that is, artists "who committed to the page painful or difficult episodes from their pasts."[128] Catriona MacLeod highlights the presence of the authorial figure/artist herself within Doucet's own work and suggests that this is historically a defining trait of autobio comics created by women, and not necessarily of those created by men.[129] Due to the high levels of her international exposure, there is no doubt that her work has served as a touchstone for other artists. Her depiction of epilepsy in particular resonates with the personalized autobiographical work of David B., whose *Epileptic* (1996–2003) was also published by L'Association, both of which can be seen as early forerunners that anticipate Iasmin Omar Ata's *Mis(h)adra* (2017).[130]

Above all else, however, one must consider the provocative nature and the unique qualities of Doucet's comics. As Roger Sabin puts it, "Julie Doucet took the kind of women's autobiography pioneered by undergrounds like *Wimmin's Comix* into uncharted waters."[131] Her work in *Dirty Plotte* was at once a multilayered and purposely crafted autobiographical portrait, a masterful indictment of patriarchal society, and a lucidly ironic challenge to the prominence of the male-centered gaze in comics. The separate publication of *My New York Diary* continues these through-lines of her general comics style, yet it also consistently emphasizes hallmark aspects of the modern urban experience. In this work, autobiography becomes, in part, a vehicle for understanding the circumstances of everyday life in the city; and reciprocally, city life becomes a conditioning force for the individual everyday experience. Kevin Ziegler puts this connection well when he writes, "By emphasizing the unflattering events of her life, Doucet creates uneasy self-portraits that catalogue the grit and filth of her urban experiences."[132] The present exploration emphasizes the way her compositional strategies reinforce concepts such as urban density, urban confinement, and ultimately, too, urban alienation. This analysis is additionally important given that critics have noted the tendency to overemphasize the perceived crudeness of Doucet's style at the expense of her intriguing and purposeful composition.[133]

As the beginning of a short review of the work dating from 1999 conveys, "Basically, *New York Diary* is a sad, desperate, highly personal account of her move to New York City and the gradual decline of her health, her relationship with her dubious boyfriend and her mental state. [. . .] As always, the artwork in the books is detailed and complex, evoking, in this case, a claustrophobic New York of tiny apartments, crowded streets and smokey bars."[134] *My New York Diary*'s significance derives from the way that what MacLeod calls "the feminist focus of the text" resonates with its urban theme.[135] One can see Doucet's work as a feminist rewriting of the characteristically hedonistic themes of underground comics, but it is also part of a longer history of comics focused on urban alienation. That is, the comic is in part a feminist complement to the themes established by Frans Masereel in his early twentieth-century visual narrative as discussed earlier in this chapter. Like the Belgian artist's single-panel work, Doucet's comparatively complex page layouts also deal with the fundamental theme of establishing and sustaining human connections in the modern city. In both cases the human senses constitute the point of entry into larger concerns. As it is with Masereel's urban hero, the freedom of Doucet's protagonist is curtailed by her urban circumstances, and she aspires to something greater than those circumstances would seem to allow. Her character embodies an ennui and urban detachment that contrast somewhat paradoxically with the overstimulation of her senses: she is indeed, as one critic puts it, "alienated and repressed in a male-dominated world."[136]

Also important is the way that working life figures into Doucet's urban story. To continue the comparison with Masereel's *Passionate Journey*, common to both comics is the theme of an inner conflict between a working self and a potentially actualized everyday self. Masereel's narrative focused on a male factory worker to explore the way that the human senses were dulled by industrial drudgery. As a metonym for the condition of the international proletariat, he sought release from the dehumanizing expectations of a labor harnessed by capitalist production. Doucet's narrative recalls and updates this central theme in underscoring the need for self-actualization, yet she inverts the relationship between work and freedom as Masereel had established it. Readers of *My New York Diary* are thus "witness to the anxieties of being female and, specifically, being a female cartoonist."[137] Her comic links artistic production with the creative expression and the relative autonomy that Masereel's male protagonist, by contrast, seems to find in his leisurely movement through public space.

The content of the graphic diary includes exteriors of "the squalor of Washington Heights, their new neighbourhood in Manhattan," but mostly depicts interior scenes (see figure 2.3).[138] At the beginning of the comic, exterior urban scenes are overwhelming enough that Doucet's protagonist seeks refuge

Figure 2.3—Doucet, *My New York Diary* (Montreal: Drawn & Quarterly, 1999: Spring, Part 1, 4–5)

inside. Readers necessarily feel trapped in the drawn apartment due to the comic's formal aspects. The work remains fixated on a three-rows-per-page layout that suggests a normative arrangement of two panels per row. Yet very few pages actually achieve what would be seen as a standard six-panel layout. Instead, Doucet mostly alternates between five and eight panels per page. She accomplishes this through a consistent compositional agitation. She intermittently introduces a third panel to one or more of the rows, and frequently fuses what might otherwise be two images into a single landscape panel. In some instances, she changes the height of one or more panels, fashioning irregular panel shapes that span more than one row. From time to time, she switches to a thick black hyperframe for the background of panel arrangements that foregrounds six, four, or even as few as three panels to a page. The effect of these choices is to create a form of compositional anxiety that destabilizes the reader's connection with her work. Overall, the page layout of *My New York Diary* suggests regularity but instead delivers only irregularity and persistent change. This compositional choice suggests a correspondence between the quintessentially shifting character of urban life and the mental state of city dwellers. It is significant that the protagonist finds in interior domesticity no safe haven from the constant change and anxiety of urban life.

Jonas Engelmann is one of very few critics who have thought to explain Doucet's work by referencing urban theory. He writes of the artist, "She obviously felt overawed by the life in the metropolis and this fact takes possession of every single panel," adding that "Walter Benjamin characterized a similar experience at the beginning of the 20th century."[139] In analyzing *Diary*, one could easily also turn to the early twentieth-century work of Georg Simmel for an account that portrays modern city life as overwhelming. Either way, what Doucet does in her comics work is reveal this hallmark condition of the urban experience through pictorial detail. Ziegler writes that "Doucet's autobiographical graphic narratives often include countless overwhelming images, hyper-dense visual compositions that are difficult to interpret."[140] It is common, in this respect, for critics to note the clutter of Doucet's interiors (see figure 2.3). The truth is that the artist's obsessive approach to the object-world depicted on the page is more than an attempt to merely denote the squalor and messiness of cramped urban living.[141] Instead, it is at once testament to what Simmel described as the anxious personality type who is unsettled by the constant change and frequent agitation of city life. *My New York Diary* functions at both of these levels, the denotative and the connotative. Barbara Postema's masterful analysis of a single panel from the comics collection demonstrates that the denotative representation of iconicity in her comics also makes possible connotative signification and symbolism.[142]

It is important to acknowledge the dual functioning of such aesthetic "messiness." That is, Doucet's panels are indeed cluttered at the levels of both represented content and formal composition. Postema writes of "the almost obsessive-compulsive representation of 'stuff'" in *My New York Diary*.[143] In fact there are so many objects in the artist's panels that one struggles to discern each item from the next. One critic likens the cluttered dwelling to a garbage dump, and another notes its surreal qualities.[144] Doucet's autobiographical persona "merges with her disorderly surroundings."[145] The lack of free space on the page has been seen to "provoke feelings of panic" and induce a claustrophobic response.[146] Manifesting a property of comics memoir as composed by women artists more generally, Doucet's autobiographical persona "is present in almost every frame."[147] Given the way in which character description is infinitely restarted by the visual form of comics—in comparison with description's more limited role in narrative prose[148]—the repeated appearance of the protagonist amidst such clutter strengthens the suggestion that she is dehumanized. Like other objects within the frame, she is doubly imprisoned—compositionally within the panel border, diegetically within her boyfriend's New York apartment.

While Julie Doucet's comics cannot be reduced to such an interpretation alone, *My New York Diary* nevertheless suggests that the metropolis can be a fraught space for women. Urban apartment living offers Doucet's autobiographical persona a potential refuge from the anxieties she feels outside on the city streets, but it is simultaneously a claustrophobic and limiting space. Given the way Doucet relentlessly emphasizes the theme of urban confinement, it is important that the comic finally offers a release of sorts. The marked nature of the "messiness" in Doucet's urban panels becomes strikingly clear at the end of the collection. It is at this point that the protagonist is freed from material clutter and by extension from her cluttered mind-set, one besieged by both gendered and urban forms of control. As Englemann writes:

> In the last panel of the comic Doucet disengages from the strict constructedness of the rest of the comic. She dissolves the limiting borders of the panels and of the social framework, which allows her protagonist, Julie, to transgress the constructedness of her disease, her female body, and her life in the city. A New York brass band, which stands metonymically for the determining forces she has experienced in the city, virtually blows her out of the metropolis.[149]

In the end, Doucet's autobiographical persona leaves the confining male-dominated domestic space of her boyfriend's apartment. As she ventures outside, the content and form of the images suggest a rebirth of sorts. These final pages are, as Postema writes, "empty and spare"—a clear contrast with the compositional style established throughout the comic.[150] The emptiness of the city streets and the marked clarity of their drawn style function as a comics metaphor. These details convey a newfound inner confidence and acknowledge that a space of possibilities has opened up in the messiness of the protagonist's urban life. Ana Merino argues that, despite the confinement she has experienced in New York, "what fascinates is her ability to remain solitary and indestructible on the inside."[151] There is room once again for her to seek out her urban passions in a way that is potentially unconstrained by patriarchal and urban forms of dehumanization. The implication is that relative freedom exists in assuming some control over your own work, and it is important that this relative freedom is linked in graphic and metaphorical terms with the freedom to be found in the city streets.

CARVING OUT A SPACE FOR SEXUAL AND ROMANTIC PASSIONS IN MODERN MADRID

As two comics from twenty-first-century Spain suggest, it is crucial that city dwellers be able to pursue their urban passions unhindered by normative social structures. In considering the message of these two comics, the links between urban spaces and normative perspectives on gender and sexual orientation are brought into relief. Raquel Córcoles (Reus, 1986) draws comics that center on a young professional woman who moves from a small town and seeks sex and romance in Madrid. Her digital design process leads to a clean or polished style that remains quite far from replicating the radical feminist agenda or visual messiness of an underground Wimmin's Comix pioneer like Doucet. Yet in her use of quotidian themes, Córcoles echoes the need for women to carve out a social space of their own amongst the urban multitudes. Rafael Martínez Castellanos (Madrid, 1965) also focuses on Madrid. His comic represents the daily life of a gay couple living in the capital city's central neighborhood of Chueca. The story of his protagonist characters Leo and Ray functions as a way of thinking through the contribution that urban spaces can make to sustaining the transnational politics of gay identity. As these two works both showcase, comics are a complex representational space. They may reflect normative social values, hold them up for scrutiny, and even challenge them. Though each does so in its own way, these comics explore what it means for residents to claim their right to the city as a use-value, or put another way, as a space in which to pursue the human passions.

Otherwise known as Moderna de Pueblo, Raquel Córcoles began blogging in 2010 (see modernadepueblo.com).[152] She graduated with a degree in journalism and has also had her work published in *El Jueves, Cuore, El País*, and *GQ*.[153] It is important to emphasize that she contributes to the need for more women's voices in comics.[154] Her output must be contextualized among other women artists in Spain, many of whom have established a web presence: Flavia Álvarez, Raquel Riba Rossy, Anastasia Bengoechea, Marga Castaño, and Esther de la Rosa; and also Meritxell Bosch, who was a candidate for an Eisner Award.[155] Córcoles is at times even described as a pioneer in the realm of web comics.[156] Though her comics images are composed and circulated digitally, their production nevertheless recalls the zine culture of the 1980s in certain respects. For twenty-first-century artists, the internet is often seen as an alternative publishing realm that promises the autonomy, creative freedom, and readership that often attracted earlier generations of artists to photocopied and self-circulated print fanzines. As Julie Doucet was able to do in the context of zine culture, Córcoles has used this alternative digital realm as a way to break into print publishing.

Her first book, *Soy de pueblo: Manual para sobrevivir en la ciudad* (I'm a small-town girl: Manual for surviving in the city) (Glénat, 2011), was created with the assistance of graphic designer Marta Rabanán after Córcoles was named as a finalist in a competition for young comics artists.[157] The title of the comic transparently communicates its premise. Its protagonist, like many young women who move to the big city, is caught between two worlds.[158] While she aspires to take full advantage of what the urban environment has to offer, she also sees through the pretensions of those around her. In this sense the comic participates in a long-standing theme of visual cultural production in Spain juxtaposing life in the country with life in the city and ties in to the broader comics legacy launched with Töpffer's engagement with this theme (ch. 1). In Spain this tradition in its contemporary form reflects in particular the waves of urban immigration that brought unprecedented numbers of new residents to Madrid beginning in the 1960s.[159] As evident in films of that decade, such as director Pedro Lazaga's *La ciudad no es para mí* (The city isn't for me]) (1965), urbanization and modernization became connected in the popular imagination. In *Soy de pueblo*, the self-styled small-town modern woman showcases the struggle to define oneself in the big city. The contrast between the two social spaces is a constant throughout the comic. Two early pages depict, on the left: the city, its buildings, and promise of celebrity culture; and, on the right, the small town and its shrunken world of possibilities (2011: 8–9). The urban atmosphere is consistently changing and chaotic: the protagonist loses her bag (2011: 10), has unexpected visitors to her apartment (2011: 13), gets lost and finds herself alongside a small child who is also lost (2011: 15), and struggles with under-employment (2011: 16–17). Intermittently, on selected pages whose

Figure 2.4—Córcoles and Rabadán, *Soy de pueblo* (Barcelona: EDT, 2011: 32)

white background is largely untouched (2011: 11, 19, 33, 59, 67), she gives advice to other newcomers to the city surrounding the lessons she has learned upon moving to the metropolis.

Perhaps most important, this is an environment not unlike that of Winsor McCay's suburban America (ch. 1), one in which visual images, marketing, and consumerism saturate city life and shape the urban experience. To wit, the condition of being "de pueblo" [from a small town] is defined on the first page as being from a place in which there is no *El Corte Inglés*, a noted department store chain (2011: 3). On its very cover, the artist's autobiographical persona declares the comics manual to be "More useful than your mother's Tupperware!" thus foregrounding the consumerist culture she satirizes throughout her work. The artist draws attention to the aspects of this culture that are specifically tailored toward women using humor and acute visual sensibility. For example, on two pages she crafts covers for fictitious men's magazines to illustrate the absurd image of women that drives mainstream publishing (2011: 22–23), and later she self-reflexively draws a Moderna de Pueblo action figure (see figure 2.4) that comes with leisure accessories and beauty products (2011: 32).

These themes of urban life are continued in her second print comic, *Los capullos no regalan flores* (Dickheads don't give you flowers) (2013), which quickly reached its ninth print edition and has also been published in France, Brazil, Portugal, Singapore, and Malaysia.[160] Here as well the artist's comics persona continues to follow her whims and desires in the big city. An early full-page design features a quintessential urban scene and first-person narration that declares: "Sí realmente quería empezar una nueva vida en la ciudad. Quizá era lo mejor que me podía haber pasado. Así que me prohibí dramatizar y me convencí de que entre tanta gente no tardaría en encontrar a alguien mejor. Solo tenía que . . . Salir a buscarlo" [Yes I really wanted to begin a new life in the city. It was possibly the best thing that could have happened to me. So I told myself to stop being melodramatic and I convinced myself that with there being so many people out there it wouldn't take long for me to find someone better. I only had to . . . Go out to find him] (2013: 13).[161] As in *Soy de pueblo*, the urban environment is the explicit background against which Moderna de Pueblo explores the passionate life of her central women characters. Importantly, she lampoons the tendency toward conformity experienced by both men and women in the city. The comic delivers a humorous critique of the beauty-obsessed culture that pervades magazines and advertising, and also a send-up of various avatars of the male urban hipster. Instead of a manual for city living in general, the artist organizes her work as dating advice. In chronicling a search for sex and romance in the urban environment, she cautions the reader regarding ten different types of dickheads. These *capullos* are each given a number, and it is significant that the last one is a *capulla*, as the protagonist addresses her complicity in a larger pattern of dating relationships.[162] The narrative arc of the comic suggests that if young women are to enjoy urban living, they must see through the prefabricated myths of what a happy life should look like.[163]

The connection between the urban theme and the dating theme in *Los capullos no regalan flores* is established through the world of appearances. As she uses her protagonist to engage themes of "love, work, music, fears, desires," she focuses on the superficiality of consumerism.[164] One of the artist's key concerns throughout is to scrutinize the consumerist drives that threaten to turn young urban women into mere copies of one another.[165] Moderna de Pueblo underscores that images of eternal youth and normative perfection—touched-up images, beauty products, health regimens, and the like—are in fact incompatible with the pursuit of true urban passions. Here there is an interesting resonance between the content and the form of her work. In aesthetic terms, the digital design of her images foregrounds their two-dimensionality. Instead of drawing each figure's image from scratch as would occur in the creation of a hand-drawn comic, Córcoles copies and pastes a single image of a given character, modifying it only slightly as necessary in a given scene, for example, facing right instead of left, mouth open versus mouth closed, arm up instead of arm down. In light of her chosen themes, this is not a limitation, but rather a provocation that further underscores the contrast between appearance and substance. Her page design and digital process thus emphasize the serialized consumerism and cookie-cutter conformity of the urban environment that her comics critique.

Otherwise known as Rafa, Rafael Martínez Castellanos is a self-taught artist and the author of an acclaimed comic, *Chuecatown* (2002), whose transposition to live-action cinema increased its visibility. Director Juan Flahn's eponymous film version of the comic (*Chuecatown*, 2007) has received far more critical attention than Rafa's hand-drawn work.[166] Yet, while the film differs in somewhat significant ways from the comic,[167] both assert the connection between gay identity and Madrid's centrally located Chueca neighborhood. As a brief review points out, the comic is important, in part, for the way in which it intersects with broader publishing trends. That is, "from a strictly gay literary perspective, *Chuecatown* is symptomatic of the increasing demand for and availability of homosexual literature in Spain that a growing number of publishing houses are trying to meet. Notable among them are Egales, the first gay and lesbian publishing house in Spain, founded by Mili Hernández in 1995. Another is Odisea, founded in 1997 by Oscar Pérez, who in 1999 initiated the Premios Odisea."[168] The *Chuecatown* comic was in fact published by Odisea, and was followed up by two sequels, all of which were grouped together and released in a single volume in 2007.

The artist bio from the first volume of the comics series specifically indicates Rafa's use of the ninth art for the purposes of urban social transformation. His story of Leo and Ray's arrival and life in Chueca is thus intended to prompt consideration of larger social issues surrounding LGBTQ populations. In telling this story through comics form, Rafa continues and departs somewhat from the depiction of sexual identity in comics of the Spanish Transition to democracy after the death of dictator Francisco Franco in 1975. Such earlier depictions, in line with the explosion of cultural production associated with what became the Madrilenian Movida, were seen as intentionally shocking as artists sought to provoke a reassessment of normative ideologies.[169] Importantly, too, the Movida was itself connected with the urban space of Chueca.[170] Against the background of this countercultural movement and its urban legacy, *Chuecatown* is notable for its relatively subdued and residential tenor.

While the urban area of Chueca is clearly identified in the title of the work and in selected scenes, outdoor representations are largely eschewed in favor of interiors. The first page, for example, shows the couple arriving at their new address in the neighborhood, which is located next to a gay video shop (2002: 7). On occasion readers note exterior views of their balcony (2002: 11), a few sidewalk scenes (2002: 17, 27, 29–31, 44), the facade of a bookstore (2002: 34), and the central Plaza de Chueca (2002: 32), yet the comic's emphasis tends to be on residential and leisure spaces such as bedrooms, bathrooms, dining rooms, bars, and parties. The characters, who physically take up most of the panel space, tend to be the clear focus of the images (see figure 2.5). As Leo and Ray have sex, make friends, drink, party, and enjoy the company of others in Chuecatown, an everyday and relatively unspectacularized vision of their life together emerges. As one reviewer puts it, "Had Leo and Ray been a heterosexual couple, all this would seem commonplace, if not downright banal. However, the fact that the comic exists at all says more than the actual plot."[171] In this way the comic makes a strong political statement that Jorge Pérez attributes to its being "written as a reaction to the marginalization, in the legal sense, of the LGTB collective."[172] Rafa's characters make a claim to city space by merely following their urban passions in an instantly recognizable area of Spain's capital city.

Understanding the relationship of *Chuecatown* to wider issues of gay identity entails delving into the urban history of the represented neighborhood. The comic's most important aspect may be the way that the work dialogues with a specific urban space on and off the page—even if this dialogue is largely implicit. In order to appreciate this largely implicit dialogue, one must understand the larger social and transnational scope of its spatial significance. Given the international positioning of Madrid as a modern city and of Chueca as an internationally known gay district, this means taking the pulse of queer issues not only in Spain but also beyond.

Scholarship suggests that the model for Chueca was unknown in Spain before the 1980s, and was imported from the US.[173] It can be seen as a response to

Figure 2.5—Martínez Castellanos, *Chuecatown* (Barcelona: Odisea, 2002: 32)

the Castro in San Francisco, New York's Greenwich Village, Marais in Paris, or London's Soho.[174] It is important to recognize that the association of such urban spaces with a politicized gay identity sometimes risks imposing a homogeneity that does not reflect the diversity of its inhabitants. As Jill Robbins notes in the context of discussing the zone's proximity to other sites and institutions, "the people crossing through the Chueca Plaza could be characterized—that is, stigmatized and/or empowered—not only by their sexual orientation, but also by their labor membership, artistic interests, fashion sensibility, social class, military status, and/or physical disability."[175] Yet the neighborhood is not immune to normative and ideological socioeconomic forces that shape the urban experience on the whole. For instance, as a social space, the area has been shaped by "a capitalist market economy and by a great influence of international tourisms, especially from Europe."[176] It is an expensive neighborhood.[177] In addition, by some reports "transsexual and transgender individuals are being pushed out of the community."[178] That said, however, it should not be ignored that the area has long been associated with socially disempowered populations.[179] In the late twentieth and early twenty-first centuries, it has "become a national epicenter of the LGBT civil rights movement creating change in Spanish society."[180] It is home to a relatively high number of LGBT-owned businesses and has become a symbol for sexual diversity.[181] It is quite unique in this respect, as it is "the most influential LGBT community in Spain and the only one with a fixed physical and social structure."[182] This reputation famously led to Madrid's hosting of Europride 2007, which was attended by more than two million people.[183]

Because Chueca is an epicenter for the broader LGBT civil rights movement, Rafa's referencing of it in this comic is highly symbolic in political terms. The artist's depiction of Leo and Ray's enjoyment of its residential and consumer spaces necessarily carries along with it the cumulative weight of progressive social change. Implicit in this is the shift in official discourse—one not necessarily complemented by practice—away from the prosecution and persecution of homosexuality under the former dictatorship in Spain.[184] Contemporaneously with the publication of the artist's three-volume series, the LGBT rights movement experienced some notable successes. As Santiago Fouz-Hernández notes, "In 2005, Spain became the third country in the world to legalize gay marriage and, a year later, pre-op transsexuals were able to alter their name and gender legally on national identity cards."[185] As his characters carve out a space for their pursuit of happiness in an urban environment, Rafa dialogues implicitly—and later in the series, explicitly—with the politics of gay identity in Spain. In the end, Leo and Ray get married.

Both Moderna de Pueblo and Rafa use comics in order to claim the city as a use-value for its inhabitants. *Chuecatown* arguably accomplishes in cultural production what its referenced neighborhood arguably accomplishes in urban terms: that is, "in making gay people visible, Chueca epitomizes the new democratic Spain."[186] Similarly, *Soy de pueblo* and *Los capullos no regalan flores* by Raquel Córcoles render in visual terms the passion-seeking experiences of women in the city. In dealing with normative and ideological social forces, each artist in her or his own way recalls the hallmark themes of *The Passion of Man* and *Passionate Journey* almost one hundred years earlier. Whereas Masereel relied on heterosexual male protagonists as a symbol of the quintessentially modern struggle to carve out a space of one's own in the urban environment, Córcoles and Martínez Castellanos expand upon this comics legacy. What all these texts share, however, is a need to confront the obstacles that stand between an urban community and full access to the potential of the cities in which its residents live, work, and seek the passions of everyday life.

DAISHU MA'S *LEAF* (2015): THE NATURAL WORLD AND THE SENSUOUS CITY

Daishu Ma is a Chinese-born artist whose career trajectory speaks to a global positioning. She left Chengdu, China, to study art in London at the Central Saint Martins College of Art and Design, and she currently lives in Spain, after having worked in Shanghai. Her wordless twenty-first-century graphic novel *Leaf* (2015) won the Cheltenham Illustration Award and has been republished also in France, Sweden, and the US.[187] One reviewer has compared the comic to *The Arrival* (2007) by Shaun Tan, praising its focus on "a single moment [that] has the power to change us forever." It could also be described in the words used by Santiago García to characterize Peter Kuper's graphic novel *The System* (1996). That is, Ma's work is similarly "an updating of the collective social portrait in the style of Ward's *Vertigo* and of Masereel's *The City*, told without words, although with a page design divided into panels and in color."[188] Overall, Daishu Ma's graphic novel contemporizes the form and themes of Masereel's early twentieth-century work with a focus on the natural world.

   In particular, *Leaf* returns to the theme of the urbanite's enjoyment of the city and underscores the fundamental importance of the human senses in catalyzing social change in urban areas. Through its "hundreds of soft pencil illustrations" arranged in multipaneled pages, Ma's graphic novel conveys the imbrication of nature and technology in the modern city.[189] The artist's imaginative scenes portray an urban environment in flux. A vast system of machinery pulls blue energy from the natural world into systems of production that sustain a drab metropolis. Yet in this greying city, the comic's protagonist finds a leaf that radiates a soft yellow glow. This discovery sets off an entire investigation by the protagonist into the city's luminary-circulatory system. The youth's traversal of various spaces of the city leads to an intimate knowledge of how this urban system of production functions. *Leaf* thus blends themes of nature, wonder, and knowledge with insights into the conditioning forces of industrial power. Above all else, it transposes to the page the Marxian premise regarding urban passions introduced at the beginning of this chapter. The reader shares the protagonist's sensory enjoyment of the natural world's visual splendor, and in this way a sensuous engagement with the city becomes the catalyst for urban knowledge.

While all of the comics discussed in this chapter continue Masereel's thematic legacy, namely, the theme of carving out a space in the modern city for passionate life, *Leaf* also boasts formal connections with the early twentieth-century wordless picture novel. In this respect, it is important to recognize that Masereel was not unknown in China, even in his own time. In an English translation of two short texts originally written in Chinese, Sean Macdonald makes some interesting remarks on the development of comics in China. His introduction to the texts asserts the political importance of word–image combinations "at a time when Marxist-Leninism is emerging as a type of discourse, not only in politics but also in the arts."[190] The translated text written by Lu Xun (1881–1936) mentions Masereel specifically and confirms that its author had looked at *The Passion of Man* and *Passionate Journey*, along with four other novels in pictures.[191] In addition, Tie Xaio's article "Masereel, Lu, and the Development of the Woodcut Picture Book (連環畫) in China" further explores the Belgian artist's substantial influence. Importantly, Masereel was introduced to Chinese readers "not just as another Western artist, but as one of the European masters of mass-oriented public art."[192] His oeuvre provided woodcut artists in China with a model for explicitly linking visual narrative with social democratic politics. It is known that several of Masereel's works, including *The Passion of Man* (1918), were reprinted by a Chinese press in September of 1933, and visual art echoing his style took on a role in revolutionizing the popular masses.[193]

Replicating Thomas Mann's praise of the artist in the European context, Chinese intellectuals of Masereel's time similarly emphasized the importance of the intelligibility of visual narrative.[194] Evidence suggests that during the 1930s in Shanghai, other prominent artists who were impacted by the Belgian's work, such as Tao Wen, adopted not only its form but also "the themes of Masereel's narratives including the allure and danger of the city, the misery of social inequality, and the suffering and sacrifice of masses."[195] Significantly, Ma is attentive to both of these thematic and formal issues in *Leaf*, even if she adds a notable amount of narrative complexity. At the level of the image, her depictions and themes are quite intelligible. Focusing on a single leaf, she is able to weave themes of industrialization, the machine age, community, knowledge, and organic beauty into her comic. Threading through the graphic novel's many-paneled pages and episodes are a tubing system that connects the rural outskirts of the city with its central street corners and alleys (2015: 8–9, 90–91), and with a giant blue-hued factory billowing smoke up into the atmosphere (2015: 33, 66). Ma depicts the protagonist as one of a vast number of urbanites who work seated in interconnected cubicles that overflow with mechanical dials. Each workstation is connected, via tubing, to large screens that track the circulation of blue energy around the city (2015: 16–17). The blue shading is pervasive in Ma's panels throughout large portions of the graphic novel: in exterior streetlamps, interior bulbs, and television screens in residences, as well as an intriguing tree in a central town park. In a magnificent two-page spread, this tree's blue luminescence attracts and entertains adults and children, who cluster around it and stare in awe, sharing the warmth of a communal environment (2015: 22–23).

The color yellow is rarely seen early on in the graphic novel, but it becomes increasingly more prevalent as the narrative evolves. The first time it appears, the protagonist has just dozed off while holding the blue leaf (2015: 13). In terms of comics form, the way in which yellow appears within a given sequence of panels is quite significant (see figure 2.6). The second panel on a nine-panel page features small glowing spots of yellow outside the window, while all remaining panels are blue-hued. The protagonist is asleep in the first panel, and wakes up in the third panel, as if having possibly dreamt the content of the second panel. Looking around as if to consider whether the yellow color was or was not part of a dream, the youth closes the window and nods back down again in slumber. The second time yellow appears, the comic returns to and deconstructs this dream trope in the context of an auspicious bus ride. This time the protagonist wakes up from a nap as a woman entering the bus passes by in the aisle. Outside the bus window there is a conspicuous, floating yellow leaf (2015: 34). Immediately exiting the bus, the protagonist arrives at a mysterious door whose streetlamp is curiously yellow, and not blue. An ornate leaf is displayed above the door, which is shaded in yellow emanating from the lamp (2015: 35). A full-page panel zooms out from the scene to show that many residences in this building cluster have soft yellow glows emanating from their windows (2015: 36). From this moment onward (2015: 37), the color blue does not appear again for another twenty-three pages (2015: 60).

This substantial yellow sequence of the graphic novel (2015: 34–60) is important because of the way in which it connects the yellow hue with an organic nature that existed prior to the construction of the city's form. As the sequence unfolds, the protagonist undergoes a sort of shift in social consciousness. A woman on the second floor of the building who is a collector of leaves, and who seems to be either a scholar of the natural world or a natural scientist, regales

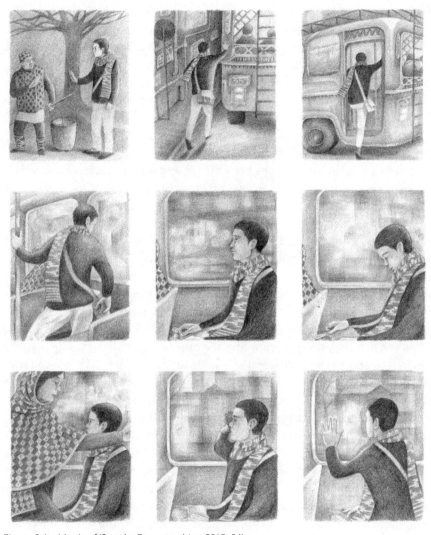

Figure 2.6—Ma, *Leaf* (Seattle: Fantagraphics, 2015: 34)

both protagonist and reader with an urban tale. This is the story of a man who, before the city existed, built a rudimentary home on the very site that would over the course of time become the building in which they are talking to each other.[196] After hearing this story, the protagonist shows the yellow leaf to this natural-scientist character. She studies the leaf, consults books, compares species, and via some scientific process mixes the leaf with other organic materials in a glass jar. During the protagonist's journey home, other urbanites begin to take notice of the yellow substance it contains (2015: 55). After another nap, it becomes clear that the yellow substance is expanding. Rushing out to the street with it in hand, the youth drops the glass jar, and it breaks open. Now outside of the jar in the open air, the yellow leaf is sucked into one of the city's tubes. The ubiquitous blue hue of the pages subsequently returns, coming to pervade the entire city (2015: 60–61).

After some thought, and assisted by an older man's knowledge of the city's tubing system, our protagonist decides to take action. Entering a specific tube of which only the old man seems to be aware, the protagonist gains entry to the factory and is amazed to find an abundance of glowing yellow spots inside of it. An empty control room provides access to the factory's blueprints, which contain the information necessary to shift the system's entire output from blue to yellow. Pointing, staring, or smiling, the other urbanites—including both the older man and the natural scientist—seem to immediately take notice (2015: 92–93). After this moment the color blue does not reappear in either the city or the graphic novel. Interestingly the comic's final pages suggest the completion of a cycle. Its blue-hued beginning pages depicted a single bird taking flight from a rural nest and joining a number of others in the sky over the town (2015: 3–5). The yellow-hued finale shows a single bird arriving and sitting on the urban windowsill of what seems to be a second-floor window (2015: 95). The relationship of the bird at the story's end to the bird at the beginning of the tale is ultimately unclear. Readers may want to conclude that the shift over the course of the book has a cyclical natural theme. In this sense the opening–closing emphasis on the bird could speak to a cyclical natural rhythm of migratory patterns. Perhaps, on the other hand, the birds leave because of the blue hues and return because of the yellow hues. It is also unclear whether the yellow factory and the blue factory are the same or different places. That there is a certain lack of specificity in the graphic novel's plot seems intentional.

Those few critics who have written about the graphic novel have underscored that its form makes interpretation problematic. "You're never quite sure exactly what is going on in *Leaf* and the meaning of the story is definitely open to interpretation," writes Gareth Branwyn.[197] Summer Hayes characterizes *Leaf* as "simultaneously cautionary and celebratory," noting that "even with all the book's languorous, wending turns, readers will easily follow the larger themes surrounding the cost of industry."[198] Chris Gaveler notes the story's focus on "the paradoxical role of nature in an urban setting."[199] Though some aspects of the story are far from clear, however, thematically there is a consistent emphasis. Branwyn's comment that "spot colors, namely blue and yellow, are used as a narrative device" is particularly helpful in this regard.[200] It is perhaps better to say that what these colors do is underscore the protagonist's—and therefore also the reader's—sensuous engagement with the urban environment.

The power of Daishu Ma's urban narrative can be traced to the role that the human senses play within it. The artist's recuperation of the human senses in theme is reflected also in the comic's formal aesthetics. This resonance leads her toward the targeted use of color in a way that goes beyond Masereel's patterns of stark relief. The move beyond black-and-white images—Ma's targeted use of yellow and blue—suggests a push to think beyond simplistic social binaries and introduces a degree of complexity to the story.[201] This formal decision at once reinforces the theme of the complex relationship between human action and the natural world. While Masereel's wordless novels tended to romanticize the rural areas untouched by industrial machinery and associate the densely populated urban areas of the machine age with capitalist exploitation, Ma takes a more nuanced view. "Though the labyrinths of buildings and machines might recall *Metropolis* at times, these city-dwellers are not dehumanized cogs in an industrialized underworld," writes Gaveler.[202] Technology in the graphic novel is neither inherently evil, irredeemable, nor something whose power can be renounced entirely. Instead, as the artist's use of color highlights, *Leaf* poses a question regarding the responsible use of technology and industrial power. It asks readers to consider the ways in which human beings harness the natural world and the social ends toward which that natural power is pushed. In the end, Ma's graphic novel is less about thinking and more about feeling. Namely, *Leaf* is about feeling connected to the natural world and making the machines that our industrialized, technological society has produced work in harmony with a more responsible set of social values.

Despite the lack of clarity regarding plotlines, one easily concludes that the graphic novel prioritizes yellow-hued power over blue-hued power. This is easy enough to see from the comic's yellow front and back covers and the interior yellow pages included at the beginning and end of the book. The color yellow is also used to illuminate the same sets of objects that shone blue in the beginning, for example, light bulbs in houses, vehicle headlights, and exterior streetlamps. This displacement of blue by yellow is tied to a sense that material urban progress results from a transformative change of social consciousness. The protagonist's journey has a transformative effect on the city, but for this effect to be achieved, a new sense of social responsibility must be forged and must inform the material urban environment for production. The substantial middle section of the comic that was hued in yellow (2015: 34–59) can be seen as the protagonist's ideological awakening. It is significant that the human senses ignite this awakening, one that is then strengthened through knowledge, and which then leads to social action. It is the protagonist's ability to engage the city at a sensuous level that precipitates a journey from alienated urbanite to a disalienated actor, one capable of effecting an urban transformation carried out also in the interests of the other city dwellers.

Those emphasizing *Leaf*'s "quiet complexity" or suggesting that there is "a gentle quiet at the center of this work" perhaps downplay the artist's commitment to social transformation.[203] Daishu Ma in fact demonstrates a connection to two central tenets of Marxian thought. Not only does she underscore the importance of the human senses in creating social transformation, she also shows an awareness of the dialectical principle outlined by Marx and urbanized by thinkers such as Lewis Mumford. In brief, this dialectical principle communicates that "mind *takes form* in the city; and in turn, urban forms condition mind."[204] The final pages of *Leaf*, wherein a range of urbanites are captivated by the small glowing yellow spots that float through the city streets, are a metaphor for the potential of urban life once the human senses have been emancipated. The blue-hued city has conditioned the minds of its inhabitants to a certain form of urban social production. Yet the yellow-hued city brought into being at the graphic novel's end indicates that new forms of urban life are possible. As *Leaf* dramatizes, such new urban social worlds are possible only to the degree that urbanites are able to imagine them and act to bring them into material existence.

In conclusion, this chapter has continued to document the tendency of comics to represent, reflect, and comment on the modern urban experience. Artists discussed here have innovated by imbuing this general theme with an emphasis on passionate life in the city. At the same time, each has also innovated in terms of the formal aspects of comics. Visual artists such as Hogarth, Töpffer, and Outcault (ch.1) had demonstrated a certain social realism in their work. Frans Masereel transposed observable social realities into a heroic-tragic key, one informed by class consciousness. His wordless novels exalted the sensory aspects of city life, and they harnessed the power of our collective urban desires to comment on the conflicted present and possible futures of the modern city. Will Eisner expanded out from the comics panel in series to fashion a whole-page design that recalled the single-image work of earlier woodcut novel artists such as Masereel. His emphasis on the Jewish American experience and the theatricality of life in the city allowed him to explore the passions as they relate to religious faith, sexuality, capitalistic opportunism, solitude, communion, and song. Julie Doucet's autobiographical persona attempted to carve out a space of her own in the city, but found herself alienated by the urban and gendered forces that impacted her life. The visual excess of her graphic style conveyed the disordered presentation of the protagonist's life, its physical and emotional messiness, and the agitated monotony of her panel frames resonated with readers as a symbol of her urban confinement. The young women protagonists created by Raquel Córcoles sought sex, romance, and community in the city and embodied the drive to enjoy the life of the streets on one's own terms. The artist's polished digital design both reflected the trappings of the urban leisure economy and drew attention to its superficiality. Rafael Martínez Castellanos's comic can be read as strong support for transnational gay identity politics. Also anticipating the legalization of gay marriage in Spain in 2005, its central gay couple experienced Madrid's Chueca district as a use-value serving the human passions. Daishu Ma's graphic novel ultimately recalls Masereel's graphic style and social themes. *Leaf* draws on a long history of wordless comics to celebrate the sensuous dimensions of city life and the role of the human senses as a catalyst for social change. The plans that implement new ideas for constructing urban worlds are very seldom so emancipatory, however. As the comics selected for exploration in the next chapter document all too well, the structure of the modern city is often in conflict with human desires.

CHAPTER 3

URBAN PLANNING, BUILT ENVIRONMENT, AND THE STRUCTURE OF CITIES

This chapter questions a central premise of modern urban planning. That is, it matters very much whether the intended goal of planning is merely to change the structure of the city's built environment or whether it is to change urban social relationships. Manipulation of the urban form is undoubtedly a tool used to solidify power and privilege. Introducing changes to the built environment is, as history has proven, somewhat of an easy task. Existing structures can be demolished, new walls can be constructed and new roads built. This much is made evident by the large-scale planning carried out by Baron Haussmann in Paris and, as explored later in this chapter, by Robert Moses in New York. Yet it must be recognized that there is a certain conceptual violence involved in the separation modern urban planners routinely invoke between the city's material built environment and its larger social context. In this light, there are two main critiques of the modern planning tradition with which we must contend. The first was put forth by American urban historian Lewis Mumford (1895–1990), and the second by French urban philosopher Henri Lefebvre (1901–1991). While both thinkers are important for understanding the urban comics representations that follow, this chapter invokes Lefebvre more thoroughly than it does Mumford. That said, they share a common rejection of the modern planning tradition.

Lewis Mumford roundly criticized nineteenth- and twentieth-century city planning for being overly mechanistic. He tied the formal structure of the city to the industrialization in which its construction was carried out. That is, as mines and mining communities were connected to industrializing urban centers through railway construction, the rectilinear logic of the railroad influenced the approach of city planners.[1] This meant that city building as a social practice was notoriously out of touch with the "organic events and organic patterns" that Mumford associated with humanity and humanness.[2] In part because of a systematic scientific and social neglect of the urban form, he argued, the modern metropolis had become a monstrosity.[3] His book *The Culture of Cities* took modern planners to task, asserting that "current thinking about cities proceeded without sufficient insight into their nature, their function, their purpose, their historic role, or their potential future."[4] Despite the deplorable state of the modern planned city, however, Mumford was confident that urban planning could help.[5] He believed that "genuine planning is an attempt, not arbitrarily to displace reality, but to clarify it and to grasp firmly all the elements necessary to bring the geographic and economic facts in harmony with human purposes."[6] As he wrote in the introduction to the 1970 reedition of *The Culture of Cities*, the time had come to reinvigorate city planning: "We have now reached a point where these fresh accumulations of historical insight and scientific knowledge are ready to flow over into social life, to mold anew the forms of cities, to assist in the transformation of both the instruments and the goals of our civilization."[7] If urban planning was overly mechanistic, it was nonetheless salvageable. In the end, Mumford believed that planners who acknowledged the interconnection of city building with wider questions of social life and humanity as a whole could have a positive impact on our collective urban futures.

Henri Lefebvre, like Mumford, was also critical of the modern planning tradition. The two thinkers coincided in underscoring the need to explore the historical links between industrialization and urbanization.[8] Yet Lefebvre's critique ran much deeper. He believed that the social practice of city building was, from the outset, conditioned and co-opted by the capitalist forces from which it had developed. Thus, in his view it was not possible to reform the modern planning tradition without also effecting a radical change in urban society as a whole.[9] Modern urban planning, argued Lefebvre, is a bourgeois science. It necessarily structures the city in the class interests of capitalists, and it unfolds under the watchful eye of the modern state. Historically, it arises during the nineteenth century and is driven by a specialized class of planners. Since the 1800s, its top-down approach has ultimately failed to create "an urban reality for users" and instead has constructed the city in the interests of "speculators, builders, and technicians."[10] Bolstered by the complicity of city planning, Lefebvre states, capitalism survived throughout the twentieth century "by producing space, by occupying a space."[11] He insisted that while the city's built environment can be planned, its less tangible and more crucial aspects cannot. Thus, he opposed the city as a practico-material and architectural fact to an essence of city life that he called "the urban."[12] In the French theorist's work, this term connotes the vibrancy, spontaneity, and ever-shifting movement of the city's living social form: thus, "the urban, defined as assemblies and encounters, is therefore the simultaneity (or centrality) of all that exists socially."[13] Urbanism, on the other hand, is thus the enemy of the urban, which it seeks to suppress and even destroy.[14] In *The Survival of Capitalism*, Lefebvre asserts, "It is worth remembering that the urban has no worse enemy than urban planning and 'urbanism,' which is capitalism's and the state's strategic instrument for the manipulation of fragmented urban reality and the production of controlled space."[15] From this perspective, urban critique involves attending to the existing structure and ongoing reconfiguration of city space. In particular, this means recognizing that urbanism's manipulation of the material built environment of the city cannot be understood without investigating its relationship to broader social issues. These are issues regarding capital accumulation, control, access, and resistance.

In *Writing on Cities*, for example, Lefebvre contends, "Planning as ideology formulates all the problems of society into questions of space and transposes all that comes from history and consciousness into spatial terms. It is an ideology which immediately divides up."[16] Thus, the city is not to be understood as a collection of buildings, but instead as a spatial form whose very structure expresses a social relationship.[17] Urban populations are constrained and controlled by the city's spatial form. They nevertheless seek to resist being controlled by this form and the social power it represents. Here the built environment is understood as one of urbanism's main tools. The material structure of the city aids planners and developers in establishing and maintaining a systematic control of urban populations. Opposed to the lived space of the city—the use-value it holds for its inhabitants—Lefebvre also theorized the notion of conceived space as a key tool of the planner.[18] The city's built environment is a direct product of this conceptual planning vision, one that the thinker compared to the bird's-eye view of the city from above. In the end, no discrete border can be drawn between lived space and conceived space, for they are both implicated in what the urban theorist calls spatial practice. Yet it is at this level of analysis that one can see a defining tension emerge. On one hand, there is the spontaneously lived space of the city dweller, what Lefebvre called the urban. On the other hand, there is the conceived space of the planner, which finds expression in the city's relatively static built environment.

In *Introduction to Modernity*, Lefebvre provides a wonderful metaphor for this relationship between lived urban space and the built environment of the city, the latter understood as the result of the planner's conceived space. He uses the metaphor of the city as a living creature to address the relationship between the city and the urban as a defining tension, an interconnection, and even a contradiction. The constructed city in this sense represents the values of contemporary urbanism made material. It expresses the urbanist's view of the built environment as a collection of objects, grouped together in a theoretically empty space that can be modified to suit any given purpose. The urban, on the other hand, is a moving, living process. Thus, in a section titled "Notes on the New Town (April 1960)," Lefebvre writes:

> A living creature has slowly secreted a structure; take this living creature in isolation, separate it from the form it has given itself according to the law of its species, and you are left with something soft, slimy and shapeless; what can it possibly have in common with this delicate structure, its ridges, its grooves, its symmetries, its every detail revealing smaller, more delicate details as you examine it more closely? But it is precisely this link, between the animal and its shell, that one must try to understand. [. . .] This community has shaped its shell, building and rebuilding it, modifying it again and again according to its needs.[19]

In this metaphor the city is the hard shell of the living urban animal. This shell may be modified over time, but at any given instant it represents a given set of social values. The question Lefebvre asks, however, is whether or not that hard shell—the built environment of the city considered at any particular moment in time—truly represents the interests of all of the city's inhabitants. Not all urbanites possess an equal power to structure cityspace in their interests, and most find that they must adapt to an urban project that may not suit their needs, much less their desires.

In the third volume of his *Critique of Everyday Life* and subsequently in *Rhythmanalysis*, Lefebvre continues in this somewhat poetic mode as a way of addressing urbanism's tangible consequences. Industrialization and urbanism under capitalism have thus been responsible for the "splintering of space and time in general homogeneity, and the crushing of natural rhythms and cycles by linearity."[20] In general, urbanism eschews natural rhythms and favors the strict law of linear development. There are thus two threats that can be leveled at urbanism's production of city space. The first is material. Lefebvre is often cited for his statement that only "bulldozers and Molotov cocktails can change the dominant organization of space."[21] To be successful, his work suggests, revolutions must transform this dominant spatial organization in some material way. Yet resistance is arguably just as important as revolution. The second threat to urbanism is to develop a form of spatial thinking that challenges its logic. The urban figure of the rhythmanalyst emerges in Lefebvre's theory in just this way, that is, as a potential threat to the linear logic of planning. The novelty of this urban figure is that the rhythmanalyst seeks to reconstitute the discourse surrounding use-value, human passion, and desire. These are now conceived as a reaction to contemporary urbanism. The rhythmanalyst recaptures the lived temporality of urban life and asserts it as a challenge. This challenge is then leveled against the urbanist's linear, conceptual, and simple, geometrical spatial approach to the production of city space.[22]

The central premise of this chapter's investigations borrows from both Mumford's insistence on the social meaning of the city's spatial form and Lefebvre's more pointed critique of urbanism. While the previous chapter focused on comics representing the urban passions of city dwellers, this chapter explores the structure of the city's urban form itself. The passions, desires, fears, anxieties, joys, hopes, and dreams that breathe life into the urban experience constituted the central themes of works by Frans Masereel, Will Eisner, Julie Doucet, Raquel Córcoles, Rafael Martínez Castellanos, and Daishu Ma (all ch. 2). Urbanites in works by those artists called upon the human senses in order to enjoy the city as a use-value or a lived space. Even so, their struggles necessarily implicated the structure of the city itself. Whether in the form of Masereel's imposing buildings, Eisner's tenements, or the close quarters of Doucet's depictions of apartment living, the urban built environment tended to both confine and dehumanize city dwellers. Moderna de Pueblo's young women protagonists and Rafa's central gay couple sought to carve out a space in which to pursue sex and romance, despite heteronormative social values and amidst gendered patterns of superficial consumerism. Daishu Ma's take on the city pitted a young city dweller and a small group of committed actors against an oppressive urban infrastructure that very few others in the comic's diegesis seemed to question. Although the present chapter interrogates the urban planning vision more directly, it thus builds on the analytical thread already established by continuing to explore the tension between urban structures and everyday urban experiences. In truth, a sensuous view of the city and a structural view of the city are two sides of the same coin.

The comics in this chapter speak to Mumford's denunciation of urbanism's mechanistic and linear logic and Lefebvre's Marxian urban critique in different ways. Overall, the sequential arrangement of these comics contributes to the fashioning of an arc of sorts. The early sections of this chapter deal with the representation of urban spatial structures that connote control. Here the linear monotony and top-down process of urban planning are presented as forces that disorient and dehumanize the individual city dweller. Along the way, the notion of individual and collective resistance to urbanism is introduced. This resistance takes many forms. For example, in a relatively realistic denunciation of urban drudgery, soporific urbanites are barely able to imagine escape from their urban monotony. Their imagination takes them only as far as to daydream of consumer-driven leisure travel. Next, in a fantastic comics narrative, a man attempts to investigate and escape from a city, only to find he is powerless to do so. Another fantastic graphic novel asserts the curved line against the linear tradition of modern planning in the context of a dystopic city. The end of the chapter focuses on the resistance to urbanism at the level of the community and the individual. A historically motivated graphic novel depicts the challenge raised by Jane Jacobs to the urbanistic plans for New York City developed by Robert Moses, even if it does so with some ambivalence. In the last collection of comics analyzed, the day-to-day movements of an individual flâneur resonate markedly with the virtues of the rhythmanalyst as described by Lefebvre.

THE LINEAR MONOTONY OF THE METROPOLIS: HARITON PUSHWAGNER'S *SOFT CITY* (1969–1975)

Hariton Pushwagner was born in Oslo, in 1940, as Terje Brofos. He reportedly started drawing at four years old and continued amidst no small amount of psychic and family turmoil.[23] He was later educated formally at Norway's National Academy of Fine Art. In the late 1950s and throughout the 1960s, he lived a bohemian lifestyle, traveled extensively, and used psychedelic drugs. Along the way he met a number of musical, artistic, and literary luminaries: in Paris, pianist Bud Powell; in Ibiza, Picasso; in London, William S. Burroughs.[24] Over the years he earned a celebrity reputation for being a strange personality. He renamed himself as Hariton Pushwagner in the early 1970s, at a time when, as his biographer puts it, he was "on the verge of madness and suicide."[25] In the twenty-first century, he is a widely recognized graphic artist with exhibits of his work taking place across Europe. The 2008 exhibition of *Soft City* was named "one of the highlights" of the Berlin biennial for contemporary art by the *New York Times*.[26] A Norwegian documentary was released in 2011 recounting "his topsy turvy life."[27] In 2012 there was a show at the Milton Keynes Gallery in the UK. There were eight gallery exhibitions of the artist's work in 2016 in Norway alone.[28]

   Pushwagner is also known for a host of other artistic works. Early on in his career, he illustrated the science-fiction books of Axel Jensen, his friend and mentor.[29] His "Apocalypse Frieze" (1973–1993) depicts "military factories churning out war machines and carnage" and consists of seven large panels produced over two decades.[30] "The Pill" (2010–2011) shows off his hand-colored graphic work. Another acclaimed creation is *A Day in the Life of a Family Man* (1980), whose illustrations are quite similar to those in *Soft City*. As "a wickedly funny set of pink, grey and black silk screenprints conceived with Jensen in 1980, [this work] brings billboard advertising, surveillance technology and TV-as-placebo into the picture."[31] Pushwagner's painting *Jobkill* (1990) is currently owned by Norway's National Museum. The importance of his graphic work is increasingly noted in academic circles, even if extended analyses are hard to come by. One important exception is a 2010 thesis written in Norwegian. Nicole Benestad Nygaard situates the artist in a comics history running from Rodolphe Töpffer (ch. 1) and Frans Masereel (ch. 2), and places his work in dialogue with the scholarship of Scott McCloud, Thierry Groensteen, and other noted theorists.[32]

The artist's epic urban novel in pictures, *Soft City*, was drawn between 1969 and 1975. It was admired by Pete Townshend and Steve Winwood, lost, found again, and finally released by Norwegian publisher No Comprendo in 2008, following a "messy legal dispute."[33] There seems to be no real clarity on how it was lost, but indications suggest it disappeared when the artist moved to Norway at the end of the 1970s.[34] Critic Martin Herbert notes that the time of the work's composition was a turbulent one. The specter of assassination and violence hung over the late 1960s, residue from the Chicago Democratic Convention of 1968, the Charles Manson murders, and the loss of Martin Luther King and Robert F. Kennedy. "By common consensus the counter-culture fell apart, authority consolidated, and hopes for revolution were visibly dashed on the rocks."[35] Critics have noted that the influence of William S. Burroughs's *The Soft Machine* (1961) is palpable in *Soft City*, and they have also signaled its resonance with the themes of significant earlier and later films, novels, and music albums.[36] These include Fritz Lang's *Metropolis* (1927), Aldous Huxley's *Brave New World* (1932), Stanley Kubrick's *A Clockwork Orange* (1971), and Pink Floyd's *The Wall* (1979).[37] Such connections speak to the artist's criticism of a persisting social urge to control, separate, alienate, and dehumanize people. Chris Ware regards *Soft City*'s themes as highly pertinent today, noting the continued "threat of an oppressive urban architecture" and the possibility that "we are also headed for such a horizonless walled existence."[38]

Pushwagner masterfully pursues the theme of urban disconnection in its most radically mundane form, that is, by focusing insistently and obsessively on the built urban environment. The unnumbered pages of *Soft City* begin with four two-page spreads: first a solid black background, and subsequently, views that get closer and closer to a sprawling urban building hand-drawn in pencil against a white background. Pushwagner's style here and throughout the comic suggests a world of stark contrasts. In particular, his images pit the pencil trace of human artistry against the monotonous urban logic of the rectilinear grid. In these early pages, a massive, unadorned, geometrical building gradually takes shape. Its windowpanes stretch from left to right margin on the double-page spread. There is text accompanying this sequence of images: "Good morning everybody . . . Look . . . Here comes . . . The sun." The sun that finally appears on the fourth two-page spread is tucked away in the upper-left corner behind what has now become an enormous building. This detail is representative of the subjugated role played by the natural world in what is a nightmarishly mundane world of white-collar urban labor productivity and consumer capitalism.

Already, as these opening pages establish, the theme of the imposing urban form and its linear logic is more important than the plotline. In fact, there is little plot of which to speak. There are no central actors. As Chris Ware notes, "the reader is left with no real person with whom to identify, no memories or 'character' with whom to empathize."[39] Instead, Pushwagner crafts the story of an urban multitude. Its unremarkable subjects are ordinary men, women, and children who sleepwalk through their daily urban routines.

In a brief review, Douglas Wolk has offered up a concise summary of *Soft City*'s contents that is worth revisiting here:

> Its oversize pages depict city life as an identity-annihilating, cookie-cutter horror. [. . .] After waking up and taking their daily "Life" pill, countless identical men in hats wave to their wives and babies, go to their identical cars and flow in a river of traffic to mammoth parking garages and grids of office workstations. The women push carts down the aisles of gigantic supermarkets in a mute frenzy of consumption; a powerful boss watches scenes of tanks and factories on an enormous screen. Then everyone repeats the pattern in reverse. At home, they watch military atrocities on TV, retreat to their beds and take a pill marked "Sleep."[40]

As Wolk's summary conveys, action is almost nonexistent in *Soft City*. Pushwagner's detailed urban scenes convey static concepts more than they do dynamic situations. On the whole, the comic evacuates the city's potential as "a theater for social action." Lewis Mumford was himself one of the greatest proponents of this idea of the urban social theater, which was clearly expressed in the 1937 essay "What Is the City?"[41] Yet another touchpoint for this idea would be English writer Jonathan Raban's work of nonfiction titled, interestingly enough, *Soft City* (1974). In terms that echo Mumford's seminal work, Raban's famous portrait of metropolitan life in London asserted the "intrinsic theatricality of city life" and described its spaces as "lit stages awaiting a scenario."[42] The subtle interaction between the individual, the collective, and the wider social environment that Mumford and Raban attribute to the city also arguably finds its way, for example, into Will Eisner's visual tales of Dropsie Avenue (ch. 2). Therein, Eisner's images invoke the trope of the dramatic spotlight to foreground highly expressive faces, and with them, the emotions, struggles, and passions of his characters. By contrast, however, in Pushwagner's *Soft City* there is no space for social theater in an environment so saturated by serial replication and the dehumanizing effects of commercial-industrial control.

Pushwagner eschews any hint of social play in his graphic novel. The brute material fact of the built environment overshadows any passions, desires, or emotions its urban inhabitants might experience. *Soft City* is a work in which "a numbed world unfolds in relentlessly repetitive detail."[43] This detail takes the form of "teeming supermarkets, endless rows of white-collar workers' desks, vast perspectival views of densely windowed apartment blocks," and the like, all contributions to what are "seemingly endless vistas of commercialism."[44] The artist "draws thousands of vehicles or desks or workers in symmetrical perspective with a thin, uneasy line, receding into infinitesimal marks at the horizon."[45] In this way, the lives of city dwellers are portrayed as identical, and the urban form itself is revealed to be potentially infinite in its extension.[46]

Some of the comic's most fascinating vistas are those saturated with the artist's characteristically repetitive detail. One intriguing page features a collection of almost identical businessmen in ties whose empty stares are directed at the reader. As if replicating the caricature studies of Hogarth and Töpffer (both ch. 1), these faces of bureaucratic capitalism crowd the image. Yet, where those earlier caricaturists may have prioritized physiological variation and simultaneously its associated social types, here it is difficult to differentiate one visage from the next. Homogeneity replaces heterogeneity. Rather than individuals whose traits are communicated through dramatic facial expression or graphic convention, these faces seem to be mere visual patterns on a sheet of wallpaper. The attentive reader will be able to find certain subtle quirks expressed here or there on the page. Yet overall the graphic improvisation and spontaneity of line for which Töpffer was known is here notably absent, as Pushwagner's style approaches a serialized uniformity.[47] Careful breaks from this uniformity only serve to reinforce the homogeneity of this urban working population as a defined social group. For instance, only one woman appears on the page. She is lost in the crowd of men, whose lost facial expression she replicates. In addition, this woman and one of the men depicted have thought bubbles emanating from their heads, visually marking them as different from the pack. Potentially, the appearance of these thought bubbles might have indicated two individuals who think for themselves, who are not yet completely sheep. Yet the content of their thoughts shows otherwise. Each person is shown admiring herself or himself in a mirror, a detail whose parallel across gender lines suggests the vacuous nature of urban conformity at the largest scale. More generally, the thought bubble is used as a formal element throughout the comic in precisely this way. It initially suggests a subtle break from urban homogeneity but, in the end, merely reaffirms the inability of members of the collective to differentiate themselves from the rest even in mind-set.[48]

Similar with regard to the artist's penchant for repetition is the lengthy sequence that follows. Over the course of the next thirty pages, Pushwagner depicts the monotonous commute to work. Unnamed urbanites pack into their shared-ride vehicles and sit in bumper-to-bumper traffic that is seemingly endless. One two-page spread features a margin-to-margin traffic jam of identical vehicles driven by identical hat-wearing businessmen who are crammed in, four to a car. The reader's point of view is anchored in the front seat of one of these vehicles, such that we can see two hands on the steering wheel, and the rectangular rearview mirror in the upper right of the vista. The latter is itself a visual container for an endless sea of vehicles that trail behind. The serial replication of this car traffic is vast and ultimately dehumanizing. It is important that the traffic is confined to the lower fourth of the page height. The result is that three-fourths of the page is filled with looming, ostensibly identical high-rise buildings. There seem to be hundreds and hundreds of rudimentary rectangular windows in these buildings, each drawn painstakingly by hand in Pushwagner's characteristic thin pencil line. The buildings themselves boast no ornamentation whatsoever. Nor can a boundary between one and the next be spotted. The linear monotony of the built environment to which they contribute is overwhelming and results in a compelling visual parallel to the theme of a monotonous urban existence.

The details of this scene are crucial to its overall significance. In the lower right-hand corner of the image a single thought bubble can be seen. In it a car passenger imagines himself fishing on a lake. As in the previous instances, this thought bubble functions as a minor disruption that only serves to highlight the uniformity of the scene. Its potential significance is minimized by the obsessive visual detail of the urban commute. In this and other images featuring very similar layouts, perspectives, and content, the vastness of the urban monotony seems to require the full attention of its city dwellers (see figure 3.1). Escape in body is impossible; escape in mind is a futile exercise. The fact that Pushwagner follows this two-page spread with a lengthy series of single-page commuting scenes that echo its content, theme, and composition only drives home the point. Interestingly, the only use of color in *Soft City* is reserved for the streetlights in this commuting sequence. Readers first see green lights in the distance, then yellow and red, red and yellow up close, and finally green again. This is a slow-moving, urban experience bereft of any passion or spontaneity whatsoever. As with the comic's infrequent use of thought bubbles, the seemingly spontaneous appearance of color only serves to highlight the lack of spontaneity in *Soft City*'s urban environment. The only rhythm in these scenes is the slow, plodding advance of mindless commuters along a Cartesian urban traffic grid. This is not a natural rhythm, but instead one imposed by the linear and dehumanizing social form of the modern built environment. What is so compelling is that Pushwagner's detailed line work communicates this linear monotony just as well as does his represented content.

Though there are human beings depicted throughout *Soft City*, it is clear that this is an object world rather than a human one. Or rather, in line with the visual effect of the famed cubicle sequences in Jacques Tati's cinematic

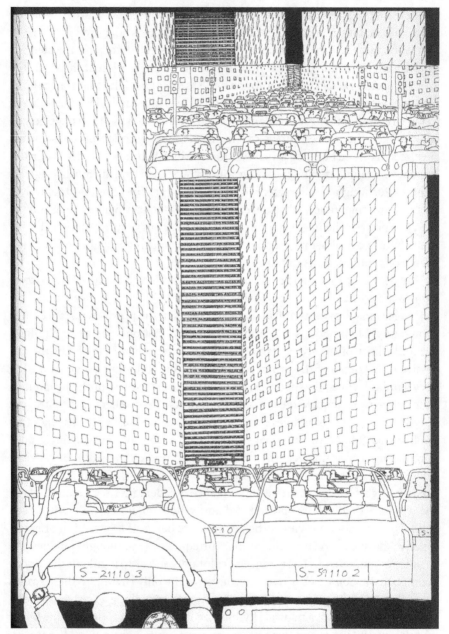

Figure 3.1—Pushwagner, *Soft City* (New York: New York Review of Books Comics, 2008: no pag.)

masterpiece *Playtime* (1967), this is a world in which humans are threatened with being reduced to mere objects. Pushwagner's city represents the stultifying effects of a planning carried out in the name of pure commerce and accumulation. It appears on the page worthy of the disdain that Mumford held for what he called the "sprawling giantism" and the "tentacular bureaucracy" of the Megalopolis.[49] Yet more specifically it also demonstrates that the urban has been devoured by the suburban. The suburban, in Mumford's terms, was synonymous with the uniform, the identical, and the inflexible.[50] Gone, here, is the social diversity of the urban downtown that, for example, was foregrounded in the fantastical comics narratives of Winsor McCay (ch. 1). In its place the reader finds what Ware calls an "impersonal, oppressive, seemingly futuristic military-industrialized complex/city."[51] The words of Sherman Sam perhaps best sum up the dehumanizing city environment drawn by the artist: "We exist, Pushwagner seems to suggest, merely to feed the urban machine."[52] While urban dehumanization in *Soft City* is unavoidable in both graphic and thematic terms, in the next comics text it is presented in a less direct manner.

THE TYRANNY OF PLANNING: *SAMARIS* (1983) BY BENOÎT PEETERS AND FRANÇOIS SCHUITEN

Benoît Peeters and François Schuiten are collaborators and master craftsmen of the ninth art. Their accomplishments have earned them the highest praise as practitioners of the Franco-Belgian comics tradition, such that one critic writes that they are "aujourd'hui considérés comme des figures emblématiques du monde de la bande dessinée" [today considered to be the emblematic figures of the world of the BD].[53] Interestingly, they have known each other since childhood. Benoît Peeters was born in Paris in 1956. At the age of twelve, he attended the same Sainte-Barbe School in Brussels as did Schuiten, but later returned to France to study philosophy at the Sorbonne in Paris. There he worked under none other than Roland Barthes. Peeters developed his writing and soon published his first novel *Omnibus* in 1976 with acclaimed publisher Minuit. He returned to Brussels in 1978, where he reconnected with Schuiten and continued his literary production.[54] He has turned increasingly to the world of comics and is also known for his theoretical analysis of the form. François Schuiten was born in Brussels in 1956, the same year as Peeters. After attending the Sainte-Barbe School, he stayed in Brussels and continued his studies at the Saint-Luc Institute during 1975–1977. His accomplishments in the world of design are numerous. Schuiten has worked in film and animation, has designed fifteen postal stamps, and has left his artistic stamp on the interior of the Luxemburg Pavilion at the University Expo in Seville, as well as metro stations in both Brussels and Paris.[55]

As these brief bios of the creative team suggest, Peeters is the writer, and Schuiten is the graphic artist. Schuiten's comics designs are heavily architectural, owing perhaps to no small amount of family influence. He comes from a family of architects. His father, Robert Schuiten, and his mother, Marie-Madeleine De Maeyer—not to mention, also, his brother and his sister—are or have been architects.[56] The passion Peeters holds for literary narrative has also marked the pair's collaborations. He is drawn to comics creators known for their narrative and highly conceptual work, having written, "The works that I have been most fascinated by are those of Rodolphe Töpffer, Winsor McCay, Hergé, Fred, Art Spiegelman or Chris Ware."[57] In artistic terms, both Peeters and Schuiten each bring something highly unique to the table. Yet it is the resulting fusion of stunning architecture and compelling narrative that has become the hallmark aspect of their collaborations. As one critic has remarked, architecture in their work has a narrative function—it is constitutive of narrative.[58] Thus, it is no surprise that their noted *Cités obscures* series—translated into English as both *Cities of the Fantastic* and *Dark Cities*—is deeply urban in concept and execution.

The comics series centers on ten cities: Alaxis, Armilia, Blossfeldstadt, Brüsel, Calvani, Mylos, Pâhry, the agglomeration known as Sodrovno-Voldachie, Urbicande, and Xhystos.[59] Interestingly, in 1996 the creators published a *Guide des cités*, where they make the case that "the Cities are best described as 'a distorted mirror image' of our world that is similar in many aspects and strikingly different in others."[60] The reader's exploration of these cities is frequently carried out from the vantage point of an outsider character. As Stefanie Diekmann has noted, this outsider is alternately a visitor, traveler, vagrant, stranger, or investigator.[61] The knowledge readers form of the cities, like the knowledge these outsiders can glean in their travels, is necessarily incomplete. Moreover, as Peeters has written, there is a fundamental instability to the *Cités obscures*: they "display a construction which is both highly structured and always on the point of falling apart, an immense jigsaw puzzle, where every piece that completes the imaginary universe has the simultaneous effect of making it impossible to totalize."[62] The result is, as Diekmann writes, that "the Cities of the Fantastic are not designed to be lived in."[63] In this sense, what the critic identifies as a current of "cultural pessimism" running through the series should also be understood as a recognition of how saturated the city is by the ambitions of modern urban planning and their dehumanizing effects.[64]

The representation of the cities throughout the comics series both reflects and undermines what Lefebvre called the "triumphant and triumphalist" character of urban modernity.[65] To explain, the built environment of the modern city is produced as a triumph of capitalist urbanism's monumental drive.

Modern cityspace is shaped through the systematic subjugation of urban life to the needs of urban production and accumulation. This triumphalist discourse of urban modernity seeks to complete its control of a constantly changing urban reality—remember Lefebvre's metaphor of the animal and its shell, which was introduced earlier in this chapter. Yet triumphalist discourse ignores the key limitation that urban life cannot be totally planned. That is, as much as ideological underpinnings of urban capitalism would have its city dwellers believe differently, the urban plan is always incomplete. This is revealed over the course of time, as urbanism must seek periodically to reconfigure and tighten its grip on the city. Within the urban fabric, there are always contradictions to be resolved, and spaces of resistance to be claimed. What the *Cités obscures* series does so well is reveal urban space as the battleground between attempts at a totalizing urban control, imposed from above, and attempts to reveal and combat hidden machinations of urban power, carried out from below.[66] In neither case can the urban be understood completely and totally. Instead, its structure undergoes a continual metamorphosis and is knowable only in pieces, whether this is considered from the perspective of the urban planning vision or the disalienated urbanite.[67]

With this context in mind, architecture is important on four interrelated levels in the *Cités obscures*. First, Schuiten's stunning images contain references to real-world architectural styles and are pertinent to place-bound debates. Each city's architectural style is somewhat distinct. In the case of *Brüsel*, for example, critics have shown the comic's relationship to the urbanistic discourse surrounding the Belgian capital.[68] Second, architecture structures Peeters's complex comics narratives. This is true at a general scale of the series as a whole, which revolves around specific urban spaces, buildings, and communities. Yet it is also the case that the built environment of the city often takes on the more active role of plot device. As is the case below in the analysis of *Samaris*, the depiction of city structure itself intensifies the comic's themes of alienation and actively pushes readers toward certain realizations crucial to the storyline. The characters of the graphic novel are somewhat two-dimensional by contrast. It might be said that the real drama is the one that unfolds between the protagonist, the walls of the city itself, and the reader. Third, the glut of architectural references throughout the series is part of a larger aesthetic method. In describing the work of Peeters and Schuiten, critics routinely use phrases like "ludic patchwork," "multiplicity," and "pastiche."[69] Importantly, such architectural pastiche has a literary complement. References to a range of literary authors, filmmakers, and architects abound in scholarship on the *Cités obscures*. This list includes Franz Kafka, Italo Calvino, Jorge Luis Borges, Jules Verne, Julien Gracq, Fritz Lang, Terry Gilliam, and Víctor Horta.[70] Fourth, however, the architectural-literary aesthetics of pastiche are not without a political resonance. In her analyses, Diekmann connects the term with Fredric Jameson's politicized notion of postmodernism as "cannibalization of all the architectural styles of the past."[71] This last point is deserving of further emphasis. She draws on Jameson, Umberto Eco, and Thomas More in establishing what she refers to as "the interdependency of architectural and political order" as a central conceit of the series.[72] Following a long tradition of representing imaginary cities, the architectural and the political are deeply intertwined in this ambitious comics project.

Les murailles de Samaris (*Samaris*) (1983) is a suitable example of the general trends that govern the collaborations between Peeters and Schuiten. It is the first book in the *Cités obscures* series of graphic novels, though it was originally published in the magazine *À Suivre*.[73] Despite its title, the narrative begins not in the city of Samaris but instead in Xhystos, one of the ten named Cities of the Fantastic. The protagonist Franz Bauer is chosen by the council in Xhystos to travel to Samaris in order to investigate a possible deceit. Previous travelers to Samaris have not returned, and the council hopes that Franz's trip will provide them with the information they lack. Before leaving, he spends one last night of passion in bed with Anna, whose own younger sister Clara has been lost in Samaris. The subsequent journey is long and arduous, and requires multimodal transport. After switching from train to altiplane, to aerophile, and finally boat, Franz finally arrives at the mysterious city. Upon checking into his hotel, he launches his investigation. Quite soon he meets a woman named Carla, whose name, readers will note, is an estranged echo of the name of Anna's sister, Clara. Other than this seeming human connection, he wanders around the city alone, often getting lost amongst its tall walls. He grows progressively suspicious of the city's built environment, thinking to himself: "At times, I had the ridiculous idea that this mysterious city had been conceived uniquely to trick its visitors. Architecture designed for the sole purpose of confusing travelers" (2017: 34). The notion of the deceitful city is here introduced.

Weeks go by, and Franz comes to realize that the entire city is a theatrical stage of sorts. Its walls move as if for him alone, shaping and constricting his urban experience quite literally. It turns out that the city is a giant mechanism of sorts. Its walls move on tracks. In truth, he has been seeing only the facade of the city, while its real source of power—carrying out the manipulation and deception of its visitors—has been hidden from his view. Having reached this realization, he remarks to himself, "The streets, the houses, popped up where I went—a moving maze that followed my footsteps, an unbelievable place where no path was ever the same twice" (2017: 41). The comics text also hints at yet another urban deception when Franz soon discovers an ancient book. It reads: "Born like the plant, the town will develop like the plant, untainted by impurities, it will be nourished by those it captures" (2017: 46). The protagonist's next thought, communicated in monologue narration, spells out the nature of the city's deception: "In order for Samaris to continue, it needed to frequently change its look, by capturing the visitors it managed to draw in. A tentacled city, like the plant that it took as its symbol, it needed an endless supply of images in order to survive" (2017: 46). The allegorical resonance with Mumford's denunciation of the "tentacular bureaucracy" of the Megalopolis could not be more apparent.[74] The urban environment has become the most deceitful version of a social theater: a pure spectacle or simulation. Franz seemingly manages to escape from the walls of Samaris and return to Xhystos, where he finds that no one remembers him. Time has apparently jumped ahead at such a rate that none of the council members who sent him on the mission are the same. Begrudgingly, he marches off once again to Samaris, which he now understands as his true home (2017: 54).

Les murailles de Samaris is no exception to the larger trends involving real-world architectural style in the work of Peeters and Schuiten outlined above. In line with the broader conceit of the series, Xhystos is known for its Art Nouveau architecture. Its design privileges "iron girders, structural engineering and art deco," recalling such real-world influences as "Víctor Horta's Brussels and Hector Guimard's Paris."[75] As the opening pages showcase, via a slow zoom into a closer view of some elegant buildings with flower-stem flourishes,[76] Schuiten's architectural renderings are a visual marvel on the page. Yet architecture is also intricately involved at the level of the graphic novel's plot, which ties together the two cities of Xhystos and Samaris. Though their relationship is still somewhat unclear at the end of the comic, each city nonetheless represents an avatar of the possible links between the city's spatial form and urban social structures of institutionalized power.

The case of Xhystos is relatively straightforward. The city was originally built as a fortress and now houses a governing council, such that the connection of architecture with both militaristic and bureaucratic social power is clear enough.[77] Recurring vistas of its grandiose towers, buildings, bridges, and stairways from the outset of the comic communicate the city's role as a fictional mirror for real-world social-architectural forms. It is the seat for the interconnected powers of capital and the bourgeois state, a fusion that is synonymous with the planning of the European city during the long nineteenth century.[78] Its construction brings to mind the monumental city, the "triumphant and triumphalist" design that for Lefebvre is synonymous with urban modernity. An early exterior of a tall, narrow building labeled "Registres et Inscriptions" (Records and Registrations) (2017: 13) is one such visual anchor for this triumphant bourgeois urban landscape. The panel in question is tall and narrow to match the building's shape, an example of what Peeters, in his contributions to comics theory, calls a "rhetorical" layout.[79] The horizontal variation of the rhetorical layout also appears in an early depiction of streetcar travel in Xhystos (2017: 18). In this way, a neatly ordered urban social world finds its expression in an equally ordered panel layout. Comics form recapitulates architectural and urban form. This approach to page organization conveys an initial confidence in the relatively stable urban governance structure of Xhystos as represented on the graphic novel's pages.

Samaris seems to be a contrast to Xhystos in every way, at least initially. It illustrates equally the premise that the city's built environment is an expression of the social powers that sustain it. Yet these social powers are somewhat more mysterious than those in Xhystos. Instead of the highly visible forms linking Xhystos with the bourgeois state and the urban governance council, the power structure of Samaris is hidden from view. Here, Lefebvre's understanding of urban capitalism is instructive. His view emphasized the pervasive and structural alienation of urbanites from the material conditions that govern their own lives. For instance, in *Rhythmanalysis* he wrote of the monstrous nature of capital: "The brave people, as you said, not only move alongside the monster but are inside it; they live off it. So they do not know how it works."[80] Franz Bauer's experience in Samaris must be seen in light of the reality of such urban alienation. As Franz disalienates himself from the city's spatial and social form, that is, as he becomes more knowledgeable regarding how it works, he manages to move from thought to action. Hearing a buzzing noise from behind a door, he breaks through it, only to find that the door and the hotel interior wall were thin facades (2017: 39). Intriguingly, this panel appears at the bottom right of a two-page sequence, such that in turning the page, the reader is complicit in accelerating the pace of the storyline. This feature is a testament to the innovative style of the comic's creators.

The sequence that follows is heavy with action as Franz tries to escape from a vast urban machine of moving walls, collapsing facades, steel girders, cables, and gears (2017: 40–48). The leisurely urban wanderings that characterized his arrival to Samaris are refashioned here as an adrenaline-induced fugue (see figure 3.2). The structure of the city is threatening. He is frequently placed in physical danger of falling, of being crushed by walls or girders, or of becoming tangled up in cables. At one point, he sees the figure of the man who checked him in at the Samaris hotel. In this moment a careful modification of visual perspective reveals to both Franz and the reader that the employee is a mere cutout constructed in two dimensions. In addition, he appears to be attached to a hotel desk that is also a mere facade or theatrical set (2017: 43). This instance is a clear call back to self-referential comics strategies used, perhaps most famously but not exclusively, by Winsor McCay, in particular, his use of the very same trope of comics characters who are revealed to exist in only two dimensions.[81] On the very next page, Franz encounters dummies of real

Figure 3.2—Peeters and Schuiten, *Samaris* (San Diego: IDW, 2017: 43)

people he has met, and he even believes that he sees Carla's dummy in a storage box that is easily confused with a coffin (2017: 44). The depiction of such two-dimensional and counterfeit human figures only serves to heighten our awareness that the city itself seems to be alive, a terrifying urban environment that devours human life.

The formal properties of the comic shift radically during this extended action sequence as a way of representing the protagonist's urban anxiety and conferring it visually to the reader. The views of Samaris as a consuming city-machine are equally as stunning as the earlier vistas of the governance seat of Xhystos. Yet the colors are noticeably darker. Earlier, in Xhystos and in Samaris, the tones were largely warm. But here light yellows, oranges, blues, and purples have shifted to a colder palette of dark blues and purples, with striking uses of green. The page layout and panel structure have also changed considerably. Whereas the page layouts of earlier sections were structured along both horizontal and vertical axes, mimicking the architectural design of buildings, here the horizontal axis of the panel layout is predominant. The careful calibration of content to panel is largely but not totally eschewed in favor of large panels of greater width. A row structure emerges, now unbroken by panels of varying heights. The effect is to push the reader's attention ever forward, accelerating the pace of the story.

It is also quite significant that the colder color palette established in Samaris is replicated in Xhystos once Franz Bauer returns to his place of origin at the end of the graphic novel. This establishes a visual and thematic continuity between the two cities. Not only is Samaris revealed to be "a hoax, a sham, a *trompe l'oeil* city," but Xhystos, upon Franz's return is equally rendered as a deceitful dystopia.[82] As he appeals to the council in a final scene, the panels stretch out vertically to a dizzying degree as if illustrating his lack of social agency. Moreover, a subtle shift in perspective reveals that the council elder speaking to the protagonist is himself a stage set constructed in two dimensions rather than a living human being (2017: 54). At this point in the story, Xhystos shares a core property of Samaris: its dehumanizing alienation of the individual. The story reveals that what seemed to be the triumphant urban modernity of Xhystos is really no different than the manipulation and deceit to be encountered in Samaris.

In truth, each of these built environments is complementary to the other.[83] The industrial urban-machine landscape of Samaris is fashioned as the structural precursor of the urban capitalist modernity represented in Xhystos.[84] The conceptual distinction between the two cities is ultimately revealed to be a misperception of the individual, rather than an objective fact. Underneath the shine of the modern urban marvel lies a social power seeking to sustain itself at all costs. *Samaris* confirms an insight that scholar Michela De Domenico has attributed to the Obscure Cities series as a whole: the city is both a "utopian and abstract principle, as well as a machine in which man becomes marginal, annihilated as a puppet."[85] Above all else, Peeters and Schuiten confirm in this graphic novel that if the city is a social theater—as claimed by urban historians such as Lewis Mumford and Jonathan Raban—then it is a stage upon which the most powerful actors and invisible forces enact the drama that best serves their interests.[86] In the end, *Les murailles de Samaris* dissolves a contrast endemic to the contemporary city, by relating the illusion of triumphant urban modernity (Xhystos) to the notion of the city as a carefully constructed and brutish urban trap (Samaris).

URBAN RECONFIGURATIONS: *DEAD MEMORY* (2003) BY MARC-ANTOINE MATHIEU

Born in 1959 in Antony, France, Marc-Antoine began creating comics at the age of five. "Rather timid and withdrawn," Paul Gravett writes, "panels and balloons became one way for him to share and communicate with others."[87] His passion for art and design endured, and in 1979 he began a course of study at the Fine Arts School in Angers.[88] Some time after graduating, in 1985, he founded a creative studio and graphic design business, named Lucie Lom, with his friend Philippe Leduc.[89] Today, "Mathieu is well-known in France as a graphic novelist who, with every book, expands the boundaries of the form."[90] When he won an award at the French comics festival Angoulême for the best first book (the *Alph-art coup de coeur* prize, 1991), Mathieu earned a spot among other comics luminaries. Other recipients of the award since 1991 have included Lewis Trondheim (1994), Emmanuel Guibert and Joann Sfar (1998), and Marjane Satrapi (2001), whose *Persepolis* brought new global readers to autobiographical comics narrative.[91] Mathieu is best known for *Julius Corentin Acquefacques, prisonnier des rêves*, a group of graphic novels referred to as the Acquefacques series, which at the time of this writing still await translation into English. The first book in the series was *L'Origine* (1990), which won him the prize at Angoulême. Since then he has added a number of works to the series: *La Qu . . .* (1991), *Le Processus* (1993), *Le Début de la fin* (1995), *La 2.333e dimension* (2004), and *Le Décalage* (2013).[92]

It is routine for critics to highlight the formal experimentation and playfulness of the Acquefacques comics.[93] This experimentation is evident at the level of the comics multiframe, including the book as material object, as well as at the thematic level. At times Mathieu cuts through pages of the comic book itself so that panels from subsequent pages are visible to readers earlier than would otherwise be the case. "This is not just a gimmick," as Adam

Stephanides explains; it also "enters into the book's plot."[94] This penchant for formal experimentation is continued throughout the Acquefacques series. For example, Bart Beaty describes how, in the fourth book, titled *Le Début de la fin*, the reader "is obliged to flip the book over and begin again from a second beginning, *La fin du début*, where the same images are presented, but this time with inverted colours. The two stories combine in a middle sequence in which Julius passes through a broken mirror, completing the doubling theme that is evident throughout the text."[95] In addition, *L'Épaisseur du miroir* (The thickness of the mirror) is a comics palindrome, while in *Le Décalage* (The slippage), the artist "shifts the whole album, its pages and printing, out of position, putting the front cover part-way through the book so that story pages appear on the covers and endpapers and then deliberately tears out six pages."[96] Such artistic decisions heighten the aesthetic complexity of the comics series and result in graphic novels that are easy to enjoy but also intellectually dense.

Part of the aesthetic complexity of Mathieu's graphic novels comes from his interests in mathematics, scientific principles, and "questions of entropy and chance."[97] As demonstrated by the publication of an article devoted to his work in a mathematics journal, these connections are quite robust and worthy of interrogation in their own right.[98] Yet critics have also signaled that his work suggests strong connections with provocative literary, filmic, and artistic influences. These include Jorge Luis Borges, Miguel de Cervantes, Samuel Beckett, M. C. Escher, René Magritte, Tim Burton, and David Lynch.[99] It is significant that each of these figures exploits the representational strategies of their chosen medium to draw our attention to the constructed nature of their artistic texts. Following suit, Mathieu adapts this metafictional tradition to the world of comics when, for example, in *Julius Corentin Acquefacques, prisonnier des rêves*, the main character "climbs out of the panel, sees in color, [and] flies away from the pages on which he's drawn," accentuating the borders of the ninth art as a representational medium.[100]

Mathieu is well known as an artist whose work emphasizes the self-reflexive tendency of comics. As scholar of the Francophone BD (*bande dessinée*, or comic) Laurence Grove notes, "For Mathieu there are virtually no external referents, the subject of these bandes dessinées is the bandes dessinées themselves."[101] As an artist so concerned with self-reflexivity, including the representational properties and production of visual art, it should come as no surprise that Mathieu often depicts art within art.[102] A prime example of this is *Les Sous-sols du Révolu: Extraits du journal d'un expert* (2006) (*The Museum Vaults: Excerpts from the Journal of an Expert*), which dialogues indirectly with the artistic space and cultural legacy of the Louvre Museum in Paris.[103] The work was subsequently translated into English, and in 2009 the Louvre commissioned Mathieu's work as part of an exhibition titled *Le Louvre invite la bande dessinée*.[104] Yet it is the way in which the artist is able to map his self-reflexivity and formal experiments to truly compelling comics narrative that explains his critical success.[105]

Most important for the present purposes, the city is a primary theme of Mathieu's art. The urban phenomenon looms large in the Acquefacques volumes. As one critic describes it, the action unfolds "in an imaginary city which is itself a major 'character' in the series, a grotesquely overpopulated cross between Befuddle Hall from *Little Nemo in Slumberland* and the dystopian city of *Brazil*."[106] The artist's representation of urban environments emphasizes the rationality implicit in modern city planning. This rationality is not envisioned as a hallmark of urban modernity, but instead its flaw. In particular, his images call to mind the critique of the modern European city by Max Weber and Georg Simmel "as the breeding ground for rationality, capitalism and bureaucracy."[107] The extreme nature of such capitalistic-bureaucratic rationality is rendered visible in a city form that Mathieu translates to the page as "a densely built-up structure, horizontally and vertically, without free spaces, intermissions or openings."[108] This dense structure, as André Suhr notes, serves as a visual complement to the way in which comics are themselves "a very orderly, rational medium."[109] The suggestion that urban structure is similar to comics structure seems such an evident part of Mathieu's work that an image from one of his comics was chosen as the cover of the landmark volume *Comics and the City*, edited by Ahrens and Meteling.[110]

Mathieu's dense visual depiction of the dense urban environment has been described as portraying a "white-collar city." Its internally homogeneous population is composed uniquely of civil servants and thus recalls the serial homogeneity of *Soft City* discussed.[111] To wit, Beaty writes of the pages in *L'Origine* in which "Julius joins a teeming throng of near identically suit-clad men on the street, a throng which steers him, like an oarless boat on a raging river, towards the Ministry of Humor at which he works."[112] On the surface the similarity between these two visual representations could not be more striking: in both of them the modern city is a dehumanizing milieu in which individuals lose their identity in the crowds, traffic, bureaucracy, and density of the urban environment. Yet Mathieu's work is also similar to Hariton Pushwagner's in its invocation of a deeper form of urban alienation. Alienation is portrayed as an everyday quality of social life in the city, but the artist also gives expression to its more apocalyptic potential. This connects Mathieu's chosen themes not merely with Pushwagner's but also with *Samaris* by Schuiten and Peeters.

In the first book of the Acquefacques series, the depiction of urban alienation happens in an inverse way relative to the plot of *Samaris*. Instead of rendering the world a more narrow and confining space, as Schuiten and Peeters do, Mathieu positions the protagonist and reader alike against an increasingly vast spatial existence. That is, whereas in *Samaris* the protagonist Franz finds that what he thought was a three-dimensional world is instead made of two-dimensional cut-outs instead of "real" people, Julius Constantin Acquefacques is stunned to discover that the two-dimensional world he lives in is in reality contained within a larger three-dimensional world.[113] The disorientation in one work hinges on a shrinking of social space, while in the other it is tied to a rapid expansion of the known world. Each of these twists is the logical inverse of the other. In the end, they are two complementary pathways to the same deeper critique of human knowledge. As with the role of the infinite in the literary narrative of Jorge Luis Borges, for instance, the urbanites in these comics are suddenly forced to question all that they have known. This realization dilutes the significance of our human aspirations. The vast and seemingly infinite extension of the urban form in Mathieu's work reflects one of Borges's key thematic concerns: the possibility that reality at its core is ultimately ungraspable.[114] It is precisely the comics representation of the urban environment that becomes the vehicle for this philosophical insight.

There may be no better illustration of this connection between knowledge and the urban form than *Mémoire morte* [*Dead Memory*] (1999), which in a 2003 edition by Dark Horse Books, became the first of Mathieu's graphic novels to have been translated into English. An instructive summary of the comic is given by Paul Gravett, who writes that the comic is "an allegorical warning about one maverick uncovering a totalitarian bureaucracy in which the population of an overcrowded, expansive city have become interchangeable cells in a computer-controlled nervous system."[115] While this is not a volume in the Acquefacques series, it nonetheless retains the artist's insistence there that "the structural aspects of comics themselves become the story being told."[116] One example is the aforementioned page from *Dead Memory* (2003: 8) that was chosen as the cover to the edited volume *Comics and the City*. The boxes and word balloons in Mathieu's text serve as an explicit meditation on the structure of cities, while the tall narrow panels prioritizing urban apartment windows foreground a central aspect of comics in their visual theme—that of subdividing a single surface into adjacent paneled boxes.[117] *Dead Memory*'s impact hinges on the relationship between the artist's visual presentation of city density and the effects of urban alienation. City dwellers in Mathieu's comic are estranged from themselves, from one another, and from their urban environment. Moreover, the artist's urbanites remain uncertain regarding what is happening to them. They are perplexed by an apparent connection between human language and city form evident in their urban surroundings. Regardless, they must suffer the consequences of an unseen power that manipulates the structure of the built environment toward its own ends.

Dead Memory opens with the voice of a mysterious off-panel narrator who declares "Who am I? You want to know who I am? All right . . . I'll tell you.

But first let me tell you who you are . . . And what you have become. Allow me to review the facts . . . Let me refresh your memory" (2003: 4–5). These words are pressed against the bottom of the page in narrow boxes (see figure 3.3). Above them are towering vertical panels depicting, in sequence, a slow zoom into a cityscape. It is significant that in the first panel, the city is almost unrecognizable as such. The bird's-eye view Mathieu employs here hides the city's vertical dimension and recalls the role of blueprints and conceived space in the modern planner's vision. What appears in the first panel seems more like a two-dimensional map of a circuit board than a view of the city. Over the course of six panels on two pages, the artist slowly zooms in to the city from above and modulates the angle of perspective from a strict vertical view toward a side-view or horizontal positioning. In this way, one of the central circular nodes of the circuit-board-turned-cityscape is revealed, in its vertical dimension, to be a building under construction. The spiraling vertical form of this building recalls the structure of the Tower of Babel as famously painted by Pieter Bruegel the Elder. In the last panel, readers get a clear view of the protagonist of the comic, Firmin Huff. As "a civil servant in the city's massive bureaucracy,"[118] Huff is similar in characterization and also appearance to Julius, the protagonist of the Acquefacques series. The voice is shown to be emanating from a black walkie-talkie device on a stone in front of Huff, who is seated on an upper tier of the spiraling tower structure. This sequence progressively transforms what seems at first to be extradiegetic narration into a narration that is fully integrated into the graphic novel's diegesis. That is, the narrow box form of the three opening text panels, which were at first subjugated to the bottom of the page, slowly pushes upward, integrating itself into the panel frame. In the last two panels of the sequence, the narrow text box is fully established inside the panel space, and it is evident here that the voice is speaking directly to Huff: "You have all forgotten everything. . . . . . and only I still remember your past" (2003: 5). As extradiegetic narration becomes diegetic narration, this narratological transition itself mirrors the notion of the shrinking social world with which Mathieu's urbanites have to make their peace.

From these initial pages the theme of *Dead Memory* is concisely yet thoroughly introduced through the union of form and content. The association of city form with circuitry, the visual reference to the Tower of Babel, and the textual focus on memory and forgetting are key. Mathieu's comic proves to be fascinated with themes of language, information, and social alienation. As *Dead Memory* continues, the increasing memory loss suffered by the urban population is revealed through its written text. In word balloons containing dialogue amongst the city's inhabitants, Mathieu routinely has his actors stumble as they try to recall individual words: for example, "walls" becomes "w . . . walls," "communication" becomes "c . . . communication," and "memory loss" becomes "m . . .

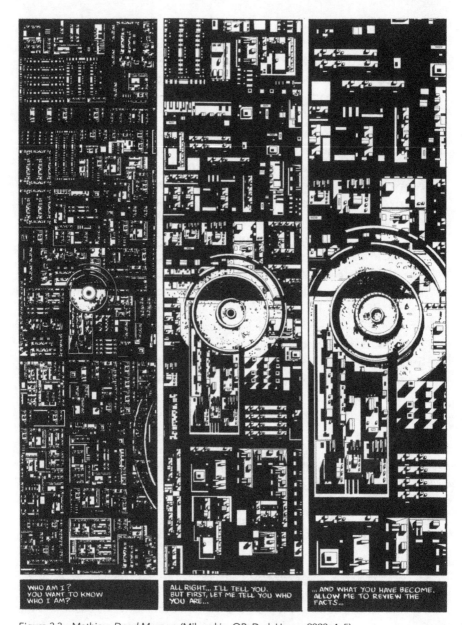

Figure 3.3—Mathieu, *Dead Memory* (Milwaukie, OR: Dark Horse, 2003: 4–5)

memory 1 . . . loss" (2003: 26, 28–29). A possible inspiration for this erosion of language, which threatens to render communication impossible, can be found in the artist's influences, particularly Jorge Luis Borges, as mentioned above.[119]

What is novel and intriguing in the comic is the way it adapts these themes to an extended visual consideration of the urban built environment, something not possible in the same way in prose literature. Here the themes of memory loss and social alienation unfold against the backdrop of an urban form saturated with billboard advertising. The city is represented as a visual spectacle. Giant advertising panels loom large above pedestrians reading, for example, "Why suffer amnesia? Memoplus kit" and "Infoplus for more information" (2003: 28). City dwellers are commonly depicted reading newspapers in the pages of *Dead Memory*, reflecting the way advertising, print news publications, and the city form were all associated with and implicated in cultural modernity.[120] They also refer readers back to the way advertising appeared in late nineteenth-century and early twentieth-century comics (e.g., Richard F. Outcault and Winsor McCay). Yet these visual representations also bring to mind the notion of the network society developed by urban theorist Manuel Castells.[121] Citizens in Mathieu's graphic novel routinely respond to instant media polls conducted in the name of "direct democracy" (2003: 29) by clicking buttons on black walkie-talkie devices carried with them at all times.

The symbolic and allegorical aspects of *Dead Memory* are perhaps subtle or obscure enough so as to present with difficulty even for readers who are fans of the artist's Acquefacques series. A less-than-favorable review of the comic written by Adam Stephanides and published in the *Comics Journal* suggests that some readers may feel disappointed.[122] Perhaps because the critic may be less acquainted with the philosophical weight and subtle construction of Mathieu's presumed literary influences—Borges, Beckett or Lynch, for example—he finds little that is familiar in *Dead Memory*.[123] Thus, he argues that it is less playful than volumes in the Acquefacques series, and that it "replaces the playfulness of those books with a serious urban dystopia."[124] This may be a fair assessment. Yet while the urban representations of *Dead Memory* have a greater philosophical resonance, they are also impressive in their own right. More easily noted is that the city is "oppressively congested," and that the book's "sense of design" eschews curved lines in favor of being "saturated with straight lines and angles."[125] Visually, the rectilinear grids of *Dead Memory* stand out on the page.[126] The triumph of the straight line is reflected in section titles such as "Rectilinear Ruins" (2003: 3), "Dead End," (2003: 35), and "Walled In" (2003: 40). The planning tradition is specifically mentioned in the comic (e.g., 2003: 13) and is a touchstone for its storyline. Recalling Mumford's critique, the inability of planners to account for the city "in all its dimensions" (2003: 16) is emphasized in its second chapter, titled "The Land Registry," wherein Huff consults an extensive two-dimensional blueprint of the urban environment (2003: 17). The overly rational nature of such linear planning is reinforced by the overly rational nature of computer memory, which gradually substitutes itself for human memory in the comic's storyline.

The central problematic of *Dead Memory* serves as a dramatization, in a fantastic key, of how easy it is for the linear legacy of planning the city's built environment to slide into excess. Early on in the comic's storyline, walls begin appearing throughout the city. "The first wall was like a foundation in reverse . . . absurdity's first stone . . ." (2003: 11). Mathieu connects this phenomenon with a social cause, as revealed in a close-up of the January 4 issue of the newspaper *The City*, which reads: "Strange Incident in the Durassier District. A wall built last night has left the Durassier district divided in two. Neighborhood quarrels may have led to its construction" (2003: 10). The number of walls continues to grow at an exponential rate, from 71 to 489 (2003: 23, 28). These sudden manifestations have a tremendous effect on the built environment of the city and, through it, the urban population. New walls close off streets, slow traffic, partition neighborhoods, isolate urbanites, and cause a general panic. The resulting society rests on a binary, as the narrator clarifies: "There remained only two kinds of people: those who built walls, and those trying to clear an unlikely path through the labyrinth of streets and blind alleys" (2003: 37). Continuing Gravett's allegorical interpretation of the comic, Mathieu thus portrays a "totalitarian bureaucracy" fixated on the structure of the urban form itself rather than on the social problems and social institutions that undergird it. This rectilinear built environment is effectively running out of control, and even the privileged planning class and its bureaucratic institutions can no longer direct the reproduction of the modern city's structure. In this fantastical scenario, there is no small dose of Mumford's critique. Mathieu in effect dramatizes planning's inability—in practice, if not also in theory—to regulate the form of a modern metropolis whose dimensions are staggering.

Yet *Dead Memory* can also be understood as an illustration of urban concepts prioritized in the work of Lefebvre. These concepts present variations on the idea that the structure of the city is an expression of the social values that undergird its production. A conversation among nameless bureaucrat-philosophers early on in the comic makes clear that Mathieu's city is a symbolic space, in line with Lefebvre's theorizations in *The Production of Space*. As the comic's protagonist Firmin Huff listens in, one of these nameless men states: "In my opinion, the notion that the city is square, not round, is rooted in our culture—we clearly prefer reason over sentiment and matter over spirit. Some symbols speak for themselves" (2003: 10). In this light, the construction of the spiraling tower that both begins and closes the graphic novel is a symbolic challenge to a simplistic planning tradition that eschews curved lines to a city form subjugated to a rectilinear grid. The shape of the tower represents an attempt—quixotic or not—to restore spirit to matter, sentiment to reason. The tower's construction can be seen as an attempt to inscribe urban space with a competing vision of society. This interpretation also recalls Lefebvre's emphasis in *Writings on Cities* on the city as a text.

Similarly relevant is an insight at the heart of the organic metaphor of the urban put forth by Lefebvre in *Introduction to Modernity*, that is, that the built environment of urban society develops as does a hard shell in relationship to the living organism contained within it. At its core, this metaphor presents a dialectical understanding of the relationship between human social activity and its shaping of the urban environment. In *Critique of Everyday Life*, the French theorist asserts, "The drama of alienation is dialectical." In fashioning the material world around us, humankind has all along been reproducing itself: "On this level, objects are not simply means or implements; by producing them, men are working to create the human; they think they are molding an object, a series of objects—and it is man himself they are creating."[127] In this sense, *Dead Memory* ties dialectical thinking to the production of both the urban form and the technological development of computerized consciousness. Mathieu's complex comics narrative manages to fuse these two seemingly disparate issues into one single social problematic. The two comics texts explored in the next section continue to represent the dialectical nature of humankind's planning activities. Yet each of these visions adheres more closely to the consequences of large-scale planning activities on the urban experience of twentieth-century New Yorkers in particular.

LARGE-SCALE URBANISM AND THE EVERYDAY URBAN EXPERIENCE

Although the two comics explored in this section both implicate the built environment of New York, they do so in different modes and from distinct vantage points. One comics work takes on a historical subject, while the other adapts a firsthand experience of the US metropolis to a fictional mode. One approaches the city from the bird's-eye view of the urban designer, while the other grounds its perspective in everyday life as experienced on the streets.

The first selection, *Robert Moses: The Master Builder of New York City* (2014), by Pierre Christin and Olivier Balez, has been described as both a "graphic biography" and "a gorgeous primer in the history of New York's urban planning."[128] The comic deals with the historical figure of Robert Moses and is framed as a balanced look at his urban impact. First released in France by Glénat as *Robert Moses—le maître caché de New York*, its original publication constituted an attempt to bring the planner's life and legacy to readers of French who may not have been specialists in architecture or urban history. In the subsequent English translation by the publisher Nobrow, Moses thus occupies a place in a series that includes biographical treatments of other famous historical figures, such as Freud and Karl Marx.[129] Because Moses is a quintessentially modern planning figure, his story reveals the disconnect between the abstraction that drives urban design and the way life is lived on the ground. The historical figure of Jane Jacobs also appears in the graphic novel as a reminder that urban renewal is not merely celebrated but also resisted at the small scale.

Rather than deal with a specific historical figure, the second selection, Ben Katchor's *Cheap Novelties: The Pleasures of Urban Decay* (1991), follows the fictional wanderings of Julius Knipl, Real Estate Photographer. Unlike Christin and Balez's work, Katchor's book is not a graphic novel but a collection of strips originally published in the *New York Press* from April 20, 1988, to March 27, 1991.[130] This is a work by a comics artist living in New York who has deep personal knowledge of how the city has changed over the years. This personal knowledge finds its way into a fictional visual narrative that nonetheless comments profoundly on the contemporary urban experience. In the words of Mark Feldman, the artist's work "addresses the structure and nature of urban modernity, urban obsolescence and decay, and the narratives and memories that exist despite and because of the seriality and fragmentation of modern urban life."[131] This critique is embedded in the daily wanderings of a fictional character who grapples at the small scale with the lasting impact of large-scale urbanism.

In line with the notion of urban planning already developed in this book, these two vantage points might be described as the view from above versus the view from below. Focused on the view from above, the planning vision is interested primarily in large-scale urbanism, in the construction of bridges, tunnels, highways, and unfortunately also in the destruction of neighborhoods. On the other hand, individual urbanites see the city by way of the view from below. Their vision is immersed in experienced temporality. At ground level, individuals and communities engage in small-scale resistance to the monumental aspirations of planners. In the end, however, while the scale at which these two graphic artists conceive of the urban phenomenon may differ, they both address the tension between top-down planning and everyday life on the city streets. The pairing together of these two comics texts is thus purposeful in that it underscores the relation between conceived space and lived space. Both texts illustrate that city design has an impact on everyday urban life. They also show that, in the best of cases, urbanites can and do resist the impact of large-scale planning.

What is so interesting about *Robert Moses: The Master Builder of New York City* is the attention it has received not just from comics readers but also from architects and planners. Reviews of Christin and Balez's graphic novel have appeared in the *Architecture Review,* in the journal *Planning Perspectives,* and on the site ArchDaily.[132] The comic was even listed in the syllabus of a course on the history of urbanism taught at the University of Montreal in 2017.[133] The writer of *Robert Moses: The Master Builder of New York City,* Pierre Christin (1938–), is a professor of literature and also "a veteran of French comics, who created the popular science-fiction series *Valérian and Laureline.*"[134] His reputation in France is superb, given that he has written comics for notable artists, including Jacques Tardi, Moebius, and Jijé.[135] His collaborator is Olivier Balez (1972–), a French artist living in Chile, with a "long record of cartoon publications directed at an adult audience."[136] Much praise has been given Balez for the artist's skill at representing architecture on the page. For instance, Florian Urban writes that his "drawings accurately and with great love of detail depict New York's architecture during the various periods of Moses's life, from the 1902 Flatiron Building [. . .] and the largely rural Long Island of the early 1900s to the numerous projects carried out under Moses."[137] The critic continues, noting that this strength shows in the graphic novel's representation of some of the planner's greatest achievements: Jones Beach (1925), the Crotona and Astoria Pools (in the 1930s), Stuyvesant Town (in the 1940s), the Verrazano Narrows Bridge (1954), and the New York World Fair in the Flushing Meadows Park (1964).[138]

Beyond the appeal of its architectural renderings, critics have praised the "expressionist film-noir-like aesthetics of the book" and its "candid rawness."[139] A comparison is frequently made between the graphic novel and the definitive prose biography of Moses, *The Power Broker: Robert Moses and the Fall of New York,* which was a Pulitzer Prize–winning book published by Robert Caro in 1974 (and is depicted in the comic, 2014: 102). To some degree, as readers might presume was the case with Caro's book, Christin and Balez tout the planner's successes. In fact, the front and back inside covers consist of a map titled "Achievements of Robert Moses," noting specifically that it follows "after Jean-Paul Tremblay's map, published in the novel [*sic*] *The Power Broker.*" It is routine for those writing about Moses to mention what might be called "New York by the numbers." The comic participates in this discourse, noting, for example, that he created six hundred playgrounds, seven hundred basketball courts, and 150,000 homes (2014: 39).[140] Christin's writing and Balez's drawings work together to portray the benefits and legacy of the planner's work. They focus the reader's attention throughout on the monuments he created and the monumental vision that pushed his urban projects forward.

Critics seem to agree that the comic is "no lionizing eulogy" of Moses, given that it exposes the "deep flaws of his power-hungry character."[141] Christin and Balez's text thus explicitly questions and criticizes the way in which his achievements were carried out, and goes further to implicate his motivations. Using the future tense and supplemented by images of the areas affected by the planner's work, the textual narration remarks, "He will also expel, 'like cattle,' according to one Manhattan official, the city's poor and predominantly minority populations" (2014: 39). Similarly, a famous quotation by the planner is rendered as comics dialogue when Moses states: "We can't get rid of the ghettos without displacing their inhabitants. I challenge anyone to make a good omelette without breaking some eggs . . ." (2014: 73). Moses was someone who "believed in public services," but who also "razed entire neighborhoods, drove out poor and often non-white inhabitants, disfigured Manhattan's coastline with motorways, and 'protected' wealthy suburbs with low overpasses that prevented the entry of typically less affluent citizens traveling by bus."[142] At its root, Moses's personality, like his legacy, embodied contradiction.[143] As David Langdon writes, he was simultaneously a "callous idealist, builder and destroyer, social advocate and racist."[144] The graphic novel addresses his racism and contempt for the poor head-on, in addition to suggesting the unfavorable opinions he held regarding the ultra-rich and the middle class (2014: 73).[145] It makes sense to link the contradictions that arise in his planning legacy to these unexamined social attitudes.

The comic's creators seek to portray both sides of Moses's character, moving back and forth between his achievements and his flaws. The cover image is a prime illustration of this thematic ambiguity. Two ideas of Moses are condensed into a single image. Standing over a city model, he appears as a heroic planner against the American flag. Yet he is also bathed in shadow, almost blending in with the dark background. The graphic effect seems to privilege his accomplishments but also to question his personal motivations and professional aspirations. This two-sided approach to the historical figure plays out also in relatively trivial episodes of the graphic novel. Early on, a two-page spread depicts him standing over a model of the city. He is drawn from a slight low angle, and his figure nearly fills the entire recto page. Insets at upper left of the verso page show him pondering nature and aid in portraying him as a quiet thinker, his thoughts in tune with the environment (2014: 12–13). Similarly, as Moses describes his plans for parks and gardens, the comic renders the outline of a future bridge construction against a beautiful setting sun (2014: 25). Yet later the comic comments directly on his passion for building scale models, asking, "Is there a residue of a young Jewish boy's spirit, in the calculation and bubbling energy of this demiurge?" (2014: 63). The tone changes here and a few pages later, when two panels, one atop the other, juxtapose Moses with his friend Disney (2014: 68). Each man's face is portrayed in close-up along with a small-scale model representing a successful building project (see figure 3.4). The content and layout of these two panels work to draw a similarity between the builders. In each case the effect is to highlight the childish imagination

Figure 3.4—Christin and Balez, *Robert Moses: The Master Builder of New York City* (London: Nobrow, 2014: 68)

that still persists in the planning vision of the grown man. Another important effect, however, is to underscore the way that patriarchal social power becomes embodied in the figure of the "master builder," whose influence looms over his creations. Each is portrayed as larger than life, a reflection of their social power and privileged perspective. On another page, oversized images of cars blot out a map of New York (2014: 37), representing the rise of automobile traffic and the gutting of the city highway construction.[146] Here, as elsewhere, the reader must decide whether the graphic novel merely illustrates the power and impact—both the benefits and the harm—of Moses's planning vision, or whether its tone is more triumphant.

There is a risk involved in taking the graphic novel's seemingly balanced critique of Moses at face value. The principles he adhered to as a planner were far more connected with systemic inequality than the comic's historical frame would seem to allow.[147] The high opinion he held of Baron Haussmann, which is mentioned in the comic itself (2014: 40), points the reader toward an entire tradition of planners known for forcibly evicting slum residents in the interests of urban modernity.[148] An airplane sequence where passengers and readers alike see New York City from the bird's-eye view further connects Moses with a disinterested planning perspective where social concerns seem to disappear. In fact, one might argue that in chapter 4 of the text, titled "Jane vs. LOMEX," Christin and Balez's work reveals its own dissatisfaction with the biographical approach. Here the historical figure of Jane Jacobs is arguably introduced as a mere vehicle to allow a reflection on the end of Moses's career. Readers familiar with urbanism may note that while Lewis Mumford praised Moses's approach, at least in principle, Jacobs was far more critical.[149]

In 1950s and '60s New York, Jane Jacobs rose to prominence as an activist for her attacks on urban planning. The scenes of Jacobs on her bicycle, attending the 1956 Architectural Forum, and staring out of her window onto bustling Hudson Street momentarily displace the primacy of Moses in the comics text (2014: 81–86). After a brief take on the topic of Moses's declining fame (2014: 87–90), chapter 4 then returns to Jacobs. She is calm, confident, and defiant as new voices take to the streets echoing ideas from her book *The Death and Life of Great American Cities* (2014: 91). The defeat of Robert Moses's plan to construct the Lower Manhattan Expressway (LOMEX) is portrayed as a victory for the inhabitants of the city (2014: 87). What is interesting is that if Moses is portrayed as a contradictory figure, Jacobs is instead depicted as a "legendary patron saint," as Maria Popova puts it.[150] The reviewer goes on to state that "the entire book feels like a love letter to Jane Jacobs buried inside a biography of a man far less worthy of admiration."[151] On a two-page spread, the two figures square off against the background of New York's sprawling cityscape (2014: 98–99). The planner's disdain for the life of New Yorkers on the ground is here opposed to the activist's "refusal of the systemic eradication of the human, done in the name of a hypothetically better world" (2014: 99). The closing pages of the book are no less ambiguous, alternating back and forth between depictions of Jacobs and of Moses. This presentation encourages readers to sit with the idea that a large-scale struggle is unfolding over city space.

By contrast, the urban comic strips of Ben Katchor (1951–) collected in *Cheap Novelties: The Pleasures of Urban Decay* (1988–1991) deal with the way that urban change is experienced at the small scale. Even though these strips take place in a fictionalized city, their creator's experience with New York City resonates on the page. In creating the strip, Katchor has said that he called upon "all of [his] memories and dreams about New York, the city [he] was born into."[152] Today, Katchor still lives in New York City, where he teaches at The New School, Parsons. Significantly, he is the recipient of a Guggenheim Fellowship, and in 2000 he was the first cartoonist to be awarded a MacArthur grant. An interview conducted by Frederick Luis Aldama relates how the artist began drawing comics as a child, attended Brooklyn College—where he contributed illustrations to the newspaper—and founded *Picture Story Magazine* in the 1970s.[153] He has contributed to *Raw*, the *New Yorker*, the *New York Times*, and *Metropolis*, an architecture and design magazine. Beyond his "voluminous" work in print comics, he has also branched out to create works of musical theater (with Mark Mulcahy), an online comic titled *Our Mental Age*, and what he calls "radio cartoons."[154] As the child of a working-class immigrant family with roots in Poland and Russia, Katchor's connection to a Yiddish-speaking Jewish culture is important to him.[155] This connection finds its way into the themes of many of his comics and is also revealed in his choice of publication venues.[156]

In Katchor's urban comics, the artist uses the everyday experience of city dwellers to bring the attention of readers to larger social forces that can be observed only indirectly. The idea here is that historical shifts in the structure and culture of the city are felt by urbanites over time in their day-to-day lives. The effects of such larger urban shifts accumulate, displacing and rendering inaccessible the social memory of how specific places used to be. The built environment morphs, neighborhoods change, and ways of urban life disappear. To return to the metaphor established by Lefebvre, the urban animal responds to change by creating a new hard shell to reflect its new reality. Such urban change has an impact on the memory of city dwellers. Katchor himself has commented, "The layers of history I see walking the streets of Manhattan are deep enough so that there's always a stratum that feels like it's about to disappear."[157] Points of connection with those disappearing ways of urban life nevertheless persist in the visual and tactile elements of everyday urban life—a presence that is revealed in *Cheap Novelties*.

With these collected strips, Katchor has put forth a central comics character through whom readers can explore the intersection of urban place, memory, loss, and alienation. Julius Knipl's wanderings serve as a pretext for considering the oft-ignored persistence of these elements of the city past in the city present. The name of this character is itself particularly important for understanding Katchor's artistic intentions. Knipl comes from a Yiddish word referring to a little treasure, a private joy, one whose recognition "opens a private lair for dreaming right there inside the moment, on even the most bleak or shelterless street."[158] In an interview, Katchor elaborated on the meaning of such treasures, stating:

> The best ones are things I never saw the interest in before. Like, today, I was walking down the street and noticed a very faded, tattered, almost illegible old sign, a sign from—who knows?—maybe forty, fifty years ago, warning about rat poison . . . I mean, think about it: the rats are long gone, the people who posted the warning are gone, the people they are warning are gone. The sign's still there. It's a knipl.[159]

As this character name underscores, signs of the past are all around us in the dense urban environment. Though most city dwellers ignore these signs, the careful eye of someone who possesses a sensitized spirit can render them visible.[160] As a real estate photographer interested in urban buildings in particular, Knipl's profession emphasizes his ability to spot privileged points of intersection with the city's past. Through these points of intersection, character and reader alike are invited by the comics artist to contemplate disappearing ways of urban life prompted by their residue. Katchor's comics themselves underscore the importance of such contemplative activity for urbanites who live "in a state of chronic overstimulation."[161]

With a "Box Brownie camera strapped to his back like a pilgrim's knapsack,"[162] Knipl bucks the trend of the distracted and disinterested city dweller. Unlike the anaesthetized urbanites in Pushwagner's *Soft City*, the disengaged or alienated characters in *Samaris* and *Dead Memory*, and the powerful planners and committed activists in *Robert Moses*, he neither impacts his urban environment nor is consumed by it. Instead, Knipl appears to be a sort of "unlikely urban archaeologist" who investigates "delis, abandoned warehouses, lost neighborhoods and dusty storerooms."[163] In a sense this character is also a fictional proxy for Katchor himself, who sees himself as a sociologist.[164] More than a scientist, however, Knipl is an urban flâneur with a contemplative interest in the urban form. The flâneur—in brief, one who wanders through the city without a clear direction or purpose (see ch. 1)—is an observer of modern urban life and a participant in the sensuous aspects of the urban experience.

Recognizable in literature before the now-classic attention given to the practice of flânerie in the work of Charles Baudelaire, the flâneur reappears in the urban philosophy of Walter Benjamin and is given new life in the radical urban practices of the Situationists in 1960s Europe.[165] The flâneur's mode of being in the city is detached rather than driven, philosophical rather than practical, and contemplative rather than consumerist. From the perspective of institutionalized urbanism, the art of flânerie is impractical. Those who practice this art are never stationary and are always on the move. Attending to this quality is crucial for understanding the form of urban practice enacted by Knipl. He is, as one critic has written, "an observer, a Whitmanian wanderer, whom we rarely, in the sixteen years of his ongoing serial, see at rest."[166] Katchor thus uses tropes of observation, wandering, and contemplation to reveal the deep distinction between the surface and actuality of urban life.[167]

Knipl's detachment is perennially evident as he reflects on the changing nature of urban life. City space and panel space are connected through interesting effects in Katchor's hands as he suggests in visual terms the urban alienation that has been so important to a whole tradition of urban geography. The ephemeral nature of the urban experience in the Knipl comics is clearly connected with an intent to broach themes of political economy.[168] The artist's focus on experiential, visual, and tactile aspects of city life can be seen as an attempt to engage an "historical materialist consciousness."[169] Formally speaking, most pages in *Cheap Novelties* feature a regularized pair of four-panel strips. Each first panel of the Knipl strips foregrounds a material object, a promotional item bearing the name and profession of its protagonist. For example, the words "Julius Knipl, Real Estate Photographer" are inscribed on a business card, a keychain, a pocket knife, a can opener, and a snow globe with a building inside (2016: 5, 6, 7, 9, 11 . . .). The list goes on and on. This prioritization of objects is relevant to the themes of Katchor's comics, which foreground an object world consisting of "the low-end artifacts of urban decay."[170] To wit, Aldama writes of how "with great acuity [Katchor] probes how humans interact with objects—especially those discarded and laid to waste."[171]

Nevertheless, the urban built environment is itself the most privileged object in the artist's work. From the tactile urban experience, Katchor directs our attention to circuits of mobility and patterns of consumption that pervade the city and its built environment.[172] In one highly representative episode consisting of nine panels broken down into two rows, Knipl enters a building's elevator and touches a floor button (see figure 3.5). What immediately catches his eye is the distinctive signature of a certain elevator inspector. This launches him and the reader into a contemplative mode of thought, represented in the text of panels 5–8. The text in the panels' narration boxes note of this inspector, "He was here five years ago on April 27 / to examine not only the elevator's mechanical

Figure 3.5—Katchor, *Cheap Novelties: The Pleasures of Urban Decay* (Montreal: Drawn & Quarterly, 1991: 19)

operation / but more importantly to peer into the dismal void that lies at the heart of most buildings. / These dark and friendless shafts are a necessary adjunct to the economy / and so our welfare depends upon their maintenance" (2016: 19). As Knipl ponders the more poetic aspects of the elevator's value within the vast infrastructure of urban commerce, the accompanying narration personifies the elevator shaft in ways that reflect modern urban alienation. It is friendless yet seems to yearn for connection with others. Moreover, this poetic contemplation identifies a split within the object that is Marxian in tone. The elevator's mechanical operation and its role as an adjunct to the economy is a clear statement of its exchange-value or the benefit it brings to flows of urban commerce. Yet this perspective is juxtaposed with the personification already noted and the text's emphasis of the elevator's location at the "heart" of the building. This bodily metaphor,[173] the mention of dismal voids and dark, friendless shafts, all imbue the elevator with signs of consciousness and feeling. These decisions thus convey, philosophically and aesthetically speaking, the possibility of a use-value that lies beyond the accumulative logic of exchange demanded by the city economy.

This strip's images further reflect this contemplative mode by asserting a relative disconnection with Knipl's immediate circumstances and point of view. This might be considered an example of the interdependent relationship of text and image as classified by Scott McCloud's typology. In this sequence, rather than visually represent the physical experience of traveling inside an elevator car or Knipl's ponderings as mediated by thought bubbles, we have direct images of sights/sites incongruent with the protagonist's experience. There is an image of the building's exterior, from afar, depicted from a point of view that is highly unlikely to have been part of Knipl's experience. In subsequent panels readers see the machinery, then the shaft of the elevator. Next is an improbable image of a cut-out both revealing the hidden elevator shaft and rendering visible interior floors of the building. Though these images are clearly not directly observed by Knipl, neither do they seem to be taking place in his imagination. The rhythm of Katchor's images works with the contemplative tone to suggest that these are direct images of the objects shown, unmediated by the consciousness of his character. Through this process, readers experience a close comics equivalent of indirect discourse in prose literature, as evidenced in the last panel's narration text: "Mr. Knipl understands why these men, of all the city inspectors, deserve to have their names publicly displayed in a suitable, transparent-faced frame." That is, the narrator of Katchor's strips maintains a relatively objective or omniscient tone while simultaneously replicating aspects of Knipl's inner speech—and even approaching the elevator's own intuitive understanding of its place in the machinery of the built environment.

This representative example demonstrates Katchor's uncanny ability to turn a mundane experience into a profound contemplative statement on the nature of modern city life. Critics have frequently emphasized the artist's unique approach to those nonrational word–image connections that are evident in the former example. Generally speaking, Katchor divides text from image and distinguishes subtly between his character and the narrator of the strips.[174] There are times when elements of the comics narrative itself must be inferred, "because the words do not relate closely enough to the panels."[175] Frank L. Cioffi writes that "the words appear to be an extension and explanation of the images, but in fact offer little help at all in explaining the overall para-world that Katchor has created."[176] The artist seems to pride himself on the relative disconnection of images and text in his work.[177] In order to make sense of his strips, readers must be comfortable with the artist's predilection for disconnection and confusion. Ultimately, the word–image relations in *Cheap Novelties* can be tied to the themes emphasized by Katchor. His artistic choices regarding comics form dovetail with the urban conditions he portrays: the disappearance of urban ways of life, strained social connections, changing urban morphology, and the resulting loss of place-bound memory. All of these forces impact the small scale of the everyday as experienced by Julius Knipl, who is undoubtedly a stand-in for a great many city dwellers who have watched the built environment change around them over the years, and not always for the better.

Ben Katchor's urban comics resist the totalizing control of experience often attributed to the built environment in their focus on the contemplative subjectivity of the individual city dweller. Julius Knipl sees beyond the city as designed by planners to perceive the urban in its temporal dimension. He is able to glimpse, instead of a static set of structures imposed from above, how things were, and perhaps even how they might be. While not as disruptive to urban design as Jane Jacobs and her ideas were to Robert Moses in the 1960s, Knipl's fictitious wanderings and philosophical musings similarly emphasize the small-scale experience of the city. Yet *Cheap Novelties* also introduces a theme that the next chapter addresses in greater depth. By focusing on the intersection between memory and building structure, between artistic representation and the object world (including his artifacts of urban decay), Katchor establishes the crucial importance of the tactile dimension of urban life. Chapter 4 continues to explore this tactile dimension of the city, not merely on the comics page itself, in two dimensions, but in three dimensions. It does this by emphasizing the work of comics artists who more ambitiously seek to connect the ninth art with architecture and a real-world, material, tactile experience of comics.

In conclusion, the comics analyzed in this chapter all emphasize the material structures of cities at the expense of the human stories that unfold within them. Hariton Pushwagner's *Soft City* depicts an object-world: city streets filled with stationary traffic, garages filled with parked cars, office buildings filled with mindless workers who dream of the same palm tree—the latter a symbol of a leisure-driven vacation. Here the critique of modern planning's destructive linearity as voiced by Lewis Mumford and the insights of Henri Lefebvre's theory loom large. *Samaris* (1983) by Benoît Peeters and François Schuiten links spatial urban form to bourgeois urban planning, deceit, and treachery in urban governance, and arguably even capitalistic urban ideology. *Dead Memory* (2003) by Marc-Antoine Mathieu expresses an apocalyptic anxiety about the future of modern urban life and depicts what happens when the reciprocally informing relationship between the urban environment and social life turns sour. *Robert Moses: The Master Builder of New York City* (2014), by Pierre Christin and Olivier Balez, and Ben Katchor's collection *Cheap Novelties: The Pleasures of Urban Decay* (1991) both prioritize the difficulty of staying connected to the spontaneity and use-value of the urban. This is particularly challenging when urbanites are faced with a planning culture and built environment that seems to have no regard for the human. The comics selected for the next chapter continue to focus on the material elements of urban life. Yet here comics architecture and tactility are seen as a meaningful presence and a force of innovation rather than a loss.

CHAPTER 4

ARCHITECTURE, MATERIALITY, AND THE TACTILE CITY

The comics form is intimately linked with urban culture. Because of its versatility, comics artists are able to exploit their visual and tactile medium to highlight its connections with the material urban experience in various ways. As the examples in this chapter illustrate, architecture can be seen not merely as a craft that constructs the visible and material city but also as a theme of comics, and even a structural property of the ninth art. It must be noted that the links between architecture and comics are robust. Scholars, architects, and comics artists alike have explored these connections from a variety of perspectives. A number of scholarly volumes investigate the case of the Franco-Belgian BD: from *Attention travaux! Architectures de bande dessinée* (1985) by Lionel Guyon, François Mutterer, and Vincent Lunel, to Pascal Lefèvre and Christophe Canon's *Architecture dans le neuvième art/Architectuur in de negende kunst* (1996), Isabelle Papieau's *La banlieue de Paris dans la bande dessinée* (2001), and Jean-Marc Thévenet and Francis Rambert's *Archi & BD: La ville dessinée* (2010). Other areas of the globe are explored in Diane Luther's *Neo Tokyo 3: Architecture in Manga and Anime* (2008) and Mélanie Van Der Hoorne's *Bricks and Balloons: Architecture in Comic-Strip Form* (2012). As these and other studies make clear, there is more than one way to approach the intersections of comics art and architecture.

The first is to contemplate the visual art created by practicing architects. This approach would yield quite a lengthy list of important figures: perhaps most notably Le Corbusier, but also French architect Doucin, Danish architect Mikkel Damso, the Russian architectural collective known as Quiet Time, and so on.[1] A second way would be to explore the role of architecture in comics and graphic novels created by non-architects, specifically, the appearance of individual buildings or architectural themes as represented content on the page. This perspective has already figured into a number of comics works discussed throughout this book, albeit in the form of an urban studies method of which architecture is but one component. Readers should remember the discussion of Winsor McCay's city skyscrapers (ch. 1), Will Eisner's New York tenements (ch. 2), and Hariton Pushwagner's monotonous parking garages and office buildings (ch. 3). Along these same lines, one could also consider other comics that are more explicitly and intentionally focused on architecture: from Andreas's *Le triangle rouge* (1955), based on the work of Frank Lloyd Wright, to Jimenez Lai's *Citizens of No Place: An Architectural Graphic Novel* (2012).[2]

These two approaches are somewhat complementary, as the reader of *Bricks and Balloons* will note. At a certain level, it becomes difficult to meaningfully distinguish between comics drawn by architects and architectural themes in the work of comics artists. Though Van Der Hoorne's volume has been seen as catering more to architect readers than comics readers,[3] she nonetheless takes great care in bridging the gap between both groups. There are important similarities and differences to be noted when discussing the creative endeavors of both architects and comics artists. Certainly spatial considerations are a shared concern, in that "a single picture is not sufficient for architects and strip artists; they require sequences of images to tell their story—particularly so that the reader can move between various spaces or adopt different angles of approach to the same space." Nevertheless, the scholar also writes, "the comic strip is a final product while an architectural drawing is a resource."[4] My own view is that one should avoid overemphasizing this distinction, yet it is nonetheless a crucial one for the scholar of cultural and artistic products.

Architectural drawing is a mediation of sorts. The image can be said to mediate between the architect's imagination and the constructed building. It may be a stepping-stone, an intermediary stage of a larger process wherein a fluid idea is gradually refined. For the comics artist, however, the image is undeniably a final product. Once it is printed and placed on the market, further changes to the product are highly improbable. Both kinds of images—the architectural and the comics image—are fashioned by larger social forces and subject to the wider cultural imaginary. Yet the comics image enjoys a stronger materiality in the following sense: unlike the architectural image, it cannot be reduced to being a mere stepping-stone toward an unrealized ideal. Once published and put into circulation, comics resist the fluid pull of reconfiguration and instead offer a greater sense of solidity. In the end, it may be better to compare the comic or graphic novel to a finished building, rather than to an architectural drawing, sketch, plan, or design.

This chapter is not about architects or urban designers whose comics creations emphasize space and buildings. Certainly the first part of the chapter does use an example that points to the intersection of architectural practice and comics production. Instead, however, it is concerned with the innovative ways in which artists choose to highlight the materiality of the comics text.[5] These are instances of urban comics whose themes and artistic form can be seen as architectural. I use the term "artistic form" to reference not just dynamics such as panel composition and page layout, but moreover the very tactile experience of reading itself. Organizationally, this chapter begins with a single study of comics architecture in two dimensions. Yet it goes on to investigate the ways in which three different artists have extended their creativity off of the two-dimensional page and into a third dimension. This is a dimension that is not merely visual, but tactile. Above all else, this creative extension brings comics into the material yet imaginative realm of the urban experience.

Comics scholar Ian Hague's insistence on the multisensory nature of comics provides a useful orientation for general readers. In *Comics and the Senses* (2014), Hague acknowledges his debt to critics such as Roger Sabin, Mel Gibson, Charles Hatfield, and Ernesto Priego, and he takes issue with ocularcentric approaches to comics, such as those to which Scott McCloud has been seen as contributing.[6] In chapter 4 of his book, Hague underscores "tactile interactions with books as desirable and pleasurable,"[7] and he explores how touch is implicated in the material architecture of comics. He asserts that one need consider the quality of paper used, hardness, flexibility, weight, size, shape, and the act of page turning.[8] There is also the relevance of tactility to the collection, enjoyment and preservation of comics, where touch is simultaneously regarded as both a taboo and a fetish.[9] Yet my interest in comics and tactility goes beyond what is discussed in Hague's text. Beyond the literal (if underacknowledged) sense in which the comic is a material object, the visual representation of architecture in comics itself functions as a reminder of the tactile and spatial world. What this means is explored in the first section below, which uses a famous architectural comic as an example.

JOOST SWARTE AND *THE COMIX FACTORY* (1980)

Dutch artist Joost Swarte (1947–) is perhaps most well known for giving a name to the *ligne claire*, or clear line, style of comics in 1977.[10] In the interim this term has been applied internationally to the work of artists like Jason Lutes and Chris Ware in the US, Pere Joan from Majorca, Spain,[11] and not least of all Belgian cartoonist and creator of *The Adventures of Tintin*, Georges Remi, who is otherwise known as Hergé. Swarte is a highly recognized comics artist in his own right. He is a major figure in comics publishing, having even been knighted by the queen of the Netherlands on account of his contributions.[12] He started the

Dutch comics magazine *Modern Papier* in his twenties, cofounded the major publisher Oof & Blik with Hansje Joustra in 1992, and founded the magazine *Scratches* in 2016. The latter was conceived as a way of bringing the work of Flemish, Dutch, and international artists together in one English-language publication.[13] In 1990 Swarte founded Stripdagen, a biennial international comics festival in Haarlem, Netherlands.[14] His art has been frequently published in the *New Yorker*, and he has also designed postage stamps, cover art for European CDs, and posters for major events such as the Holland Animated Film Festival.[15] Initially published in Dutch magazines such as *Vrij Nederland* and *Humo*, Swarte's characters Jopo, Dr. Ben, and Dee have attracted international attention.[16] Indeed, his comics work has been widely influential despite the fact that English translations seem not to have been made readily available until the publication of *Is That All There Is?* (2012).[17]

Swarte is also a designer and an architect. While in school for industrial design studies, he was attracted to what he saw as the comparative artistic freedom offered by American underground comics.[18] He counts Robert Crumb among his most important influences, admitting also, of course, the impact of Hergé on his style.[19] Though interest in both comics and architecture/design competed for Swarte's attention early on in his career, one might say that today a relative equilibrium has been reached. He increasingly does "architectural work and stained-glass windows, even creating furniture and fonts."[20] Along with the group of young architects known as Mecanoo, Swarte worked as a designer of renovation plans for the Toneelschuur Theater building in Haarlem, from 1995 until its opening in 2003.[21] In this way, as Catherine Slessor writes in an article published in the *Architectural Review*, his "distinctive cartoon style" has influenced building design itself.[22] As Ann Miller discussed with him in an interview published in the pages of *European Comic Art*, he also enjoyed a leading role in the conception of the new Hergé museum in Louvain-la-Neuve, Belgium.[23] Swarte's comments there reveal that he considers the clear line style to be a point of connection between comics and architecture, the appropriate vehicle for delivering a precise clarity of expression.[24] In the words of author and comics critic Douglas Wolk, "Swarte is more concerned with formal purity, and with making the deep structures of cartooning visible. He pares his art to mechanical, hard-edged vectors and curves: caricature triple-distilled into symbolic visual shorthand, with every line canted just so."[25] Though he may prefer "hard-edged vectors and curves," the Dutch artist's use of represented space is far from rigid. Swarte's comics provide many examples of how his architectural vision prizes fluid movements and open or interconnected spaces.[26]

Regarded as one of the "'serious' cartoonists of the 1970s," Swarte has influenced generations of creators.[27] Wolk notes that his "geometrically precise, nearly architectural drawings are the bridge between the Tintin creator Hergé

Figure 4.1—Swarte, *The Comix Factory* (1980: cover of *RAW* no. 2, reprinted in *Read Yourself RAW*, New York: Pantheon, 1987)

and contemporary artists like Chris Ware."[28] It comes as no surprise, then, that the American comics artist was asked to write the foreword for the *Is That All There Is?* collection. As Ware has himself acknowledged in interviews published in 1997 and 2006, he is greatly indebted to Swarte's graphic style.[29] The Dutch artist's influence on American comics can be traced to the appearance of his images in Spiegelman and Mouly's foundational magazine *Raw*.[30] In fact, Swarte designed two of the eleven *Raw* covers, more than any other artist.[31] The cover known as *Comix Factory* was designed especially for *Raw* #2 (1980) and is a striking example of Swarte's architectural comics vision. This image was particularly important for the young Ware, who conceived the cover of his own self-published *Lonely Comics and Stories* (1992) as a direct homage to it.[32] Due in part to its privileged position on the cover of *Raw* but also to its inherent visual complexity, the *Comix Factory* cover is arguably the most reprinted of Swarte's images.[33] In Ware's estimation, it is simply "one of the most perfect cartoons ever drawn."[34]

Though itself two-dimensional, the *Comix Factory* cover provides a good introduction to the architectural, spatial, and ultimately three-dimensional and tactile qualities of urban life. The scene is a bustling building interior with a prominent window to the city outside (see figure 4.1). The visual density of the image reflects the density of urban life in its careful delineations of intersecting spaces, adjoining rooms, and building floors. A high window draws attention upward and outward toward towering buildings, as if to emphasize for readers the vertical dimension of the modern city. A window frame divides its panes of glass into what appear to be numerous small panels, evoking the traditional panel structure of sequential art. Faithful to the title of the image, those actors drawn within the Comix Factory are engaged in the restless work of production. This much is conveyed through the prominent display of bulky props, the mise-en-scène of the image as a whole, and particularly the depiction of scaffolding and a business office. The implication of all of these visual elements, anchored by the prominent window, is that the comics produced in the factory are intimately connected to the material production of the city itself.

A brief discussion and analysis of *Comix Factory* can elucidate the various ways in which Swarte's architectural vision figures into his comics. Of particular importance is how the artist creates visual complexity through the depiction of multiple architectural levels within a single panel frame. One identifies a foreground, mid-ground, and background in the image. Yet the oblique viewpoint of the image—it is focused more or less directly on the back corner of the room where two walls meet—makes it possible also to distinguish two axes of depth. These run from the reader's eye toward the back left wall and the back right wall of the room, respectively. The eye passes more easily toward the back left wall, drawn by a depth axis that draws the reader down from a middle tier, left along a walking corridor, and finally up the back left wall to a high window with a city view toward the outside. It is significant that letters placed in the individual panes of this window form a reverse view of the words "Comix Factory." The fact that this title of the image is at once the name of a building is an interesting duality that should not be lost on readers interested in the confluence of architecture and art. Height is another factor complicating this represented interior scene. There are three vertical tiers to the image. Linked with the middle tier through laws of visual perspective, the reader looks down on a street-level interior and also up toward the rafters. The horizontal depth and vertical tiers of the image are important insofar as they collectively fashion an open architectural space. In terms of comics readership, this allows a fluid eye movement to roam as the reader sees fit throughout the various spaces depicted in the image.

The visual sense of structure and order in the image comes not from the conventional use of separate panel frames and gutters, but instead from the represented architectural form itself. Accordingly, the spatial and architectural logic of the building's interior presents relatively autonomous groupings of images. Each is distinguishable from, but nonetheless seamlessly connected to, the others. Thus, one might describe the content of *Comix Factory* by attending to each of a number of subgroupings of visual elements in the image. A car is parked in the immediate foreground on the street level of the warehouse. In the lower left, a scriptwriter works under pressure. This pressure is rendered in visual symbolism through what might be seen as an urban comics counterpart to the sword of Damocles. An I-beam inscribed with the word "DEADLINE" hangs ominously over his head. Above him, two men stand by a camera on a tripod and a phone, discussing plans for the day's shoot. Under a row of scaffolding, along the street-level walkway from left to right, Swarte depicts a worker carrying a toolbox, three images of Jopo de Pojo—hair coiffed, preparing for a comics role—and three seemingly identical dogs leashed to a railing outside a room labeled W.C. Two sets of feet are visible under the swinging door of the water closet, suggesting two individuals standing very close to each other, as if they were embracing in the relative intimacy of this enclosed and largely concealed space. Above the scaffolding three men are hard at work constructing a comic strip set. Above them, in the rafters, are rows of other strip sets waiting to be lowered by theater cables. At the back right wall, behind the scaffolding, W.C., and hanging sets, is an area that is almost entirely obscured. One can see the lines used to hold up the hanging comic strip sets, as well as props such as a palm tree and city buildings waiting to be utilized in a future comics scene. From these key details one can imagine that the Comix Factory is capable of staging a seemingly endless range of representational possibilities. Curiously, one also sees the feet of a man who appears to be hanging from the rafters. It is unclear what the man is doing up there in the top vertical tier of the image. It seems not out of the realm of possibility that he has hanged himself—whether from the stress of work or the drudgery of routine, one cannot tell. That he receives so little attention—from other workers, and perhaps even from less attentive readers of the comics scene—adds to the impersonal feeling of the image. The verticality of *The Comix Factory*, its crowded enclaves, and linked architectural spaces collectively serve as a stand-in for key aspects of the modern city as a whole.

Swarte's composition of the interior scene underscores that the building is half factory and half theater. Thus, it is part workplace and part art-space. This dual perspective on the image resonates with the opinions of critics. For instance, Ware's comments draw attention to the work or production side, underscoring the Comix Factory as "a joke on comics as a sleazy, low-budget sort of quasi-movie business."[35] Martha B. Kuhlman, on the other hand, emphasizes the art or representational side: "By representing the comic strip as an elaborate theater set with the characters waiting for their cue, putting on makeup, and learning their lines, Swarte's cover exposes the mechanisms behind the form, and alludes to processes that artists typically conceal."[36] The tension between clarity and concealment is particularly pronounced in the image. Exploiting what Pascal Lefèvre calls nonvisualized space, Swarte's overall design prompts us to contrast what can be clearly seen on the page with the *hors champ interne*, or "the supposed 'hidden' space within the borders of the panel itself."[37] The W.C. room in the right foreground of the image and the back-right wall where production materials are stashed are potent areas of concealment. In addition, the man hanging from the rafters is mostly concealed behind rows of comic strip sets. Yet the image reveals as much as it conceals. *Comix Factory* takes us "behind the scenes," so to speak. Its graphic excess and ornate architectural arrangements systematically reveal intersections between the processes of creative imagination and the materiality of industrial production.

The urban theme is also explicitly entangled in these tensions. Not only is comics linked with industrial production and artistic representation in this image, it is also directly connected with the city, whose form it likewise reveals and conceals. The multitiered building interior serves to remind us of the city's vertical dimension. Various visual elements within the panel are prominent reminders of the urban experience. The scaffolding and the car, for instance, would fit equally well in the representation of an exterior urban scene. The set materials awaiting use in one of many comic strips include three building shapes colored in grey, green, and beige. Most important of all is the street-level channel on the factory floor that leads the eye up toward the high window through which tall buildings can be seen. This window not only frames an image of the city outside the factory but also reveals the power of architecture—material architecture this time, and not comics architecture—to conceal, to separate and even to wall us off from the larger world. This power of architecture operates both in urban life more generally and on the comics page. In this latter sense, the built environment of the city, the "outside" of which we catch only a fragmented glimpse through the window, is yet another hidden space within the panel frame (or *hors champ interne*). Yet it simultaneously alludes to what Lefèvre calls the *hors cadre*—non-visualized space that is left outside of the panel frame. In this instance, the *hors cadre* is, by extension, the modern city as a whole. The spatial form of the urban environment is suggested through interior architecture, concealed through the spatial architecture internal to the comics panel as per Lefèvre, and revealed in its exterior form through the window frame.

It is this larger understanding of the urban toward which *Comix Factory* gestures. It is a curious depiction of industrialized urban modernity. As Lewis Mumford notes in *The City in History*, the modern city is a form whose construction is intensely linked to industrialization. As a factory scene, Swarte's image captures the "change from organized urban handicraft to large scale factory production" that transformed the industrialized cityscape.[38] It accomplishes this in a way that is both literal and symbolic. First, the image's meaning turns on the historical relationship solidified between comics, the city, and the printing industry in the early twentieth century.[39] Second, it also serves as a nod to the postindustrial context in which cultural production becomes more intimately linked with urbanized capital accumulation strategies.[40] Swarte's image portrays the art of comics as an industrialized cultural product. There is a certain humor in the notion it conveys, that is, that all comics are put together at a specific site in the city—as if the Comix Factory were akin to newspaper production, print journalism, or, in Ware's phrasing, the sleazy movie industry. Yet the image also suggests, via the high window whose paneled frames capture and represent the outside world, that the city itself can be framed and viewed as a cultural product.

What is so interesting in Swarte's design is that the fluid space of the factory interior is unmediated for viewers. Strictly speaking, in terms of narrative structure or comics form, there are no fragments here of which to make sense.[41] The artist has removed the compositional panel-gutter structure of comics to reveal the behind-the-scenes action, but ingeniously he shows at once how the architecture of the modern city itself can provide that same structure and visual organization that might otherwise be provided by panel borders.[42] The paneling of the individual panes in the high window is significant in this regard. Viewed inside to outside, from the vantage point of readers, the paneled window brings focus to the fragmentation of the urban environment. Spatially, the fluid urban experience is subdivided into discrete units through the social gridding of the city—that is, the subdivision of the city into individual blocks, plots, buildings, and apartments, for example. Viewed from outside to inside, an inverse vantage point that requires an act of the reader's imagination, one peers into the Comix Factory and understands it in the context of the modern city as a space where innovations in industrial design bring structure to comics as a creative cultural form. The window in this sense serves to remind readers of the tension between fragmentation and structure in comics. Through what Groensteen calls the breakdown of the strip, narrative elements are fragmented in comics but nonetheless are synthesized into an interdependent whole that is larger than any single panel. Here the traditional comics breakdown acquires an architectural rather than a geometrical form, as the depth and breadth of building construction direct the reader's gaze. Moreover, the individual panes of the high window bearing the cartoon's title are important because they mediate the inside and the outside of the image. This window is a further architectural element in two interrelated senses: it is both an individual element of the building design and an individual element of the comics page layout. It brings to mind the more general notion of architecture as a way of bringing both of these views, interior and exterior, into a relationship. Moreover, architectural design is an art that seeks to bring disparate and even distant elements, fragments, or spaces into a structured relationship with one another.

A related and significant aspect of the image is its provocative use of iconic solidarity. Groensteen notes the reliance of comics upon related visual forms that vary across panel borders. Iconicity thus takes on a dual role that the theorist describes using the terms "separation" and "coexistence." He defines the principle of iconic solidarity in terms of "interdependent images that, participating in a series, present the double characteristic of being separated [. . .] and which are plastically and semantically over-determined by the fact of their coexistence *in praesentia*."[43] What is interesting in Swarte's image is the curious persistence of this principle of iconic solidarity. That is, despite the fact that there are no panel borders or gutters internal to the frame of the comics page, we nevertheless identify the repetition of similar iconic forms. Ware is directing our attention to this when in his foreword he refers to "multiple images of the same person, represented here by identically-dressed actors in various stages of waiting for the cue to their literal moment in the spotlight."[44] Thus, Swarte's most recognizable character, Jopo de Pojo, appears three times on the factory floor (and can be seen a fourth time poking his head through a hole in the strip under construction atop the scaffolding). Each of these iconically similar visual renderings coexists with the others in the same, albeit variegated, space. The pronounced lack of comics panel structure may trick viewers into believing that these are three (or four) different characters. Yet it is more appropriate to view this multiplication of figures as a visual joke of sorts. The humor in this case stems from the way Swarte's image plays with the iconic solidarity and even the iconic redundancy of recurring characters in action and adventure comics, as depicted using traditional panel-and-gutter structures at least.[45] It is the architectural layout of space internal to the image that makes it function so compellingly as a comic, despite the lack of discrete panels, transitions and gutters.

There are two primary effects of the overall visual complexity of *Comix Factory*. For one, the image is a self-reflexive commentary on comics production as an industry and an art. In this sense, Wolk is right to assert that the artist is concerned "with making the deep structures of cartooning visible." Yet it is also a visualization of the material links between comics, architecture and the city. Swarte's professional engagements as both a comics artist and an architect prompt readers to contemplate the connections between the two art forms on and off of the comics page. Despite the fact that the image discussed here is two-dimensional, the artist's exploitation of depth of field and innovative depiction of vertical tiers force viewers to confront the multidimensionality of spatial form. Even if it lacks tactility, other than that of the material comics page, Swarte's architectural vision here reminds us of the three-dimensional nature of space and architecture in the real urban world.

Each of the other artists discussed below takes this notion of the materiality or tactility of comics one step further. In every case the theme of the urban experience encourages readers to see the tactility of comics in relation to the real city in which comics circulate as cultural products. Mark Beyer provides his readers with tactile trading cards depicting the urban adventures of his characters Amy and Jordan. Seth creates 3D versions of buildings from his imagined town of Dominion. First, however, Chris Ware pushes the comics multiframe to its limits in a boxed-set assemblage that ensures readers are highly aware of the tactile and material dimensions of comics.

CHRIS WARE'S *BUILDING STORIES* (2012)

Born in Omaha, Nebraska, and living in Chicago, Chris Ware (1967–) has cultivated a reputation that extends far beyond Anglophone readership markets.[46] For instance, *Jimmy Corrigan: The Smartest Kid on Earth* (2000) was famously the first foreign text in fifteen years to win the best book prize in the International Comics Festival of Angoulême in 2003. His work has progressively been received as a high-status comic even by those in literary fields who can no longer ignore the narrative potential of graphic art. *Jimmy Corrigan* was also the first graphic novel to win the *Guardian*'s First Book Prize in 2001, and, interestingly, author Zadie Smith's edition of the literary anthology *The Book of Other People* includes a comic by the artist.[47] Indeed, Ware's work has been described as being "precisely balanced between the literary and the artistic."[48] This notoriety in literary circles has even led to a public mural commissioned by Dave Eggers in 2001: "Ware's spare, four-panel artwork appears as a 20-by-13-foot wall mural on the upper façade of a three-story building in San Francisco's Mission District at 826 Valencia St."[49] It may not be surprising that in *Comics versus Art*, Bart Beaty has written about Ware that he is "the figure best poised to make the transition into the art world following [Robert] Crumb."[50] All this, despite Ware's own ambivalence and even "disdain for the art world."[51]

Ware is known for his spatial innovation, unconventional reading patterns, and the density of his compositions.[52] His spatial innovation and unconventional formats are pronounced in the perennially disruptive design and visual experimentation of volumes in the *ACME Novelty Library* series (1993–present).[53] Aspects of *Jimmy Corrigan* emphasize the materiality of the reading experience or challenge the two-dimensionality of the text in interesting ways. Some images, for example, require readers to "rotate the book by 90° to continue reading, which clearly marks out the existence of that book as a spatial entity that has a tangible substance upon which the reader is able to act."[54] Along with many other cut-outs, the comic also features a zootrope that can be cut out from the pages and assembled by readers. Such complexity impacts and can even disrupt reading.[55] This potential disruption is taken to an extreme when one realizes that a single page in the comic may have two different cut-outs printed on each of its two sides—thus making it impossible to cut them both out! Ware thus pits the aesthetic value of his page against the use-value of his cut-outs. In his study of *Jimmy Corrigan*, Thomas A. Bredehoft uses the notion of architecture as a way of thinking through the "two-dimensionality of the comics page" versus the two-dimensionality of the comics panels read in sequence.[56] He acknowledges that the artist's "three-dimensional irruptions into his two-dimensional comics [. . .] challenge a familiar set of boundary lines: the ones conventionally drawn between author and character, author and reader, reader and character."[57] Yet in the end Bredehoft uses three-dimensionality to explain narrative, rather than—as I prefer to do—see it as a link fashioned to underscore the relationship between a text and the tactile world in which it is enmeshed.[58]

It is significant that what Beaty describes as Ware's disdain for art does not carry over to architecture. In truth, Ware is undoubtedly one of the most important figures bridging the worlds of architecture and comics. He was heavily influenced by Joost Swarte, yet in turn he has also influenced many other architects. These include, for example, the architectural Irish team Odos Architects, who have themselves collaborated with strip cartoonist BrenB.[59] Beaty reminds us that critics have repeatedly seen in Ware's work the "complexity," "geometrical design," and "technical precision that can be found in architecture."[60] It is undoubtedly true that readers must approach Ware's comics more deliberately than they might other visual works due to the density of their composition.[61] Yet rather than focus on how narrative temporality operates in Ware's comics, it is important to pause and appreciate the architectural construction of his pages. Ware's hallmark compositional density is on display in *Jimmy Corrigan*, where page architecture sometimes takes the form of various sizes of panel blocks layered on top of one another in irregular stacks. There are times when the result almost seems an ornate brickwork pattern.[62] One is reminded of statements made by Ware himself, where the artist has nurtured a correspondence between comics and architecture more than once. In one particularly striking statement, he invites readers of his pages to "consider the composition all at once, as you would the façade of a building."[63]

Architecture plays a role not only in the content of Ware's work but also in his page composition and the more material, tactile aspects of the comic. Beaty writes, "The apotheosis of Ware's architectural and performative approach to the page would be his intricate *Building Stories* work."[64] Focusing on this project allows us to consider the materiality of the comic in a slightly different way than we might when looking at *Jimmy Corrigan*. *Building Stories* (2012) is undoubtedly urban—architectural and spatial—in both content and form. It represents the enduring everyday lives of residents of an apartment building but also prioritizes the space and memory of that building itself. As critics have noted, Ware even "represents the building as a character."[65] Moreover, *Building Stories* is a work "where architecture, with its diagrams and cut-aways, dominates both style and story form. (Part of the novel is narrated by a Chicago walk-up; Phil, the main character's husband, is an architect)."[66] Readers have no choice but to wonder at the pervasive formal innovation that characterizes Ware's use of the comics medium.

It is hard not to be dazzled by how he has pushed this innovation beyond its limits in the work's intriguing spatial and even architectural layout. One scholar gives voice to the perplexing feelings readers often have when confronting this large box of interdependent comics: "Your first question is likely to be: what the hell am I looking at? The title, *Building Stories*, suggests a book, but the rattling box in your hands suggests something closer to a game or a jigsaw puzzle. The truth lies somewhere in between. Inside the box are fourteen objects. Two of them are clearly books of the species *codex*."[67] In an interview, the artist himself has referenced the motivation for the work's complex composition:

> For a long time I'd been wanting to do a book that didn't have a beginning or end, a book that you didn't know where to start and you didn't necessarily know where it finished, but once it was in your mind it would start to, kind of,

coalesce. Design approaches like this have been done before by Dave Eggers and *McSweeney's*. So if one opens [*Building Stories*], there are fourteen books inside of the box itself, ranging in size from a giant newspaper-format-thing that opens up very large to accommodate the larger pages to some very tiny booklets. Also some strips of paper, and a hardcover.[68]

Below, we will return to this idea of how the ensemble materiality of *Building Stories* is one of many reminders that, as Ian Hague has put it, "materiality matters" for comics creators.[69]

The comic has received attention from both geographers and scholars in the humanities. It is highly significant that Jason Dittmer's "Narrating Urban Assemblages—Chris Ware and Building Stories" was intended for delivery as the 2013 *Social & Cultural Geography* Plenary Lecture at the annual meeting of the Royal Geographical Society.[70] The geographer maps the compositional complexity of Ware's work to an existing geographical discourse. In the process, he makes the argument that geography as a discipline should be more interested than it has historically been in cultural texts and specifically in the way space is used in comics. Dittmer is conversant in important scholarship on comics and the city and demonstrates a passion for artistic considerations. In particular, the attention he devotes to Joseph Cornell's box tradition, which undoubtedly informs Ware's product, is quite welcome.[71] His central argument is that Ware's work "provides not only an account of the urban as an assemblage, but also indicates more broadly the way in which comics might be used to narrate urban assemblages in ways that highlight their multiplicity and plurivocality."[72]

Also interesting is that scholars in the humanities have been referring to urban studies in their analyses of Chris Ware's *Building Stories*.[73] For example, Daniel Worden's article "On Modernism's Ruins: The Architecture of 'Building Stories' and *Lost Buildings*" explores connections with Walter Benjamin, Mies van der Rohe and architectural critics.[74] He asserts that "Ware's 'Building Stories' gestures to a possible way out of melancholy through the shared experience of living in the built environment and its potential to render the private sphere public."[75] Matt Godbey's article "Chris Ware's 'Building Stories,' Gentrification, and the Lives of/in Houses," which is included in the same book as Worden's essay (*The Comics of Chris Ware: Drawing Is a Way of Thinking*), seeks "to consider Ware's keen interest in the experiential power of architectural space and the building's place in the context of ongoing debates about Chicago's gentrification."[76] To do this Godbey mixes in the work of gentrification scholars and urban geographers (e.g., Neil Smith, Logan and Molotch, Sorkin . . .) as well as urban thinker Jane Jacobs (ch. 3).

Ware's choice of *Building Stories* as a title can be interpreted in multiple ways: 1) the work draws attention to the act of constructing stories, from the verb 'to build'; 2) the work consists of stories or narratives that are set in buildings, 'building' used here as an adjective to differentiate these from 'street stories' or 'park stories'; and 3) the work foregrounds the integration of individual stories or levels of a building into an articulated whole, playing on the use of 'story/stories' in American English as a synonym for the 1st, 2nd, 3rd floor of a building.[77] It is interesting that Art Spiegelman, who was influential in bringing attention to Ware's talents through *Raw*, gives his preferred definition of *story* in architectural terms: "a complete horizontal division of a building."[78] At the level of content, the materiality of place is a persistent theme in the boxed-set graphic novel. Intriguingly, it is by imbuing the central building in the work with a consciousness and a memory that Ware brings greater awareness to the theme of materiality. For instance, a number of pages in "September 23rd, 2000," a separate book included in the *Building Stories* box, represent the thoughts of the three-story walkup (see figure 4.2). These thoughts are conveyed to readers in more than one way. There is a form of first-person interior monologue to which readers have direct access, that is, "You shoulda seen me in my heyday. [. . .] My new copper cornice gleaming bright, jaunty awnings lazily half-lidded, sheltering my sculptured stone stairway . . . why I woulda grabbed you by the legs and made you live in me!"; but there is also a more nuanced form of indirect discourse, that is, "So with all 3 of its floors once again occupied, and though recently ready to resign itself to being a 98-year-old has-been whose days were numbered [. . .]."[79] The building reflects on its long life and attempts to quantify the routine events, intimate feelings, and tragic occurrences that have unfolded on its premises. This amounts to a form of architectural consciousness, which recalls the elevator-centered example from Ben Katchor's *Cheap Novelties* (ch. 3).

The pronounced architectural presence in *Building Stories* must not be seen as separate from the work's presentation of a more human drama. The main human protagonist is an unnamed woman who is very often lonely and depressed. She lost her left leg below the knee in a boating accident as a young girl. Given the critique of ableist conventions in art sustained over decades by scholars working in the interdisciplinary field of literary and cultural disability studies, it is immediately striking that Ware uses the trope of physical disability as a vehicle for pathos.[80] On the other hand, as Margaret Fink has argued using an explicit disability studies framework, in Ware's work "this particular representation does valuable theoretical work by positing an alternative understanding of disability rooted in the ordinary."[81] One must note the breadth and depth of the correspondence he develops between the human protagonist and the building.[82] Not only are both similarly portrayed through introspection, feelings of loss, and the reality of time's passing, but each negotiates a relationship with the other that is material and emotional. Life in the building

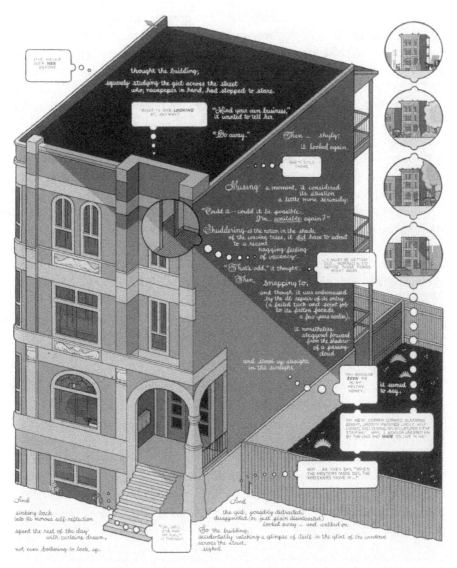

Figure 4.2—Ware, *Building Stories*, "September 23rd, 2000" (New York: Pantheon, 2012: no pag.)

is portrayed in terms of the remembrance or presence of tactile relationships. At one point, the building's consciousness explicitly indulges in the simple pleasures of the closeness and affective touch of the protagonist, "her warm ear pressed lightly to my floor . . . such refinement and poise in her repose." This is a story of cohabitation or coexistence between a human consciousness and an architectural consciousness. The unnamed protagonist speculates on the thinness of the walls and ceilings of the building, draws the building in her diary and then scratches the image out, and is frequently portrayed navigating the interior and exterior stairs of the building. The building is a silent witness to the protagonist's struggles, if not a companion of sorts. For example, while she waits for a date to call her again, the building thinks to itself: "Sigh, you'll live honey . . . oh the poor thing . . . I shouldn't make fun of her . . . though you don't have to be a hundred years old to know that boy's never going to call her back . . . I've seen it happen a thousand times before." There is an affective correspondence between the protagonist's self-image and the building's self-image. As one page reveals, "The building, sadly ignorant of the rejuvenating powers of renovation (or even restoration) rather enjoyed the companionship of its upper level inhabitants, embarrassed as it was by its crumbling walls, sagging floors, and cracking windows." Architecture is definitively humanized.

Thierry Groensteen's term "arthrology" can be applied and expanded here to account for how the relationships between building and human protagonist are portrayed on the pages of *Building Stories*. In *The System of Comics*, Groensteen employs this term, "from the Greek *arthron*: articulation," to capture the process by which "comics submit the images of which they are composed to different sorts of relations."[83] Arthrology is, then, the "entirety of these relations," which, as he goes on to explain, are spatial in nature.[84] The arthrology of *Building Stories* envelops human drama and architecture in a singular articulated framework. Not only are the pages composed of interlocking blocks, suggesting the notion of brickwork as mentioned above, but, in addition, Ware frequently mixes interior and exterior perspectives in a single view. Such views cut away the roof or side walls of the Chicago walk-up to reveal a character's actual or potential movements throughout the building's interconnected spaces. As in the example of Joost Swarte's *Comix Factory* above, this architectural approach to composition dispenses with the traditional comics gutter, or space between panels. Instead, Ware uses the walls, doorways, and interior architecture of the building itself as mediators between spaces. This choice to use building architecture to convey comics architecture (i.e., a traditional panel-and-gutter structure) is striking. Moreover, it provides a formal and artistic complement to the themes of estrangement and connection that are developed in the content of *Building Stories*. Where comics traditionally use the absence of the gutter, a nondiegetic space between panels, Ware elevates a diegetic architecture, one internal to the story, to the level of structural mediation.[85] Thus, the very walls of the building bring a visual structure to graphic sequence and become a compelling metaphor for the separation and connection that characterize modern urban dwelling.

Though these spatial and architectural dynamics are largely internal to the page layout, it is crucial to understand how Ware brings them into a third dimension. Dittmer notes how the notion of assemblage in *Building Stories* has an architectural and spatial quality in the visual modality. He emphasizes Ware's ability "to reveal the city as multiplicity,"[86] but it is necessary to specifically underscore the intersection of the material or tactile qualities of *Building Stories* with the wider urban experience. It has been said that "the tactility of print is a fundamental aspect to engaging with the work."[87] Ware's conception of the comic as a boxed ensemble or assemblage maximizes the number of covers, folds, creases, and material objects that the reader must manipulate. The sense of touch thus becomes much more important than it might be in a single comic book binding. Here, readers are somewhat less able to "lose themselves" in the process of reading. We are constantly reminded of our own embodied spatiality as we sift through the comics objects included in the boxed set. Thematically speaking, this materiality of the *Building Stories* multiframe calls us back to the key dynamic experienced by both the human protagonist and the building protagonist of the work—which is, namely, the centrality of touch as a mediator of experience and feeling.

There is yet another way of understanding the architectural structure of the boxed-set / graphic novel ensemble in light of an urban context. Readers are instructed that they can peruse the various material fragments included in *Building Stories* in the way they see fit. This undirected perusal is thus in a sense comparable to the urban art of flânerie. The fact that the trajectory of readers is self-directed brings to mind the effortless wandering through the city practiced by the urban stroller (dramatized in Ben Katchor's comics). Readers can allow their touch and their attention to drift throughout the material segments of *Building Stories* based on a whim, much as if they were wandering along one of many pathways through the city. The tactile dimension thus brings our comics perusal closer to the form of urban wandering that takes center stage in the work of our next comics artist.

MARK BEYER'S "CITY OF TERROR" TRADING CARDS (1980)

If Chris Ware's reputation has arguably gained him the greatest international reach of contemporary Anglophone comics artists, the reputation of American Mark Beyer (1950–) is perhaps the most understated relative to his importance in the wider comics world. This contrast is even more intriguing when one juxtaposes Ware's experiments with oversize work to Beyer's small frames. The vibrant color of Ware's clean panel architecture stands in contrast to Beyer's textured black-and-white design and frequently irregular frames. Where Ware gives us expansive visual fields, Beyer gives us condensed innovation. In the trading cards project under study, this is innovation that fits in the palm of the hand.

To be clear, Beyer does not lack for an international reputation. In fact, his work has received significant levels of attention in Japan, France, Spain, and Germany.[88] Bart Beaty finds cause even in his book devoted to the European graphic novel of the 1990s to mention that Beyer is, along with Lynda Barry and Gary Panter, one of the "three central figures in the early 1980s American comics new wave."[89] The reference is hardly out of context when one acknowledges the substantial impact American comics have had on European style. This impact is due not only to Robert Crumb and the 1960s underground but also to subsequent patterns of influence sustained through the 1980s and '90s. Like Swarte, Beyer was himself invited to design a cover for *Raw* (no. 6, 1984), and his work frequently appeared in the pages of the iconic comics magazine.[90] Moreover, as Spanish scholar Santiago García emphasizes, Mark Beyer was a key player in breaking the ninth art form away from limiting conventions. García lists him by name as one of the artists in *Raw* known for "their shared interest in graphic experimentation and their rejection—institutionalized by the magazine—of the genres that had been associated with the comics of youth and consumer culture: fantasy, science fiction, superheroes, and so on."[91]

Beyer's works published outside of *Raw* include *Tony Target* (1977), *A Disturbing Evening and Other Stories* (1978), *Death* (1980), *Dead Stories* (1982), *Agony* (1987), and *We're Depressed* (1999). Although long-form explorations of Beyer's work are rare, readers of comics scholarship necessarily come across countless references to the artist. Such concise references suggest that his comics aesthetic is the epitome of stylistic innovation.[92] Part of the reason for the lack of extended scholarship on Beyer may be related to the fact that he struggled to find venues for his unique style and format. "Generally acknowledged as one of the most important artists in underground comics history," Jeff Zaleski writes, "Beyer is also one of the medium's most under-published."[93] While extremely active in the late 1970s and 1980s, he largely moved away from comics in the 1990s.[94] Art Spiegelman has himself commented on Beyer's continual struggle to find publishers, suggesting that this difficulty came from the fact that the artist failed to conform to the "mainstream underground" style that came to be expected of contemporary artists.[95] Nonetheless, Spiegelman insists on calling him "one of the most important third-generation cartoonists."[96]

As a fitting tribute to this reputation, an in-depth retrospective of Beyer's work was held in the Urban Arts Space (Jan. 8–Feb. 23, 2013) at The Ohio State University, which also houses the Billy Ireland Cartoon Library and Museum. Curated by Thomas Arlen Wagner, the exhibition included 130 items, 70 of which were original works.[97] Like many other comics artists, Beyer has also turned to commercial art—*New Yorker* covers, as well as album art and posters, for example. Yet he is most well known for his black-and-white strips depicting the misadventures of his two primary characters.[98] *Amy + Jordan* was originally a series of weekly strips published from 1988 to 1996 in the *New York Press* and was collected in book form in 2004. The 2010s have brought about a resurgence of interest in his work. Nearly thirty years after their publication in 1987, the Amy and Jordan stories from *Agony* were reprinted by New York Review Comics in 2016. Invited to pen an introduction to this reprinting was none other than Colson Whitehead, a prominent author of speculative fiction who went on to win the 2016 National Book Award for Fiction and the 2017 Pulitzer Prize for Fiction. It is difficult not to see the inclusion of Whitehead's introduction as a clear move to brand Beyer as a 'literary' comics artist. Yet here the term "literary," so often objectionable to comics artists and scholars, is not as out of place as it might be elsewhere. That is, one must remember Beyer's own statement that *Agony* is "a novel."[99]

As depicted in *Agony*, and elsewhere, Amy and Jordan are a pair of alienated urbanites who stroll the city and repeatedly and repetitively encounter "horrendous and often fatal situations."[100] The strips have been described as "hilariously grim," a characterization that can be applied to both the content and the form of *Agony*.[101] Beyer's graphic style here is quite design intensive, and the resulting effect has led to comparisons with Art Brut.[102] He relies on what comics scholar Douglas Wolk has called "creepy-crawly patterns and barely recognizable geometric distortions of people and things."[103] He uses "a geometric style to convey a flat depthless world."[104] Yet shapes, lines, and textures fill nearly every open space, sowing a form of visual chaos. While perhaps not quite as cluttered as the urban interiors of Julie Doucet's *My New York Diary* (ch. 2), the chaos Beyer creates on the page finds a necessary complement in the chaos of the modern city. One is reminded of early twentieth-century urban thinker Georg Simmel's famous declaration that the fast pace of city life heightens nervous stimulation in the individual.[105] The urbanite thus must adopt a "blasé attitude" or a "state of indifference" in order to cope with the overwhelming nature of the urban experience. Amy and Jordan seem to float from one misfortune to the next with very little sense of agency. They are overwhelmed, dissociated from what happens to them, and in a constant state of underexpressed agony. They each embody an estrangement that operates at multiple levels. They are estranged from themselves, from each other, and from their urban environment, as if embodying the multidimensional nature of alienation adapted by Henri Lefebvre to the urban experience.[106] Amy and Jordan's own state of indifference regarding what happens to them in the modern city is seemingly contagious. Readers must adopt a similarly blasé attitude in order to cope with their frequent injuries and deaths, which never seem to stop the action from relentlessly continuing to move forward. In this way, Beyer cultivates an urban attitude in readers (in the sense articulated by Simmel). Deep attachments with represented characters are no longer possible for the reader, nor are they necessary. In this way, Beyer's work manages to restage in artistic form the social shift from rural to urban modernity suggested by theorists from Marx to Simmel, Lefebvre, and Marshall Berman.

As Chris Mautner remarks in a review of the reprinting of *Agony*, Beyer uses "his grotesque and at times primitive art style to create a hellish and unrelenting nightmare for his protagonists, where the basic question isn't 'will things ever get better' but 'what type of misery awaits us around the corner?'"[107] Indeed, the corners, the twists and turns, and the streets and buildings of the modern city loom large in Beyer's banal and yet violent urban tales. "'What Amy and Jordan go through are exaggerations of everyday occurrences,' says Mark Beyer, creator of the comic-strip sadsacks. 'Maybe you go into a grocery store and somebody's rude to you. Maybe it's some odd phrase, maybe you say something nasty, and suddenly it creates a strange feeling between you and another person.'"[108] Amy and Jordan's adventures blend the everyday routine and the exceptionality of death in an explicitly urban treatment. Beyer's characters are "besieged by urbanity."[109] The city is the setting for "nihilist slapstick," but it also presents the continual threat of violence.[110] What happens to the pair of urbanites demonstrates the power of the urban experience to dehumanize the individual. Immersed in the site of consumer culture par excellence, they are themselves consumed by the city and even killed by it.[111] This is the source of *Agony*'s dark humor: life is a living death, one that the urban experience threatens to turn into a common joke.[112] While the urban environment is perhaps just as alienating as it is in Hariton Pushwagner's *Soft City* (ch. 3), Beyer's reaction is a wry humor rather than almost total resignation.

Agony is full of striking urban scenes. In the first few pages, Amy and Jordan are fired from their jobs and drift through the streets to enter a horror cinema screening. Afterward, a ghoulish creature cuts off Amy's head and enters an aquarium to drop the head in a tank of fish. By the end of the small book, the pair of protagonists have somehow survived a rural escapade and have made it from hospital to prison to transit bus to motel to park to neighboring town and back. In the closing panels, Amy and Jordan fall from the sky through the ceiling of an apartment, for which a lease has already been signed in their names. They appear to be saved, for the moment at least, from the ill effects of their urban precarity.

In the most general sense, the storyline parallels the urban–rural translocations of Masereel's *A Passionate Journey* (ch. 2).

While the two-dimensional escapades of Amy and Jordan deserve attention in their own right, here I focus on an example that allows us to explore comics' relationship to the tactile urban experience. The two-page spread titled "City of Terror" appeared in *Raw* no. 2 (1980) and was accompanied by a set of "City of Terror" trading cards, complete with real bubble gum. It is significant that authors who seek to underscore Beyer's distinction as an innovative artist tend to mention these oft-referenced cards as a shorthand.[113] They are perhaps the quickest way to point to both Beyer's innovation and the representational variety of the comics medium. The trading cards are also a fascinating contribution to the urban comics tradition. In the simultaneously dark, nonsensical, and tragicomic urban story that is "City of Terror," the pair arrives home to their city apartment only to find it has been broken into. A dog they met on the city sidewalk outside ventures inside and begins to eat Jordan's bubble gum cards, which have been strewn all across the floor. After eating the cards, the dog escapes the apartment. Chased by the couple, the dog is run over by a vehicle. Filing a report at the police station, they learn that the dog was a dangerous criminal. In appreciation, the State then rewards Amy and Jordan with a pack of personalized bubble gum cards. Most important, however, is that the surreal fourteen-panel story is accompanied by an insert of six tangible "City of Terror Trading Cards." The inclusion of trading cards and bubble gum in the comic's diegetic narrative and also in the form of a tangible prize for readers works to fuse the urban world of the comic's characters with the urban world of the comic's readership.

In the original *Raw* magazine #2—and reappearing later in the *Read Yourself Raw* anthology (1987)—six out of a possible eight trading cards were included (all eight appeared in the reissue). The very existence of the cards plays upon the informal networks of exchange particular to other trading cards. Their nonsequential numbering implied the existence of a vast collection of 88 cards, and the backs of the cards prompted readers to buy them all. There are: 12, "The Supermarket Line"; 42, "No Parking Anytime"; 38, "Three Card Monte"; 21, "Isolation"; 3, "Blasting the Bugs"; 17, "Mugged by a Dog"; 76, "Chased by Buildings"; and 20, "Agoraphobia." Each card highlights urban themes in concept, name, and image, and the backs of the cards bear paragraph descriptors that function as mini-stories linking to Amy and Jordan's serialized urban escapades. For example, card 76, titled "Chased by Buildings," reads, in its entirety:

Jordan picked up Amy after work. It seemed like a good idea to take the short cut through the financial district. This part of the city was generally very quiet at night. You could feel the silence and the enormous weight of the tall buildings which, in the shadow, seemed to be almost leaning over. They turned a

corner and started walking down a narrow alley. Suddenly they heard something moving. It sounded like bricks scraping together. Jordan turned around
slowly and saw that they were being chased by four small office buildings. They
started running as fast as they could. Luckily there was a subway stop nearby.
The buildings were unable to get downstairs due to their enormous size.[114]

Here, Beyer's dark humor stems from the fact that the threat of violence that
pervades the modern city is rendered literally, with the buildings personified
as aggressors (see figure 4.3). The front of the card depicts these four buildings in typical geometrical style, but fashioned with arms and legs. There are
two buildings with faces in profile, and two merely with windows—the latter
examples displaying a faceless visage that seems all the more menacing for lack
of features. The fact that the buildings are unable to follow Amy and Jordan
into the subway is another point of humor that forces readers to imagine the
material difficulty of a city's built environment trying to navigate itself. Jokes
aside, however, the urban symbolism of the encounter is clear enough. The
threat of the small office buildings illustrates the essential unpredictability of
the modern urban environment in contrast to historical forms of rural living.
The city exerts a material force that structures the lives of its inhabitants. As
the ending of card 76's storyline makes clear, the material structure of the city
is not merely a vehicle for controlling urbanites. It also provides the possibility
of spaces of refuge. This dual and even paradoxical aspect of the city's built
environment is one that regularly figures into the work of urban theorists.[115]

While the "Chased by Buildings" card in particular exemplifies the significance of the urban theme for understanding Beyer's work, the others follow
suit. Card 12, "The Supermarket Line," conveys the drudgery of urban living,
as patterns of consumption and exchange triumph over the city's use-value.
To wit: Amy spends four hours in the supermarket queue and, as intimated
on the cardback, leaves exhausted (see card 13 "Collapsed on the Street"). Card
21, "Isolation," deals with a fundamental aspect of urban alienation. Alone in
her apartment with only the television to keep her company, Amy tries to
make human contact: "She knew a lot of people in the city, but most of them
disliked her. She had attempted to phone a few friends earlier in the evening
but felt that she had been rebuffed by most of them. They probably sensed the
intense depression she was experiencing and wanted no part of it." This card in
particular begins to articulate explicitly the dark humor that underlies Beyer's
creation of the trading cards as a group. After all, what good are trading cards
if readers have no one to trade them with? The false claim that there are eighty-
eight cards in the full set takes this joke to another level, as relationships of
exchange—should they even occur with fans possessing six of the eight cards—
are necessarily cut short. Of course, these are trading cards in name only. "City

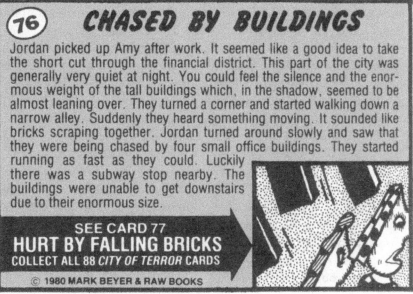

Figure 4.3—Beyer, *City of Terror*, "Chased by Buildings" (1980: card #76, reprinted in *Read Yourself RAW*, New York: Pantheon, 1987)

of Terror" exploits the tactile nature of the cards strategically to shift its urban critique from the two-dimensional page to the three-dimensional social space in which its readers find themselves. At face value, the cards are fashioned as handheld objects of exchange. Yet since no exchange is really possible, they are in truth objects of art, with a use-value for those who possess and enjoy them. Humor blends with implicit social critique as well, resulting from the fact that the relationships of exchange-value upon which the idea of the "trading cards" are predicated are unmasked as a mere cozenage.

In the end, the cards allow Beyer to forge a much more immediate tactile connection between comics and the city than would have been possible in mere two-dimensional representation alone. Taken in general terms, this is something that Ware also accomplishes, of course. Yet, while Ware uses the materiality of the comics multiframe to showcase the tactile links among space, architecture, and narrative, Beyer engages a more explicitly critical mode of art. The "City of Terror" trading cards are a nod to the tactile circuits of urban consumption wherein images become the objects of exchange. This decision creatively represents the triumph of exchange-value over use-value that Marxian theorists such as Henri Lefebvre have attributed to modern urban life. In sympathy with a diegetic comics world that reinforces the blasé attitude of urbanites, the cards assert a tactile bond between the reader and the Amy and Jordan characters. This bond is somewhat curious. In a sense, it is less exceptional than one might think, as it emphasizes the power of comics as a material object more generally. That is, the cards constitute an incursion into three-dimensional space that serves merely to underscore the way in which the tactile nature of the material object always mediates readers' connection to comics. We connect with Amy and Jordan not because of any traditionally "literary" notion of characterization, but because of their textured graphic representation. Beyond being a darkly humorous joke, the materiality of the trading cards exaggerates the fact that despite Amy and Jordan's lack of deep characterization, we nonetheless come to appreciate their relevance to our own circumstances in visual and immediate terms. With the pocket-sized *Agony* release and the "City of Terror" trading cards that fit into the palm of your hand, Mark Beyer manages to definitively collapse the diegetic world of comics narration into our own urban world.

SETH'S DOMINION

Seth (1962–), whose birth name was Gregory Gallant,[116] goes about bridging the urban world of his comics with our own in a way that is no less tactile than the example of Beyer's "City of Terror" trading cards. Born in Clinton, Ontario, Seth moved to Toronto in 1980 to study at the Ontario College of Art and now lives in Guelph, Canada.[117] Overall, his original graphic style draws on eclectic influences. The comics artist puts creator of *Peanuts* Charles M. Schulz (1922–2000) "at the top of the list."[118] This list would also include a fair number of cartoonists who are less well known to contemporary audiences, but of significance given their contributions to the *New Yorker.* Two prime examples are Ludwig Bemelmans (1898–1962), author of the *Madeline* series, and Peter Arno (1904–1968), who enjoyed a reputation for "mocking the cultured urbanites of the day."[119] Seth's early comics work included contributions published in the notable Vortex Comics series *Mister X* (1983–1990), created by Dean Motter.[120] Interestingly, *Mister X* is set in a place called Radiant City—a name that itself suggests a connection with Le Corbusier's eponymous urban design project—and its central character is an architect. While Seth has not systematically dealt with architect characters in his work, he has consistently emphasized architecture in dealing with the urban experience. Santiago García writes that Seth shares with Chris Ware, among other concerns, a focus on "the marked importance of the design and materiality of the book" and "nostalgia for pre–World War II products and buildings."[121] As we will see, these two concerns are deeply intertwined in his artistic work, both on and off the comics page.

Seth has been one of the Montreal-based comics publisher Drawn & Quarterly's "flagship authors" since the beginning.[122] In 1991 he began the long-running series *Palookaville,* which reached its twenty-third volume in 2017 and serves as a vehicle for many different stories set in city and town environments. The graphic novel *It's a Good Life, if You Don't Weaken* (1996), for example, was also originally part of *Palookaville,* appearing in volumes 4 through 9. The separate publication of material from volumes 10 through 15 of the series as *Clyde Fans: Book 1* (2004) presents a similar case. Other book-length projects by the artist, however, have been composed outside of that series: *Wimbledon Green: The Greatest Comic Book Collector in the World* (2005), *George Sprott: 1894–1975* (2009), and *The Great Northern Brotherhood of Canadian Cartoonists* (2011). His works tend to represent solitary male figures against a backdrop of urban sociality from which they are seemingly estranged. Daniel Marrone writes in his 2013 dissertation exploring the artist's comics that "urban perambulation [. . .] is in fact a persistent feature of Seth's work."[123] His characters wander the city's streets and contemplate its architecture, in the process demonstrating the modern urbanite's tendency toward isolation. This common thread runs throughout what are very clearly distinguished works.[124]

There is much to be explored in Seth's comics. Previous scholarship has tended to emphasize their connection with themes of nostalgia, frozen time, memory, and authenticity.[125] In addition, critics have explored how the artist tends to indulge in a sophisticated metacommentary on visual representation in general and comics in particular.[126] The visual and narrative tone Seth establishes through his style is arguably the most complex aspect of his comics. One scholar writes that "Seth's work is known for its nostalgic warmth, but lying underneath is a razor-sharp honesty."[127] One should not mistake this emotional honesty for a clear vision of events. Seth prefers a more complex view of memory to any straightforward understanding of its completeness or accuracy. He cultivates a distance between his readers and characters through a curious combination of a detailed present specificity, on one hand, and a generalized lack of knowledge about the past, on the other. In this respect it is quite intriguing that he names fellow Canadian Alice Munro as perhaps his favorite author.[128] Munro is a short-story author who is the recipient of the 2013 Nobel Prize for Literature, yet her work is very similarly focused on tone. Both artists explore the profundity of the quotidian and foreground understated emotional responses to underlying social conditions and striking events. In both Munro's prose fiction and Seth's comics, the full scope and the precise nature of these conditions and events are unlikely to be clearly or even satisfactorily explained.[129]

The presence of the city in Seth's work has hardly been ignored by critics. Nonetheless, the urban has tended to figure into analysis of other themes rather than to be explored in its own right. The exception to this is the clear attention that has progressively coalesced around his physical models of city buildings, as discussed below. Yet the influence and the symbolism of the city are pervasive throughout Seth's comics works themselves. The urban environment is extremely important in shaping the mood of the artist's stories and reflecting the isolation of its characters. In his study *Palookaville: Seth and the Art of Graphic Autobiography* (2016), Tom Smart explains this connection in a way that masterfully brings the artist's own urban experiences to bear on the themes and moods he establishes throughout the landscapes of his comics creations:

> And while these [comics] landscapes bear similarities to Seth's own home bases—Toronto's Cabbagetown; Bayfield; Tilbury; Strathroy; London—he draws them in dispiriting tones. They are impersonal, and at times even dangerous. A big city looms at the limits of a neighbourhood or town; an avenue or alley lies off the beaten track; a dismal factory and apartment are in some nondescript corner of a place way out back of nowhere-land. In general, the places that comprise Seth's comic book theatre are downcast, filled with melancholy, angst and anxiety. They seem to be shaded with the characters' own feelings of loss, alienation, hopelessness and despair at having missed out on opportunity because time has passed them by and left them to wonder at the nature and depths of their failures.[130]

The name Seth has given to the fictional southwestern Ontario town that figures throughout his works is Dominion.[131] Though he admits he may not have set out with this idea in mind, he has confirmed in an interview that, over time, "Dominion has developed into a place where I now know all my stories take place."[132] Drawing on his own urban experiences, Seth fashions a concordance of sorts between the city's atmosphere and the moods of his protagonists. In his comics, the city itself is just as subject to time's unrelenting push forward as are its inhabitants. As Smart points out, Seth's characters endure loss, alienation, hopelessness, and despair. In parallel, the city's buildings are themselves lost to time, demolished or neglected, replaced or forgotten.

This city of Dominion, which its creator has said is "about the size of Hamilton, Ontario," first appeared in *Palookaville*.[133] Particularly in the depictions appearing in *Palookaville*, an interesting correspondence is constructed between the reader's experience of the city on the page and the diegetic experience of Dominion by Seth's characters. His urbanites act as contemporary flâneurs who lose themselves in introspective reflection as they cross street after street.[134] Seth's pages are constructed to emphasize their spatial aspects almost as strongly as their temporal flow. They are made to be traversed in terms of an urban spatiality; said another way, one moves the eye from one panel to the next by simultaneously shifting from one city block to another. Here, Seth frequently employs spatial *raccords* of the type attributed to Frank King's innovation in *Gasoline Alley*. Julian Ferraro asserts these as a defining aspect of Seth's work, writing that this "full-page single image partitioned by a series of panels, is typical of his practice."[135] Whether these *raccords* take the form of a full-page layout or merely a three- or four-panel strip, in both cases this choice foregrounds the intericonic gutter as a diegetic marker or mediation between spaces on the page. In a sense, this usage collapses the reader's structural experience of the page with the character's wanderings. Beyond the notion of the gutter as a grammatical element of comics, here it also constitutes a fold between the spatial layout of Dominion and the embodied and necessarily urban experience of the readers. At both levels—as a diegetic event and regarding the reader's experience—Seth prioritizes "browsing and non-linear narrative pleasures" at the expense of strict emplotment.[136] The wandering of the reader's eye coincides with the character's wandering of streets, and the pace of comics reading thus begins to coincide with the pace of diegetic walking.[137]

One might think of the following aspects of Seth's creative work as points on a sliding scale of representational materiality: 1) the iconic drawings of streets and buildings on his comics pages, 2) the iconic and indexical photographs of building models included in his comics, and 3) the tactile building models constructed and displayed outside of his texts. That is, first, to name a recent example, *Palookaville* volume 23 includes an entire section devoted to "Some Small Paintings," a sampling of works exhibited at the Renann Isaacs Contemporary Art Gallery in Guelph in 2014 and 2015. Many of these are urban scenes. They feature, for example, the Dominion Building, Main Street, Skyline, Warehouse, Motor Inn, Factory Corner, and Town Hall. One step further along the sliding scale there is the question of the photographic image. Actual snapshots of the artist's tactile Dominion building models appear somewhat obtrusively in the work *George Sprott (1894–1975)* (2009), for instance, and arguably point outside of the comics text to the actual objects fashioned by Seth in the real world.[138] These might be taken as complements to the way comics bookend a section of photographs depicting the Crown Barber Shop in *Palookaville* 22.[139] Finally, even further along the sliding scale, Seth's 3-D tactile models of Dominion's buildings take the materiality of comics representation to its limits and brush up against the visual technology of power exercised by the urban planner. Together, these three points located along a sliding scale of materiality bring up questions pertinent to urban geography. These questions hinge on debates over the dialectical exchange between materiality and the cultural imaginary. While these debates themselves have an extensive philosophical resonance and theoretical history, in urban geography they can be summed up by asking two important questions: How do material urban realities structure or impact the ideas we have about urban life? And how does our social imagination—in the larger sense, not solely individual or collective—impact cities understood as material spaces?

Seth's comic *George Sprott 1894–1975* proves to be quite significant in considering these questions. Its oversize dimensions emphasize the materiality of the book, as García mentioned above, recalling the oversize dimensions of *Soft City* (ch. 3). Also, its intercalation of photographic images alongside comics panels allows us to consider further the connection of comics with tactile materiality outside of the text. First, *George Sprott* asserts its own materiality in ways that go beyond the standard arguments regarding the routine tactility of comics.[140] Candida Rifkind notes that it is "a very big book (14 by 12 inches) that is awkward to read without a table, to transport in a bag, or to fit onto a standard bookshelf: it is not a book designed for casual and impromptu reading. Instead it demands attention."[141] A single photograph of one individual building model takes up an entire oversized page in the comic. On the graphic novel's unnumbered pages, readers see, in order of appearance, the CKCK television station (see figure 4.4), the Melody Grill diner, the Radio Hotel, the Coronet Lecture Hall, and the Narwhal Books building. These large-page-spanning photographs "have been lit so that the models cast a shadow, emphasizing their materiality."[142] Rifkind distinguishes Seth's efforts from those of the architect in this way: "While the architectural model is usually mimetic (a representation

Figure 4.4—Seth, *George Sprott (1894–1975)* (Montreal: Drawn & Quarterly, 2009: no pag.)

of a real building) or projective (a plan for a future real building), Seth's models are retrospective fictions."[143] I regard as important the role these photographs play as a mediation of sorts. They break with established patterns of comics narrative to draw attention to the comic's nature as a material construction. Yet they simultaneously point to the material products of the urban imagination off of the page. At one level, their appearance in the book is no different from other compositional or narrative strategies used by Seth to disrupt the reading process. They function in tandem with the print–image combinations of the book to call attention to the incomplete, and thus constructed, record of its main character, whose circumstances readers must ultimately interpret for themselves. At another level, however, they are a form of image more immediately connected with the world outside the book. That is, while comics exploit iconicity along a varying scale, photographic representation is both iconic and indexical. In serving as an index or actual imprint of the real world, the photograph boasts a direct link—and here in comics, a semiotic link—with the material world beyond the borders of the book.

Seth's tactile 3-D models of the city of Dominion should also be considered in their own right. Responding to a question asked by none other than underground comics pioneer Robert Crumb, Seth once described his building models in his own words: "They are made out of FedEx boxes. I cut them up and glue them together with a glue gun and paint them with house paint. They are about this big [*gesturing about a foot tall*], each one. Some of the skyscrapers are bigger."[144] Perhaps once regarded by the artist as more of a hobby, the 3-D models have gradually attracted a significant amount of attention and perhaps even acclaim. "This city is a craft project transferred to the gallery," asserts Rifkind.[145] It is significant that Seth's city models have been displayed at least twice in prominent galleries. In 2007 Chris Ware curated an exhibit at the Phoenix Art Museum in Arizona that included the work of Kim Deitch, Jerry Moriarty, Gary Panter, Ron Regé Jr., and Seth. A catalog of the event was also released as *Uninked: Paintings, Sculpture and Graphic Work by Five Contemporary Cartoonists*. In 2015 Andrew Hunter curated an exhibit dedicated solely to Seth's Dominion at the University of Lethbridge Art Gallery in Regina, Saskatchewan. Josephine Mills, director and curator of the art gallery, reflects on the exhibit in a brief catalog that includes photographs. And of course the 2014 documentary film *Seth's Dominion* by Luc Chamberland similarly draws attention to the artist's cultural production, blending both comics and tactile models. The model buildings have even captured such a level of attention that "Dominion has now been mapped and archived as an interactive web-based 'heritage site.'"[146]

The name of Dominion itself brings up an implicit connection with the power to organize space exercised by modern urban planners. Ferraro shifts this discourse into the comics mode when he writes that "Seth's Dominion City has become not only the setting for an ever growing number of institutions, characters and stories, but also a repository for, and embodiment of, the author's expressed nostalgic longing for a past time and place of his own creation, subject to his own control."[147] The comics artist's creations may very well be what Rifkind calls "retrospective fictions," distinct from architectural practice. Yet there is in Seth's cultural production something of the planner's eye. The need to see everything from the bird's-eye view, to have visual command over urban space as conceived from above, reveals itself on Seth's comics pages but also, and even more powerfully so, in the 3-D models of Dominion's buildings. It is significant, as originally noted by Matt Seneca, that "one of the striking things about the model Dominion is the complete absence of people."[148] One might be tempted to conclude that Seth's preference for the planner's perspective obviates the need for people, or by extension and in Lefebvrian terms, that conceived space triumphs over the lived space of the city. Such an approach, however, severs the intimate links between the 3-D town model and the personal narratives represented in Seth's 2-D comics pages.

It is interesting that Seth himself downplays the connection between his models and his comics work, stating, for example, "It is not really a comics project, I suppose. It is more an inner world that I'm interested in."[149] Yet Ferraro has been right to assert, "For all their three-dimensional materiality, the models retain much of the visual vocabulary of Seth's cartooning style."[150] There are both stylistic and methodological similarities to underscore in the artist's approach to both 3-D and 2-D composition. Seth uses a similar process of amalgamation to create both his buildings and his characters, drawing from his experience piecemeal and changing details to fashion what he considers to be a better product.[151] Thus, while Seth's models of Dominion have been seen in terms of a lack,[152] I would say that it is more appropriate to view them as a presence, a representation of the connection between the imagination and the material tactile world. Seth thinks of the cardboard city as a "unifying element" for his stories and characters.[153] The Dominion project has in common with planning culture a certain gravity of intention: "Seth's referencing of historical imagery and design stands out, and appeals all the more, because his work is neither ironic nor superficial."[154] Yet this intention, as he puts it, gravitates more toward "emotional resonance" than toward "architectural accuracy."[155]

The next and final section of this chapter, however, does trade in architectural accuracy. The specificity of recognizable buildings from Barcelona's cityscape feed into both the content and structure of the graphic novel under study. This investigation in a sense carries this chapter full circle, returning to how the materiality of urban space is important at the level of 2-D comics representation, as was the case in Swarte's *Comix Factory* image. While there are no direct links to the tactile world here as in the work of the previous three artists, materiality is implicated in the way the graphic novel uses the architectural imaginary to stoke the specificity of the tourist imagination.

BARCELONA'S SPECTACULAR ARCHITECTURE

The Catalonian capital of Barcelona is almost synonymous in the global imagination with the architectural innovation of Gaudí. Antoni Gaudí i Cornet (1852–1926) was born in Reus, Catalonia, and moved to Barcelona to study at the Llotja School and the Barcelona School of Architecture, graduating from the latter in 1878. His works both anticipated and departed from the noted characteristics of Catalan Modernism. As Marià Marín i Torné points out, for example, the architect's "Casa Vicens was finished [in Barcelona] in 1888, while Hôtel Tassel by the Belgian Victor Horta, considered to be the first modernist house, was finished [in Brussels] in 1893."[156] Through his constructions and continued legacy, Gaudí was able to craft what Mari Paz Balibrea calls "a Barcelona identity for the global audience."[157] In 1984, and by an extension carried out in 2005, a total of seven of Gaudí's projects were added to the list of World Heritage Sites: Parc Güell, Palau Güell, Casa Milà, Casa Vicens, Sagrada Família, Casa Battló, and Colònia Güell. In light of the worldwide reputation his oeuvre has earned the architect in the cultural sphere, Gaudí's impact on global reader markets should not surprise. This impact has now manifested itself in the world of comics, in the process drawing on a trend established in prose literature.

As scholar Edgar Illas writes, the search for the "next and definitive 'great novel of Barcelona'" is one that has accelerated in the twenty-first century.[158] The built environment of the Catalonian capital figures prominently in a slate of recent historical novels. Illas notes that these serve in part as guidebooks that introduce readers to the city and its history, under the guise of literary entertainment. Most interesting, however, is that "the massive consumption of these books by Barcelonans, and Catalans and Spaniards in general, reveals how natives also establish a merely 'tourist' relationship with their own city and its past."[159] Readers now consume urban spaces in the literary imagination in ways that parallel the visual consumption of the city in the wider tourist imagination. One significant example is the novel *La clave Gaudí* (*The Gaudí Key*) (2007) by Esteban Martín and Andreu Carranza, which uses Gaudí's architecture as the catalyst for a mystery plot. In parallel to such examples from prose literature, Barcelona's urban spaces have also been central to a whole tradition of comics. For instance, noted collaborators Miguel Gallardo and Juan Mediavilla built their comic *Fuga en la Modelo* (1981) around an escape from the city's centrally located prison. In 1987 Victoria Bermejo edited a collection of comics titled *Barcelona: 10 visions en historieta*, which was supported by the municipal government.[160] The edition included work by Gallardo, as well as by other comics artists such as Pere Joan and Emilio Manzano, and functioned in part as a tribute to the visual and architectural splendor of the Catalonian capital. The 2017 graphic novel titled *The Ghost of Gaudí*, written by El Torres and illustrated by Jesús Alonso Iglesias, capitalizes on both of these publishing traditions. It takes advantage of the literary market's penchant for dramatizing historical data in the form of the mystery story. Yet it also exploits the comic's ability to graphically represent Barcelona's urban architecture on the page.

The connection of the comic with Gaudí's life and works is made quite clear. Its own mystery is fueled by the continuing mystery surrounding the architect's personality as derived from his curious projects. As Marià Marín i Torné explains, we must rely mostly on his works as a way of getting to know the person himself.[161] That said, there are some things that are known. In real life, the architect's life was cut short when he was run over by a tram.[162] In one of the comic's opening scenes (2017: 10–11), the protagonist Toñi (short for Antonia) sees an old man who steps into an intersection right in front of a tram on Barcelona's Gran Vía. She risks her life to save him and is herself hit by the vehicle. She survives, yet while disoriented she speaks with the man, who appears not to be suffering any injuries from the incident. The scene ends abruptly. During her recovery in the hospital, she asks about the old man, and a doctor informs her that he must have been a figment of her imagination (2017: 15). This man is, of course, the ghost referred to in the graphic novel's title. Not only does the manner of Gaudí's death figure prominently in *The Ghost of Gaudí*, however, his buildings lend their names to the chapter structure of the graphic novel. Its numbered chapters are named after specific constructions designed by the famed architect: Casa Vicens, Güell Pavillons; Güell Palace, Casa Calvet, Park Güell; Casa Battló, La Pedrera; and, of course, La Sagrada Familia. Much in the style of the *Da Vinci Code* books and films, *The Ghost of Gaudí* aims to capitalize on the popular imagination through familiar elements of urban cultural history.

At the center of the plot are a series of horrific murders connected with Gaudí's monuments in Barcelona. A detective named Jaime Calvo (Jaime Skinner in the English translation) is called in when a disemboweled body is found in the first house created by the Catalan architect. The first death is Ignacio Pombo, real estate developer, found at Casa Vicens (2017: 24), where the site's old gardens have been turned into a "a horrendous apartment block" (2017: 17). Other bodies turn up over the course of the comic, implicating an expanding web of intrigue and capital interests. The second murder is revealed when a body is dropped from a moving van at the at the Güell Pavilions (2017: 29). The cadaver is María Bonet, head of the biology department at a local university (2017: 34), who had "altered the original design" of the pavilions. The third death is that of Luis Barberà, who turns up dead at Casa Battló with mosaic tiles covering his corpse. The victim was a banking consultant and treasurer of a Gaudí foundation who had been accused of embezzlement (2017: 64). It turns out that all three victims were members of the same foundation council as Pere Montull, who has links to the Department of Heritage. In due course it is revealed that the murders are being committed by a serial killer named Trencadís. Yet the detective correctly surmises that there is more than one

Figure 4.5—El Torres and Alonso Iglesias, *The Ghost of Gaudí* (St. Louis: Lion Forge, 2017: 7)

culprit involved. These culprits, he states, "are not motivated by economic gain. They are motivated by a name. Gaudí. [. . .] they murder whoever they think is corrupting Gaudí's work" (2017: 24, 42). Tony Manso, who wears a Gaudí mask, turns out to be Montull's accomplice in the murders.

The name Trencadís is important, as it refers to the mosaic-tile technique used by Gaudí in some of his most famous architectural constructions. In a scene from the graphic novel that takes place at Parc Güell, for instance, Montull explains in the text for readers that the method involves "using recycled materials to create such a symphony of color, in such beautiful flowing designs" (2017: 52). Opposed to the notion of a clean uninterrupted surface, the trencadís method prizes unevenness and texture created through the union of disparate materials. It carries with it a social meaning. As scholar Josep Miquel Sobrer writes: "In symbolic terms, trencadís exalts the poor, the broken, the outcast; in artistic terms, it creates an illusion. [. . .] Trencadís is a perfect material metaphor: it elevates the lowly into the lofty, it makes one of the broken many."[163] Readers of *The Ghost of Gaudí* are introduced to this technique just as they are exposed to other historical works connected with the city: the poetry of Verdaguer (2017: 26) and the renaissance of Catalan culture and politics known as the Renaixença, for example (2017: 37).[164] The mosaic-tile becomes a persistent reference. A white trencadís design covers the two inside covers and separates each chapter from the next. In these pages, a tactile surface is suggested visually. Metaphorically, these images also contribute to the graphic novel's theme of a social cohesion fashioned out of disparate elements. At the level of the plot, too, they are important, as a conversation between the detective and the judge reveals when they map the contradictory elements of trencadís as an artistic practice to the contradictory motivations of the criminal(s) (2017: 65).[165]

Iconic representations of Gaudí's architectural constructions are perhaps the most striking references in the work. At the level of content, readers see depictions of each of the locations highlighted in the four chapter titles. Yet at the level of comics form, Gaudí's eye for curved lines is also quite present in the panel construction. The first page of the graphic novel after the white trencadís design boasts a black hyperframe.[166] Upon this hyperframe are layered five colorful images detailing the city of Barcelona, and then interiors and exteriors of Gaudí's constructions (see figure 4.5). The panel frames of these images are curved, irregular shapes, mimicking the design of exterior and interior windows in Casa Battló.[167] The next page contains only four "panels," of La Pedrera, the Sagrada Família, and a bloodied Gaudí guidebook and map. Here there is a slow transition from irregularity toward straight lines. The last of these four panel frames is a rectangle, almost as if to signify a shift toward the more linear layout of industrialized comics (2017: 7–8). These irregular frame shapes against a black background recur at two important points in the narrative: at the scene of the first murder in Casa Vicens (2017: 14), and later in La Pedrera, in the climactic scenes leading to the final standoff at the Sagrada Família (2017: 79). Readers also see an echo of this within the content depicted at Casa Vicens, where the detective stares through windows with internal glass panels framed in irregular shapes (on both 2017: 18 and 19). By adapting Gaudí's visual style and preference for irregular shapes into the page design, the creators ensure that their graphic novel is saturated with references to the real-world architect.

The appeal of *The Ghost of Gaudí* is certainly not unrelated to its masterful story and page design by El Torres and Jesús Alonso Iglesias. Nevertheless, it is necessarily the case that Barcelona's architectural splendor is a key intertext for the graphic novel. It cannot be ignored that its thematic core stakes a claim to the visual and tactile legacy of an internationally famous architect. In this respect, it is important to understand the way in which the comic fashions strong links with global touristic discourse. As many scholars have noted, Gaudí is one of the main building blocks of "the city's touristic cultural provision and, more generally, of its constructed image and personality."[168] If Barcelona is one of many global cities that function as "symbolic urban landscapes," then Gaudí is its main symbol.[169] The Olympic Games of 1992 brought national attention to the city and its urban architecture in a way unprecedented since, perhaps, the World Fairs of 1888 and 1929. Continuing to exploit the city's built environment for the touristic vision, "2002 was declared the Year of Gaudí, heralding the 150th anniversary of the architect's birth with a range of exhibitions, floodlighting projects, open days, and merchandise."[170]

That the graphic novel is conscious of the architect's role in global tourism is made clear in its text. The graphic novel's character Montull gives voice to the urban cultural discourse that sustains such dynamics, stating, "In a way, Gaudí *is* Barcelona. His vision, his genius, they comprise the soul of this city" (2017: 36, original emphasis). In addition, direct attention is given in the comic to the benefits of tourist revenue and the potential negative impact of tourist behavior. In the course of the investigation, as the body count rises, Gaudí monuments are closed to the public, causing the loss of tourism fees (2017: 66). Early in the graphic novel, tourists are shown gawking, littering, pointing, and taking photos outside the Sagrada Família (2017: 21). Inside the monument someone is shown in close-up consuming ice cream as a voice from off yells, "Madam! This is a church!" (2017: 22). The prominent depiction of a gift store in the building acts as a further nod to these links between the architectural legacy of Gaudí and wider patterns of consumerism (2017: 22). In a sense, the comic's loose if highly visual connection with the value and continuing preservation of Gaudí's works is true to the architect's vision. During his lifetime, Gaudí himself "expressed the need to conserve monumental remains and to use them to enhance the beauty of the city."[171] In the current reality, this need to conserve has interacted with mass tourism and strategies of capital accumulation that have accelerated since the architect's death. The identification of Gaudí with the urban space of Barcelona is unavoidable and in a sense totalizing. As Josep Miquel Sobrer writes, "today Gaudí—and all that the name Gaudí has come to represent—is virtually untouchable; to decry Gaudí would be to decry Barcelona, if not Catalonia."[172] In the end, the graphic novel both decries and exalts Gaudí, narrating through the visual power and tactile touristic memory of his creations the contradictory yet still emblematic role of the architect in the urban imaginary.

In conclusion, the comics discussed in this chapter demonstrate that architecture is a creative art boasting many connections with comics texts. Comics can serve as a purely imaginative visual and architectural space. On the page, comics creators can design city environments and urban dramas with a relatively unrestricted freedom. Yet in the work of skilled creators, architecture is not only a theme but a compositional strategy that becomes a way of fusing the comics imagination with concrete, material influences and products outside of the text. Whether by suggesting three dimensions through an innovative 2-D page, as in the case of Joost Swarte, or by extending into a third, tactile dimension in various ways, the comics discussed in this chapter question the perceived boundary between art and architecture. Chris Ware is one of three artists who go much further than mere visual representation to remind us of the material and tactile nature of the urban experience. His complex architectural-themed comics multiframe highlights the importance of touch to the reading experience, while also suggesting a drifting urban vision. The urban environment is crucial to Mark Beyer's *Amy + Jordan* series as a whole, but in his intriguing set of tangible "City of Terror trading cards" he pushes off the page to engage with the idea of urban exchange. Seth's tactile models of Dominion's buildings, constructed over the course of a decade, in truth build off of complex urban representations from his comics. These models are best thought of as a strategy that complements the material comics text and photographic images in asserting the tactile connection between comics and the city. While greatly indebted to the work of a historically important architect, *The Ghost of Gaudí* is also a point of transition toward the final chapter of this book, which is focused on the comics representation of the fantastical city. In exploring urban comics from Argentina, Uruguay, France, England, Japan and Brazil, the last chapter looks at what happens when comics creators exercise their freedom to play with and beyond fantastic genres, including the occult/mystery story, alien-invasion science fiction, disease/epidemic, suspense/terror/horror, and even magical realism.

CHAPTER 5

DANGER, DISEASE, AND DEATH IN THE GRAPHIC URBAN IMAGINATION

This chapter deals with urban comics whose pages boast graphic and sometimes fantastic depictions of danger, disease, and even death. It is important to recognize that these themes historically have been linked with the built environment of the city. In his landmark book *Cities of Tomorrow*, urban historian Peter Hall borrows the phrase "The City of Dreadful Night" from the work of a Victorian poet as a way of pointing to nineteenth-century conceptions of urban threats and fears.[1] This phrase becomes the title for the second chapter of Hall's book, which explores the living conditions of slum cities as varied as London, Paris, Berlin, and New York. As this evocative phrase conveys, fears surrounding urbanization were certainly palpable during the eighteenth and nineteenth centuries. This was a time when the pace of urban commerce accelerated, the density of urban living increased, and living conditions themselves became more cramped. These changes were seen to correlate with an increased potential for disease transmission. In addition, the industrialized automation brought by the rise of factories—combined with the prominence of the railway, and mechanized urban transportation systems such as the trolley (e.g., implicated in Antoni Gaudí's death, ch. 4)—further confirmed the city as a space of risk, injury, and fatality. These and other urban fears were not so easily quelled as time went on. That is, the perennial threat expressed through the discourses of density, disease, and bodily harm, if not outright death, has continued to inform our understanding of what the city is—and also our collective fears of what it might become. A concise history is necessary in order to understand how the comics artists discussed in this chapter bring these hallmark discourses of urban threat to life in the pages of their visual representations.

One might say that the bourgeois practice of modern city planning emerged, in part, as a response to some of the urban fears just mentioned. Nineteenth-century planners such as Ildefons Cerdà and Baron Georges Eugène Haussmann sought to alleviate the cramped conditions of the metropolis through the destruction of old buildings and the creation of new streets. The broad avenues introduced in both Paris and Barcelona were partially an attempt to mitigate density in central areas of the city. These quintessentially modern urban plans cannot be fully separated from miasmic theories of health circulating at the time. Odors were themselves thought to cause disease, as David S. Barnes explores in his discussion of the Great Stink of Paris, which occurred in the summer of 1880.[2] Thinking the city at a larger scale, as these planners did, simultaneously had the effect of slowing the spread of contagion and mitigating its threat to urbanites. Nineteenth-century urban planners intentionally integrated nature into city design hoping to contribute to urban health. Haussmann's tree-lined boulevards were both aesthetic and practical in this sense, as was Cerdà's intention to "ruralize the urban" through the design of green spaces on every city block.[3] Such strategies, it was hoped, might counteract the effects of what was known as "bad air" or "night air" by helping to foster clean circulation patterns. Yet even as germ theories replaced such miasmic theories regarding the transmission of disease in due course, urban fears evolved and continued to shape the modern city and its social imaginary.

Notions of health took a more psychological turn in the twentieth century but were still deeply entwined with discourses on city living. Georg Simmel's work in particular sheds light on a specifically urban anxiety, one that was prompted by exposure to the built environment itself and came to be recognized as a threat to mental health. In the essay "The Metropolis and Mental Life" (1903), he explored the onslaught of stimuli present in urban environments and theorized regarding the mental resources that could help individuals to cope with states of chronic overstimulation. "The metropolitan type," Simmel wrote, "creates a protective organ for itself against the profound disruption with which the fluctuations and discontinuities of the external milieu threaten it."[4] The links he established between the metropolis and mental life are merely one prominent example of how the urban form has been seen as impacting the psychological health of the modern city dweller. Interestingly, the idea that the constantly shifting conditions created by urbanization could destabilize the human psyche had been prefigured in discourse surrounding the railway. In the mid-nineteenth century, the rise of the "steel horse" stirred the public imagination and quickly became a symbol for the dangers of industrialization in general. Mobility studies pioneer Wolfgang Schivelbusch documents the reality of illnesses and disorders that were linked to the cultural imaginary of nineteenth-century train travel in his book *The Railway Journey: The*

Industrialization of Time and Space in the Nineteenth Century (1986). Such conditions included "railway spine," "traumatic neurosis," and "commotion."[5] The excessive velocity of train travel was itself widely regarded as a destabilizing force on the human organism.

The effect of the metropolis on the urbanite's inner life and the dangers of train travel for the passenger were among many physical threats to the human body intensified by rising industrialization and urbanization. These latter two forces became deeply interconnected over the course of the nineteenth century.[6] Accidents resulting in injury certainly occurred both on and off the railroad track. The large industrial machinery of the modern era constituted another threat to the well-being of factory workers. By extension, these fears surrounding the railway and mechanization in general can be seen as an expression of more deeply rooted anxieties about urban modernity as a whole. The dangers that were increasingly associated with industrialization and transportation— dangers both imagined and real—were certainly reflected in cultural production. Thus, it was no surprise that numerous early twentieth-century visual artists expressed collective fears about what Santiago García calls "the velocity and violence of contemporary life."[7] The legacy of such cultural representations of urban threat can be traced through publications of the late twentieth and early twenty-first century, as evidenced in the sections that constitute this chapter.

Culture was deeply implicated in how planners and social reformers imagined urban space. Part of the impact of culture can be seen in the development of a kind of metaphorical thinking that became pervasive in discourse surrounding the modern city. Thoughts of danger, disease and death were seldom far from the minds of modern urban dwellers. The city is, after all, that dense social space where such common fears could circulate rapidly. The circulation of such discourse led to two outcomes that are of interest for our purposes.

First, urban planners took to organic metaphors for the city. If the metropolis was a site of danger, disease, and death, then the role of the planner was to render its urban fabric healthy again. Against this conceptual background, the city was seen in metaphorical terms as a living organism. Drawing on seventeenth-century scientific insights into the circulation of blood in the human body, urban streets were imagined as a circulatory system.[8] Trees and green spaces were the city's lungs. The sewers underneath the modern city were themselves seen as the "organs of the metropolis" by Haussmann.[9] In another significant use of this organic metaphor, Ildefons Cerdà famously portrayed the planner as a surgeon, and the city's tissue as a human body awaiting the planner's scalpel.[10] This broadly resonating approach is expressed quite incisively in his *General Theory of Urbanization* (1867), wherein Cerdà writes of the planner's activity in medicalizing terms: "Introducing the scalpel into the most intimate and recondite areas of the social and urban organism, one discovers the original cause alive and in action, the fecund seed of the grave illness that corrodes the entrails of humanity."[11] The metaphor of surgery is perhaps an apt way to describe the invasive approach that modern planners used in carving up the city. Urban areas deemed as problems were identified, delineated, and excised. Planners such as Cerdà and Haussmann gutted the central areas of their cities in the interests of regularization and modernization.[12]

A second outcome of metaphorical thinking about the urban environment was that certain populations were themselves associated with disease given their location in the city-as-body. As Hall reports, the New York tenements, for example, were seen as "centres of disease, poverty, vice, and crime, where it is a marvel, not that some children grow up to be thieves, drunkards and prostitutes, but that so many should ever grow up to be decent and self-respecting."[13] Yi-Fu Tuan characterizes the modern city as a "disorienting physical environment in which tenement houses collapse on their inhabitants, fires break out, and heavy traffic threatens life and limb."[14] Despite the work of social reformers, urbanites were seen to be both conditioned and limited by their environments. Thus, they were frequently written off by the powerful and pushed out of the central city by renewal schemes that focused on the built environment at the expense of urban social life. Or else they were neglected and forgotten, left to the crowded conditions portrayed, for example, in Richard F. Outcault's *Hogan's Alley* (ch. 1). Given the co-opted interests of what Henri Lefebvre calls a bourgeois science, urban planning necessarily preserved the city as a space produced in the interests of the privileged few and imagined the lower classes as a disease that might be excised from the urban body. Significantly, however, an entire countertradition has also reappropriated the same organic metaphor that pervades the modern planning tradition. Lewis Mumford did so in calling for a drastic shift in planning practices.[15] Henri Lefebvre used the metaphor of the city as organism as a way of combatting the rampant urbanism that was destroying the spontaneity and use-value of everyday urban life.[16] And Jane Jacobs (ch. 3) inverted the relationship between the organic metaphor and the surgical operations of planning. This inversion can be seen in her daring assertion that planners were themselves causing harm to the living organism of the city, rather than alleviating it.[17]

The urban comics discussed in this chapter are implicitly indebted to these historical circumstances. Yet they transpose persistent urban social fears surrounding danger, disease, and death to a more fantastical key. On the comics page, urban fears are often reinterpreted in a metaphorical mode and distilled to their emotional essence. Yet the discourse of imminent threats to urban life is preserved in their representations all the same. Whether the artists explored here employ tropes of science fiction, the occult mystery story, dystopian fiction, historical crime fiction, or magical realism, the city's form is central to their

treatment of urban fears. In each case, the modern city proves to be a dangerous environment for both the individual urbanite and the urban collective to
navigate. Moreover, these artists find innovative ways to integrate the urban
form into their imaginative comics cartographies at the levels of both content
and form.

ALIEN INVASION AND DISEASE TRANSMISSION IN THE RIVER PLATE (BUENOS AIRES/MONTEVIDEO)

Science fiction (SF) emerged, or so the argument goes, in industrialized and
technologically advanced nations. The works of literary figures from England,
France, and the US have long been associated with SF as a genre—canonical
authors being Mary Shelley (1797–1851), Jules Verne (1828–1905), and H. G.
Wells (1866–1946), for example. Yet theorists have been relatively slow to acknowledge contributions by authors and artists from other global spaces. Here
an exploration of two graphic novels from the Latin American River Plate region assists in expanding beyond the Anglophone urban geography of SF. Texts
introduced earlier in this book may also be seen in terms of science fiction
tropes—*Samaris* by Peeters and Schuiten and *Dead Memory* by Marc-Antoine
Mathieu (both ch. 3) being notable examples. Yet the SF themes of two comics
from Argentina and Uruguay are perhaps more immediately recognizable as
part of the genre, due to their themes of alien invasion and a mosquito-borne
epidemic, respectively. It is important that the storylines of these two comics
unfold in specific urban environments. In the process, the visual texts thereby
connect with long-standing discourses of the city as a site infused with threats
of danger, disease, and death.

First there is *The Eternaut*, by writer Héctor Germán Oesterheld (1919–1977)
and artist Francisco Solano López (1928–2011). Originally published in Argentina in installments of the magazine *Hora Cero* (1957–1959), founded by Oesterheld himself, it was later released as a single volume.[18] This graphic novel has
received increasing popular and critical attention in the twenty-first century,
is available in both Spanish and English editions, and has also been translated
for publication in Croatia, France, Greece, and Italy.[19] Its storyline begins with
an unexplained lethal snowfall, as seen through the eyes of a group of friends
who function as a collective hero, rather than a heroic individual.[20] Favelli,
Lucas, Herbert, Polsky, and Juan Salvo are gathered together in a suburban area
of Buenos Aires. After Polsky dies suddenly from contact with the radioactive
snow, the remaining members of the group don protective suits and venture
out in search of provisions. As things escalate, they find that an alien invasion
is upon them. The invading force includes several types of creatures—*manos,*

gurbos, *cascarudos*, and *hombres-robot*. Battling their way through the city's built environment, the group of friends soon discover that the center of the invasion is the Plaza de los Congresos, a noted site located in the very center of Buenos Aires.

Second, there is the graphic novel *Dengue*, which was also created by two collaborators: writer and journalist Rodolfo Santullo (Mexico, 1979–) and artist Matías Bergara (Uruguay, 1984–). Originally published in Spanish by Editorial Estuario in Montevideo (2012), three years later the comic was released in English under the same title by Humanoids in Los Angeles (2015). The story opens with an indication that constant heat and humidity have affected seasonal change. This shift has done away with winter, converting the Argentine–Uruguayan River Plate region into a zone that is just as tropical as Managua, Nicaragua. The risk of mosquito-borne illness has become a threat of epidemic proportions, and those who venture outside must thus wear protective suits. These suits quite clearly recall those appearing in Oesterheld and Solano López's *Eternaut*. Moreover, in due course, *Dengue*'s plot intersects with a more traditional alien invasion narrative, as it is revealed that human-mosquito hybrids are now seeking out their own right to live in the city of Montevideo.

As should already be clear from these brief introductions, these two comics texts are exemplars of urban SF. They transpose collective fears surrounding the city into a fantastical, visual mode. Here, depictions of the Latin American capitals of Buenos Aires and Montevideo resonate implicitly with long-standing urban anxieties surrounding notions of danger, population density, disease transmission, and even death. Most important, the comics connect themes of alien invasion with depictions of local urban spaces. Looking more closely at each pair of creators and their comics texts provides a better understanding of how the built environment is central to their visual exploration of collective urban fears.

The Eternaut was an early instance of science fiction in Latin America in which local urban space played a crucial role.[21] It bucked a tradition whereby even Latin American writers of science-fiction stories tended to situate their narratives in the industrialized Anglophone or Francophone world. While earlier SF in the Spanish language had centered on places in the industrialized Anglophone world, *The Eternaut* was among the first to use a Latin American city—Buenos Aires, not Paris, London, or New York—as the central site in its narrative of an alien invasion.[22] In the words of Martin Hadis, "until Oesterheld came along, aliens had mostly stuck to their old and well-rehearsed routine of invading U.S. or European cities."[23] By rooting its storyline in the streets of Buenos Aires, the comic's creators laid their own claim to the science-fiction genre. While Oesterheld was able to draw on a number of influences, including Verne, his intent was clearly to establish an autochthonous strain of science fiction.[24]

To wit, he writes: "My stories are all filled with allegory and have a message to convey. They all try to express something, and they try to do so in a way that is ours, that is Argentine: neither that of Bradbury, nor of Arthur C. Clarke, nor of Italo Calvino, nor of any of the great sci-fi masters. Just that: ours."[25]

The level of praise bestowed upon the comic by readers, critics, and scholars should not be underestimated. As Andrea Bell and Yolanda Molina-Gavilán explain, *The Eternaut* inaugurated the "'first golden age' of Latin American sf."[26] Among readers, it tends to be recognized as "Argentina's most well-loved science fiction comic series."[27] In the context of publishing, it is "the alpha and omega of a national tradition, the prototypical humble pulp that climbed to the top of the national stage and achieved an international influence."[28] Oesterheld has been described as "the most important comics writer in Argentine comics history, if not in the world."[29] The figure of the Eternaut is "un icono cultural y político" [a cultural and political icon], and his image has appeared in the real world, for example, in a train station mural in Rivadavia, Buenos Aires, and a political campaign advertisement.[30]

The widespread affection for both this work and its creators is not unrelated to Oesterheld's rejection of the SF genre's colonialist legacy and its habitual need to represent only the established centers of industrialized world power. Joanna Page has explored *The Eternaut* as an "allegory of imperialism," and other critics have connected it to Peronism and the Cold War, as well as the more recent politics of Néstor Kirchner (2003–2007) and Cristina Fernández de Kirchner (2007–2015).[31] These political approaches gain greater force when one considers that Argentina's Dirty War of 1976–1983 greatly impacted both of the comic's creators. While Francisco Solano López was able to flee to Spain to escape persecution, Oesterheld and his family were victims of repressive measures and violence perpetrated by the government on its own citizens. The creator was one of some thirty thousand people who were forcibly disappeared, with the likely year of his death being 1977. The war led directly not only to his own disappearance but also to the disappearance and death of all four of his daughters.[32] Oesterheld's posthumous reputation only grew after the Argentine defeat in the Falklands War and, as signaled by scholars, the iconic character he created with Solano López lives on as a symbol that is not merely associated with Argentina but is moreover linked to the universal human condition.[33]

From beginning to end, Oesterheld and Solano López portray Buenos Aires as an exceptionalized and fantastic site representing what are nonetheless more historically grounded urban fears. The lethal snowfall, which is the first sign of the invasion,[34] refers in part to what is an unlikely weather event for the capital city of Argentina. According to a short piece prefacing the English edition of *The Eternaut*, snow has been observed only twice in Buenos Aires in living memory.[35] Thus, when readers "realize that any contact with the phosphorescent flakes means almost instantaneous death,"[36] they are responding to Oesterheld's clever use of local conditions in forging a compelling metaphor of estrangement. From this point forward, the graphic novel's depiction of danger and death relies on its presentation of the cartographic imaginary. This in itself proves a fine example of what Fredric Jameson has underscored as the spatial significance of science fiction in general.[37] Darko Suvin, founder of the journal *Science Fiction Studies*, lauds the work of Verne as "the triumph of imaginary cartography."[38] Yet here it is significant that *The Eternaut* represents the triumph of an iconic, extratextual urban cartography, that of the real built environment of Buenos Aires itself: "Any reader who takes it upon himself or herself to visit Buenos Aires after reading *The Eternaut* will instantly recognize the tiled sidewalks, the styled lampposts, and the many landmarks depicted in these pages."[39]

Iconic representations of specific sites in Buenos Aires are fundamental to the structure of the work and its narrative emplotment. The action slowly moves from the suburban areas of the Argentine capital toward the center of the city, proceeding along General Paz Avenue, and passing by the noted River Plate Stadium, where the narrative pauses for a somewhat lengthy siege. The alien invasion is highly destructive of the urban environment. For Argentine readers in particular, the visual experience of seeing key landmarks in Buenos Aires destroyed carries a heavy emotional weight.[40] At one point, the larger-than-a-tank-sized *gurbos* run straight through some central buildings, and the accompanying text notes, "Amid the deafening crash of the buildings collapsing, their steps echoed, like the blows of a pile driver."[41] More systematically, the inclusion of a long list of concrete street names lends further urban legitimacy to *The Eternaut*'s depiction of place. One notable example is a long march revealing to the protagonists and readers alike that familiar streets such as "Once de Setiembre, 3 de Febrero, O'Huiggins, Arcos, Cuba, todas las calles que cortaban Pampa estaban bloqueadas por edificios en ruinas" [all the streets intersecting with Pampa were blocked by demolished buildings].[42] Also depicted are the Plazoleta Falucho and the Plaza Italia.[43]

These destructive urban movements culminate in a scene at the Orchestral Pavilion in the Plaza de los Congresos (see figure 5.1).[44] This site is one of the most easily recognizable for readers.[45] Joanna Page writes of this scene, "The futuristic domes and transmitters contrast sharply with the quasi-photographic precision with which the central monument is drawn, audaciously mapping science fiction topoi from the First World onto a clearly identifiable local space."[46] The plaza appears in a full-page spread, approximately two-thirds of the way through the comic. This artistic decision to opt for a page-spanning image itself does away with the panel-and-grid structure of the traditional comics page. Moreover, this act echoes in formal terms the destruction of the city grid effected by the invading alien forces at the level of content. Adding

Figure 5.1—Oesterheld and Solano López, *The Eternaut* (Seattle: Fantagraphics, 2015: 254)

to this simultaneous disruption of the urban/comics grid is the inclusion of an inset or *incrustation* at lower right, a formal presence that comics theorist Thierry Groensteen has described as a further challenge to a traditional comics structure.[47] This formal disruption of the page anticipates the destruction of the plaza itself. In subsequent panels, a barrage of missiles falls from the sky, launched by the military to obliterate the alien forces.[48] Soon after, a nuclear bomb is detonated, and the text reads: "Before our eyes, in the center of the city, the terrible phantasmagoria of a mushroom cloud bloomed . . . Buenos Aires . . . atomized . . ." The denouement of the comic then moves to the outskirts of the destroyed city as the remaining characters reflect upon their losses.

Perhaps because it is a more concise comic, Rodolfo Santullo and Matías Bergara's *Dengue* is less thoroughly iconic in its representation of Montevideo than *The Eternaut* was in relation to Buenos Aires. Yet it is similarly urban in orientation. The comic implicitly references the work of Oesterheld and Solano López from cover to cover. Santullo and Bergara's graphic novel employs tropes of the hard-boiled detective novel to progressively reveal an urban threat of epidemic proportions. Changing weather conditions have allowed the spread of a virus transmitted by mosquitos, resulting in human mutations and the creation of dangerous mosquito-human hybrids. The story begins when the protagonist Sgt. Pronzini takes on the investigation of a simple murder but evolves when he joins television reporter Valeria Bonilla in asking questions that point to an even larger web of crime. Working together, and with the help of a mosquito-human hybrid, the pair exposes a deep conspiracy between the "Instituto de Estudios Dípteros" [Institute for Dipterous Studies] and its investors. This conspiracy is one perpetuated to make money on the sale of pesticides, sky domes, anti-bug suits, and more. In the end, the investigators manage to uncover and correct for a vast capitalistic strategy to profit off of the mutations. By the comic's conclusion, the mosquito-human hybrids are relocated as part of a resettlement process, Bonilla's journalistic reputation skyrockets, and Pronzini is left where he started, suspicious of what may be unfolding behind the scene.

Referencing *El Eternauta* explicitly in the dedication and implicitly through a visual resonance and thematic harmony, the original Spanish edition of *Dengue* consciously appeals to the notion of a common River Plate canon for SF graphic novels. Santullo and Bergara make the pervasive resonance between their comic and *El Eternauta* explicit by including a dedication to Oesterheld, Solano López, and even Juan Salvo (the Eternaut character himself) on the back inside cover.[49] In clear homage to *The Eternaut*, the protective suit that appears on the cover of the Spanish version of *Dengue* is quite similar in design to that originally drawn by Francisco Solano López. Visual echoes of *El Eternauta* are also observable throughout *Dengue*. Not only is there the frequent appearance of that suit—although here it protects against mosquito bites instead of a lethal snowfall—there is also the growing emphasis on nonhuman life-forms (see figure 5.2) and the key role of a soccer stadium in heightening the dramatic action of each story. The depiction of the stadium in *Dengue* here recalls its equivalent moment from *The Eternaut*. The massive construction nearly fills the panel frame and is captured in a general shot, from a distance.[50] In both stories, the stadium has a similar role to play. In the first, it becomes the site of a great battle between the military and the alien beetles; in the second, it becomes an indicator for the level of threat posed by infected mosquitoes. In *Dengue* the stadium is initially closed as a temporary measure, that is, through the construction of a sealed roof, supported through public and private funds.[51] The mosquitoes find their way in, nonetheless. When the first soccer player dies, a new level of fear sweeps the city, due to the ease with which the disease and its mutations will surely spread in a dense urban environment.

Such urban fears are reaffirmed in a prologue included in the original Spanish-language edition written by Ian Watson, the well-known author of *AI: Artificial Intelligence*. Yet, interestingly, Watson's prologue is absent from the English-language edition. Therein, Watson emphasizes how the key vocabulary of the comic—for example, the words "epidemia" [epidemic], "apocalipsis" [apocalypse], "mutación espontánea" [spontaneous mutation], and "guerra

Figure 5.2—Santullo and Bergara, *Dengue* (Los Angeles: Humanoids, 2015: 11)

biológica" [biological war]—figure prominently within a critique of capitalism's own adaptive/mutating behavior. Part of this prologue reads: "y que no le quepa duda de que el capitalismo dará con la manera de sacar beneficios hasta de la epidemia más espantosa [and readers should have no doubt that capitalism will find a way to extract benefits from even the most frightening epidemic]." Those who are bitten three times become large human-mosquito hybrids with very few human attributes still visible. Yet there are seeming advantages to allowing the threat to continue. As Dr. Richard Kanakis, an employee from the Dipterous Studies Institute, states on camera just before being dragged off by army officials, "There's a cure! [. . .] But dengue's big business now! Millions of dollars in safety domes, air purifiers, masks, suits, and so on! It's a money-making behemoth that simply cannot be stopped!"[52] The absence of Watson's prologue from the English edition might be taken as one indicator of a dilution of the graphic novel's ideological and anticapitalist critique.[53]

By contrast with *The Eternaut*, the specific urban cartography of *Dengue*'s Montevideo is subdued (see figure 5.2). Iconic, identifiable depictions of urban scenes are relatively infrequent. Parks seem like they could be anywhere. Street names are lacking. Whole sections of the city seem to be abandoned, as when a tank carries Sgt. Pronzini and a crew through what could just as equally be a war-torn zone of Oesterheld and Solano López's comics version of Buenos Aires. In *Dengue*, however, the buildings that appear in panel backgrounds are basic outlines, an approach more akin to the more rudimentary style developed by Will Eisner for the Dropsie avenue graphic novels (ch. 2). Visual representations of the city share certain attributes: blank streets, small groups of suited pedestrians, and, perhaps most important, a constant mist of pesticide hovering above the streets. This mist, while also a reminder of classic visual depictions of the hard-boiled metropolis, limits what both characters and readers can see. The urban buildings' collective lack of definition can thus be seen as having a clear purpose relative to the broader narrative. This lack of definition replicates the disorienting experiences of the comic's characters for readers by extending that disorientation via a narrative focalization. Despite the relative lack of iconic specificity in the comic, there are nevertheless reminders that this is an urban tale unfolding in Montevideo. The Ministry of Defense appoints Commander Pablo Kaneda to drive the mosquitoes out of the city. Kaneda soon reveals that his plan is to "force them towards the suburbs" and then kill them all. As in *El Eternauta*, the center of the city is a crucial part of the action. Beyond their explicit violence, Kaneda's remarks also bring to mind bourgeois fears of lost territory and the assertion of social and urban power by a planning class staking claim to the city center. "We have the downtown and the main neighborhoods covered: Punta Carretas, Pocitos, Punta Gorda, etc.," he states in a tactical briefing.[54] Later the narrator notes that people "no longer go to the waterfront or Prado Park for a stroll."[55]

Both *The Eternaut* and *Dengue* illustrate how urban fears can become metaphorized in comics. The fantastical approach taken by the creators of these comics render the urban discourses of death and disease much more immediate and their effects much more visible. Yet the theme of alien invasion, whether in Buenos Aires or Montevideo, also serves to reveal how urban populations take stock of and respond to threats. Oesterheld and Solano López showcase the potential for urbanites to band together to confront an outside threat collectively, while Santullo and Bergara dramatize the tendency for powerful urban communities to define themselves through exclusion of the other. In each case, the built environment of the city is central in communicating to readers the emotional weight of the story being told. The next section turns from Latin America to Europe and shifts from classic themes of SF to the unique combination of the mystery/esoteric tale as invoked by one of the form's leading practitioners. Still, it provides another example of how comics artists portray city dwellers as being in a constant state of vulnerability, threatened by forces beyond their control.

JACQUES TARDI AND THE URBAN MYSTERIES OF PARIS

French comics artist Jacques Tardi (1946–) started drawing comics in his twenties and has earned a reputation as both a critical and a popular success.[56] In his book-length study of European comics, Bart Beaty notes, "Since at least the 1960s, artists like Jacques Tardi and Moebius have sought to create possibilities in magazines (*Pilote*, *Métal Hurlant*) and publishing houses (Futuropolis) for serious-minded literary comics that pushed the boundaries of the medium."[57] The fact that his works have also sold particularly well seems not to have tarnished Tardi's reputation.[58] The artist was one of eleven creators who provided a cover for *Raw* magazine, and in 1985 he was awarded the Grand Prix de la Ville d'Angoulême.[59] Because of these and other accomplishments—not ignoring the routine publication of his work with esteemed comics publisher Casterman over the years—he tends to be seen as a "serious cartoonist."[60] As Thierry Groensteen confirms, mention of his name has become almost obligatory in any listing of the greatest comics artists.[61] Yet he has also worked with L'Association to open up new pathways to comics publication for younger generations of artists.[62]

Tardi has collaborated with other artists quite often but is also known for his single-authored comics work. His drawings have accompanied scripts written by Manchette, as is the case with *Griffu*, and by Pierre Christin (see ch. 3), in the case of *Rumeurs sur le Rouergue*. He has also adapted novels, including "*Brouil-lard au pont de Tolbiac*, *120 rue de la Gare*, *M'as-tu vu en cadaver ?*, *Casse-pipe à la nation* (all by Léo Malet); *Jeux pour mourire* (Geo-Charles Véran); *Le secret de l'etrangleur* (Pierre Siniac); *Le cri du peuple* (Jean Vautrin); [and] *Le petit bleu de la côte ouest* (Manchette)."[63] Tardi is also sole creator on projects wherein he both writes the original script and breaks down the narrative into original images. While the artist is also well known for his comics depictions of the First World War,[64] he is perhaps most widely known in the global popular imagi-nation for his creation of "la série fantastico-policière" [the fantastical-police series] *The Extraordinary Adventures of Adèle Blanc-Sec* (1976).[65] Published beginning in the 1970s, the action of the series unfolds between 1910 and 1920 in urban Paris.[66] Whether solo or working in collaboration, Tardi is highly skilled at blending tropes from literary genre fiction into comics form. While some comics readers and theorists may believe that the ninth art needs to distinguish itself more clearly from literature, in Tardi's case, the connection with literature is more often than not celebrated. This seems to be not merely attributable to his preference for literary adaptations.[67] Jordi Canyissà, for one, notes that "la literatura és un element essencial per configurar el particular univers creatiu de Jacques Tardi" [literature is an essential element in shaping Jacques Tardi's particular creative universe].[68] It is perhaps precisely due to this unique fusion of literary ambition and comics form that it can be said, as Joachim Sistig does in the title of his article on the artist, that Tardi is "un auteur sous influence" [an author of influence].[69] Because Tardi's name is veritably synonymous with the visual mystery tale, it is important for readers to understand that the literary mystery tale upon which the artist draws heavily in his Adèle Blanc-Sec comics is subject to two distinct influences during the nineteenth century.

The first influence owes its genesis to the formation of the modern police force as protector of the class interests of accommodated urbanites, and the built environment as the product of the bourgeois science of urban planning. The creation of detective units such as the Sûreté in Paris (~1812)—and, mod-eled after it, Robert Peel's Metropolitan Police Force in London (~1829), not to mention Scotland Yard (~1842)—prompted a new spin on the mystery story. The macabre tales of Edgar Allan Poe (1809–1849), for example, are simulta-neously hallmark expressions of the modern urban detective genre. Some of Poe's most famous stories feature a detective named C. Auguste Dupin, whose superior intellect presents a challenge to the crime and disorder of the mod-ern city. Perhaps more important, Eugène Sue's serialized novel *The Mysteries of Paris* (1842–1843) similarly contributed to the popularization and global spread of the urban mystery genre. This legacy capitalized on interest in the modern urban life to turn the city into a space of intrigue and ultimately, too, an adventure topography. First and foremost, Tardi's comics protagonist Adéle

Blanc-Sec is, as Michael Cuntz explores, "a relative of Eugène Sue, author of the *roman feuilleton* called *Les Mystères de Paris*, a serialized novel published in newspapers (Adèle is exploring the new mysteries of Paris in the different adventures centered around her character)."[70] Explicit references to Edgar Allan Poe, Mary Shelley, and Sherlock Holmes in the Adèle series have also been investigated by comics critics, and implicit connections are likely to be patently obvious to readers familiar with those traditions.[71] Tardi's protagonist Blanc-Sec is a journalist who nonetheless operates very much as a detective, displaying the intuition and intellect of this literary type. Yet in line with the twentieth-century shift toward hard-boiled detective fiction—in line, that is, with the now classic typology established by Tzvetan Todorov[72]—these investigations render her vulnerable to ongoing threats perpetrated by organized power structures. As Adèle states in episode 4, "three attempts on my life have been made—using the pretext of providing me with information on my mummy."[73] This vulnerability stems from the fact that, as theorized by Todorov more broadly, the temporality of the crime in these comics narratives unfolds simultaneously to the temporality of its investigation.

The second factor influencing Tardi's comics series is the interest in the occult that flourished in the late nineteenth and early twentieth centuries. In the case of fin de siècle Europe in particular, international movements like Theosophy, headed by Helena Petrovna Blavatsky,[74] inspired renewed belief in notions of hypnotism, mesmerism, magnetism, Spiritism, and the like. The impact of these occult traditions on Tardi's Adèle series is quite pronounced, as the artist's plotlines center on monsters such as pterodactyls, mummies, and ghosts, as well as esoteric topics running from telepathy to demon worship. What is so interesting in the Blanc-Sec series is the way in which these two discourses are blended, that is, how occult and mystery themes irrupt into the social framework prioritizing the journalist's rational investigation.

Both thematically and formally, Tardi's comics emphasize the way in which competing discourses and disparate elements can hide a single organizational principle. Scholars have noted that Tardi's comics foreground their heterogeneous composition without seeming incoherent—referring to both his mixing of literary forms such as detective fiction, esoteric/fantastic literature, and the feuilleton, and also to his references to visual representations such as photography, engraving, illustration, film noir, and Technicolor.[75] Yet it is important to note the social end toward which the artist pushes these influences in his urban comics series.[76] Tardi is particularly attentive to the way in which social power is systematically maintained, and also the way in which social hierarchies are implicated in the space of the city and its surrounding regions—at times subtly and at other times more overtly. Thus, he leverages interest in both occultism and the mystery genre precisely as a way of revealing hidden forms of social power. In the artist's storylines, the drive to expose and understand fundamental forces in the universe is one that overlaps, to a large degree, with the drive to expose and understand the power wielded by social elites. The result is Tardi's portrayal of a dualistic city, such that there is a sharp divide between the city's real organization and practices and what might be seen by more routine observers.[77]

The connections with occultism forged by the artist are crucial in that they mirror the way in which systematic social power can either remain hidden or be ephemerally revealed. The strange event at the center of a given tale is sometimes explained away through rational means, but sometimes not. Thus, Tardi oscillates between affirming the premises of either the occult or the mystery tales, but in both cases he emphasizes themes of social power. In episode 2 of the Adèle Blanc-Sec series, for instance, the "Eiffel Tower" demon Pazuzu turns out to be a human being in costume and mask. Similarly, the demon of the catacombs in episode 4 turns out to be a high-profile public figure, one whose face and identity are kept hidden even from readers.[78] Yet in episode 1 the man named Boutardieu's pterodactyl-linked psychic powers are presented as quite real—and after being killed by gunshot, the character notably returns in the third episode of the comic in spirit form, summoned from the beyond by a medium (Tardi 2010: 35). Similarly fantastic in spirit, episode 4 tells the story of a cult that somehow places Adèle into a trance from afar and lures her to their lair against her conscious will. In episode 3, readers also encounter a very real prehistoric man, referred to as "the pithecanthropus," who has been reanimated by a mad scientist.

As these examples demonstrate, there is an ambivalence in the series that adds to the sense of mystery and never fully affirms a rational or scientific worldview. Common to both of these tendencies, however, is Tardi's intention to denounce. As one scholar puts it, "structural hierarchies, scientific reason, the ideologies of progress and respectability—these are the very harbingers of madness and folly" in the Blanc-Sec series.[79] The creator thus challenges not merely traditional scientific beliefs but also the routine faith many urbanites have in their social institutions. As a result, Adèle's ongoing investigations of unexplained phenomena allow her to reach new levels of social understanding. Tardi's approach to the mystery adventure comic is thus to discover and defamiliarize the class structures of modern society, holding them up to scrutiny by the reader. Just as important, the artist maps these insights into the hierarchies and ideologies of social power to the spatial dimensions of the modern city.[80]

In the essay titled "Paris au Pluriel: Depictions of the French Capital in Jacques Tardi's Comic Book Writing," Cuntz outlines two main axes to Tardi's spatial approach to the urban comic.[81] First, the series positions Paris as the center of a global and colonial spatial web that radiates outward, thus along a horizontal axis. The critic describes Adèle Blanc-Sec's city as "one of the uncontested centers of the world, picturesque and powerful [. . .] It is a cosmopolitan city as well as a colonialist metropolis."[82] Merely in following the storyline, readers effectively trace the horizontal spatial extension of colonialist power, from central Parisian streets into its urban and rural peripheries. Such is the case with the first episodes, where Marseille, Nantes, and Lyon appear, and with the storylines that feature monsters transported from afar, including for example the prehistoric man from Siberia that figures in episode 3. These spatial connections are arguably not presented as an affirmation of France's colonialist history, but rather as a challenge to it.[83] Second, as Cuntz explains, there is a vertical dimension to Tardi's urban comics' spatiality. The artist explores at once the metaphorical underbelly and the literal underground of Paris. This can be seen in the role played by the city's sewers, which were famously referred to by modern planner Baron Haussmann as the "organs of the metropolis." In episode 4, for example, Adèle Blanc-Sec finds herself below ground in the catacombs. Yet the vertical dimensions of such urban storylines extend both downward and upward. Readers are exposed not merely to the depths of its underworld, but also to the dizzying heights of the modern city. In episode 1, for example, Adèle ventures both down into tunnels beneath the Seine and also up into the Eiffel Tower to unravel the mystery of the cult of Pazuzu, demon of the southwest winds and propagator of the bubonic plague.[84] Overall, the movements of Tardi's protagonist through urban space further emphasize these vertical and horizontal dimensions of the modern city. She is highly mobile, symbolizing an accommodated urban class and "belonging to the affluent few who can afford motorcars, moving easily from the center to the outskirts of the city."[85]

Tardi is regarded as a creator who puts significant effort into representing his city of residence.[86] In his original comics visions, Paris becomes a monumental city, one whose iconic sites are rewritten in the narrative mode of the mystery/occult tale.[87] Readers experience what has been described as "a certain precedence of architecture over people."[88] The second episode, *The Eiffel Tower Demon*, centers on "not only the city's most recognizable landmark but *the* most emblematic picture postcard view as the location for the final showdown."[89] Also playing key roles in the series are the Pont Neuf and the Louvre, for example.[90] Yet Tardi also subverts or challenges the monumental city by restaging it as a set of sites where both occult forces and also systemic forms of social power are revealed. In the fourth episode, "a blood-dripping corpse with a goat's head is hanging from the Arc de Triomphe du Carrousel," with another dead body left hanging on the fence marking the boundary of the Tuileries garden.[91]

The city in the Adèle Blanc-Sec series is not merely the background against which crime, social hierarchies, and other mysterious forces are revealed. Tardi goes further and attributes to it a certain agency, such that the urban itself is a hidden or unacknowledged source of power. His drawn architectural city "supposedly manifests the hidden truth of human beings, forging the outer landscape with the inner."[92] This idea informs the development of an interlinked topography and style that the artist borrows from urban noir.[93] That is, it is not merely the rich and the powerful who control the fate of individual urbanites. The city-labyrinth itself—perhaps due to a power imbued within its spatial form by the bourgeois interests that have constructed it—is able to mete out its own punishment on the inattentive city dweller.[94] No doubt, the representation of occult forces in Tardi's series symbolizes repressed challenges to the social structure and the modern state.[95] But the artist's mystery/occult storylines can also be seen as expressions not merely of a social power but of a properly urban power. Helgesson gives a nod toward this urbanistic theme when he writes that "the [Eiffel Tower] demon functions as a metaphor for that which the tower, as an icon of modernity, contains but conceals."[96]

A concise exploration of selected aspects of episode 1, "Pterror over Paris," reveals how the occult and mystery tales are combined in Tardi's work with a commentary on the modern city, its built environment, and urban forms of social power. Here the occult storyline introduced on page 1 precedes even the appearance of Adèle Blanc-Sec as protagonist. The first page of the episode begins with a wide panel depicting an outside view of several buildings in the Jardin des Plantes. The importance of architecture is signaled in the upper-left-hand corner of the page by a building that extends beyond the panel boundary through a half-inch of white space in the hyperframe to touch even the upper limit of the physical comics page itself. This feature—the very first image the reader sees, in fact—conveys the primacy of architecture and built environment in the series as a whole. It also exploits an apparent breach in traditional comics form to skew reader expectations—not only in form but in theme and content, readers should prepare themselves for the unexpected and the strange. As revealed in three successive panels on the page's bottom row, a 136-million-year-old egg is breaking open from the inside. As a result of the reader's active participation in turning the page, a pterodactyl breaks out from the shell and subsequently also breaks out of the glass display case housing it in the Jardin's Museum of Natural History. On the next page, the pterodactyl also breaks through the Museum's glass ceiling and flies off into the night. As revealed later, a man with significant psychic powers in Lyon has birthed the dormant creature and is attempting to control its actions from afar. The triple rupture of a barrier on the comic's page (eggshell, glass case, museum ceiling) serves to reinforce the occult theme of a paradigmatic break from the rational and scientifically modern world, of which the museum building is itself a concrete symbol.

Scenes that advance the occult drama of the animal's psychic control and the "pterror" it causes on the city streets are interspersed with scenes of the urban social world of modern Paris. Early on, the comic's presentation of this urban world focuses on landmarks that connote the social power of discourses and institutions from science and medicine to bourgeois planning and governmental control. Public order and governance is portrayed in a scene unfolding in a police station of the 12th *arrondissement* (2010: 6), and the depiction of the archway and architecture of L'Élysée (2010: 9). The world of science is threatened by the pterodactyl's attack on George Plot as he closes the Pharmacie Pasteur (2010: 7). Urban infrastructure is implicated in an accident on the Change bridge caused by the beast, the depiction of the train station (2010: 13), and, later, the depiction of the modern subway (2010: 28). Tardi repeatedly fills panels with close-up images of newspaper stories (2010: 8, 9) and actors grasping newspapers (2010: 10, 11, 12), thus illustrating dense circuits of urban information exchange and the increasing fears of city dwellers in response to rumors of the creature. Here, too, readers can see the capital city as a colonialist space or center for empire. At the "behest of the government," a hunter named Justin St. Hubert returns from Africa to hunt down a pterodactyl in the streets of Paris (2010: 19).

How Tardi depicts the buildings in Paris is quite significant. There is a high degree of modulation of the relation of panel size and shape in regard to the buildings being presented. This not only confirms the general usage of the variable frame, which "stretches, compresses, and dilates the rhythm of the reading,"[97] but additionally implicates the architectural and spatial dimensions of the city in each variance. At times, the panels are tall and narrow, to prioritize the vertical dimension of the city (e.g., 2010: 14). More frequently, wide panoramic or postcard views of the cityscape convey the visual splendor of the city—an aspect of Tardi's work that has been frequently noted. Significantly, however, a portion of the panel frame sometimes breaks away from its standard rectangular shape and morphs to outline the shape of a specific building feature, as is the case with the depiction of the train station's clock tower in this episode (2010: 13). Somewhat regularly, Tardi uses an exterior establishing panel to introduce a specific urban site. Such panels tend to boast a larger panel size, use bold colors, and are frequently less cluttered in composition, namely, to have no dialogue or lengthy narration. The lack of dialogue and narration in such establishing architectural exteriors is marked, particularly when one considers Tardi's penchant for excessive text.[98] The image of L'Élysée (2010: 9) communicates the monumentality of urban architecture in precisely this way (see figure 5.3). It is larger than any other panel on the page, and the height of the panel goes well beyond the height of the building, leaving room for an extended flagpole. The blue, white, and red of the French flag are set against a

Figure 5.3—Tardi, *The Extraordinary Adventures of Adèle Blac-Sec*, Vol. 1 (Seattle: Fantagraphics, 2010: 9)

vast expanse of surrounding sky, conveying the stability and dominance of the government. The respect communicated here visually is, of course, undermined in the next cluster of smaller panels as public opinion, motivated by fears of the creature, turns against the government, and Lépine, prefect of police from 1899 to 1912, steps down. Tardi's straightforward manner of representing architecture and its ornate details functions as a clear synecdoche for "triumphant and triumphalist" urban modernity and the magnificence of Paris understood as a monumental city.[99]

This very same use of architectural form is simultaneously a visible signifier that points to forms of power that are hidden from view. That is, one can either take the representation of these buildings at face value, or one can see them as more complex indices of Tardi's social themes. In one respect, they are clearly denotative signs. Intended to ground the Adèle stories in a modern urban milieu, they provide important spatial context and even atmosphere. Yet in terms of comics form, they can also be seen as subtle exploitations of what Pascal Lefèvre calls the *hors champ interne*. The theorist draws attention to the way in which diegetic space is hidden not mere by the framing of the comics panel (*hors cadre*), but also "to the supposed 'hidden' space within the borders of the panel itself (in French called *hors champ interne*): for instance figures can overlap one another and hide parts from the eye of the viewer."[100] In "Pterror over Paris" and other episodes in the series, the clearly manifest architectural surface is at once a visual reinforcement of Tardi's themes of hidden social power. The exterior surface of the buildings at once presents their monumental signification and also hides their inner machinations. Whether monument, postcard image, or panorama, such building exteriors and their implied but nonrepresented depth of field complement, in visual terms, Tardi's deeper explorations of social power—specifically its systematic obfuscation and ephemeral revelation.[101]

THE VERTICAL DYSTOPIAN CITY IN *BLAME!*

While the monumental city takes center stage in the occult/mystery tales of Jacques Tardi's *Adèle Blanc-Sec*, readers of *Blame!* (1998–2003) encounter a dystopian urban environment. This manga series created by Tsutomu Nihei (1971–) showcases the artist's fascination with the technologically networked city of the future. Science-fiction is clearly a touchstone for both the creator and the fans of his work; the appearance of alien and hybrid life forms will recall SF themes from *The Eternaut* and *Dengue*.[102] Yet the series, which is "set several hundreds, maybe a few thousand years into the future," nevertheless hinges on much more contemporary, turn-of-the-twenty-first-century anxieties

about the place of humankind in the cosmos.[103] Nihei seems to be particularly
concerned with the idea that architecture, urban planning, and technology
are already changing our collective human futures—and not necessarily for
the better. The priority given to urban space provides a point of connection
between Nihei's and Tardi's works. Both artists employ architecture as a visual
signifier for the core values of a contemporary human society. The French creator conveys a tension between the modern monumental city and entrenched
forms of social power and privilege. In his vision, the individual monument,
landmark, or building becomes representative of a more pervasive structural
or systemic inequality. The act of reappropriating these monuments within the
framework of the visual occult/mystery story can be seen as a playful challenge
to the urban social power they symbolize. This approach reveals and perhaps
undermines the hidden legacy of nineteenth-century urban social power in
France. Yet the Japanese creator's approach is more extreme.

The approach to spatial representation encountered in *Blame!* has earned
its creator comparisons to contemporary comics artist Moebius, the imaginary
prisons depicted by eighteenth-century Italian draftsman Giovanni Battista
Piranesi, and the haunting designs of Swiss artist H. R. Giger.[104] As these references imply, there is a vastness that manifests in the artist's products—through
his world building, his storylines, and his line work. His urban worlds juxtapose
cramped conditions, where threats lurk behind every corner, with vast chasms
and endless landscapes. In every case Nihei brings these worlds to life on the
page with intricate detail. The artist has created what critics have called "a
post-apocalyptic saga set in a world of mega-skyscrapers," or, in other words, "a
sterile and inhuman atmosphere which comes from technological aberration
of the city and its structures."[105] Writing that there are "obvious indications of
human irrelevance," Keith Leslie Johnson states, "For Nihei, the world is alive
in its deadness, but it does not necessarily live for us."[106] Humans are present
but seemingly irrelevant in this world of architectural forms that seem to exist for themselves. Perhaps it is better to say that any trace of human presence
in the artist's landscapes is diluted within a vast and spectacular architectural
extension. Endless combinations of metal, concrete, wires, and tubing forge a
dehumanized and dehumanizing landscape that is paradoxically the product
of human work.

It is interesting to note that while in manga, historically speaking, "little
attention is paid to the setting in which the stories take place," settings nonetheless became more important in the 1970s and '80s, in part due to European
influences.[107] As an expression of this shifting tradition, Nihei's chosen setting—
his vast dystopian urban world—is crucial to his story. One might even say
that in *Blame!* the setting is the story. As in cyberpunk in general, "architecture,
then, bears a considerable symbolic burden" in Nihei's work.[108] The series under

study depicts not some future version of Tokyo specifically, but rather a place called "The City, a structure that was constructed on earth but has become so enormous, it effectively has become a new, artificial world."[109] Somewhat like the Neo Tokyo of Katsuhiro Otomo's *Akira*, Nihei's urban setting is a "city of chaos and violence."[110] Its human population seems to have been largely wiped out by alien or robotic forces. Survivors live in small groups as scavengers, still in hiding and constantly on the move. The city's passages, tunnels, stairwells, and elevators are all in various states of neglect and decay. The protagonist, who is named Killy,[111] navigates the alternately enclosed and vast open spaces of Nihei's endless urban sprawl. Equipped with powerful weapons, he fights and dispatches the enemies he encounters along the way. Beyond mere survival, it is difficult to know what he seeks. Even positive reviews of the manga tend to underscore that it is noticeably thin on plot and characterization. One reviewer writes that the work has "almost no story to speak of, virtually no characterization, and generally consists of little more than atmosphere, mood, and bursts of spectacular violence."[112] Others draw similar attention to its infrequent dialogue, lack of "well-defined characters," and the fact that "the plot here is a thin MacGuffin."[113]

What is known about the storyline of *Blame!* can be summed up concisely: "The world has become an endless metal labyrinth, populated by people hunted by unknown forces for their genetic material."[114] There are a variety of beings in this labyrinthine world: not only The Authority, who seem to be benevolent robotlike overlords, but also a variety of insectoid, spider-like, and humanoid creatures.[115] Given the complexity of the plot relative to its explanation in the graphic novel itself, accounts differ as to whether the protagonist is helping The Authority—seeking to save humanity and to reestablish a connection to the Net that has been destroyed over time—or whether he is, on the other hand, trying to "unseat the sinister 'Administration' that holds sway over all."[116] Yet the graphic novel more than makes up for this ambiguity in its visual presentation.

A great part of the visual enjoyment of reading *Blame!* comes from Nihei's ability to shift back and forth from enclosed spaces to vast panoramas, a duality that highlights the extreme vertical dimensions of his dystopian city. It should come as no surprise that the comics artist studied architecture in the US, a reference that is almost obligatory for anyone writing about his work.[117] Luis Miguel Lus Arana goes further than most critics when he acknowledges Tsutomu Nihei's place among the many who have left architecture to dedicate themselves to the comic: Guido Crepax, Milo Manara, and Luiz Gê, in the 1960s; Daniel Torres and Miguelanxo Prado, in the 1980s; and in addition the continuing scenographic or architectural work of creators such as Marc-Antoine Mathieu (ch. 3), François Schuiten (ch. 3) and Joost Swarte (ch. 4).[118] In contrast, for example, to the clear line style associated with Hergé and that arguably finds expression in Tardi's work, *Blame!*'s creator pursues a "dark aesthetic."[119] He "contrasts the use of fine lines, engravings reminiscent of past centuries, with dark shading where shapes seem to come out of the shadows."[120] This preference for fine lines and dark shading informs Nihei's development, throughout the graphic series, of a range of "architectural zones with no sense of logic or contiguity."[121] The artist's dark aesthetic tends to reinforce his preferred themes of psychological disorientation and emotional dislocation.[122] Nihei's characters and readers alike become lost in a seemingly infinite urban space where human belonging and emotional connection to place prove elusive.

Blame!'s emphasis on the vertical dimension of The City is particularly important in mobilizing hallmark urban anxieties and fears. This is true in two respects. First, there is the awe one feels when staring up at a grandiose edifice or down on the city from above. In some cases, this awe translates into a fear of heights or a form of vertigo. Nihei translates the feelings of awe, anxiety, and/or fear generated through an experience of the extreme vertical city to the comics page in his compelling visual representations. Stairwells are often used to this effect by the artist, and they give the impression of a vertical labyrinth. Stairs are a recurring visual trope and a constant reminder of the hero's vertical journey. They often saturate the image plane (foreground, mid-ground, and background), such that the artist's visual depictions of them have been seen as reminiscent of Escher.[123] But the verticality of Nihei's dystopian urban world is evident throughout the pages of *Blame!* in other ways, as underscored from its very first images.

The two panels on the title page introducing the first episode ("Log.1 Net Terminal Gene," 2016: 3) and a single-panel double-page spread that follows (2016: 4–5) prioritize the vertical dimension of the city in the content and form of the image. All three panels represent different perspectives on a single scene. Killy and a small child walk side by side on a long narrow bridge connecting two massive structures. The two title-page panels are themselves vertical in orientation. One shows the pair from an oblique bird's-eye view that reveals them as specks in contrast to the massive concrete walls and a gap between them that seems to be of almost infinite depth. The other shows their backs as they walk away from the reader. This view introduces the characters but also provides a more textured view of their surroundings. Readers see the unevenness of the concrete bridge surface, gain a sense of its state of neglect if not also decay, and also catch a glimpse of the concrete-and-wire constructions that tower over the pair of travelers. The two-page spread that follows captures the extension of the same bridge from a side-view. The panel's perspective is drawn from a point positioned in the middle of the chasm over which the bridge spans. In this view the extreme vertical depth can once again be seen but is complemented by a seemingly infinite horizontal extension. The walls of the massive structures

Figure 5.4—Nihei, *Blame!*, Vol. 1 (New York: Vertical Comics, 2016: 103)

seem to go on forever in both dimensions. This double-page spread masterfully inaugurates the series by calling attention to extension, depth, and expanse as the key coordinates for *Blame!*.

Throughout the series, Killy must traverse narrow bridges constructed crudely of cement, tubing, and fraying wires (2016: 103), many of which twist and turn, extending out past the vanishing point of linear perspective (2016: 246–47, 255). These architectural renderings are archetypal representations of the primal fear of falling (see figure 5.4). Scenes of vertical shafts (2016: 332) and narrow ledges (2016: 344) also reinforce this fear. Given the structure of Nihei's fictional urban world, one of the most common manners of death in the series is to fall—frequently after a target is shot, of course. The vertical dimension also acquires a symbolic value, in the context of the hero's journey, as Killy has ascended some five thousand levels of the massive structure.[124] While even casual readers cannot ignore the visceral verticality and architectural symbolism of Nihei's dystopian series, they may nevertheless miss out on its relationship to matters of scale. That is, *Blame!* also links the individual experience of a vertical modern urban environment to the social project of city building. As Lucy Hewitt and Stephen Graham write in the journal *Urban Studies*, "Interest in the development of the vertical urban axis has, therefore, been a central strand of the modern architectural imagination [. . .] urban development processes have [. . .] stretched far into the spaces of the air and sky, signaling corporate status, political and economic centrality, and technological mastery as they reach for ever-greater vertical extension."[125] Nihei's comic in essence draws on a strong tradition from science-fiction prose literature where the vertical dimension of cities both connotes an immediate personal anxiety and symbolizes an unchecked social power. *Blame!* thus resonates also with the work of H. G. Wells, J. G. Ballard, and William Gibson, for example, whose works depict "future urban complexes structured around extremes of vertical extension and distanciation."[126]

Blame! can be classified as a work of "design science fiction," where the artist carries out speculative activity regarding the end result of current planning trends.[127] The series depicts an urban world that has grown at a rate so fast that human life has become incidental to its own expansion. Johnson writes of the series, "One of the most obvious indications of human irrelevance in this new biopolis is its vast scale."[128] The content of the comic makes explicit reference to patterns of urban expansion that are out of control. The world readers experience throughout the pages of *Blame!* is one that has been created by "self-guided machines" called Builders.[129] These Builders operate in the interests of an automated urban planning that prioritizes growth over coherence: they "blindly construct, deconstruct and reconstruct the environment."[130] The question of scale determines how one sees the artistic form of the comic. Johnson gives the examples not only of a room Killy must traverse that is the size of Jupiter, but also a time break expressed through the gutter between certain panels that implies the elapse of "more than a million hours of endless trudging."[131] In his estimation, Nihei's architectural representation and page layouts attempt to stage for readers "a space-time which simply cannot be processed in 'physical terms,' which must be either 'transposed onto some relative human metric or 'sublimed.'"[132]

In order to appreciate the dystopian vision that underlies *Blame!* readers must keep in mind how the notion of scale is implicated in the historical practice of urban planning. Nineteenth-century urban designers such as Haussmann and Cerdà—and twentieth-century planners such as Robert Moses (ch. 3)—mobilized the notion of scale to craft the quintessentially modern city. That is, the modern city is modern, in part, because it has been designed on a larger scale. When Winsor McCay's comics protagonist Little Nemo (ch. 1) tours the slums and uses his magic wand to turn them into wide avenues and stately mansions, the size of the buildings and the breadth of the avenues are their hallmark qualities. Such a push to think the city at a much grander scale can be seen, too, in the twentieth-century work of Le Corbusier. His high-rise towers extended the city upward rather than outward. The progressive enlargement of the modern city along both the horizontal and vertical axes moves past the point of no return with Nihei's unrecognizable and disorienting megalopolis. This form takes urban scale to the extreme, exacerbating the psychological effects of the city on urbanites, that is, the chronic overstimulation noted by Simmel and the urban alienation noted by Lefebvre. The ultimate result of enlarging the scale of urban planning is the production of a built environment that decisively dehumanizes the individual. Well into the twentieth century, theorists like Lewis Mumford argued that cities had been allowed to grow recklessly, with little attempt to articulate existing planning traditions with social needs. The reaction of Jane Jacobs (ch. 3) to the grand vision for New York put forward by Moses was precisely to argue for an urban form that would be livable—one that would correspond to the needs of the people who actually live in cities. An appreciation of the use-value of the city, as detailed earlier with reference to a variety of comics artists (ch. 2), demands that it be planned at the human scale. Yet Nihei's urban world is definitively a dehumanized city where "people are an afterthought." The fact is that these "environments, in their scale, design, etc, are not designed with humans in mind."[133]

The notion of the organic metaphor of the city is also important in *Blame!* It is both a visual touchstone and a theoretical concept. As always, this metaphor can be mobilized in different ways depending on the needs of the urban discourse at hand. Nineteenth-century planners used the notion of the city as a body in carrying out a top-down form of restructuring that gutted central parts of the city and displaced urban residents. This usage of the metaphor thus justified a form of invasive urban surgery. On the other hand, twentieth-century activists such as Jane Jacobs marshalled the organic metaphor to combat top-down planning, alleging that such conceptual violence destroyed the interconnected web that made cities vibrant places in the first place. Nihei's use of the organic metaphor in his comics series, however, calls to mind Lewis Mumford's evocation of the city as monstrous thing. The "tentacular bureaucracy" and "sprawling giantism" Mumford attributed to the unplanned megalopolis is effectively automated in the role given to the Builders in *Blame!*[134] Set in motion some time ago, and carrying out their work without attending to the needs of human urbanites, these science-fiction Builders stand in for a privileged class of planners, whose inattention to the city as a social form was so bemoaned by Mumford. Judging from Nihei's pages, the results of their work provide some evidence of "organic complexity."[135] Frequently in *Blame!* "the artificial elements, bridges, catwalks, cables, pipes, look like the organs and entrails of a mechanical body."[136] Yet while on the page "the city is seen as a living organism, a pool of cells continuously evolving,"[137] the organic complexity of the urban is represented as somewhat distinct from the organic quality of human life. The tendency is for Nihei to represent people as black dots (e.g., 2016: 322–23), thus as insignificant specks cast against the vast factory of urban expansion. The insignificance of human life is also a theme of the next comic, though this unfolds in the much more human and historical context of nineteenth-century London. Whereas Tsutomu Nihei's work implicitly denounces the triumph of technological and architectural planning and its dehumanizing effects, *From Hell* zooms in to imagine the horrific crimes perpetrated by the notorious serial killer known as Jack the Ripper.

LONDON AND PSYCHOGEOGRAPHY IN *FROM HELL* (1989–1996)

Alan Moore is sometimes placed in the category of "superstar comic book writers" who emerged in the 1980s and '90s.[138] His other high-profile works include *V for Vendetta* (Moore and Lloyd, 1982–1988), *Swamp Thing* (1983–1987, which won Moore the Best Writer Kirby Award of 1985–1986), *Watchmen* (Moore and Gibbons, 1986–1987), and *The League of Extraordinary Gentlemen* (Moore and O'Neill, 1999–2007).[139] One scholar specifically attributes Moore's larger success to his emphasis on urban themes.[140] Works like *Watchmen*, *The Ballad of Halo Jones* (Moore and Gibson), and *Promethea* (Moore, Williams, and Gray 2000–2005), in particular, rely heavily on the built urban environment.[141] *From Hell*, his collaboration with artist Eddie Campbell, returns us to the Victorian

London that for scholar Peter Hall was synonymous with the phrase, "The City of Dreadful Night." The Whitechapel area of London, in which the Jack the Ripper murders occurred in 1888, was among the city's worst slums.[142] To tell the story of the serial crimes committed there is thus at once to delve into two distinguishable but interconnected aspects of urban fear. That is, as Yi-Fu Tuan writes in chapter 12 of *Landscapes of Fear*, "Fear of the city as a physical environment cannot be neatly isolated from fear of the city's human denizens."[143] At its core, the graphic novel is concerned both with the fears residents had of one another and the way those fears drew from and permeated their urban environment.

Alan Moore has stated definitively that the comic "isn't history. It's fiction."[144] Nevertheless, there is an element of historical verisimilitude at play in *From Hell*. The comic is somewhat directly inspired by Stephen Knight's *Jack the Ripper, The Final Solution* (1977). It is important to keep in mind that Moore "doesn't assume that Knight's conspiracy plot is true or even probable, he just considers it good story material."[145] Faithful to that text, the graphic novel centers on the figure of William Gull, a Freemason and royal physician loyal to Queen Victoria herself. As Knight's conspiracy plot would have it, the Queen's grandson, Prince Albert Victor, secretly marries a lower-class urbanite named Annie Crook and has a child with her. A group of women finds out and tries to blackmail the crown, at which point the Queen asks Gull to dispose of them. This he does with astonishing brutality. Thus, *From Hell* both "establishes and disrupts expectations of historical authenticity"; it employs "Knight's hypothesis, among others, to anchor the motives and identity of the killer for his broader purposes of analyzing Victorian society."[146]

The comic originally began its publication in Stephen Bissette's *Taboo*, "an anthology that was, at least, intended to be a horror anthology."[147] As co-creator Eddie Campbell made clear in 2002 at the University of Florida's Comics Conference, the resulting graphic novel had a tough road: it was cost prohibitive and even banned in some locations. Due to the nature of the murders, *From Hell* is explicit about misogynistic violence toward women and its connection with a patriarchal social structure. Simultaneously, it also foregrounds the connection of the crimes with architecture and urban space. Moore and Campbell's graphic novel is, as Elisabeth Ho has pointed out, part of a broader trend of "Ripperature," or literature focusing on the renowned serial crimes committed in Whitechapel. It is one among "a group of texts published in England in the late 1980s and mid-'90s that mobilize themselves around Jack the Ripper and treat him not as a literary character but as a measure of national character."[148] Even if the source material on which it is based has been discredited, what is so compelling about *From Hell* is how its urban theme provides a link between the fear of crime and fear of the machinations of social power in London's built environment. Scholarship has noted that it weaves a "complex Victorian narrative tapestry" and that its themes are apt for an interrogation of "Victorian sensibilities and social realities."[149] Its readers certainly "get a detailed image of what London looked like by the end of the nineteenth century"—an image that references specific urban locales.[150]

Campbell's art is crucial in forging the volume's aesthetics of urban fear. Dominic Davies writes that "*From Hell* replicates the grid of the city through the nine-panel, gridded page of the comic."[151] In the words of Simon Locke, the emphasis on a nine-panel grid works to bridge the "stark black and white of Campbell's art" with Moore's deterministic worldview that runs through the comic. The result conveys a sense of the depressed urban existence of the residents of Whitechapel, people trapped in circumstances of grim and grinding poverty, caught in claustrophobic social and economic circumstances with little room to manoeuvre and less chance of escape."[152] Recalling the use of the panel grid to emphasize confinement in the work of Julie Doucet (ch. 2), the monotony of the panel frames here reinforces the urban environment as a space of imprisonment. Yet *From Hell* is a contribution to true crime rather than the development of an autobiographical persona, and given its intertext it is significantly more gruesome in its depiction of violence.

Campbell not only brings Moore's vision to life; he also crafts a compelling visual portrayal of Victorian London's architectural and urban aspects. *From Hell*'s emphasis on urban and architectural themes—specific visual references to space and place in London—the comic also brings to mind the movements of the nineteenth-century flâneur.[153] This connection is not as surprising as it might seem when one considers, as Tom McDonough does, the significance of crime for Walter Benjamin's original interrogation of the wandering urban figure.[154] Benjamin himself had written that "no matter what trail the flâneur may follow, every one of them will lead him to a crime," and as McDonough illustrates, the urban wanderer may be seen as a detective or, just as easily, as a criminal.[155] Mentioning the concept of the flâneur explicitly, scholars writing on *From Hell* have noted "Gull's increasingly intense detachment from the time and space of Victorian London,"[156] and many have privileged its fourth chapter as the point in the narrative where the physician's urban wanderings are of most note. In order to pave the way for a concise urban analysis of that chapter in particular, readers must appreciate how Moore's interests and Campbell's art work together to fuse themes of violent crime and the supernatural with flânerie on the comics page.

As a teenager, working as an apprentice at the Northampton Arts Lab, Moore had adopted a characteristically "open attitude towards the potential boundlessness of artistic practice," yet he developed a deeper interest in occult and supernatural themes precisely when later writing the character of Dr. William

Gull.[157] Moore has declared an interest in Aleister Crowley, Tarot, Kabbalah, and their connection to linguistic systems, and in *From Hell* he includes pointed references to figures such as Crowley and William Blake, who posited a spiritual reality behind the world of visible things.[158] Manifesting a connection with such mystical traditions, Gull's irrational thinking induces the character to believe he possesses a way of communicating with the supernatural or even a perverse God.[159] Along with its mystical theme, critics have explored in depth *From Hell*'s explicit depiction of violence and the symbolic and systemic meaning it possesses. Violence is central in terms of both content and form—in the unbearable scenes of disembowelment (in particular, chapter 10 of the comic), and in the strategies of both narrative and visual composition used by its creators.[160] More important, however, the physician's irrational thinking is connected in Moore and Campbell's text with the urban form. The mystical reality Gull perceives is projected upon the city of London, and implicated in its historical planning. This mystical reality is systematically linked both to a patriarchal social structure and to misogynistic violence. Gull's character is simultaneously pushed into violent acts by two sets of forces: one emanating from the social structure of Victorian England, and the other emanating from behind the veil of London's built environment. As Björn Quiring puts it, "Gull sees the perpetual city both as a kingdom and as a corporate male body brought into being by infinite, interrelated, symmetrically arranged series of imperious bloody acts."[161] The physician sees it as his task to perform the murders in the interests of the crown while also contributing to a larger goal. As he puts it, "Great works have many purposes. To aid her majesty's but one . . . the rest are mine alone" (4: 33).[162]

The concept of psychogeography is an unavoidable point of reference for understanding how the supernatural and the urban are fused in chapter 4 of Moore's story. While there may be a loose connection with the psychogeographical method of the Situationists, as used in this context psychogeography is "a means of divining the meaning of the streets in which we live and pass our lives (and thus our own meaning, as inhabitants of those streets)."[163] Moore borrows the idea not from the Situationists but instead from British writer Iain Sinclair, and he prominently includes an excerpt of the latter's work as an epigraph for chapter 1 of the graphic novel. If Sinclair the psychogeographical writer can be understood as "a channel for the cultural legacy of place," then Dr. Gull can also be understood as a channel for the mystical legacy of place.[164] It is in chapter 4 of *From Hell* that this notion is most clearly revealed through the main character's wanderings through London. Therein, Gull educates his coachman Netley in "the historical significance and [. . .] arcane relevance" of specific sites to his task.[165] As Annalisa Di Liddo explores, the physician and his coachman roam the streets "in search of evidence of the city's masonic structure, where the historical reminiscences of places overlap with Gull's own perception of reality."¹⁶⁶

Chapter 4's images begin on the recto page (4: 1) with a site-specific notation that the action begins on "Brook Street, London. August, 1888." Yet it is equally important that the verso page—as per the custom throughout *From Hell*—contains an epigraph in white text against a black page background. In this case, the epigraph is from Vitruvius, the Roman architect and engineer who wrote treatises still discussed today in twenty-first-century architecture programs. The epigraph consists of two full paragraphs that are cited at length. These paragraphs contain a self-reflexive meditation on the difficulty of putting thoughts on architecture into writing. Vitruvius notes the distance between the architectural principles and practices he describes and the reader's knowledge. There is a risk, the Roman author writes, that the "unusual nature of the language" used to describe architecture may lead to what he calls "obscurity of ideas." It is necessary for him to be concise, Vitruvius states, for if he is not, the result will surely lead to "indefinite notions" in the mind of the reader. Indirectly, but crucially nonetheless, these paragraphs introduce themes of great relevance to Dr. Gull's psychopathy: the distance between the word and the thing, the possibility of flawed communication, the power of memory, and the transcendent importance of ideas such as precision and symmetry. That all of these themes are introduced to readers of *From Hell* in the context of a meditation on architectural language is equally significant since, for Gull, urban architecture becomes the mystical link with forces unperceived by his fellow Londoners.

This is the chapter in which Gull receives the directive from Queen Victoria to murder the blackmailers (4: 2–3). Seemingly not long after receiving his orders, Gull and his driver Netley ride through town as the physician lays out the task before them. Toponyms crowd the word balloons on the page, starting a long listing of sites that will continue throughout the chapter: for example, Oxford Circus, then Oxford Street, then Gray's Inn Road heading to King's Cross . . . (4: 4–5). With Netley listening, Gull compares the "great work" of doing away with the women named by Queen Victoria with the "great work" that led to the construction of the city of London itself (4: 6–7). Chapter 4's formal features must be understood in relation to the established pattern of the comic's aforementioned nine-panel grid. Here, the stress in Gull's emphasis on "great work"—a phrase he uses to describe both the killing of women and London's historical urban planning—is mirrored in the inclusion, on each page, of at least one large panel. These large panels disrupt the regularized nine-panel page structure of the graphic novel on the whole. In fact, as chapter 4 of *From Hell* moves on, the panel structure allows progressively larger panels to occupy the page (see figure 5.5). These grow to cover two or more rows. Among this

Figure 5.5—Moore and Campbell, *From Hell* (Marietta, GA: Top Shelf, 2006: ch. 4, 26)

pattern of enlargement there are, for example, large panels depicting St. Luke's (4: 13), St. George Bloomsbury (4: 16), the obelisk known as Cleopatra's Needle (4: 20), St. John's (4: 26), Christ Church at Spitalfelds (4: 32), St. Paul's (4: 34), and finally a skyline of London (4: 38), which closes the chapter and appears in red as the cover art for the volume. (As readers will learn from the comic's text, red is the Druidic color of magic, 4: 37.) Chapter 4 contains many more large panels than do chapters 1–3, and thus this formal shift in the comic's visual layout simultaneously marks a tonal shift in the story's narrative by underscoring the grandiose dimensions of Gull's demented commitment to his murderous task.

London's urban architecture is envisioned in chapter 4 as a gateway to another spiritual realm. This gateway is one that has been historically stained with blood. As Gull puts it, "The greater part of London's story is not writ in words. It is instead a literature of stone, of place-names and associations, where faint echoes answer back from off the distant ruined walls of bloody history" (4: 9). As he continues to tour the city with Netley, the physician recounts story after story of murderous death that has taken place in the city, imbuing the sites they visit with significance. Sharing word balloons with urban toponyms such as those mentioned in the previous paragraph are references to masonic killings (4: 29), the Sun god of Egypt (4: 12, 20), the murder of Mani, the Teutonic Lunar deity (4: 10), the pagan ideas of the architect Hawksmoor (4: 13), and the existence of magical and misogynistic powers (4: 24). Confirming William Blake's faith as that of a Druid (4: 12), Gull invokes the Druidic belief that "locations were empowered by suffering" (4: 27) and introduces the idea that in Druid churches "mortar's mixed with blood, lending the stones vitality to do their work though all their architects be dust" (4: 31).[167] As Gull has Netley connect the sites they have visited on a map, the reader sees that they form a pentagram (4: 36). The chapter closes with the physician's words "Our story's written, Netley, inked in blood long dry . . . engraved in stone" (4: 37–38).

Gull's commitment to bloody misogynistic violence in *From Hell*, as scholars have noted,[168] is the expression of a mythologized and historical system of patriarchal power. Yet it is at once very important to recognize the links of this social system of patriarchal power with the production of the modern city. The ritualistic spilling of human blood in which the physician Gull participates is a crime perpetrated on women that of necessity must be understood in relation to the practice of urban planning, specifically. Here we have an occult rendering of the organic metaphor of the urban discussed in chapter 3 of the present book. In Gull's demented account of things, the urban form becomes a human body somewhat more materially, in the sense that human blood is mixed with mortar, and ritual sacrifice contributes directly to the grandeur of the city. While nineteenth-century urban planners may have used the organic metaphor to position themselves discursively as surgeons, Gull is himself an actual surgeon. He employs the scalpel to render in both material and symbolic terms the patriarchal violence of planning's metaphorical thinking. There is no small amount of conceptual violence here. As William Gull carves up the bodies of his female victims, he also performs a conceptual violence on the city itself. He turns both the female body and the body of the city into a symbol rather than a lived reality.[169]

The body and the city are both seen as symbolic texts that become tools of urbanized patriarchal power. Maps, in this respect, are crucial visual elements of *From Hell* that suggest this urbanized power. It is of note that maps appear in the body of the graphic novel itself but also in Campbell's drawn city-map appendices, which are included at the end of the published volume.[170] At one particularly important moment in chapter 4, a large panel represents Gull and Netley marking the sites they visit on a map and connecting them via straight lines with a ruler (4: 19). In his analysis, Davies refers to this in particular as an event that is "uncannily reminiscent of Haussmann's urban restructuring."[171] Haussmann imposed a geometrical design on the city of Paris and connected monuments via straight sight lines and wide boulevards that communicated the power of imperial urban planning. It is also relevant that Elisabeth Ho's analysis uses Lefebvre's critique of the monumental city to analyze *From Hell*. She cites the urban theorist's assertion "To the degree that there are traces of violence and death, negativity and aggressiveness in social practice, the monumental work erases them and replaces them with a tranquil power and certitude which can encompass violence and terror."[172] It might be said that Gull's grandiose plans for London engage directly with violence, death, and terror at the scale of the individual in order to effect an urban transformation at the social scale. It should not be lost on readers that the flattened two-dimensional spatiality of the modern cartographic vision does a conceptual violence to the lived experience of the city streets. Significantly, too, this conceptual violence is reiterated in the formal aesthetics of the graphic novel, as Campbell's nine-panel grid carves up the representation of London's city's space and as this regularized grid is periodically destabilized through the interruption of larger panels.

Given that their themes overlap, it is worth reading the general coordinates of Moore and Campbell's graphic novel against Jacques Tardi's Adèle Blanc-Sec series. Both employ the urban landscape as the stage on which occult forces and forms of social power disrupt the lives of urbanites. As we have seen, the monumental city in each work functions as a symbol of state and social power, whether in Paris or in London. Violence meted out upon the female body by patriarchal organizations is crucial to both works. Tardi's violence, however, is neither as grotesque nor as lethal as that depicted in *From Hell*. Perhaps more important still, Tardi's selection of a female protagonist is effectively the inverse of the role *From Hell* assigns to the female victim. Contrasted with Gull's victims in the East End, Adèle Blanc-Sec is a comparatively privileged urbanite. While the royal physician actualizes the patriarchal legacy and conceptual violence of London's urban planning in his brutal crimes, Blanc-Sec strives to avoid being caught up in the plans and speculations of various urban actors in Paris. As the next example shows in the mode of magical realism, the ability to dream the city is crucial for urbanites who, due to the danger and death that pervade the modern city, are necessarily forced to confront their own mortality on a daily basis.

THE UBIQUITY OF DEATH IN *DAYTRIPPER* (2010)

Co-created by Fábio Moon and Gabriel Bá (both 1976–), *Daytripper* has been acclaimed within and beyond Brazil. Its creators grew up in the neighborhood of Vila Madalena in São Paolo, Brazil. They began producing stories as adolescents and went on to study plastic arts.[173] Publishing their early work in Portuguese—titles such as *O girasol e a lua* (The sunflower and the moon) (2000), *Meu coração, não sei porque* (My heart, I know not why) (2001), and *Mesa para dois* (Table for two) (2006)—they started working directly in English with *De:Tales: Stories from Urban Brazil* (2006), which was nominated for the Eisner Award in 2008.[174] *Daytripper* (2010) is their second collaborative work in English, and it won the Eisner Award for Best Limited Series in 2011.[175] It was first published in ten installments by the Vertigo Comics line of DC Comics from February through November of 2010, and only later collected in book form. Notably, it was the number one title on the *New York Times* best seller list in March 2011.[176]

The comics series' broad appeal and international circulation have invited a variety of opinions. Critics have suggested that its publication in English by DC Comics—prior to being translated into other languages, including even Portuguese—is a clear marketing strategy.[177] The title *Daytripper* itself recalls the way in which Brazilian artists partnered with Anglophone musicians and their standards, resulting in a greater international audience. A case in point is the hit cover of the Beatles' song "Daytripper" released by Sergio Mendes and Brasil '66. As David William Foster underscores, "in Brazil, there is an association of the cultural vanguard with the English language."[178] Yet, as he also points out elsewhere, the twin creators were already publishing in English with their volume *De:Tales: Stories from Urban Brazil* (2006).[179] Critical assessments of the comic vary considerably. While one detractor has claimed that *Daytripper* is not graphically innovative, another underscores the innovative aspects of both its aesthetic and narrative aspects.[180] Some have mentioned that it exploits racial stereotypes, while others have celebrated the comic's compelling visual storytelling and focus on cultural hybridization.[181] Rather than disentangle and comment on these issues, in what follows I prioritize the comic's urban aspects.

Before being collected in one volume in 2011, Fábio Moon and Gabriel Bá's *Daytripper* was originally published as ten separate comics installments. Each installment follows the main character, Brás de Oliva Domingos, through a given moment or moments in his life. Brás writes obituaries for a São Paolo newspaper and aspires to be a novelist. As critics routinely mention, the moments in his life are told out of chronological order,[182] such that the ages of the protagonist vary across and even within installments. First, Brás is 32 years old, then 21, 28, 41, 11, 33, 38, 47, then various ages, in the penultimate installment, and finally 76, in the last.[183] What makes the comic so unusual is that the protagonist dies at the end of each segment. While this conceit perhaps suggests the importance of remaining aware of one's own mortality in order to enjoy life to the fullest, it also can be seen in terms of a magical realism where each of the deaths does in fact occur. As Jonathan Liu writes of Brás in a review published in *Wired* magazine, "each day in his life *did* happen to some extent because the chapters allude to the people and incidents in previous chapters."[184]

Brás's numerous deaths simultaneously work as a representation of our collective urban fears. Death is everywhere in the modern city, and the improbability of a single person dying so many times becomes a synecdoche for the fate of the urban multitude. Moon and Bá do not seem to be unaware of the connection between their comic's focus on a single character and the allegorical reading of modern life in Brazil. Their text turns on associations between Brás and the national scale. The protagonist's name has prompted scholars to consider connections to another great work of Brazilian literature—*Memórias póstumas de Brás Cubas* (1880) by Machado de Assis.[185] As this reference makes clear, there is an intent throughout the comics series to grapple with issues of importance for Brazilian society as a whole.

The cultural hybridization and religious syncretism some would claim are the bedrock of Brazilian national identity are foregrounded in the themes of *Daytripper*. What is more, the comic strives to be expansive in scope, portraying not only São Paolo, but also other cities such as Salvador and Rio de Janeiro.[186] The creators have spoken on their desire to use real locations to activate the reader's imagination.[187] One will find, for example, images of the Edifício Martinelli in São Paolo, the first skyscraper built in Brazil, and the Chapada da Diamantina national park.[188] While many scenes of the comics series are clearly urban, others focus on the natural world—either adjacent to the city (the urban beach) or within the city (green spaces, parks). Space is thus important in the comics series, but its role in the protagonist's deaths is less direct than it might be. That is, while the creators had arguably devoted their earlier work *De:Tales* to what Foster calls "hostile urban textures," by contrast

Daytripper "is in general remarkably benign about big-city day-to-day living, which, one could assert, only serves to put into greater relief that moment of violent death when it arrives."[189]

Readers of the comic will necessarily observe scenes of Brás's deaths in which the crowded conditions of the metropolis and/or the mechanized danger of industrialized urbanization play a role. Such is the case when the protagonist is shot in a bar by a stranger (2011: 11–12, 31–32), hit by a delivery van while crossing a busy street (2011: 79–80), jolted by an electrical wire as he tries to disentangle his kite (2011: 128), and killed in a car crash on the way to Rio (2011: 152). Even if it does not in fact claim Brás's life, the comic's representation of the TAM Linhas Aéreas airplane disaster of July 17, 2007—known as one of the worst accidents in Brazil's history—stands as a reminder of the large-scale interurban transportation accidents with which contemporary readers will be familiar (2011: 138–39).[190] The fact remains that these forms of death are represented alongside others less directly connected with urban modernity (suicide, murdered by a neglected friend, heart attack . . .). Even these manners of death, however, may be seen as being potentially linked to the stresses of the modern metropolis. Regardless, Foster's point above is well taken. Here the modern city is not solely the cause of death but also a stage for the human drama of mortality.

While *Daytripper* invests heavily in the built environment of the city, its narrative drama simultaneously draws from somewhat more universal themes of earthly suffering and transcendence. Moon and Bá are just as concerned with the broader human condition as they are with specific urban locations. It is significant that their protagonist is a fledgling journalist aspiring to be a novelist. His day-to-day work of writing obituaries is portrayed as a relatively unimaginative task compared with the promise of writing novels. There is thus a tension established in the comics series between the drudgery of quotidian city life and the promise of mental—and frequently rural—escape. Themes of adventure, leisure, travel, and love engage the imagination of the protagonist and reader alike and offer a respite. This dichotomy, of course, parallels the contrast between a material, earthly, and mortal plane of existence, and a spiritual or immaterial form of transcendence. In this juxtaposition there is no small suggestion that earthly existence draws its meaning from the finality of death. That Brás dies suddenly and repeatedly throughout *Daytripper* in a variety of ways strengthens this suggestion. Yet the comic's form contributes to this idea just as strongly as its content.

In formal terms, this is a complex comics text. In terms of creative process, the twin comics artists from São Paolo share a partnership that has been called "symbiotic."[191] In an interview, the pair has stated that Moon designs the pages, but Bá designs the moments in which a person is dreaming, including also the pages between chapters in the complete edition of the comics series.[192] Note, too, that this collaboration also included Dave Stewart as colorist, known for his work on *Hellboy*—and the washes and palette he employs are crucial to the comic's tone.[193] Thus, both creators are involved in the drawing and page layout—with Gabriel Bá signing his name to full-page illustrations that are quite important to the overall effect of *Daytripper*. One critic has written that what McCloud would call action-to-action and scene-to-scene transitions predominate throughout, yet I believe this characterization leaves to the side the imaginative and oneiric qualities of the work.[194] This is unfair precisely because dreaming is so central to the theme and form of the comics series. It is worth attending to Bá's use of the full-page image not only because he disrupts the logical transitions captured by McCloud's terminology but also because his page design frequently uses the urban image to further the contrast between material and immaterial modes noted above.

Generally speaking, the use of the full page in comics is significant, in and of itself, as it is more likely—in terms of the formal aspects of the ninth art—to prioritize the emotional impact of a moment rather than an action or scene per se. Bá's imaginative composition in *Daytripper* takes this effect to the extreme. His full pages appear once per comics installment—the cover of each individual issue published in 2010 has been incorporated into the complete text published in 2011. There is a dualism implicit in the periodic alternation of the full page with the paneled layout. Thus, the very alternation of his full-page images with Moon's paneled comics emplotment represent two complementary views on the urban.[195] This dualism, in line with the urban theme of the comic, can also be seen in urban terms. Moon's panels use action-to-action and scene-to-scene transitions to reflect the Brazilian city as an embodied space. Bodies are constrained in the city, pushed along from one place to another, one event to another; as such, minds are themselves routinized. Yet Bá's striking urban images prioritize the nonlogical, imaginative mind. In their use of the urban form, they convey the sense that the city is a dream-space, in addition to being a site of danger and death. The juxtaposition of images by Moon and Bá gives the work a dynamic tension, reflecting the human condition of being caught between waking and dreams, and between life and death.

The image chosen as the cover of the complete *Daytripper* volume comes from the first installment (2011: 9) and best expresses the role of the urban form in the comic as a whole (see figure 5.6). Brás sits on an urban bench, a dog by his side, and a newspaper in his lap. Multiple pages of the newspaper hover in mid-air, blown away by the wind. The pages are drawn as abstract shapes, with folds that intimate the wings of a bird, and thus they serve as a visual metaphor for the flights of fancy that animate the ideas of the novelist.

Figure 5.6—Moon and Bá, *Daytripper* (Burbank, CA: DC Comics, 2011: 9)

A brightly colored oneiric scene builds upward from the figure on the bench against the white background of the page. Though neither a word balloon nor a thought balloon, the funneling shape of the scene nonetheless evokes these forms of traditional comics art. Yet its content is more that of an "imagination balloon." The images represent not necessarily concrete words or thoughts of the protagonist, but rather various muses or conditions for the artistic imagination.[196] From bottom to top these include: an ashtray of spent cigarette butts, a typewriter, a coffee cup, an urban scene, and finally a boating scene. Visual elements of these last two are blended together such that buoys of the boating scene are superimposed over the towering building, and the lights atop the tall streetlamp almost appear to be buoys floating on the water. The vertical progression of the scene—the funnel shape whose narrowest part is rooted in the figure of Brás on the bench—requires that readers read through the city to arrive at the boating scene. In this way, the image parallels the comic's theme of the modern city as a limiting and conditioning space as juxtaposed with the escape promised by leisure space and the transcendence evoked through the symbolism of water.[197]

Due to the association of the full-page image with escape and transcendence, it is not surprising that many of the ten original covers for *Daytripper's* comics installments do not directly showcase the urban form. There are many full-page scenes representing water and nature (2011: 33, 153, 201, 225). Yet others represent urban form indirectly. In one such scene, Brás sits in a chair surrounded by boxes of belongings on the floor (2011: 57). Bá leaves scant detail above and around the figure, and seems to purposely be using the white page background to convey the introspection and contemplation of his protagonist. Below the chair, the inverted image of an urban apartment window can be seen, detailing many guests inside and connoting a human warmth that eludes Brás in the current moment. This image foregrounds the contrasting urban themes of density and loneliness, that is, that one can be surrounded by many other urbanites in the crowded city and still feel alone (cf. Doucet, ch. 2). Another image also employs a targeted illustration of urban architecture. Bá depicts Brás's father. Holding his newborn son in his arms, he is located by a short wall and at the top of an outdoor urban stairway (2011: 81). Here the use of the built environment is not meaningful in itself but instead works as a synecdoche for the larger urban context of São Paolo (cf. Eisner, ch. 2). This scene is drawn inside of a larger representation of Brás's father, this one much older than the former. In this image, Bá asserts the city as the enduring context within which our human drama of aging—of birth and of death—unfolds.[198]

Daytripper's thematic and formal dualisms thus both ultimately prioritize the role of the urban. The alternation of urban scenes and rural scenes parallels the alternation of panel layouts and full-page layouts. In both cases the modern city is connected to the discourse of earthly suffering (whether physical harm, emotional agony, familial strife . . .) and at once contrasted with notions of escape (whether adventure, travel, leisure, joy, love . . .). The protagonist's deaths reaffirm the notion that the modern city is a dangerous place, yet they also mobilize the urban image in order to emphasize the theme of spiritual transcendence. Beyond even this, however, what is so interesting in Moon and Bá's theme of pervasive danger and periodic death coincides with the multiframe of their comics series. That is, the episodic rhythm of the story coincides with the episodic rhythm of its publication. In this way, content approaches form. *Daytripper* plays with beginning, finality, and starting over in such a way that the comic as aesthetic object and the comic as industrial product almost square up with each other. Moon and Bá's creation can also be taken as a metacommentary on the comics imagination. It is the creative power of the imagination that links the storyline, centered on journalist-novelist Brás, with the context of the comics series' co-creators themselves as artistic producers. Comics are themselves illustrative of the power that dreams have for contemporary urbanites. In channeling our collective urban dreams or urban nightmares into work on the page, comics artists seek a form of transcendence, a communication with forces larger than themselves, with audiences beyond their home cities. In linking urban and rural spaces together through the moments of our collective human drama, *Daytripper* showcases the power of the ninth art to reflect on our contemporary urban circumstances.

In conclusion, the comics analyzed in this chapter exploit genre conventions in order to portray the city as a dangerous place. On their surface, the urban fears in *The Eternaut* and *Dengue* are related to alien invasion, radioactive snowfall, and mosquito-borne illness. Yet these SF tropes serve as metaphors for powerful if sometimes nuanced obstacles to social cohesion in urban communities. In *The Extraordinary Adventures of Adèle Blanc-Sec*, Jacques Tardi fashions a wider urban and social critique using the occult/mystery story format. In truth, the supernatural—unmasked or not—provides a way of addressing the urban social power of Paris, and by extension, the colonial powers of greater France. Tsutomu Nihei's *Blame!* evokes the staggering architecture and constantly shifting infrastructure of Tokyo. In formal terms, the artist's expansive vision, vertical drops, and distant angles quickly disorient readers and point toward the logical and dehumanizing conclusion of large-scale urban design. Alan Moore and Eddie Campbell's graphic novel *From Hell* fictionalizes historical fears using a true crime story, linking urban sites with a patriarchal and misogynistic urban violence carried out in Victorian London. The finality of death as part of the human and urban condition looms large in the magical realism of *Daytripper* (2010), which is the perfect choice to end *Visible Cities*. Here co-creators Fábio Moon and Gabriel Bá underscore the ubiquity of danger and death in urban environments. Perhaps most important, they convey an acceptance of the fact that that all things must come to an end.

CONCLUSION

To bring *Visible Cities: Urban Images and Form in Global Comics* to a close, it is worthwhile to return to how I outlined this project in the introduction. This book was not meant to be an exhaustive treatment of global cities in comics. Neither was it meant to be broadly representative of themes addressed in the comics medium as a whole. It did not attempt to tell an encyclopedic history of the ninth art, or to catalogue the way in which cities are represented in comic. First and foremost it has been an urban contribution to the interdisciplinary landscape of comics studies.

Within the scope of such an urban contribution to comics interdisciplinarity, the five chapters of this book have covered quite a bit of ground. Readers have traveled over North America, South America, Europe, and Asia. Together we have explored the way that the form, themes, and style of urban comics resonate across the eighteenth, nineteenth, twentieth, and twenty-first centuries. These chapters have mixed the work of some of the most renowned comics artists with others who are less well known in the Anglophone world. The vignettes provided in each chapter have provided introductory material about the artists that is suitable for all readers while also analyzing an individual work in greater depth. Most important, each chapter has grouped together a handful of significant comics according to a theme of urban research.

More than anything else, I hope to be leaving readers with a better understanding of why spatial theory and urban geography are relevant disciplines for the study of comics. This is true in more than one sense. Cities are represented in comics as content, where they provide the setting for comics storytelling, function as symbols of modernity, and reveal the patriarchal and normative social and state powers that shape the lives of contemporary urbanites. Yet they are also implicated in the structure of comics as an industrialized art form. Urbanization and industrialization have developed in tandem. In the historical city and the urban imagination, each is implied in the other. Comics form cannot be theorized without recognizing the way that industrial production brought a certain regularization to art that is palpable in the twentieth century. Echoes of the rhythms and punctuated beats of the comic strip survive in twenty-first-century comics and graphic novels. At the same time, it is also useful to see the historical regularization of urban space—its division into plots, blocks, grids, and avenues—as a touchstone for comics form. The panel-and-gutter structure of the traditional comics grid recalls the emergence of the planned modern city.

The idea that terms like "comics," "cities," and "space" must be studied in relationship to one another is not new. In making the case for urban theory in comics studies, I have drawn on insights from books edited by Jason Dittmer, and Jörn Ahrens and Arno Meteling. Yet as this book has charted out, there is much more work to be done if we are to thoroughly understand the depth, breadth, and variety of urban representations in global comics. Moreover, in building upon novel theories and approaches, *Visible Cities* has continued to open up new avenues for comics research. The intersection of art and architecture, in particular, deserves greater attention. Ian Hague's work on multisensory approaches to comics and tactility squares quite well with the aims of urban scholarship and the work of artists such as Chris Ware (ch. 4), Mark Beyer (ch. 4), and Seth (ch. 4). The importance of contemporary political struggles to secure what Henri Lefebvre called "the right to the city" for minoritized and marginalized groups—women and LGBTQ urbanites, for example—is reflected in the urban comics of Sophie Yanow (ch. 1), Julie Doucet (ch. 2), Moderna de Pueblo (ch. 2), and Rafa (ch. 2). The city is a space of gathering, but also conflict, in the work of William Hogarth (ch. 1), Rodolphe Töpffer (ch. 1), Richard F. Outcault (ch. 1), Daishu Ma (ch. 1), and Franz Masereel (ch. 2). It is a spectacle in the comics of Winsor McCay (ch. 1), Hariton Pushwagner (ch. 3), El Torres and Jesús Alonso Iglesias (ch. 4), and Tsutomu Nihei (ch. 5). It is a contemplative space in the strips of Ben Katchor (ch. 4), and it is a space to be contemplated in the *Raw* cover by Joost Swarte (ch. 4). The patriarchal power structures that have driven the production of the modern city are also specifically rendered visible in urban comics, once again in the work of Sophie Yanow (ch. 1), but also in texts created by Pierre Christin and Olivier Balez (ch. 3), and Alan Moore and Eddie Campbell (ch. 5).

Though many scholars still avoid making connections between comics and prose literature—due to what is a conflicted history, to be sure—genre comics and genre literature both share in an urban legacy. This goes far beyond the literary pretensions of Will Eisner (ch. 2), and the moniker "graphic novel" that perhaps incites more ire than it deserves. For a rich literary legacy involving cities one need merely consult the science fiction themes of works by Benoît

Peeters and François Schuiten (ch. 3), Marc-Antoine Mathieu (ch. 3), H. G. Oesterheld and Francisco Solano López (ch. 5), and Rodolfo Santullo and Matías Bergara (ch. 5). The examples of the fictional and fictionalized occult mysteries of Jacques Tardi (ch. 5), El Torres, and Jesús Alonso Iglesias (ch. 4) and Alan Moore and Eddie Campbell (ch. 5) deserve to be read against or along with literary versions of the detective story. Finally, Bá and Moon's *Daytripper* (ch. 5) might even be considered a magical realist narrative in the comics form. It is perhaps only once the ninth art receives the respect it is due within publishing, scholarly, and social circles that these connections between prose literature and comics texts will spark greater interest among critics.

To be clear, urban comics are not a genre. They do not hold to a single convention or set of principles. Instead, they represent the hallmark attributes of the urban itself: variety, diversity, whim. Artists covered in this book use a range of methods: engravings, woodcuts, black-and-white drawings, targeted use of color, vibrant color palettes, and even digital composition. Their themes, as listed in the introduction to this book, are inexhaustible. The city is not a simple idea, but rather a right to which both artists and urbanites must stake a claim. We all personalize our connection with cities. And yet we must realize that the city exists not just for us alone but for all who live, work, and seek passion within it. My hope is that this book will encourage scholarship to pay more attention to the way the city is represented in global comics. At the same time, it is important for scholars to look beyond canonical comics artists for new creators in parts of the world that have been less frequently studied. In particular, *Visible Cities* has brought Spanish-language comics into this broader discussion, correcting for what has been, in my view, an unfairly marginalized position within the field. But there are other urban comics stories that need to be told as well. I thus look forward both to seeing more English translations of global urban comics, and to further innovative interdisciplinary scholarship exploring visible cities not covered here.

NOTES

1. Adapting the cultural studies method articulated by Raymond Williams (2007: 152), I outline the dimensions of an "urban cultural studies" approach in previous publications: the monograph *Toward an Urban Cultural Studies: Henri Lefebvre and the Humanities* (Fraser 2015) and the two-part inaugural editorial of the *Journal of Urban Cultural Studies* (Fraser 2014a, 2014b).

2. *GeoHumanities: Art, History, Text at the Edge of Place* (2011) is edited by Dear, Ketchum, Luria, and Richardson, and *Envisioning Landscapes, Making Worlds: Geography and the Humanities* (2011) is edited by Daniels, DeLyser, Entrikin, and Richardson. Chapters of note in the books include Cocola 2011; Cosgrove 2011; Hones 2011; Luria 2011a, 2011b; Richardson 2011.

3. Both *The Spatial Humanities: GIS and the Future of Scholarship* (2010) and *Deep Maps and Spatial Narratives* (2015) are edited by Bodenhamer, Corrigan, and Harris. See Ayers 2010 and Holmes 2010.

4. *Comic Book Geographies* (2014) is edited by Jason Dittmer, and *Comics and the City* (2010) is edited by Jörn Ahrens and Arno Meteling.

5. Groensteen 2008: 91.

6. Ahrens and Meteling 2010: 4.

7. Couperie et al. 1968: 155.

8. Qtd. in Groensteen 2014.

9. Groensteen 2013; Morgan 2003; cf. Wartenberg 2012. Also see the resonance of this idea in Santiago García's assertion, in the context of discussing Töpffer's images, regarding "the innate narrative capacity of drawing" (2015: 36).

10. Dittmer, ed. 2014: 16–17.

11. Suhr 2010: 231.

12. Richard F. Outcault's *Hogan's Alley*, which corresponds to a comics period of "mass production and the creation of serial images" (García 2015: 48), is an example.

13. Roeder 2014: 117; also Blackmore 1998: 18.

14. See, e.g., Appadurai 1996; Repetti 2007.

15. Lent 2014: xiv–xv.

16. D. Johnson 2016: 106.

17. Kelp-Stebbins 2014: 7.

18. Oslo is arguably implicit in *Soft City* (1969), and Tokyo is implied in the fictional *Blame!* (2000). In addition, the woodcut novels of Frans Masereel do not appear to be references to specific cities but might be seen in connection to common patterns of twentieth-century urban living across Europe, and perhaps to places where the artist spent considerable time: Ghent (Belgium), Berlin (Germany), Geneva (Switzerland), or Paris (France), for example.

19. On African comics see also Hunt 2002; Otu 2016; Seck 2018. The following Oneafrica. org blog post was initially important in directing me to further resources on African comics artists: "African Comics by Bunmi Oloruntoba/A Bombastic Element (guest-post)."

20. See the arguments of Repetti 2007: 16–19.

21. See Barnett 2017.

22. See Lumbala 2009: 189.

23. Repetti 2007: 28.

24. See Mugavazi 2017.

25. See Thierry Smolderen's *The Origins of Comics* (2014).

26. The exceptions to this are *Chuecatown* by Rafael Martínez Castellanos (as noted in the body text, a film version with English subtitles does exist), and the comics of Raquel Córcoles, though the popularity of her works indicates that English translations may be on the way.

27. See, e.g., Dittmer, ed. 2014; Fitch 2017; Mak 2013; Vieira 2011; Bainbridge 2010; Uricchio 2010; York 2013. As Glen Weldon notes in *The Caped Crusade* (2016), Batman started out in New York City. It was not until two years after *Detective Comics* issues #31 and 32 that scriptwriter Milton "Bill" Finger coined the name Gotham City (Weldon 2016: 24).

28. Equally at home in this book would be urban representations of Beirut (Lebanon), Berlin (Germany), Fiume (Italy; now Rijeka, Croatia), Jerusalem (Israel), Saigon (Vietnam), and Tehran (Iran). Yet while such analyses of comics texts created by David B., Guy Delisle, Jason Lutes, Sylvain/Bruno Ricard and Christophe Gaultier, Marjane Satrapi, and Marcelino Truong would have been interesting in their own right, I concluded that paying attention to these texts would have diluted the coherence of this book's urban approach.

29. Where not originally written in English, the vast majority of these comics have been made available in translation. The sole exceptions are the brief comics text "Un cocodril a l'Eixample" (Pere Joan and Emilio Manzano, in Catalan, 1987), *Chuecatown* (Rafael Martínez Castellanos, in Spanish, 2002; although a 2007 film adaptation is available with English subtitles), and *Moderna de pueblo* (Raquel Córcoles, in Spanish, 2012). My hope is that with the rise of interest in comics from Spain—a tradition that has been largely neglected in Anglophone comics publishing and research—these titles will soon be made available in English as important texts from Latin American already have been: for example, *The Eternaut* (Argentina) and *Dengue* (Uruguay). Note that a comprehensive introduction to comics in Spain appears as the first chapter of my recent book *The Art of Pere Joan: Space, Landscape and Comics Form*.

30. This pattern of one image per text is in line with fair use guidelines recommended by the Society for Cinema and Media Studies, provided that the image is not gratuitous and is linked to critical analysis.

CHAPTER ONE

1. Smolderen 2014b: 8.

2. Jeet Heer and Kent Worchester's volume *A Comics Studies Reader* skips over Hogarth but does include an essay by David Kunzle on Töpffer.

3. See Bindman 1997: 7, 9.

4. See the discussion in Bindman 1997: 11–15.

5. See Kunzle 1973: chapter 10, which is titled merely "Hogarth."

6. Perry and Aldridge 1971: 31.

7. Bindman 1997: 37.

8. Bindman 1997: 37.

9. See Bindman 1997: 11, 15.

10. See Bindman 1997: 37–39.

11. Smolderen 2014b: 16–17, citing the autobiographical notes published in Hogarth 1955.

12. See Bindman 1997: 98–99.

13. Bindman 1997: 30; see also Smolderen 2014b: 10.

14. Bindman 1997: 30.

15. See Perry and Aldridge 1971: 31.

16. Bindman 1997: 37.

17. In Kunzle, this is not Molly but Moll Hackabout (1973: 304), and the critic notes the resonance with Daniel Defoe's *Moll Flanders* (1973: 307).

18. Referring visually to personalities that were of note at the time, the Madam is Mother Needham, and the lecherous man is Colonel Francis Charter. Smolderen's analysis includes descriptions and illustrations of these panels (2014b: 10, 11, 13, 15, 16, 17). See also Bindman (1997: 93, 118) for discussion of plates 1 and 5.

19. This "Venetian picture story dating from the preceding century" is titled *The Mirror of Destiny of the Prostitute* (ca. 1657), Smolderen 2014b: 10, also 14. David Kunzle traces this theme through historical investigation back even further in chapter 9 of *The Early Comic Strip* (1973).

20. Using the phrase "conflicting views," Meskin and Cook 2012: xxi.

21. See Perry and Aldridge 1971: 12.

22. McCloud 1994: 16, cited in Holbo 2012: 21.

23. See Bart Beaty's remarks in *Comics versus Art* (2012: 204–5).

24. On this disagreement see Meskin and Cook 2012: xxxi; Lopes 2009: 17; Carrier 2000: 55. Note that contemporary artist David Hockney created a version of *A Rake's Progress* (1961–1963) (see Bindman 1997: 64).

25. See the note in Kunzle 1973: 1.

26. On the latter, see Kunzle 1973: 1.

27. Though not in the disciplinary context of this comics debate (thus in the context of comic art, rather than comics art), Michele Hannoosh writes of Hogarth, "One might say that the images themselves narrate; the captions are not part of the composition, but merely translate the moral already stated by it" (Hannoosh 1992: 195; Hogarth is discussed 193–201, but Hannoosh does not mention *A Harlot's Progress* by name).

28. Note that Kunzle 1973 also gave Hogarth his due in extensive considerations, but this focus was displaced over time, perhaps because of the priority given Franco-Belgian scholarship—arguably more closely aligned with the Swiss artist Töpffer—in the study of comics even in Anglophone contexts. Miller and Beaty (2014: 18) provide a brief overview of debates over Hogarth and Töpffer in the history of comics.

29. Smolderen 2014b: 5.

30. Smolderen 2014b: 3.

31. See Smolderen 2014b: 5–8.

32. This is from Kunzle 2007: 162

33. Bindman 1997: 29. See also Thom 2013, who similarly relies on Habermas.

34. See McPhee and Orenstein 2011: 32–33; Bindman 1997: 101; Kunzle 1973: 358–59.

35. These essays, « De l'essence du rire et generalement du comique dans les arts plastiques, » « Quelques caricaturists français, » and « Quelques caricaturists étrangers, » are explored in Hannoosh 1992.

36. Hannoosh 1992: 195.

37. This connection is a requisite part of comics scholarship, as explored thoroughly by historians of the ninth art such as David Kunzle (e.g., 1990: xix).

38. Hannoosh 1992: 252.

39. Hannoosh 1992: 255.

40. Hannoosh 1992: 252.

41. See the discussion in Hannoosh 1992: 253.

42. As commented by Hannoosh 1992: 254.

43. Kunzle 1973: 358, 359.

44. Carrier 2009: 109.

45. On the continuation of Hogarth's legacy and the figures associated with it through the late eighteenth and early nineteenth centuries, see Kunzle 1973.

46. McPhee and Orenstein 2011: 4; see also Heer and Worchester's introduction 2009: xii; also Groensteen 1998 (cited in Grove); Grove 2005: 39–40.

47. See Grove, McKinney, and Miller. 2009a: v.

48. García 2015: 37.

49. Kunzle 2007: 158, 183; see also García 2015: 29–30.

50. For more see Smolderen 2014b: 22; Kunzle 1990:1; 2007: 158, also 57.

51. See Kunzle 1990: 28; Rossiter 2009: 43.

52. He is described as a "schoolmaster, and then university lecturer," Kunzle 2007: 120.

53. See Kunzle 2007: 57.

54. Kunzle 2007: 120, 126; see also Smolderen 2014b: 34.

55. Kunzle 2007: 3; also Kunzle 1990: 29.

56. See Miller and Beaty 2014: 9.

57. The first quotation is from Smolderen 2014b, already cited above in the text.

58. Kunzle 2007: xi.

59. Kunzle 2007: xi.

60. Miller and Beaty 2014: 9. See selected translation of Töpffer (1845) in Figueiredo 2016. Of interest here is the connection between comics and the concurrent technology of the railway, discussed in Smolderen 2014b: 46, and also Kunzle 1990: 377–78.

61. Smolderen (2014b: 47) admits that Töpffer did not create a theory of comics or sequential art explicitly, but that his creative work amounts to such a theory.

62. Heer and Worchester 2009: 13.

63. Kunzle 2007: 3.

64. Kunzle 2007: 47.

65. Kunzle 2007: x; also 5–7.

66. Kunzle 2007: 51, 90.

67. Kunzle 2007: 59.

68. Kunzle 1990: 38. Interesting, too, is the statement that "*Monsieur Jabot* is, simply, the first modern comic strip or, better, graphic novel" Kunzle 2009a: 173; On the debate over publication/distribution dates as they relate to Töpffer and his personal circumstances, see Kunzle 2014: 117–18. Also of interest, Töpffer is frequently given credit for taking control of his own production and distribution systems; see Smolderen 2014b: 47.

69. His first public hit was *La Bibliothèque de mon oncle*, Kunzle 1990: 30. *Festus* is a "satire on science and scientists" (Kunzle 2007: 78), and *Pencil* expressed "disillusionment following the July Revolution in Paris" (Kunzle 2007: 83).

70. Grove et al. 2009: v.

71. Grove et al. 2009: v.

72. On the Genevan's integration of time, see Heer and Worchester 2009: 13.

73. Kunzle 2008: 114.

74. Kunzle 2007: 114.

75. See Kunzle 2007: 37–38.

76. Kunzle 2007: 38. The narrative of *Festus*, as the critic makes clear, perhaps makes this contrast most explicit. It is important that this contrast is carried out in such a way that both the rural and the urban psychology are ridiculed.

77. On one hand, in Kunzle's estimation Töpffer was "ever railing against systems, whether social, political, religious, or pedagogic," he held a certain "sympathy for the French (if not Genevan) working classes," and he viewed Geneva as a "nanny state," Kunzle 2007: 62, 89, 94. Yet on the other hand, he adopted a conservative stance on the divisive issues of his day and was opposed to the radical ideas that were sweeping Europe. See also Kunzle 2007: 59–60, where the decision to critique the practice of dueling is considered a relatively "safe" choice by Töpffer.

78. Kunzle 2007: 16.

79. Kunzle 2007: 3, 111.

80. See Kunzle 2007: 95; also, 1990: 51.

81. See Kunzle 2007: 108.

82. Kunzle 2007: 15.

83. Kunzle 2007: 111–12.

84. Traugott 2010: 357n74.

85. Traugott 2010: 148.

86. Kunzle 2007: 70, 66, 88; 1990: 66; respectively.

87. See Kunzle 1990: 71.

88. Kunzle 2007: 112.

89. "The history of comics begins)—not taking into consideration the long history of combining pictures and words since Ancient times and the tradition of illustration, caricature, and picture stories in the eighteenth and nineteenth century (William Hogarth, Wilhelm Busch, Rodolphe Töpffer)—with the emergence of comic strips in American newspapers around 1900" (Ahrens and Meteling 2010: 4). As Ann Miller points out, the debate over whether comics are a distinct contemporary form or part of a wider historical tradition of visual representation "reveals a strategic maneuver on the part of those who prefer to see it as part of the artistic tradition" (Miller 2007: 16; quotation is from García 2015: 15).

90. See Perry and Aldridge (1971: 95), who reserve this honor for the *Little Bears and Tigers* by James Swinnerton, which ran in William Randolph Hearst's *San Francisco Examiner* in 1892. This sort of milestone, of course, can likely be pushed back even further by scholarship on the origins of comics. In the body text of this section, I do not mean to affirm one or another perspective, merely to give readers a sense of how Outcault has been traditionally seen in the field. See Richard Marschall's chapter on Outcault, which begins by debunking the artist's association with many "firsts" in comics (1989: 19).

91. The titles of the essays are "'Hully Gee, I'm a Hieroglyphe': Mobilizing the Gaze and the Invention of Comics in New York City 1895" (Balzer 2010) and "Every Window Tells a Story: Remarks on the Urbanity of Early Comic Strips" (Frahm 2010). Luks's continuation of the Yellow Kid creation is perhaps traditionally downplayed in discussion of early American comics. Consider Waugh's statement that "Luks, however, never quite arrived at the true, low-down vulgarity of Outcault, who, with all his penetrating humor, certainly, in this period, rarely achieved any sense of refinement" (1974: 7).

92. Gubern 1972: 20; Waugh 1974: 3; Smolderen 2014b: 143, citing Blackbeard 1995.

93. Buster Brown was created during a brief stint at the *New York Herald* (Couperie et al. 1968: 21).

94. Waugh 1974: 9. See Roeder 2014: 150; Outcault ran the agency from 1907 until his death in 1928.

95. Waugh 1974: 6.

96. Balzer 2010: 22.

97. García 2015: 42–43.

98. See García 2015: 43 concerning the titles, authors, and disputes related to these comics.

99. This is a common idea in comics scholarship, noted, for example, in Gubern 1972: 31. Yet as Balzer indicates, it is misinformed. Richard Marschall, Richard D. Olson, and Bill Blackbeard have allowed us to understand that yellow was already in use years before 1896 and that it appeared also in an earlier *Hogan's Alley* cartoon from May 1895 (Balzer 2010: 21). The Yellow Kid also appeared earlier, on July 7, 1895 (Becker 1959: 10).

100. Perry and Aldridge 1971: 95, 112. Sources disagree on whether this appeared on 18 February 18 (Balzer 2010, drawing on Waugh 1974) or February 16 (Perry and Aldridge 1971: 95, 112).

101. Balzer 2010: 21.

102. Coulton Waugh attributes rising sales to The Yellow Kid (cited in Balzer 2010: 20–21; see Waugh 1974: 1–10). Balzer ultimately seriously questions this argument in his study, suggesting that accounts of the color engineering of yellow print and the importance of the Yellow Kid comic were exaggerated (Balzer 2010: 21). See also Sheridan 1942: 57.

103. García 2015: 16; citing Harvey 1994: 7; also Gubern 1972: 21; Couperie et al. 1968: 19.

104. "slum saga" (Marschall 1989: 25); "immigrant ragamuffins" (Marschall 1989: 21); "area urbana proletaria de Nueva York" (Gubern 1972: 20). Put another way, he depicted "the generally unsavory doings of the citizens of a New York slum" (Couperie et al. 1968: 19).

105. Sheridan 1942: 17; Waugh 1974: 2.

106. See Riis 2004: 6 on juvenile crime.

107. See Canemaker 1995; Sheridan 1942: 17; also Becker 1959: 13.

108. Sheridan 1942: 17.

109. Marschall 1989: 27.

110. Perry and Aldridge 1971: 95, 112.

111. Marschall 1989: 25.

112. See Marschall 1989: 21 and also the arguments made by Meyer 2012.

113. Murray 2004: xii. The reference to India is from Riis 2004: 3.

114. The image appears in Waugh 1974: 4.

115. The image appears in Smolderen 2014b: 107.

116. While perhaps not actually as common as his language suggests, Marschall notes that "invariably, somewhere in each cartoon, [is] a kid falling from a fire escape" (Marschall 1989: 27).

117. The image appears in Becker 1959: 12.

118. Smolderen 2014b: 4; see also the reference to Hogarth in Marschall 1989: 22.

119. See Smolderen 2014b: 5.

120. See, for example, Couperie et al. 1968: 19; Smolderen 2014b: 141.

121. Smolderen 2014b: 5.

122. Balzer 2010: 26–27.

123. Smolderen 2014b: 5; Kunzle 2007: 114.

124. Balzer 2010: 30; Balzer defines the comic in terms of its urbanity (2010: 30–31).

125. Smolderen 2014b: 141; García 2015: 46.

126. Note, for example, that Rudolph Dirks, famous for *The Katzenjammer Kids*, which eventually overtook the Yellow Kid in popularity, also used balloons (Waugh 1974: 8, 11).

127. Balzer 2010: 21.

128. Balzer 2010: 22; see also Becker 1959: 11.

129. See Balzer 2010: 23, 25.

130. See, e.g., Marschall 1989: 28.

131. "The comic section, not the comic strip, was his legacy and is his monument" (Marschall 1989: 38).

132. Compare the statements in Roeder 2014; Marschall 1989: 76; Heer 2006: 112; and Robb 2007: 246.

133. On Shulz, Crumb, Spiegelman, and Ware, see Heer 2006: 109–10; Shannon 2010: 190; Roeder 2014: 191; and García 2015: 156. McCay also influenced Maurice Sendak (Crawford 2007: 58).

134. Heer 2006: 111; the descriptor "pivotal" appears also on page 120.

135. Roeder 2014: 5.

136. See Roeder 2014: 6.

137. See Heer 2006: 112. He also freelanced for *Life* (Marschall 1989: 77).

138. He produced 821 episodes of *Rarebit* versus only 508 known episodes of Little Nemo (Roeder 2014: 157).

139. Marschall 1989: 91. In the mid-1920s he returned to New York's *Herald-Tribune* (Marschall 1989: 92).

140. Couperie et al. 1968: 35. George Herriman, author of Krazy Kat, shares this honor with McCay in that text.

141. García 2015: 45.

142. See Smolderen 2014b: 149.

143. He arguably brought "the achievements of the other graphic arts" to bear on the comic (Couperie et al. 1968: 205).

144. On time in Töpffer, see Roeder 2014: 7.

145. See the description in Couperie et al. 1968: 183.

146. Roeder 2014: 7, 92.

147. See Smolderen 2014b: 157.

148. See Roeder 2014: 7.

149. See Groensteen 2007: 60–61.

150. Smolderen 2014b: 149; see also 157. On spectacle see Smolderen 2014: 157; Roeder 2014: 109.

151. See discussion in Smolderen 2014b: 149, 154.

152. See Roeder 2014: 7.

153. Roeder 2014: 8. His success was notable in both areas; Smolderen writes of his "pioneering venture in film animation" (Smolderen 2014b: 152).

154. Crafton 2013: 33; see Marschall 1989: 89–91; also Roeder 2014. For more on the Gertie animated film, see Blackmore (1998: 26–27).

155. Crawford 2007: 59–60.

156. See Morton 2010.

157. Labio 2015: 312. McCay's work perhaps represents a unique point of entry into the architectural aspects of comics, one that will be continued in ch. 4 of this book.

158. Critics have long noted McCay's "grandiose architectural constructions" (Couperie et al. 1968: 29; also that "McCay was a master of architectural perspective," Couperie et al. 1968: 209). It is of interest that his roommate in Chicago, Jules Guerin, was "later a noted illustrator specializing in architectural and travel subjects" (Marschall 1989: 77). Roeder notes his "command of architectural drawing" (2014: 157). "McCay's early-twentieth-century comics reflected the visual perspectives on the city afforded by new forms of public transportation like the elevated commuter train lines and amusement park rides" (Roeder 2011: 25–26).

159. See Roeder 2014: 157.

160. Roeder 2014: 158, 160, 181. Readers may find it interesting that Roeder then analyzes *Rarebit*'s presentation of the unhealthy city in line with Simmel's essay "The Metropolis and Mental Life" (Roeder 2014: 160–65).

161. Roeder 2014: 7.

162. Roeder 2014: 154.

163. Here I also follow Catherine Labio's idea that "McCay's broadsheets reflected their urban context (both thematically and with respect to the medium in which they were disseminated)" (2015: 343).

164. See Roeder 2014: 120.

165. Marschall 1989: 88–89.

166. This might be seen as yet another connection between McCay's and Töpffer's work, particularly in the latter's theoretical essays, as mentioned above in the text.

167. Roeder 2014: 61, 54.

168. Couperie et al. 1968: 27, also 27–29 for general comments on McCay; Marschall 1989: 80.

169. Blackmore 1998: 33; citing Inge 1990: 34.

170. Roeder 2014: 62.

171. See Marschall 1989: 151.

172. Jeet Heer sees the fact that this is a church steeple as subtle critique (Heer 2006: 107).

173. Smolderen 2014b: 155; also Roeder 2014: 54–55 on this particular image.

174. Blackmore 1998: 19–20; Marschall 1989: 80; on Outcault and class, see also Roeder 2014: 58–59.

175. This 1908 comic appears with no month or day listed in Marschall 1989: 88.

176. Marschall 1989: 88.

177. Roeder 2014: 114.

178. Roeder 2014: 114–15.

179. Harvey 2006: 3.

180. Lefebvre 1996: 168.

181. Sennett 1992; on Haussmann and control in Paris, see also Tuan 2013: 165.

182. It is an exception, according to Blackmore 1998: 24.

183. Heer 2006: 106; see also Roeder 2014: 148–49.

184. Lefebvre 1976: 22.

185. See Roeder 2014: 9.

186. Available online is the information that on June 23, 2016, Yanow offered a cartoon workshop for women veterans in connection with the White River Junction VA Medical Center Women's Clinic.

187. See comments of "deft sketches and minimal text" (Goodyear 2014).

188. Clough 2014.

189. Yanow, qtd. in Goodyear 2014. "Large open squares are the obvious places where people can converge. But I think that in terms of building social movements, a walkable city is important. Places where people literally brush up against each other on the sidewalk, where they have to be in public together and don't just see each other passing by in cars. When people aren't used to being together in the street, I think they're less likely to go to the street and demand change."

190. Yanow, qtd. in Goodyear 2014.

191. Giaufret 2016a mentions Yanow's text only in passing but also addresses Montreal's representation in comics. The quotation is from Giaufret 2016b: 116.

192. A 2015 dissertation mentions Yanow in passing, emphasizing her text's distinction between the strike as addressed to the state and the occupation of space (McKay 2015: 113–14).

193. Kettling was used by the Montreal police in the massive 2012 protests of the Maple Spring (Léger and Sorochan 2014: 92) and is also mentioned explicitly in *War of Streets and Houses* (Yanow 2014: 31). The *Battle of Algiers*, of course, engages a much more contemporary moment in French colonial history, given that the anticolonial struggle would inflame again with the Algieran War of Independence in 1954 (see Wark 2011: 83–84).

194. Singer and Langdon 2004: 49, 53, 54.

195. Rid 2009: 620.

196. Singer and Langdon 2004: 60. Chapter 2 of Singer and Langdon 2004 (titled "Bugeaud and the Conquest of Algeria," 47–90) provides a point of contrast with the spirit of Yanow's more radical engagement with the figure of Bugeaud.

197. Lambert 2012: 94; Yanow 2014: 68. An excerpt of what is arguably Bugeaud's pamphlet is introduced by Eyal Weizman in an online edition of *Cabinet Magazine* (Weizman 2006). Yanow writes that these doubts surrounding the manual are something that "the introduction [by Weizman in *Cabinet Magazine*] fails to mention" and introduces the possibility that the text translated from the French there may have something to do with the creative activities of the OuLiPo workshop.

198. In 1866 Blanqui "wrote a clandestine instruction manual for armed insurrection in Paris, explaining in detail how to build a barricade by modifying a block of buildings and thus transform a neighborhood into a veritable fortress"; "He also described a process of mining within the mass of housing, by cutting stairs, digging through floors, and piercing the walls" (Lambert 2012: 94).

199. Algiers was occupied by France in 1830 (Çelik 1997: 1, 19).

200. Named governor-general in late 1840, he arrived in Algiers February 22, 1841 (Singer and Langdon 2004: 66).

201. It is significant that "the pacification of social revolution might have directly influenced the development of modern urban planning." (Abdalrahman 2016: 424, who mentions connections between Bugeaud and Haussmann.)

202. Weizman 2012: 165.

203. Graham 2011: 12. See also Evans 2009, who adopts an urban lens on insurgency.

204. On Bugeaud, Haussmann, and Algiers, see also Sagan 2015: 53–55, who cites Weizman.

205. Weizman 2012: 164. Also, "Architecture is a great framework with which to enter the world of politics, because every political act is registered in space"; "Conflict saturates the urban environment. The understanding is that every bit of construction and destruction is a certain index for political and military forces, but also of economical and societal ones."

206. See *The Production of Space* (Lefevbre 1991a).

207. Wark 2011: 94. Also "Lefebvre's moment is closely related to Debord's turn towards the situation."

208. See also the work of Barcelona-based Lefebvrian thinker Manuel Delgado Ruiz (2007).

209. Lefebvre 1976: 15.

210. This Lefebvrian distinction reappears uncredited in Weizman's comments: "The problem is also that this kind of urbanization kills everything that is important about the city: its heterogeneity, its sense of multiplicity, and its difference. The urban, we should remember, is different than the city; urban is the condition of the city, the condition of heterogeneity, and vitality that the city has. The city fabric might be considered the hardware within which the software of urban life takes shape" (Weizman 2012: 166). Compare to Lefebvre's use of the snail metaphor for the living city and its hardened shell as discussed in *Introduction to Modernity* (1995).

211. Smolderen 2014b.

CHAPTER TWO

1. Mumford 1970: 149–50; see also Mumford 1961, 1934. LeGates and Stout note that "Lewis Mumford's magisterial *The Culture of Cities* (New York: Harcourt Brace, 1938) was the first and remains the best book on the culture of cities" (2005: 10).

2. Mumford 1970: 159.

3. One of the most thorough investigations of this tension is Roy Rosenzweig's *Eight Hours for What We Will: Workers and Leisure in an Industrial City, 1870–1920* (1983).

4. Marx 1964: 139.

5. Merrifield 2002: 78, original emphasis; also 17–18.

6. See the discussion of this in *Lefebvre, Love and Struggle: Spatial Dialectics* by in Rob Shields (2005: 40); also Fraser 2015.

7. Lefebvre 2005: 26. This idea is elaborated upon in Lefebvre 1991b, 2002, 2005; Lefebvre's invocation of the notion of the "colonization of daily life" (e.g., 2002: 11; see also 2005: 26) owes to the thought of Guy Debord, with whom he had a falling out: see Mendieta 2008: 149; Debord 1961, 1995; Knabb 2006; Merrifield 2005.

8. Lefebvre 1991b: 249.

9. Lefebvre 2003: 92.

10. Merrifield 2002: 79.

11. Lefebvre 1976, 1991b. See also Fraser 2015.

12. Smith 1984.

13. *Toward an Urban Cultural Studies: Henri Lefebvre and the Humanities* (Fraser 2015) made this argument more carefully by systematically reviewing Lefebvre's legacy and concentrating on its value for the study of cultural texts. See also Léger 2006: 149.

14. Beronä 2008: 15. From 1917 to 1920 Masereel worked as a political cartoonist for *La Feuille*, and "from this experience he developed a style of woodcuts that exposed the social ills of his time and the growing threat of capitalism on the human condition" (Beronä 2001: 20); among the books he illustrated are some authored by Romain Rolland, who won the 1915 Nobel Prize in Literature (García 2015: 54).

15. Beronä 2008: 15; the quote is from Antonsen 2004: 155.

16. Antonsen 2004: 155.

17. Lanier 2007: 15.

18. Antonsen 2004: 155.

19. Antonsen 2004: 155.

20. Groß 2014: 202.

21. Lanier 2007: 15; Postema 2015: 91–92; Beronä 2001: 19–20; Beronä 1999: 90; García 2015: 58–59, 62, 159; see also Kunzle 1990: 194. The influence on Jason Lutes in his *Berlin* trilogy is not surprising when one understands that Masereel was "clearly an important artist in the German Weimar years" (see Antonsen 2004: 155). Also of note, Pascal Lefèvre mentions Masereel in passing (2009a: 25–26).

22. Lynd Ward also discovered, in Germany, the work of Otto Nückel, the latter known for *Destiny: A Novel in Pictures*. Beronä 2001: 19–20.

23. Beronä 1999: 95.

24. Beronä 2008: 41.

25. García 2015: 58.

26. Beronä 1999: 95; see also 95–98 where Beronä elaborates on this comment while referencing Ward's other works.

27. Beronä 1999: 93.

28. Beronä (2001: 19) links this tradition of the wordless novel with silent movies; García (2015: 55) notes this connection too and attributes it also to the much later work of Seth (ch. 4).

29. García 2015: 56.

30. García 2015: 56.

31. Kuper 2008: 7. See also Kuper's graphic novel *The System*.

32. This is stated clearly by Beronä 2001: 20.

33. These are highlighted in Beronä's 2008 book.

34. Beronä 2008: 16.

35. Groß 2014: 202.

36. Antonsen 2004: 154.

37. See Groß 2014: 202.

38. Groß 2014: 203.

39. Beronä 1999: 93.

40. Beronä 1999: 94.

41. Beronä 1999: 93.

42. Beronä 1999: 94.

43. Lefebvre 1969: 98; also 1976: 19.

44. See Dauber 2006: 279–80.

45. Dauber 2006: 279–80.

46. Dauber 2006: 282–84; Smith 2010: 184; Schumacher 2010: 192.

47. See Dauber 2006: 284.

48. It is common for scholarly work on comics to note the importance of *Comics and Sequential Art* (1985), for example, as Thierry Groensteen (2007: vii) does in a passing reference. See also Varnum and Gibbons 2001: viii; Perret 2001: 125. More and more, comics scholars tend to associate Eisner's definition of sequential art, and by extension McCloud's continuation of this point, with a crude reduction of what should be seen as a more expansive comics aesthetic. One example is García 2015: 26. El Refaie 2012: 22 links Eisner and McCloud's approach to sequential art. See also Beaty 2012: 33–34.

49. García 2015: 132; Beaty 2007: 111.

50. Hatfield 2005: x; Smith 2010: 184.

51. Dauber 2006: 280.

52. García 2015: 73; see also Hatfield 2005: xi, who writes about the shop production of comics.

53. Sabin 1996: 78.

54. See Schumacher 2010.

55. See, for example, Davis 2011: 260, 274n1.

56. Dauber 2006: 280; García 2015: 132, who also notes that cartoonist Jules Feiffer worked on Eisner's team.

57. See Beaty 2012: 196.

58. Astor 2005: 7.

59. Sabin 1996: 54.

60. Smith 2010: 184.

61. Helgesson 1998: 36.

62. García 2015: 132, 12.

63. Roth 2007: 465 points to the use of the term in the 1960s. The moniker "graphic novel" was in part hype but was also part of a long history of novels in graphic form, as seen in Masereel; see Sabin 1996: 165. "The first public use of the phrase [graphic novel], by Richard Kyle, was in a 1964 newsletter circulated to members of the Amateur Press Association, and the term was subsequently borrowed by Bill Spicer in his fanzine *Graphic Story World*. Many think Will Eisner invented the term, because he used it in a more commercial context, to sell *A Contract with God* (1978) to publishers" (Chute 2008: 453); in an endnote, Chute clarifies that Eisner "claim[ed] not to know the term had been used earlier" (2008: 462). See also Schumacher 2010: 201: "'I thought I had invented the term,' Eisner admitted, 'but I discovered later that some guy thought about it a few years before I used the term. He had never used it successfully and had never intended it the way I did, which was to develop what I believe was viable literature in this medium.'"

64. Smith 2010: 184.

65. García 2015: 134.

66. Hatfield 2005: 29. On the marketing of *A Contract with God* as a "graphic novel" and matters of readership, see García 2015: 20, 132, 134; Postema 2013: 135.

67. On the connections and distinctions between comics, literature, and cinema, see, e.g., García 2015: 14; Hatfield 2005: 33; Aldama 2017: 1.

68. Beronä 1999: 99.

69. Eisner 2006a: xiv.

70. Beronä 1999: 100.

71. Eisner took "a more broad-minded attitude toward nudity and sexuality displayed in the underground comics of the day" (Beronä 1999: 98). Beronä adds, "What has developed is a deluge of sexual content and various styles in today's comic market including, from the current generation, women's comics that has forced a male dominated audience of readers to reexamine sexuality from an entirely different perspective" (1999: 100).

72. García 2015: 135; Klingenstein 2007: 86.

73. Note that Frimme means "pious" in Yiddish (Klingenstein 2007: 83).

74. Harvey Kurtzman coined a word to refer to Eisner's use of rain—"Eisenshpritz" (Schumacher 2010: 197).

75. This example brings up an important aspect of Eisner's work. He is credited with explicitly underscoring that text reads as image in comics. Kannenberg 2001: 178 writes of "Will Eisner's dictum that 'text reads like an image'" Thus also, "lettering (hand-drawn or created with type), treated 'graphically' and in the service of the story, functions as an extension of the imagery" (Eisner 2008: 2). Although Kannenberg notes Eisner's dictum in the context of discussing Chris Ware, it is traceable to Outcault's earlier use of text in the Yellow Kid comics as well (see ch. 1). Similarly, the distinction between "visual" and "illustration" made by Eisner (Perret 2001: 126) is also another legacy of his deep considerations of comics. This idea is refined and elaborated in McCloud 1994 of course. See also visuals vs. illustrations in Postema 2013: 14.

76. Royal 2011b: 154.

77. Eisner 2006: ix; see also García 2015: 62.

78. The original text is from 1978, reprinted in Eisner 2006: xix; see also Beronä 1999: 98; who cites Eisner 1989: 6.

79. Groensteen 2007: 44–45; Postema 2013: 39; also Schumacher 2010: 197.

80. See Royal 2011c: 125; Smith 2010: 191, 193.

81. Smith 2010: 184.

82. Eisner, quoted in Schumacher 2010: 1, also 213.

83. Schumacher 2010: 235.

84. Smith 2010: 183, also 186.

85. This can be seen as an example of how "the scenes in Eisner's stories often end in a situation/tableau where the characters take an exaggerated posture at the height of the scene's action" (Smith 2010: 188).

86. See Smith 2010: 188.

87. See Smith 2010: 188, who refers here to Eisner's own language that envisions comics as frozen moments.

88. Note also Eisner's interest in "shapes made by light" (Smith 2010: 193).

89. See the connections made between (urban) modernity and melodrama in Smith 2010: 189–90.

90. Royal 2011b: 158; 153–54.

91. Eisner, quoted in Schumacher 2010: 214, original emphasis. See also Eisner's fragmented presentation of the city as noted by Smith (2010: 196), who emphasizes "stoops, doorways, drain grates, windows, alleys and so on."

92. Royal (2011c: 120) thus writes of "the social fragmentation of the modern urban landscape."

93. Here I draw from Smith 2010: 191 and Roth 2007: 468.

94. Dauber 2006: 290.

95. Smith 2010: 195. For more on how Eisner wanted to avoid accuracy, specifically, see Schumacher 2010: 214.

96. On the notion of autobiographical intimacy, see Dauber 2006: 290.

97. Denny O'Neil, quoted in Dauber 2006: 289.

98. Smith 2010: 196. See also *City People Notebook* and *Will Eisner's New York: The Big City* where Eisner talks about the impact a city has on its inhabitants (Dauber 2006: 290).

99. Dauber 2006: 291; see also Royal 2011c: 151.

100. Lewis 1995: 11; on Eisner and 1920s New York, see also García 2015: 134.

101. See Schumacher 2010: 224. Drawing on comments made by Royal 2011c: 121, the third book in particular represents an expansion, one could say treatment of a wider scale and a more expansive temporality of the urban experience.

102. See Royal 2011c: 135–36.

103. On Eisner's intermittent panel border, see Smith 2010: 195.

104. Some arguably follow more directly in his footsteps. One article explores connections with Joann Sfar's *The Rabbi's Cat* and JT Waldman's *Megillat Esther* (Roth 2007: 465).

105. See Ziegler 2013: 101.

106. Køhlert 2012: 24.

107. Ziegler 2013: 143.

108. Ziegler 2013: 143.

109. Chute 2014a: 7, 90.

110. She is one of many non-European comics artists who have "lived in Europe for extended periods of time," Beaty 2007: 19.

111. Ziegler 2013: 101; see also Gabillet 2009, 2010.

112. On Doucet's publication choices and L'Association, see Beaty 2007: 39–40, 245; Ziegler 2013: 101.

113. See the interview with Doucet in *Ladygunn*, Doucet 2010.

114. Beaty 2007: 60–61.

115. Beaty 2007: 113, 119, 131. On Spain, see also García 2015: 150.

116. Robbins 2001: 130.

117. Hatfield 2005: 41–43, 45, 61, 110–11.

118. Chute 2014a: 12.

119. In addition to those cited in this section, see the brief review by Cormier-Larose 2008; and Brogniez 2010; thesis and dissertation work includes Ziegler 2013; Wright 2006; Lealess 2006.

120. Respectively, Køhlert 2012: 24; Miller and Pratt 2004; Ziegler 2013: 38.

121. Wright 2006: 75.

122. Merino 2001.

123. Chase 2013: 213.

124. Though they do not mention Doucet by name, in their article "A Comic of Her Own: Women Writing Reading and Embodying through Comics," the conference planners introduce a special issue of *ImageTexT: Interdisciplinary Comics Studies*, whose articles focus on women comics artists (Brown and Loucks 2014).

125. See Wright 2006: 75.

126. El Rafaie 2012: 38.

127. El Rafaie 2012: 70, see also 39.

128. García 2015: 136, 162.

129. MacLeod 2012: 60.

130. See Engelmann 2010, who discusses David B. and Doucet together.

131. Sabin 1996: 211.

132. Ziegler 2013: 96.

133. On Roger Sabin and other critics, see Ziegler 2013: 139, 102; also Silverberg 2008: 11.

134. Niedzviecki 1999: 63; also, Wright 2006: 80.

135. MacLeod 2012: 70.

136. MacLeod 2012: 70.

137. Wright 2006: 79; on the depiction of sexuality in *My New York Diary* following more generally from Doucet's previous work, see Lealess 2006: 57 and MacLeod 2012: 64, incl. also 66, 70.

138. Ziegler 2013: 104.

139. Engelmann 2010: 52, see also 53.

140. Ziegler 2013: 104.

141. Ziegler 2013: 104–5, who reaffirms a statement made by Jonas Engelmann.

142. Postema 2013: 5. For instance, the example of the cockroach is iconic, connotative, and also indexical (the latter in the sense that it is evidence that mess has caused cockroaches to appear . . .).

143. Postema 2013: 6.

144. Wright 2006: 79; Chaney 2011: 132.

145. Miller and Pratt 2004.

146. Ziegler 2013: 105, citing Engelmann 2010: 52–54.

147. Miller and Pratt 2004.

148. On iconic redundancy as a fundamental property of comics art, see both Postema 2013 and Groensteen 2011.

149. Engelmann 2010: 56.

150. Postema 2013: 7. For a similar remark on the suitcases in that final scene, see MacLeod 2012: 69.

151. Merino 2001, quoted in Wright 2006: 80.

152. See Mollá Liñana 2017: 36.

153. Mollá Liñana 2017: 36.

154. See Fernández Recuero 2015; also Yanke 2016: 27 on her work with journalist Lucía Taboada; and finally De las Heras Bretín 2017.

155. De las Heras Bretín 2017: 25.

156. Pérez 2016: xxvi.

157. Cortés Navarro 2016: 368–69. Also noted by Mollá Liñana 2017: 36.

158. See Cortés Navarro 2016: 375.

159. See Crumbaugh 2009; Fraser 2014; Pavlović 2012; Richardson 2011.

160. Mollá Liñana 2017: 36.

161. My translation.

162. These are: 1 The Classic Dickhead (2013: 9), 2 The Elusive Dickhead (2013: 21), 3 The Dickhead Dickhead (2013: 27), 4 The Cultured Dickhead (2013: 53), 5 The Self-Involved Dickhead (2013: 71), 6 The Irritating Dickhead (2013: 87), 7 The Star Dickhead (2013: 99), 8 The Quarterly Dickhead (2013: 120), 9 The Asperger Dickhead (2013: 153), and 10 The Embittered Dickhead (2013: 155).

163. There is a superficial connection here with works of Spanish literature such as María de Zayas's *Desengaños amorosos*. Note that the third book published by Córcoles is coauthored with Carlos Carrero (Madrid, 1984) and appears to focus on the male hipster, *Cooltureta: La novela gráfica* (Lumen, 2014).

164. See Cortés Navarro 2016: 373.

165. Córcoles describes her own journey to the city in these terms—as a stock arrival. See Cortés Navarro 2016: 368.

166. The film has received much more attention than the comic. See, for example, Fouz-Hernández 2010; Pérez 2012; Sánchez González 2014; Sánchez Soriano 2016.

167. Pérez (2012: 180) admits the difference between the film and the comic but explores the film's commitment to queer politics. The film arguably exploits iconic/indexical references to specific spaces of the neighborhood to a much greater degree than the comic, and it ties the body appearance of its characters to the appearance of the neighborhood (Fouz-Hernández

2010: 91; see also Sánchez González 2014: 112–13). Also on the film versión, see Sánchez Soriano 2016: 177.

168. Gerling 2003: 144.

169. Gema Pérez Sánchez, in *Queer Transitions* (2007), whose chapter 5 focuses specifically on comics, provides an outstanding analysis of the sexual politics of this period as seen through cultural production.

170. Martinez and Dodge 2010: 231.

171. Gerling 2003: 143.

172. My translation from Pérez 2012: 186. He also sees the comic as taking jabs at the state and the Catholic Church.

173. Mira 2004: 604; Adams-Thies 2007: 55. See also Ayala Rubio 2006; Villaamil 2004.

174. See Mira 2004: 604–05; Fouz-Hernández 2010: 83.

175. Robbins 2011: 1.

176. Martinez and Dodge 2010: 238.

177. Martinez and Dodge 2010: 242. Adams-Thies also notes the high rents and points out the fact that the majority of its residents are heterosexual (2007: 55, 56).

178. Martinez and Dodge 2010: 234.

179. Adams-Thies 2007: 71, whose study offers interested readers a short history of the neighborhood prior to the dictatorship (2007: 61–82) and covers in separate sections the period spanning 1976–1988 (2007: 82–94), the period of 1988–1998 (2007: 94–108), and the period of 1998–2006 (2007: 108–25).

180. Martinez and Dodge 2010: 227.

181. See Sánchez González 2014: 111.

182. Martinez and Dodge 2010: 227, also 238, 245.

183. Fouz-Hernández 2010: 81.

184. "In 1954, the reform *Ley de bagos y maleantes* (Vagrancy Act) declared homosexuality illegal and men found to be practicing were sent to prisons called *gallerias de invertidos*)" (Martinez and Dodge 2010: 230). "The approval of a new constitution in the year 1978 eliminated homosexuality from a list of prosecutable offenses and a year later the Law of Social Danger ceased to be applied. Though the legal structures of the country may have eliminated homosexuality as a prosecutable offense, some social structures continued and still persecute homosexuality" (Adams-Thies 2007: 29).

185. Fouz-Hernández 2010: 81. On marriage, adoption, and legal gender information change, see also Sánchez González 2014: 111. Also, "In 2005, the National Adoption Law of 1987 was amended" and "currently same-sex couples can adopt" (Martinez and Dodge 2010: 233).

186. Giorgi 2002: 60, 62.

187. See Gaveler 2017.

188. Hayes 2015; García 2015: 63.

189. See Branwyn 2015.

190. Macdonald 2011.

191. See Macdonald 2011. Xiao 2013 also mentions Xun Lu.

192. Xiao 2013.

193. Xiao 2013. "If the concept of 'creative print' inspired Chinese woodcut artists and enthusiasts to see woodcut as a legitimate medium of self-expression distanced from the 'reproductive' form of commercial art, a series of 'woodcut novels' by Frans Masereel (1889–1972), the Flemish graphic artist, provided them an invigorating model of pictorial narrative that linked the expressive possibilities of creative woodcut with the social-democratic politics. In September 1933 Liangyou Press reprinted several of Masereel's narratives including *25 Images de la passion d'un homme* (1918). The reprints not only reflected Chinese intellectuals' fascination with Masereel's distinct graphic art, but was also inseparable from their changing perceptions

of lianhuanhua as an effective visual art form." Also, "In 1932, leading leftwing intellectuals such as Qiubai Qu advocated new lianhuanhua with revolutionary content as one important component of 'proletarian literature and art for the masses.'"

194. Xiao 2013.

195. Xiao 2013.

196. Hayes calls these characters "a young botanist and a wizened street sweeper" (Hayes 2015). Gaveler interprets these characters in a similar way: "She even conveys the content of a flashback story told by a leaf expert about the pioneering founder of the city" (Gaveler 2017).

197. Branwyn 2015.

198. Hayes 2015.

199. Gaveler 2017.

200. Barnwyn 2015.

201. Consider the comment by one reviewer that "the novel is not a simple tale of goodness and light triumphing over darkness and evil. Just as the tyranny-and victim-free community challenges dystopia norms, Ma's color motif creates a more nuanced plot struggle" (Gaveler 2017).

202. Gaveler 2017.

203. Gaveler 2017; Branwyn 2015.

204. Mumford 1970: 5; original emphasis.

CHAPTER THREE

1. Mumford 1970, 149–50, 159.

2. Mumford 1970: 149.

3. Specifically, for example, he bemoans the frequent destruction of open spaces in the city and the overly decorative nature of street planning. See Mumford 1970: 183–90.

4. Mumford 1970: ix, see also 190.

5. Mumford 1970: 375–76.

6. Mumford 1970: 376.

7. Mumford 1970: 9, 10.

8. On the close relationship between industrialization and urbanization, see Lefebvre 2007: 47, 134, 195; 2003a; 1996; see also Harvey 2009:305–07.

9. By contrast with Lefebvre's thinking, Mumford's approach is quite superficial. Mumford does not understand that the conceived space used by planners to reconfigure urban areas is itself arguably a product of the ideological fragmentation that is characteristic of bourgeois knowledge, or that the relations of capital are decisive in urban planning. See Lefebvre 2003, 1996.

10. Lefebvre 1996: 168.

11. Lefebvre: 1976: 21.

12. In *Writings on Cities*, Lefebvre writes of the "double morphology [of the city] (practico–sensible or material, on the one hand, social on the other)" (1996: 112).

13. Lefebvre 1976: 15; see also 1996: 117; 2003: 174.

14. Lefebvre 2003: 160; e.g. also Lefebvre 1969: 145.

15. Lefebvre 1976: 15.

16. Lefebvre 1996: 99.

17. Lefebvre's critique attributes a certain ignorance to urban planners, who seem not to or choose not to understand that "the urban considered as a field is not simply an empty space filled with objects" (2003: 40); urbanism as a bourgeois science ignores that "the complexity of the urban phenomenon is not that of an 'object'" (2003: 56).

18. See *The Production of Space*, Lefebvre 1991a: 33.

19. Lefebvre 1995: 116.

20. Lefebvre 2005: 135. See also in *Rhythmanalysis* Lefebvre's comments on the partition-ing of the working day (2006: 48); his assertion that capitalism "constructs and erects itself on a contempt for life and from this foundation: the body, the time of living" (2006: 51); the "death–dealing character" of capital (2006: 53); and its use of a method that is incapable of dealing with movement and merely attends to the inert, unmoving ("the negation of the," 2006: 55) body.

21. Lefebvre 1991b, 56.

22. See Lefebvre 2006: 21.

23. Herbert 2008: 163.

24. Herbert 2008: 164.

25. See Herbert 2008: 164; Mejlænder, cited in Herbert 2008: 166.

26. www.pushwagner.no; Also, he "was in 2008 invited to the Biennale of Sidney and also the Kadist Art Foundation, Paris, France."

27. Sherwin 2012.

28. See www.pushwagner.no; which notes: "In 2013 the exhibition "Pushwagner: Soft City," a retrospective of his work were exhibited at Museum Boijmans Van Beuningen, the Neth-erlands. It was previously shown in the MK Gallery, UK and Haugar Vestfold Art Museum, Norway. The exhibition received rave reviews in The Guardian, Icon Magazine and Frieze Magazine. Pushwagner is also represented in The National Museum of Art´s collection. Push-wagner has his own Gallery located at Tjuvholmen alle´10, Oslo, Norway."

29. Sherwin 2012.

30. Sherwin 2012.

31. Sherwin 2012.

32. Nygaard 2010. A passing reference to Pushwagner also appears in Lopes 2013.

33. Ware 2008: 5; also Herbert 2008: 163.

34. See Herbert 2008: 163.

35. Herbert 2008: 164.

36. On Burroughs, Herbert 2008: 164.

37. Herbert 2008: 165.

38. Ware 2008: 6.

39. Ware 2008: 6.

40. Wolk 2017: 18.

41. Therein Mumford writes: "The city in its complete sense, then, is a geographic plexus, an economic organization, an institutional process, a theater of social action, and an aesthetic symbol of collective unity. The city fosters art and is art; the city creates the theater and is the theater. It is in the city, the city as theater, that man's more purposive activities are focused, and work out, through conflicting and cooperating personalities, events, groups, into more significant culminations" (Mumford 2005: 93–94; see also Mumford 1970: 480; original from 1937, republished in 2005).

42. Raban 1974: 27; cited in Makeham 2005: 152.

43. Sherwin 2012.

44. Herbert 2008: 165; Ware 2008: 6.

45. Wolk 2017: 18.

46. See Sherwin 2012.

47. On Hogarth, Töpffer, see Kunzle 1985: 165–66, 185; Also, Ware (2008: 5) notes the "aston-ishing crowd scenes, where, if the reader looks carefully, individuals and personality quirks still survive despite the airless, inclined landscape of regulated humanity they inhabit."

48. This aligns with but goes further than one critic's comment that "the only glimmers of human subjectivity in *Soft City* appear in a handful of thought-balloons" (Herbert 2008: 165).

49. Mumford 1961: 533, 543.
50. See Mumford 1961: 486, where he also mentions "mechanical instrumentalities."
51. Ware 2008: 5.
52. Sam 2012.
53. Richir 2011: 61.
54. Lus Arana 2006: 256.
55. Lus Arana 2006: 255; see also Conte Imbert 2011: 249–50.
56. Conte Imbert 2011: 250; Lus Arana 2006: 233–34.
57. Peeters 2010: 111.
58. Lus Arana 2006: 234.
59. Diekmann 2010: 85.
60. Diekmann 2010: 86; interior quotation is from Schuiten and Peeters 1997: 6.
61. Diekmann 2010: 88.
62. Peeters 2010: 108. See also Diekmann 2010: 94.
63. Diekmann 2010: 88.
64. Diekmann 2010: 95–96.
65. Lefebvre 1995: 3.
66. See also Conte Inbert 2011: 255.
67. On instability, continual metamorphosis, see Diekmann 2010: 94.
68. Diekmann 2010: 87. Interestingly, Isabelle Doucet (2012) uses the graphic novel *Brüsel* by Schuiten and Peeters to discuss the broader architectural and urbanistic discourse surrounding the real-world city of Brussels.
69. Conte Imbert 2011: 250; Steimberg 2004; Diekmann 2010: 84.
70. Diekmann 2010: 91; Ramalhete Gomes 2007: 95.
71. Jameson 1991: 18, cited in Diekmann 2010: 84.
72. Diekmann 2010: 89, also 86; see also Eco 1990.
73. Ramalhete Gomes 2007: 88. The friendship and collaboration between the two artists leading to *Les murailles de Samaris* is documented in Peeters 2010; previous scholarship has looked at this work in terms of genre, science fiction, and architecture (e.g., Diekmann 2010; Baetens 2017), but I want to look more closely at the urban aspects, which include but are not limited to its presentation of architecture.
74. Mumford 1961: 533, 543.
75. Diekmann 2010: 87; also Ramalhete Gomes 2007: 90; De Domenico 2011: 242; Lus Arana 2006: 236.
76. De Domenico 2011: 243.
77. On Xhystos's history as a fortress, see Diekmann 2010: 89.
78. See remarks in Diekmann 2010: 91.
79. See Peeters 1998: 48–53; also Groensteen 2013: 46.
80. Lefebvre 2006: 54–55.
81. See Roeder 2014: 136–37. The McCay strip in question is *Little Nemo in Slumberland*, published Feb. 11, 1909, in the *New York Herald*. Roeder invokes Thierry Smolderen's phrase concerning the "wall paper aesthetic of the comic strip" (2003: 13) and notes Smolderen's attribution of this aesthetic's exploitation by McCay, McManus, and Opper.
82. On this theme: De Domenico 2011: 243; Ramalhete Gomes 2007: 93, 99; Diekmann 2010: 87; Schuiten and Peeters 1997: 130.
83. One critic suggests that this collapsing urban duality is a trope of the series as a whole (De Domenico 2011: 243).
84. Drawing from Harvey 1989: 24.
85. De Domenico 2011: 242.
86. See Diekmann 2010: 94.

87. Gravett 2013.

88. Gravett 2013; Watson 2009.

89. Gravett 2013; Watson 2009.

90. Watson 2009.

91. Watson 2009.

92. This list is based on Macho Stadler 2015: 93–94.

93. Stephanides 2004: 42; Lesage 2011; Lemay 2007; Carrier 2005; Bridgeman 2005.

94. "In the first book, for example, a rectangular hole the size of a panel is cut out from one of the pages, so that upon coming to this 'panel' the reader reads the panel that shows through on the next or preceding page" (Stephanides 2004: 42). Also see Gravett 2013.

95. Beaty 2007: 57.

96. Gravett 2013.

97. Watson 2009.

98. On a mathematical approach to the Acquefacques series, see the article by Macho Stadler (2015) published in the journal *Pensamiento Matemático* (Mathematical Thought).

99. Watson 2009 mentions Borges and Cervantes. Gravett 2013 writes that Mathieu's comics prompt connections with a range of additional figures, including Jorge Luis Borges, Samuel Beckett, Escher, Magritte, Tim Burton, and David Lynch.

100. Watson 2009.

101. Grove 2013: 277, see also 160, 210, where Grove similarly identifies Mathieu with the self-reflexive BD. Flinn 2013 also notes the artist's penchant for creating self-reflexive comics.

102. On Mathieu and the theme of art within art, see Picone 2013: 64.

103. The Louvre itself is not specifically mentioned in the book but is implied through the graphic novel's wordplay and Watson 2009. Also on the Louvre and Mathieu's work, see Flinn 2013; Howell 2015.

104. García 2015: 8.

105. See Beaty 1997: 29–30.

106. Stephanides 2004: 42.

107. The quote is from Suhr 2010: 239, who also mentions Simmel's "informational overload" (2010: 243).

108. Suhr 2010: 236.

109. Suhr 2010: 235.

110. The image is from Marc-Antoine Mathieu's *Dead Memory*, discussed in greater depth below and also reproduced in the analysis contained in Suhr 2010: 242.

111. The quotation is from Suhr 2010: 237. A note made by Herbert (2008: 165) and published with Pushwagner's work concerning *Soft City* might be better applied toward *Dead Memory*. The critic suggests a connection between the graphic novel's urban environment and "Constant Nieuwenhuys's designs for a stasis-free, anti-capitalist Situationist city, New Babylon (1959–1974), in which automated work would leave its citizens free to alter their environments perpetually via modular architectural elements."

112. Beaty 1997: 30.

113. See the discussion in Macho Stadler 2015: 94.

114. Toward the beginning of the comic, a group of experts philosophizes on the infinite nature of Mathieu's city: "The fact that the city is infinite doesn't bother me . . ." / "An acquaintance of mine, J. Akfak, works in surveying for the building department. He thinks the city is neither round nor square. He says geometry is irrelevant to infinity" (2003: 9).

115. Gravett 2013.

116. Suhr 2010: 232.

117. Suhr's comments on the "cadastral register" of the comic are relevant to this connection between comics and cities: "Here, the built-up structure of an urban space is transferred to a

two-dimensional map, laying the groundwork for a planned, rationalized city [. . .]. In these cadastral maps the close connection between comics and the city finds a most striking illustration: the map's grid of streets and blocks closely resembles a comics page consisting of panels in their grid of blank space, thus stressing the analogy between comics and the city in their respective rational organization" (Suhr 2010: 237).

118. Stephanides 2004: 43.

119. See the story "The Tower of Babel" by Jorge Luis Borges.

120. Suhr 2010: 231. Remember also the discussion of print in the work of Outcault (ch. 1).

121. See Castells 1990, 2000.

122. Stephanides writes of *Dead Memory* that "not only is it far from his best work, it's an outright failure," adding, "Is there anything more disappointing?" (2004: 42).

123. Stephanides ignores the value of the comic's hermeneutic openness; see 2004: 43.

124. Stephanides 2004: 43.

125. Stephanides 2004: 43.

126. Labio 2015: 321.

127. Lefebvre 1991: 169.

128. Pallister 2015; "Comics Review" 2014.

129. Popova 2014.

130. As Roger Sabin notes (1996: 189), *Cheap Novelties* was first released as a *Raw* one-shot in 1991. Katchor also published in *Escape* (Sabin 1996: 192).

131. Feldman 2009: 130. Note that "There are three volumes of Julius Knipl strips: *Cheap Novelties: The Pleasures of Urban Decay* (1991), *Julius Knipl, Real Estate Photographer* (1996); and *Julius Knipl, Real Estate Photographer: The Beauty Supply District* (2000)" (Feldman 2009: 129).

132. See Pallister 2015; Urban 2016; Langdon 2015.

133. Beaudet 2017.

134. Pallister 2015.

135. See Croonenborghs 2015 and Urban 2016: 659–60.

136. Urban 2016: 660. Because he is a French artist living in Chile (Newman 2015: MB2), he is sometimes mistakenly described as a Chilean artist (e.g., Croonenborghs 2015).

137. Urban 2016: 660.

138. Urban 2016: 660; Langdon 2015.

139. Urban 2016: 660; Langdon 2015.

140. See also Pallister 2015; Croonenborghs 2015.

141. Langdon 2015; Popova 2014. On the planner's bad qualities, see also Urban 2016: 660; Croonenborghs 2015.

142. Urban 2016: 660; Langdon 2015, who also notes the planner's creation of overpasses "too low for buses to bring New York's urban poor to his beaches."

143. "For each groundbreaking feat of structural engineering and political mobilization, there is another story told of his callous social engineering, the consequences of which reshaped the lives of New Yorkers as much as his architecture" (Langdon 2015). The graphic novel, of course, covers Moses's own life circumstances in depth. Another scholar mentions an "ambiguity both in Moses's personality and his social position: privileged for being born into a wealthy and well-established New York family and being educated at Yale and Oxford, and at the same time marginalized for being Jewish among the protestant elites of the time" (Urban 2016: 660).

144. Langdon 2015.

145. Comparing Moses to Orwell through the lens of class, unfavorably: see Pallister 2015.

146. The text box on this page reads: "And during this time, he will build almost all the highways that drum the beat of New York life: Van Wyck Expressway, Gowanus Expressway,

Clearway Expressways, Cross Bronx Expressway, Brooklyn-Queens Expressway, Long-Island Expressway" (Christin and Balez 2014: 37).

147. See Langdon 2015.

148. Remember an episode from Winsor McCay's comics discussed in chapter 1 of this book that also invokes Haussmann.

149. See Popova 2014, who quotes from Mumford's comments on Moses.

150. Popova 2014. The review from *Planning Perspectives* complicates this picture by exploring text from the last few pages of the comic. The reviewer feels that the book is also ambiguous in its presentation of Jacobs and alleges that Moses is today, in planning circles, once again revered (Urban 2016: 660–61), though I hesitate to adopt the latter view myself.

151. Popova 2014.

152. Katchor 2017; see also Katchor 2002: 4.

153. Katchor 2017.

154. On the latter, see Hague 2012: 106. On his "voluminous work," see Katchor 2017, interviewed by Aldama, who mentions his books "*Cheap Novelties: The Pleasures of Urban Decay* (1991 and reissued in 2016), *Julius Knipl, Real Estate Photographer* (1993), *The Jew of New York* (1998), *The Cardboard Valise* (2011), and *Hand-Drying in America: And Other Stories* (2013)."

155. Katchor 2017, wherein he states, "I'm the child of someone who was raised in a Yiddish-speaking Jewish culture in Eastern Europe."

156. The strips collected in Katchor's volume titled *The Jew of New York*, for example, represent the historical attempt by Mordecai Manuel Noah to establish a Jewish homeland in rural New York in the 1820s. See Glaser 2007; also Royal 2011b on Katchor and explorations of Jewish comics. Interesting for the present urban approach, Cohn 2009a: 366 mentions that critics such as Halkin 1999: 37 have seen *The Jew of New York* as being "preoccupied with 'the physical world of the city' over and above any concern with 'people.'" These strips and also those depicting the urban wanderings of "Julius Knipl, Real Estate Photographer" were both originally published in the *Jewish Daily Forward*. As Glaser 2007 points out, *The Daily Forward* is a formerly all-Yiddish publication. Gardner 2006: 790 notes that "Katchor is relatively unique among graphic novelists in publishing much of his work in such newspapers as the *New York Press* and the *Daily Forward* before expanding his narratives into book form."

157. Cited in Gardner 2006: 787.

158. Murphy 2002: 160.

159. Katchor, qtd. in Murphy 2002: 159–60, cited from an interview with Katchor published in the New Yorker on 17 March 1993.

160. See Op be Beeck 2006: 821, who discusses Katchor's work and writes that "we encounter (and generally ignore) dusty or gummed-up traces of the past in the material layers of shopfronts, sidewalks, and alienated commodities."

161. Gardner 2006: 791, citing from the text of *Cheap Novelties* itself, no. 91. This phrase itself resonates with ideas expressed in the work of Georg Simmel.

162. Murphy 2002: 159.

163. Gardner 2006: 791.

164. Katchor 2017. Elsewhere in the same interview, Katchor distances himself from the idea that he is directly observing human behavior, saying: "In this sense, while the urban experience is important, I'm not conducting urban anthropology. I'm creating a completely make-believe thing. In my work the world becomes malleable. There are no physical or economic limitations. As in dreams so too in my strips, I can do whatever I want in the fictional rebuilding of the real world."

165. Gardner 2006: 788. "The work of Ben Katchor perhaps best exemplifies the drives of the urban archaeologist of the contemporary past." Here there is explicit comparison to Walter Benjamin's "archivist of the arcades" or his "'chronicler' of history." As Gardner (2006: 789) also

notes, Katchor "grew up in an environment where the concerns of Benjamin and the Frankfurt School were especially relevant."

166. Gardner 2006: 790.

167. I refer readers to a statement by one critic who writes of the "truth that Katchor reveals, namely that the surface and actuality have little to do with each other" (Cioffi 2001: 111, regarding the artist's "Help Wanted" strip).

168. See Moore 2004: 480.

169. Op de Beeck 2006: 807.

170. Gardner (2006: 791) writes of how the characters at end of *Cheap Novelties* display a "fascination with or investment in the low-end artifacts of urban decay." Another great example is the strip in which Katchor focuses on the commercial urban circulation of weights made specifically to place on top of stacks of newspapers awaiting sale. Intriguingly, the artist has stated that the newspaper-weight manufacturers bit was entirely made up, but that he was surprised to receive a letter of thanks from someone claiming to be in that very business (from Op de Beech 2006: 824; qtd. in Weschler 1993: 64).

171. Katchor 2017.

172. Interestingly, "When *Village Voice* cancelled the strip in 1995, he set up an illuminated 'Julius Knipl Reading Box' for the new installments, on display in the window of a B&H Dairy, or outside the neighborhood Papaya King, literally putting his strips out on the streets" (Gravett 2001: 26).

173. The notion that the city is a body is developed elsewhere in Katchor's work more extensively. On this see Gregory-Guider 2005. Note also the human body vasculature imposed over panels or even maps in Katchor's work (see example from *The Jew of New York* discussed in Glaser 2007: 160). Also relevant, Aldama in Katchor 2017 notes Katchor's "twisted perspectives and oddly balanced geometric shaping of urban landscapes and disproportionate bodies, along with an oft-abundant verbal presence."

174. Gardner 2006: 789–90.

175. Cioffi 2001: 106 explores one such example in an analysis of Katchor's strip "The Padlock," which includes a "narrative line that must be inferred, because the words do not relate closely enough to the panels."

176. Cioffi 2001: 104–5.

177. See interview with Lawrence Weschler, cited in Cioffi 2001: 105.

CHAPTER FOUR

1. See chapter 2 of Van Der Hoorne (2012: 32–64), but also Lus Arana 2013.

2. Van Der Hoorne 2012: 47–48.

3. See Ascari 2014: 122; Van Der Hoorne 2012: 10.

4. This and previous quotation are from Van Der Hoorne 2012: 25.

5. See Thon and Wilde 2016 for a survey of existing criticism on mediality and materiality.

6. Hague 2014: 3, 92; McCloud 1993: 89.

7. Hague 2014: 98. Here the reference is to Roger Sabin and Constance Classen, but also important is Hatfield 2005: 58–65.

8. Hague 2014: 100–8.

9. Hague 2014: 93.

10. Swarte 2010.

11. For more on this artist, see my book *The Art of Pere Joan: Space, Landscape and Comics Form* (University of Texas Press, 2019).

12. Swarte 2012b.

13. Swarte 2012b; Stone 2016.

14. Swarte 2012b.

15. Swarte 2012b; Ware 2012b; Stone 2016.

16. In an interview, Swarte has spoken at length about Jopo (2012b). Critics have referred to Swarte's character as the "huge-quiffed schlemiel Jopo De Pojo" (Wolk 2012: 24) or alternately "shark fin-headed Jopo de Pojo" (Daley 2012: 56). Chris Ware writes that "Swarte's most well-known character, Jopo, [is] a disquieting amalgam of animated cartoon African-American stereotype and lily-white Euro-Tintin" (2012: 4).

17. Chris Ware's comment is revealing in this regard: "It's sort of hard to write an introduction for a cartoonist you can't completely read; aside from the English-language edition of 'Modern Art' and the few pages which appeared in Art Spiegelman and Françoise Mouly's *RAW* magazine in the 1980s, I've deciphered comparatively little of Joost's stories. I've read plenty of his drawings, however. Studied, copied and plagiarized them, actually" (2012: 3).

18. "Underground comics were really my thing," see more in the Peniston and Thompson interview, Swarte 2012b; also "when I started first of all I was influenced by the American underground. I was a design student and I saw that in comics there was a lot more freedom than there was at that time in the design world" (2010: 214).

19. He notes that Hergé "was very much influenced by cinematographic laws" and "was a master at framing pictures" (Swarte 2012b).

20. Swarte 2012b.

21. Swarte 2012b; see also Slessor 2004; Ware mentions the Toneelschuur in his foreword to *Is That All There Is?* (2012a: 6). See also Van Der Hoorne 2012: 12.

22. Slessor 2004: 68.

23. Swarte 2010: 209–15. He called upon Thierry Groensteen for assistance, among others.

24. Swarte 2010: 215.

25. Wolk 2012: 24. See also Wolk's 2007 book *Reading Comics*.

26. One might consider similarities between Swarte's image and the open space and leveled design captures in photos of the Toneelschuur space (Slessor 2004: 71).

27. Santiago García lists Swarte as one of the "'serious' cartoonists of the 1970s, like Crumb, Tardi and Swarte" (2015[2010]: 146). It must be noted that this seems a line lifted by García from Bart Beaty's *Unpopular Culture* (2007), where the critic remarks that the small commercial publisher "Futuropolis made its mark with the publication of works by consecrated 'serious' artists from the 1970s generation, most notably, Jacques Tardi, Joost Swarte, and Robert Crumb" (2007: 28). Beaty also names Swarte in a listing of "consecrated comic book modernists" along with Winsor McCay, George Herriman, Hugo Pratt, and Lorenzo Mattotti (2007: 70–71). Roger Sabin's *Comics, Comix & Graphic Novels* (1996) contains references to Swarte (1996: 183, 185, 189, 192).

28. Wolk 2012: 24.

29. See Hignite 2006: 256; also Kuhlman 2010: 87n2.

30. Jenkins 2013: 308; García 2015: 111, 172.

31. Beatty 2012: 135.

32. See the interview in Swarte 2012b; also Kuhlman 2010: 78, 81; Ware 2012: 6.

33. Ware 2012b: 4.

34. Ware 2012b: 5.

35. Ware 2012b: 4–5.

36. See continuing discussion Kuhlman 2010: 78–79.

37. Lefèvre 2009b: 157–58.

38. Mumford 1961: 446.

39. See Ahrens and Meteling 2010; particularly Frahm 2010: 33.

40. See, for example, the work of Fredric Jameson and David Harvey.

41. See Postema 2013: 1.

42. Chris Ware remarks, "It was not surprising for me to discover that his favorite film is Jacques Tati's exquisitely orchestrated *Playtime*" (2012: 5). One thinks, thus, of Tati's exceptionally imaginative use of cubicles in that film as an architectural device that mediates human relationships in space.

43. Groensteen 2007: 18. See also Postema on the "co-presence of images" (2013: 55), where her discussion cites Groensteen.

44. Ware 2012b: 4–5.

45. One can see this as connecting with Ware's thought that Swarte's image expresses "the innate compositional contradiction of comics made real" (Ware 2012b: 5).

46. García 2015: 154. Note that Ware was introduced to readers in Spain, for example, in the publication *Nosotros Somos los Muertos*, edited by Pere Joan and Max. Similarly, Ware's name comes up numerous times in *Unpopular Culture: Transforming the European Comic Book in the 1990s*, where Bart Beaty references his impact, European translations, and presence through exhibitions.

47. García 2015: 157.

48. García 2015: 168.

49. Hawthorne 2002: 22.

50. Beaty 2012: 11.

51. Beaty 2012: 55, 216.

52. On the density of Ware's comics, see García 2015: 154; Groensteen 2013: 48. On reading patterns and sequential narrativity/temporality, see Postema 2013: 120; also Groensteen 2013.

53. García 2015: 154.

54. Hague 2014: 54, also 165.

55. Bredehoft 2006: 869, 879.

56. Bredehoft 2006: 872.

57. Bredehoft 2006: 884.

58. To put this another way, this connection to the material world prompted by three-dimensionality becomes somewhat lost in his larger aim to explain how narration works in Ware. Consider Bredehoft's concluding sentence: "Whether through their participation in multilinear and two-dimensional narrative or through their invocation of the third spatial dimension, Ware's pages demonstrate how the unique architecture of comics enables these specific challenges to narrative linearity" (2006: 885–86).

59. Odos is composed of Darrell O'Donoghue and David O'Shea. Van Der Hoorne 2012: 57, 99–100.

60. Beaty 2012: 221.

61. See Groensteen 2013: 40; Peeters and Samson 2010: 125.

62. See the example from *Jimmy Corrigan* discussed in depth by Groensteen 2013: 49, also chosen as the cover for *Comics and Narration* in English translation by Ann Miller.

63. Ware, quoted in Raeburn 2004: 25; Raeburn's conversations with Ware took place in 2003, as he notes. See Raeburn 2004: 110n7; also Bredehoft 2006: 871; Beaty 2012: 221.

64. Beaty 2012: 221, who also mentions Ware's 2006 cover for the *New Yorker* in this same context.

65. Godbey 2010: 121.

66. Hungerford 2013: 150.

67. Gardner 2012.

68. Qtd. in Burns et al. 2014: 158.

69. Hague 2014: 25.

70. Interested readers should consult the explanation in Dittmer's acknowledgments section (2014: 501).

71. See Widiss 2013. One notes that in other scholarship this important background is mentioned only in passing (Hungerford 2013: 149) or even omitted entirely (Ghosal 2015). Ariela Freedman's article is a notable counterexample of this trend (see 2015: 339–41).

72. Dittmer 2014: 479.

73. Appropriately enough, one can see wide divergences of emphasis in the articles by Worden (2010), Godbey (2010), Freedman (2015), and Ghosal (2015), where themes of urbanity, modernity, artistic citation, narrative, race, and gender, for example, are given fluctuating weight according to the individual scholar's interests in Ware's text.

74. Worden also mentions Groensteen's notion of arthrology, discussed in the body text of this chapter, in passing in one of his endnotes (2010: 119 n. 23). Mauro 2010 also frequently draws from Walter Benjamin in his study of Ware.

75. Worden 2010: 111.

76. Godbey 2010: 123.

77. Olcayto (2012) mentions 1 and 2 explicitly but does not explicitly identify 3. Note that in British English and other English variations, "stories" in this usage could be spelled "storeys."

78. Quoted in Labio 2015: 315; originally from Spiegelman's *Breakdowns: From Maus to Now: An Anthology of Strips* (1977: np).

79. *Building Stories* has no page numbers. All the quotations used here come from the golden-spined book whose title page reads "September 23rd, 2000" or the oversized untitled hardcover, alternately published as *ACME Novelty Library* number 18. Note that the *ACME* version lacks one page included in the *Building Stories* hardcover and is slightly smaller in size.

80. I discuss disability studies approaches to comics and graphic novels, as well as the vibrant tradition of literary disability studies, in *Cognitive Disability Aesthetics* (2018). See also Quayson 2007; Mitchell and Snyder 2000. The notion of narrative prosthesis developed by Mitchell and Snyder is thus particularly apt when applied to a comics character who has a prosthetic leg.

81. Fink 2010: 192. Freedman notes, "The prosthetic leg is an important part of her characterization and emphasizes the work's focus on the partial and segmented body" (2015: 342). See also Comer 2016, who is more critical than Fink in his assessment. Relating to the argument in this chapter, Comer does, however, shed light on how Ware's use of disability refigures the materiality of embodiment at the level of reading by noting that the form of the work forces the reader "to return to his or her own body, and to return to the materiality of the 14 members that constitute *Building Stories*" (2016: 53). I do not have room here to pursue my own disability studies reading of the work, but it would most likely encapsulate the concerns of both Fink and Comer. Note that even Comer's assessment is ambivalent, closing with the words: "Its form may well save it at the end of the hermeneutic spiral, if there is an end, from any simple attack from the standpoint of disability studies. Even so, *Building Stories* is also a lesson in how even that which appears to be avant-garde in form and content will remain tainted by conventional representational politics" (2016: 57).

82. Worden discusses this relationship from a complementary point of view (2010: 111). Ghosal approaches Ware's work through the notion of "the human body" (2015: 78), or the body as a structuring agent but does not use an explicit disability frame.

83. Groensteen 2007: 21.

84. See Groensteen 2007: 21.

85. Relevant in this regard is the statement that "Ware brings into focus the extent to which gutters must be thought of as architectural attributes of the page" (Labio 2015: 337).

86. Dittmer 2014: 499.

87. Haddad 2016; see also Huston 2013.

88. Gehman 1987: F01. A 1994 Berlin exhibit devoted to Beyer is mentioned in Loss 2013.

89. Beaty 2007: 48; see also 103; Beaty talks about Beyer again in *Comics versus Art* (2012: 41, 135–36).

90. Mark Beyer's cover of *Raw* no. 6 (1984) appears in Sabin (1996: 179), along with a two-page spread of Amy and Jordan from the magazine (Sabin 1996: 180–81).

91. García 2015: 123.

92. E.g., see Tensuan 2006: 957.

93. Zaleski 2004: 64.

94. See Loss (2013), who states, "Beyer stopped publishing comics in the late 1990s and has returned to the form, so far as I know, only once."

95. This Spiegelman quotation is from Baetens and Fray (2015: 59).

96. Witek 2007: 4, see also 218.

97. Loss 2013.

98. Loss 2013 notes the exhibition's inclusion of a number of these other items, including "commercial art of *New Yorker* covers and commissioned album art and posters [. . .] his animated series *The Adventures of Thomas and Nardo.*"

99. Reported in Gehman 1987: F01.

100. Sabin 1996: 188. See similar wording in Zaleski 2004: 64.

101. Wolk 2007: 341.

102. Wolk uses the phrase "design-intensive" (2007: 341); on Art Brut, see Schneider 2016: 51; Sabin 1996: 188.

103. Wolk 2007: 54.

104. Schneider 2016: 51.

105. Simmel 2000: 150.

106. As explored in greater depth in Fraser 2015, Lefebvre expands Marx's formulation of alienation to fit the contemporary urban experience, one that has been pervaded by urban forms of capital.

107. Mautner 2016.

108. Quoted in Gehman 1987: F01. See also Zaleski 2004: 64.

109. Loss 2013.

110. See Loss 2013.

111. "The city prepares to consume you, or reflects your pleasure in consuming and then spitting your own body out onto the pavement. At least you've murdered yourself instead of letting someone else do it" (Loss 2013).

112. See Loss 2013: "Fittingly, city living killed Amy and Jordan"; "That is Beyer's other great subject, the one that extends through all of his work: death and its various animations, by which I mean how our existence becomes a living death"; "In so many of the *Amy + Jordan* comics, culture, which is epitomized by the city, turns life and death into meaningless jokes told on each other."

113. Bart Beaty mentions "City of Terror" bubble gum cards (2012: 135); as does Gehman (1987: F01), "Real cards with shards of real gum were bound with the issue." Robin Johnson 1990: 390 uses Beyer's cards as an example of *Raw*'s innovation, also calling Beyer's work "enigmatic" (1986: 24).

114. Also this card includes the lines: "See card 77 Hurt by Falling Bricks. Collect all *City of Terror* cards."

115. From Haussmannization onward, one could chart the development of the modern city as the outcome of a struggle between control from above and détournement from below. This duality is reflected in the work of De Certeau, David Harvey, and Henri Lefebvre, and relates more fundamentally to the Marxian distinction between use-value and exchange-value in the commodity form, which urban theorists have expanded to include the built environment of the city.

116. Tom Smart 2016: 26–27 speculates on the origin of the choice of the name Seth.

117. Seth discusses his reasons for leaving Toronto in an interview that forms Appendix B of Daniel Marrone's PhD thesis (2013).

118. Smart 2016: 39.

119. Smart 2016: 41, 70–71. Smart (2016: 19) also discusses the resonance between Seth's work and cartoonists of the Franco-Belgian tradition such as Yves Chaland (1957–1990), Serge Clerc (1957–), François Avril (1961–), and Philippe Dupuy (1960–) and Charles Berbérian (1959–).

120. See also Jenkins 2010, who mentions Seth's work on *Mister X*. The series also included work by Jaime Hernandez, Gilbert Hernandez, Mario Hernandez, Shane Oakley, and D'Israeli.

121. García 2015: 158. See further comments on Seth in García 2015: 158–59.

122. The quoted phrase is from Marrone 2013: 12.

123. Marrone 2013: 116.

124. As a side note, Seth has also done illustration work and designed the cover of Aimee Mann's *Lost in Space* album from 2002 (see Hignite 2006: 209).

125. On authenticity in *It's a Good Life, Ii You Don't Weaken*, see El Rafaie 2012: 175.

126. On self-reflexivity and auto-critique in *It's a Good Life, if You Don't Weaken*, see Mullins 2009. Marrone 2013 and 2016 contain compelling arguments about Seth's "drawn photographs."

127. Doane 2016: 75.

128. Smart 2016: 18; see also the interview with Seth in Marrone 2013.

129. As Rifkind argues, no one really knows the whole truth about George Sprott (2015: 226).

130. Smart 2016: 25.

131. Josephine Mills 2015 writes: "A fictional city set around the 1950s, Dominion stands in for mid-size Canadian centres of the mid-century era."

132. Seth, qtd. in Chute 2014b: 162. See also Mills 2015.

133. Qtd. in Rifkind 2015: 238; see also Ferraro 2015: 32.

134. Ferraro 2015: 49 writes about virtual flânerie in reference to Seth's work.

135. Ferraro 2015: 30.

136. Marrone 2013: 116.

137. I view this as an implicit suggestion of the analysis in Marrone 2013: 116.

138. See Rifkind 2015: 239 on photography as mediation in *George Sprott (1894–1975)*.

139. The Crown Barber Shop, run by Seth's spouse, exists in Guelph, but also in Dominion. A photograph of Seth's 3-D model of the shop appears in that volume of *Palookaville* as well.

140. Discussed above, the insights of Ian Hague are relevant, to which one can add Rifkind's own thoughts: "Comics have been defined by their materiality. They materialize exterior and interior worlds on the page and have been shaped by the materiality of the page" (Rifkind 2015: 225).

141. Rifkind 2015: 229.

142. Ferraro 2015: 34; see also Rifkind 2015: 239.

143. Rifkind 2015: 239.

144. Qtd. in Chute 2014b: 165.

145. Rifkind 2015: 238.

146. Ferraro 2015: 33. See Peter Wilkins and David N. Wright, "Dominion City as Heritage Site," November 2012, http://vimeo.com/53482605; and David N. Wright, "Two Dominions," Graphixia, November 2012. http: www.graphixia.cssgn. org/2012/11/1393-mapping-seth-dominion-city-as-heritage-site/.

147. Ferraro 2015: 33.

148. See Ferraro 2015: 43, citing Seneca 2010.

149. Seth, qtd. in Chute 2014b: 162.

150. Ferraro 2015: 45.

151. See Seth's discussions in Hignite 2006: 195, 199.

152. This word is used in Rifkind 2015: 241.

153. Seth, qtd. in Chute 2014b: 162.

154. Mills 2015.

155. These quotes come from Seth's discussion of taking photographs in Hignite 2006: 202.

156. Marín i Torné 2017: 272.

157. Balibrea 2017: 152; citing Pep Subirós (1992:3–4; 1999: 15).

158. See the discussion in Illas 2012: 61.

159. Illas 2012: 61.

160. Contributors include Roger, Rubén Pellejero, Laura i Mercedes Abad, Juan Linares, Garcés i Molina, Alfonso Font i Molina, Josep M. Beá, Mariscal, Tha i TP Bigart and Miguel Gallardo. Sponsorship was provided by the Ajuntament de Barcelona and the Caixa de Barcelona.

161. Marín i Torné 2017: 289.

162. See also Hughes 1992: 464.

163. Sobrer 2002: 212.

164. See Hughes 1992: 483 on the Dragon sculpture on the gate to Finca Güell and its connection to Catalanist identity.

165. See El Torres and Alonso Iglesias 2017: 22. For more on Gaudí and nature see Kent 2002.

166. "The hyperframe is to the page what the page is to the panel" (Groensteen 2007: 30).

167. See also Hughes 1992: 511.

168. Balibrea 2001: 191.

169. McNeill 2002: 255.

170. McNeill 2002: 256. See also Antònia Casellas 2009; Ganau 2008: 826.

171. Ganau 2008: 809, citing an interview with Gaudí published in the *Diario de Barcelona* in November of 1908.

172. Sobrer 2002: 209.

CHAPTER FIVE

1. This is the title of chapter 2 of the book *Cities of Tomorrow*. "The City of Dreadful Night" is borrowed from an 1880 work of Victorian poet James Thomson (see Hall 2014: 13).

2. "In the late 1870s, nearly all medical observers agreed on the fundamental causes of disease: heredity, climate, miasmas, immoderate lifestyles. Some diseases were considered to be contagious in some circumstances—smallpox and syphilis, for example—but even those could usually be traced to these fundamental causes. By the mid-1890s, all but a few holdouts considered living microorganisms the only true cause of infectious disease. [. . .] The practical strategies recommended for preventing disease, however, had changed little. Moderation, conformity with behavioral norms, avoidance of overcrowded living conditions, public and domestic cleanliness, containment and disposal of bodily excretions, and even the neutralization of contaminating odors with disinfectants figured as prominently among precautionary injunctions in 1900 as they did in 1875, or in 1840 for that matter" (Barnes 2006: 1).

3. See Resina 2008: 22. Cerdà's intentions were, however, sacrificed to a large degree in the implementation of the plan.

4. Simmel 2010: 104.

5. See the chapter on "Railway Accident, Railway Spine, Traumatic Neurosis" in Schivelbusch 1986: 134–49.

6. See, e.g., Mumford 1961: 448, who writes, "Urbanization increased in almost direct proportion to industrialization."

7. García 2015: 56. I include in this category those working in both comics and film. See chapter 2 of the present book in the discussion of Frans Masereel for more discussion.

8. See my discussion in Fraser 2011: 185; drawing on Sennett 2008: 204.

9. Gandy 1999: 24, who translates the quoted phrase to English directly from the work of Haussmann 1854: 53.

10. See Cerdà 1876; Fraser 2011.

11. Cerdà 1867, the English translation is from Fraser 2011: 181.

12. See Choay 1969 on regularization and the modern city.

13. Hall 2014: 39.

14. Tuan 2013: 146; on tenements, see also 149.

15. Mumford 1970: 6.

16. Lefebvre 1995: 116.

17. Jacobs 1992: 433.

18. Haywood Ferreira 2010: 283. Oesterheld also founded *Frontera*. Readers may also want to know that the first version was rewritten in 1969 with drawings by Alberto Breccia in the magazine *Gente* published by Editorial Atlántida (Fernández and Gago 2012: 120).

19. Hadis 2015.

20. On the collective or group hero, see Haywood Ferreira 2010: 291, who also remarks that these are "human and fallible" characters, as opposed to superheroes of the time (Haywood Ferreira 2010: 287); see also Di Dio 2012: 140.

21. Fredric Jameson (1987) underscores the spatial/urban significance of science fiction in general in his article "Science Fiction as a Spatial Genre," although the emphasis is on invented cityscapes and imagined worlds rather than the more complex case of modified real-world areas such as Buenos Aires (*El Eternauta*) or Montevideo (*Dengue*).

22. See Fraser and Méndez 2012: 38; drawing on Rubione 1995.

23. Hadis 2015.

24. Hadis 2015, who also relates that Oesterheld was an avid reader even as a child and singles out "Salgari, Defoe, Stevenson and Verne" as influences. Juan Caballero contextualizes the Eternaut as part of a wider trend of Argentina's domesticating of imported genres (Caballero 2015: 353).

25. On the autochthonous SF tradition, see also Haywood Ferreira 2010: 290. As Haywood Ferreira writes, Oesterheld attempted to diagnose the reasons why such a tradition had been lacking in Latin America: "Possibly it all comes down to the fact that we do not consider ourselves capable of being protagonists," Oesterheld said in an interview in 1971 (qtd. in *Oesterheld en primera persona* 41)." See also Rubione 1995: 229.

26. Bell and Molina-Gavilán 2003: 7; cited in Haywood Ferreira 2010: 282.

27. Page 2010: 45.

28. Caballero 2015: 353.

29. Qtd. in Haywood Ferreira 2010: 281, who cites Pilcher and Brooks 2005: 210.

30. Respectively: Fernández and Gago 2012: 122; Page 2010: 45–46; and an ad with the Eternaut bearing Kirchner's face—see Francescutti 2015: 27.

31. Page 2010: 45; on connections with Peronism and the Cold War, see Di Dio 2012. On the relation of the comic to the more recent politics of Néstor Kirchner and Cristina Fernández de Kirchner, see Fernández and Gago 2012.

32. See Mena 2015.

33. See Trabado Cabado 2017: 766; Fernández and Gago 2012: 121.

34. See Di Dio 2012: 132.

35. Hadis 2015, n. 1.

36. Haywood Ferreira 2010: 287.

37. See Jameson 1987.

38. Suvin 1979: 150.

39. Hadis 2015.

40. In the words of Martin Hadis 2015: "For us Argentines, seeing (and I use the verb deliberately) our city in ruins, our monuments and buildings either shattered or strangely disfigured by alien technologies, our streets blanketed by an eerie, iridescent snow, literally brought the idea of an alien invasion home, and sent shivers up our collective spine."

41. Oesterheld and Solano López 2015: 198.

42. See Fraser and Méndez 2012: 63, who cite from the Spanish edition of the comic: 175, 219, 221, 224–25, 229.

43. See Fraser and Méndez 2012, who cite from the Spanish edition of the comic: 226, 241.

44. See Fraser and Méndez 2012, who cite from the Spanish edition of the comic: 103, 122, 173–78. In the English version, see 2015: 254.

45. Di Dio 2012: 139.

46. Page 2010: 47.

47. See Groensteen 2007: 86.

48. The missiles destroy the buildings and cause fatalities, but the alien forces manage to protect themselves and what remains of the plaza with a special force field.

49. The Spanish edition's wording of the dedication—which does not appear in Humanoids' English version of the text—references Juan Salvo, the protagonist of that earlier work, and also underscores the importance of the protective suit he wore out into the streets of Buenos Aires as a way of avoiding injury caused by the radioactive snow that covered the Argentine capital in that graphic novel.

50. *Dengue* (2012: 15; 2015: 13) and *El Eternauta* (2004: 122–23).

51. See Santullo and Bergara 2015: 13.

52. Santullo and Bergara 2015: 42.

53. In an article in progress, I explore other such indicators that involve certain Spanish-to-English translation decisions.

54. Santullo and Bergara 2015: 31.

55. Santullo and Bergara 2015: 89.

56. According to Sistig (2008: 15), Tardi began his career at twenty-eight years old, yet other accounts push that age back further, noting the importance of his early work with *Pilote* and *Metal Hurlant* (see, e.g., Garrido Alarcón 2011). On *Metal Hurlant*, see also Cáceres 2008: 25.

57; Beaty 2007: 10.

58. Beaty 2007: 20.

59. See Picone 2009: 319; Beaty 2012: 135; *Raw* magazine was important for including international authors, among them Tardi. See García 2015: 123, also 172; Sabin 1996: 192.

60. See García 2015: 147.

61. See, e.g., Groensteen 2009b: 3.

62. Beaty 2007: 38.

63. Cuntz 2010: 106; Canyissà 2012: 69, 70–79; also on adaptations, see Gervais 1989, and the listing of works that appears in Canyissà 2012: 68.

64. See Ribbens 2011: 239; see also chapter 2 of Denéchère and Révillon 2008; Sabin 1996: 224.

65. Sistig 2008: 15.

66. The timing is such that it can be seen as capitalizing on political themes established with the movements of 1968. See Canyissà 2012: 68; Cáceres 2008; Molina 2007: par. #2; Helgesson 1998: 36–37; Beaty 2007: 26.

67. See Sabin 1996: 225: "Jacques Tardi also contributed to the genre with two *Nestor Burma* adventures, adaptations of private eye novels by Leo Malet, and *Adele and the Beast*, an album spoofing early twentieth-century thriller fiction, and starring a plucky heroine"; Baetens 2004: "La collaboration Tardi-Malet autour des 'Nouveaux mystères de Paris' est considérée par

beaucoup comme un des exemples les plus réussis d'une adaptation littéraire en bande dessi-née" [The Tardi–Malet authorial collaboration on the 'New mysteries of Paris' is considered to be one of the most successful adaptations of literature into comics]; on *120, rue de la Gare* and on Malet and Tardi, see Bliss 2016.

68. Canyissà 2012: 67.

69. Sistig 2008.

70. Cuntz 2010: 109; also, Canyissà 2012: 84: In its conception and execution, Tardi's serial-ized comic is thus "un homenatge a un tipus molt concret de literatura, la literatura de fulletó" [an homage to a very concrete type of literature, feuilleton literature].

71. See, for example, Canyissà 2012: 84.

72. See Todorov (1977), "The Typology of Detective Fiction," in which he outlines this literary form and theorizes on the temporal relationships between crime and investigation that may be established in the form's variations.

73. Tardi 2011, unnumbered.

74. See Vonnegut 1970; Blavatsky 1967, 1999[1888]. I thus disagree somewhat with the as-sessment of Cuntz (2010: 108), who writes that "Adèle's fantastic is the fantastic of the museum." This is not untrue, but what is missed in this interpretation is the appeal of the occult and its broader connections with European and Latin American literature and culture of the early twentieth century, not merely Theosophy but also such organizations as the Golden Dawn Society.

75. See Alary 2007: 72; Cuntz 2010: 104–5, who notes that Tardi draws on photography, nineteenth-century book illustrations, etchings, nineteenth-century stereoscopy and pan-orama, the aesthetics of postwar French black-and-white movies and film noir, and even Technicolor. On engraving and photography, see Bernard 2010: par. 2.

76. See Sécheret and Schlesser 2010: sec. #2, section #3; Molina 2007: par. #1.

77. See Molina 2007: par. #15.

78. "As for the demon of the catacombs, we will not reveal his name for he was a high-ranking official of the 3rd Republic!" Tardi 2011, unnumbered.

79. Helgesson 1998: 38.

80. Picone 2009: 317.

81. Cuntz (2010: 108) talks of a "centripetal horizontal extension" in the series but also "a vertical dimension: the city's horrible, bizarre and fantastic secrets hiding in the underground, in secret caves, tunnels and subterranean laboratories. All these criminal and/or insane subter-ranean activities are linked to creatures or idols from the past: dinosaurs, cavemen, and mum-mies coming alive, or ancient idols worshiped in gory cult rituals by members of the Parisian high society." Each of these axes of urban representation brings the artist's literary aesthetic into dialogue with visual representations such as film, photography, and engravings, resulting in what Crystel Pinçonnat has called Tardi's literary cartographies. Pinçonnat (2007: 5), who includes Tardi's comics in the general exploration of the nature of literary cartography, asks, "Dans la bande dessinée, quelle topographie parisienne un dessinateur comme Jacques Tardi construit-il?"

82. Cuntz 2010: 107–8.

83. Cuntz 2010: 109, who notes that "Paris becomes decentered" in Tardi's adaptations and collaborations.

84. Tardi 2010: 71.

85. Cuntz 2010: 108.

86. Cuntz 2010: 103–4.

87. Alary 2007: 75. It is easy to see how the Gaudí urban comic discussed in ch. 4 of this book invokes this same tradition.

88. Helgesson 1998: 37.

89. Cuntz 2010: 108, original emphasis.

90. Helgesson 1998: 37.

91. Cuntz 2010: 101.

92. Helgesson 1998: 37.

93. There are "two major aspects of Tardi's approach to the city: topography and style" (Cuntz 2010: 103). Cuntz (2010: 104) also notes "a specific Tardian atmosphere created by rain, fog, and snow, reflections of the city lights on wet pavement and blurred lines serving as a counterpoint to the tradition of *ligne claire*." On the connection with noir—Molina 2007: par #9; Sabin 1996: 188. "Jacques Tardi who produced strips best described as noir realism."

94. Cuntz 2010: 102. He references a certain principle of "topographical inflexibility" operative in Tardi's work and comments, "Those who shut their eyes to the possibilities offered by the maze of the city, callously following their daily routines and repetitive itineraries, will be punished severely."

95. Helgesson 1998: 37.

96. Helgesson 1998: 37.

97. See Groensteen (2007: 62), who cites from Jacques Samson's analysis of the frame in Tardi.

98. Blin-Rolland 2010: 30, citing from Sadoul 2000: 118. See also Bridgeman 2005: 116.

99; Vollmar 2011.

100. Lefèvre 2009b: 157–58.

101. Tardi's use of a non-actorialized narrative voice as well as actor dialogue also reinforces this approach to urban power in its duality. Groensteen 2011: 103. "In the cycle of 'Les aventures extraordinaires d'Adèle Blanc-Sec' (The Extraordinary Adventures of Adèle Blanc-Sec), Tardi used [. . .] a non-actorialized narrative voice, that of the reciter."

102. Nihei has stated in an interview, "I like reading science fiction" (Alverson 2016).

103. Montecalvo 2010: 4.

104. Pereira 2008: 78; Yegulalp 2016.

105. Galuschak 2006: 24; De Domenico 2012: 54.

106. Both from K. Johnson 2013: 194. Also Lebas 2009: 54.

107. De Domenico 2012: 45.

108. K. Johnson 2013: 190.

109. Alverson 2016.

110. De Domenico 2012: 51, discussing the work of Katsuhiro Otomo.

111. One scholar emphasizes this name as an example of the universal quality of Nihei's work (Montecalvo 2010: 13).

112. Yegulalp 2016.

113. Menelao 2005: 6; "*Blame!* Volume 1 [Review]" 2005: 40; see also Galuschak 2006: 24.

114. "*Blame!* Volume 1 [Review]" 2005: 40.

115. See Galuschak 2006: 24; K. Johnson 2013: 192.

116. The first account is given in a lengthy journal article by K. Johnson (2013: 192–93), who seems to understand the plot better than others have; the second is given in a brief plug for the graphic novel by Yegulalp 2016.

117. De Domenico 2012: 53. Also K. Johnson 2013: 192; Pereira 2008: 70; Montecalvo 2010: 4.

118. Lus Arana 2013: 57.

119. De Domenico 2012: 53–54.

120. De Domenico 2012: 53–54.

121. K. Johnson 2013: 196.

122. De Domenico 2012: 54.

123. De Domenico 2012: 54–55.

124. See Galuschak 2006: 24; also, Pereira 2008: 70.

125. Hewitt and Graham 2015: 924. The authors argue there and in their previous work that "critical social science has long prioritized a flat, planar or horizontal imaginary of urban space over a volumetric or vertical one" and call for "a 'vertical turn' in urban social science" (2015: 924, 925). On the experience of the view from above, see also Barthes 1979; Certeau 1988.

126. Hewitt and Graham 2015: 925. See also Hicks 2014 on the vertical cities of J. G. Ballard.

127. See Abbott 2007; Hewitt and Graham 2015.

128. K. Johnson 2013: 194.

129. Yegulalp 2016.

130. K. Johnson 2013: 193.

131. K. Johnson 2013: 194.

132. K. Johnson 2013: 195.

133. K. Johnson 2013: 196.

134. Mumford 1961: 533, 543.

135. K. Johnson 2013: 193.

136. De Domenico 2012: 55.

137. De Domenico 2012: 55; also, 57.

138. Beaty 2012: 84. Bernard and Carter (2004: 11) call Alan Moore "a disciple of Kurtzman's style." Adaptation is an important theme in studying Moore's work. See Krueger and Shaeffer 2011.

139. See Quiring 2010; and Bernard and Carter 2004.

140. Quiring 2010: 202.

141. See Quiring 2010; Davies 2017; also, "Alan Moore and Ian Gibson's *The Ballad of Halo Jones* [. . .] charts the adventures of an 18-year-old girl (Halo Joones) from the Hoop, a 'poverty reduction' district of New York—a giant ghetto moored off Manhattan in the Atlantic Ocean" (Little 2010: 148).

142. Hall 2014: 18.

143. Tuan 2013: 156.

144. Moore and Campbell 1994: 337–38; cited in Round 2010.

145. Quiring 2010: 204–05.

146. Ferguson 2009a: 203; Prince 2017: 254–55.

147. Bernard and Carter 2004: 21. As Locke (2009) notes, there was a preview of the comic in *Cerebus* 124 (Aardvark-Vanaheim, July 1989) prior to its appearance in *Taboo*. It was later published by Mad Love (Moore's company) and finally by Kitchen Sink. See further discussion in Locke 2009.

148. Ho 2006: 105.

149. Lukić and Parezanović 2016: 322; Prince 2017: 254.

150. Coppin 2003; Ferguson 2009b: 57–58.

151. Davies 2017: 338.

152. Locke 2009.

153. Lukić and Parezanović 2016: 322.

154. Benjamin 1985: 41, but also McDonough 2002: 101; both cited in Lukić and Parezanović 2016: 327.

155. Benjamin 1985: 41, cited in McDonough 2002: 101; McDonough 2002: 116–17.

156. Lukić and Parezanović 2016: 330.

157. Di Liddo 2009: 327; also "He [Alan Moore] claims to have established first contact with the irrational while writing the character of Dr. William Gull in *From Hell*" (Di Liddo 2009: 325).

158. Di Liddo 2009: 326; Quiring 2010: 205.

159. See Coppin 2003.

160. Barish Ali explores the violence of "'quotations' from other sources—for example, re-productions of William Hogarth plates and Blake illuminations, the depiction of the Elephant

Man, and visual allusions to factual photographs from the crime scene—that not only mirror the violence of Jack the Ripper, but also make the quoting of history itself an act of violence" (Ali 2005: 607–08); *From Hell* is "about the violence required to recreate, re-enact, and represent in a late-twentieth-century text the proto-serial-killer Jack the Ripper" (Ali 2005: 608); "Similarly, in *From Hell* the almost unbearable scene from chapter 10, which details every step of the murder committed by William Gull on November 9, 1888, and particularly pages 4 to 9, where the victim is savagely disfigured and ripped apart, draws its power from the regularity of the layout and the continuity of the angle of vision" (Groensteen 2013: 192n28).

161. Quiring 2010: 207. On this ritualized misogynistic violence see Ho 2006: 113; Lukić and Parezanović 2016: 325–26; Platz Cortsen 2014: 406; Prince 2017: 252–53.

162. In these notations, since the pages of *From Hell* are not numbered throughout, I use the chapter (e.g. 4) and the page of that chapter (e.g. 33) to form the reference 4: 33. All such references are from Moore and Campbell 2006.

163. Di Liddo 2009: 326 citing directly from Moore 2002: 7.

164. "Quotation from Di Liddo 2009: 326; see also Quiring 2010: 204; Wolfreys 2004.

165. Prince 2017: 257.

166. Di Liddo 2009: 326, who regards this as "the best known example of psychogeographical writing by Alan Moore."

167. See also Quiring 2010: 206.

168. As above, this list includes Ho 2006; Lukić and Parezanović 2016; Platz Cortsen 2014; Prince 2017; Quiring 2010.

169. The symbolic violence done to the city is reflected in the attitude—so characteristic of the flâneur—that one needs to "read" London "carefully and with respect" (4: 9).

170. See Davies 2017: 340–41.

171. Davies 2017: 352.

172. Ho 2006: 111–12, citing Lefebvre 1991: 222; Lefebvre is also mentioned in Lukić and Parezanović 2016: 329–30.

173. Tomé 2013: 64.

174. See Foster 2011: 139; also Tomé 2013: 66.

175. See Foster 2016: 107. Note that the pair has received numerous other awards, as mentioned in a master's thesis from Brazil (see Tomé 2013: 65): they received the Best Anthology Eisner Award in 2008, and the Harvey Award for Best Artist in 2009. In Brazil they received a variety of awards, including but not limited to the Angelo Agostini award for Best Scriptwriter in 2004; Best Designer in 2005 and 2006.

176. See Gruber 2017: 7.

177. "The fact that *Daytripper* was written in English [. . .] has, one speculates, nothing to do with Moon and Bá seeking entry into the geometric multilingualism that is part of Brazilian cultural history and everything to do with market opportunism" (Foster 2016: 118). Foster 2016: 118 noted that the comic "has been translated into French, Danish, Spanish, Italian, and Portuguese."

178. Foster 2016: 107. Brazilian readers, according to Foster, preferred content from elsewhere translated into Portuguese rather than original Brazilian material, and written in English, it was perhaps also an indication that readers abroad would be interested in Brazilian content (see Foster 2016: 106).

179. And as Jasmin Wrobel's chapter in the volume *Literature and Ethics in Contemporary Brazil* (2017) makes clear, the pair is "currently living and working in the US" (Wrobel 2017: 108).

180. "Moon and Bá don't really do anything in the comics that pushes the boundaries of the medium itself" (Liu 2011); cf. with the comment that "A novela gráfica *Daytripper* dos autores Fábio Moon e Gabriel Bá apresenta muitas inovações no âmbito da estética e principalmente no da narrativa, e muitas outras inovações ficam por conta do conteúdo da narrativa, ou

seja, nos elementos culturais expressos a partir dos traços de autoralidade" [The graphic novel *Daytripper* by the authors Fábio Moon and Gabriel Bá presents many innovations in the area of aesthetics and principally in that of narrative, and many other innovations can be observed in the content of the narrative, or rather, in the cultural elements expressed through traces of authorship] (Tomé 2013: 97).

181. "Moon and Bá merely adopt a white middle-class perspective, making use of exotic stereotypes (e.g., the attractive Mulatto woman who is compared to the Yoruba goddess Yemoja [. . .] The protagonist's only black friend, Jorge, goes crazy in one of the stories and brutally kills Brás" (Wrobel 2017: 109); See Foster 2016 on the penultimate item; Tomé 2013 on the last.

182. Foster 2016: 108; Liu 2011.

183. Tomé 2013: 75.

184. Liu 2011, original emphasis; cf. with Vollmar 2012: 69, who notes that the comic "achieves the almost impossible task of playing equally to the individual unit and the finished work by making each story an alternative version of the last day of Domingo's life, marking that point at a variety of locations along his possible timeline"; see also Álvarez Martínez 2016: 56.

185. Thus the graphic novel is said to be "loosely inspired by Machado de Assis's *Memórias Póstumas de Brás Cubas* (1880)" (Wrobel 2017: 109; see also Tomé 2013: 75–76, 108). It should be noted that the creators have said in an interview they were instead focused on the way the name Brás foregrounds associations with Brazil in the reader's mind. In the interview, the creators shift away from connections with Assis in their answer.

186. Tomé 2013: 72, also 95.

187. On the use of real places in the comic, see Tomé 2013: 106. The critic asserts that the choice to include Brazilian places and people is linked to its intent to appeal to Brazilian readers (Tomé 2013: 93).

188. Tomé 2013: 106.

189. Foster 2016: 110.

190. Tomé 2013: 74–75.

191. "While the listing of names suggests that Fábio Moon is responsible for the narrative and Gabriel Bá for the illustrations (Dave Stewart is credited with the coloring and Sean Konot with the lettering), collaboration is so close, so symbiotic between the two of them that this is a unified product with shared and exchanged responsibilities" (Foster 2016: 108).

192. Tomé 2013: 105–6.

193. See Gruber 2017: 7.

194. Tomé 2013: 82–83.

195. I hesitate to call Moon's approach traditional, as his paneled pages also boast some very innovative layouts.

196. Two other full-page images also foreground the theme of writerly creativity (2011: 105, 129).

197. On an analysis of the role of water in two chapters from *Daytripper*, see Scholz 2017.

198. The figure of the father—this time Brás himself as regards his son Miguel—reappears as a faint outline in another image and recalls this one (2011: 177).

REFERENCES

Abbott, Carl. 2007. "Cyberpunk Cities: Science Fiction Meets Urban Theory." *Journal of Planning Education and Research* 27: 122–31.

Abdalrahman, Kittana. 2016. "City Resilience amid Modern Urban Warfare: The Case of Nablus, Palestine." *International Planning History Society Proceedings*, 17th IPHS Conference, History-Urbanism-Resilience, Tu Delft 17–21 July. Ed. Carola Hein. Delft: Tu Delft Open. 423–32.

Abell, Catharine. 2012. "Comics and Genre." *The Art of Comics: A Philosophical Approach*. Ed. Aaron Meskin and Roy T. Cook. Foreword by Warren Ellis. London: Wiley-Blackwell. 68–84.

Adams, Paul. 2011. "A Taxonomy for Communication Geography." *Progress in Human Geography* 35: 37–57.

Adams-Thies, Brian L. 2007. "Perimeters, Performances and Perversity: The Creation and Success of a Gay Community in Madrid, Spain." PhD diss., Department of Anthropology, University of Arizona.

"African Comics by Bunmi Oloruntoba/A Bombastic Element (guest-post)." Oneafrica.org. 20 May 2010. Accessed 20 July 2018. *https://onafrica.org/2010/05/20/ohx1274349748/*.

Ahrens, Jörn, and Arno Meteling, eds. 2010. *Comics and the City: Urban Space in Print, Picture and Sequences*. London: Continuum.

Alaniz, José. 2014. *Death, Disability and the Superhero: The Silver Age and Beyond*. Jackson: University Press of Mississippi.

Alary, Viviane. 2009. "The Spanish Tebeo." *European Comic Art* 2.2: 253–76.

Alary, Viviane. 2007. "Tardi, sa marque, son soufflé." *MEI* 26: 71–88.

Alberghini, Andrea 2006. *Sequenze urbane: La Metropoli del fumetto* [Urban Sequence: The Metropolis of Comics]. Rovigo: Edizioni Delta Comics, 2006.

Aldama, Frederick Luis. 2017. "ReDrawing of Narrative Boundaries: An Introduction." *Studies in 20th & 21st Century Literature* 42.1: article 3. https://newprairiepress.org/sttcl/vol42/iss1/3/.

Ali, Barish. 2005. "The Violence of Criticism: The Mutilation and Exhibition of History in *From Hell*." *Journal of Popular Culture* 38.4: 605–31.

Álvarez Martínez, Juan Diego. 2016. "Entre viñetas y palabras: Las potencias de la novela gráfica." *Filo de palabra* 20: 53–58. Accessed 5 March 2018. http://revistasum.umanizales.edu.co/ojs/index.php/filodepalabra/article/view/1830.

Alverson, Brigid. 2016. "Blame! Game: Tsutomu Nihei on *Blame!, Knights of Sidonia,* and Viewing Japan Like an Outsider." *The B&N Sci-Fi and Fantasy Blog.* 25 August. Accessed 11 February 2018. https://www.barnesandnoble.com/blog/sci-fi-fantasy/tsutomu-nihei-on-blame-knights-of-sidonia-and-viewing-tokyo-like-an-outsider/.

Antonsen, Lasse B. 2004. "Frans Masereel: Passionate Journey." *Harvard Review* 27: 154–55.

Appadurai, Arjun. 1996. *Modernity at Large: Cultural Dimensions of Globalization*. Minneapolis: University of Minnesota Press.

Ascari, Stefano. 2014. Review of *Bricks and Balloons: Architecture in Comic Strip Form* by Mélanie Van Der Hoorne. *European Comic Art* 7.1: 120–23.

Astor, Dave. 2005. "Cartoonist Will Eisner's Newspaper Legacy." *Editor & Publisher* 138.2: 7.

Ayala Rubio, Ariadna. 2006. "Conformación y cambio de la identidad gay en España: El 'fenómeno Chueca.'" *Revista de Antropología Social* 15: 457–523.

Ayers, Edward L. 2010. "Turning toward Place, Space, and Time." *The Spatial Humanities: GIS and the Future of Scholarship*. Ed. David J. Bodenhamer, John Corrigan, and Trevor M. Harris. Bloomington: Indiana University Press. 1–13.

B., David. 2008. *Black Paths*. London: Self-Made Hero, 2011.

Baetens, Jan. 2017. "Un chronotope a personage ajoute: Le nouveau fantastique des *Cités obscures* (Schuiten-Peeters)." *Brumal: Revista de Investigación sobre lo Fantástico* 5.1: 113–25.

Baetens, Jan. 2008. "Graphic Novels: Literature without Text?" *English Language Notes, Special Issue* (Graphia: The Graphic Novel and Literary Criticism), 46.2: 77–88.

Baetens, Jan. 2004. "La main parlante." *Image & Narrative* 9: http://www.imageandnarrative.be/inarchive/performance/baetens_main.htm.

Baetens, Jan, and Hugo Fray. 2015. *The Graphic Novel: An Introduction*. Cambridge: Cambridge University Press.

Baetens, Jan, and Pascal Lefèvre. 2014a. "Texts and Images." *The French Comics Theory Reader*. Ed. Ann Miller and Bart Beaty. Leuven: Leuven University Press. 183–90.

Baetens, Jan, and Pascal Lefèvre. 2014b. "The Work and Its Surround." *French Comics Theory Reader*. Ed. Ann Miller and Bart Beaty. Leuven: Leuven University Press. 191–202.

Bainbridge, Jason. 2010. "'I Am New York'—Spider-Man, New York City and the Marvel Universe.' *Comics and the Cit: Urban Space in Print, Picture and Sequence*. Ed. Jörn Ahrens and Arno Meteling. London: Continuum. 163–79.

Balibrea, Mari Paz. 2017. *The Global Cultural Capital: Addressing the Citizen and Constructing the City in Barcelona from 1979*. New York: Palgrave Macmillan.

Balibrea, Mari Paz. 2001. "Urbanism, Culture and the Post-Industrial City: Challenging the 'Barcelona Model.'" *Journal of Spanish Cultural Studies* 2.2: 187–210.

Balzer, Jens. 2010. "'Hully Gee, I'm a Hieroglyphe'—Mobilizing the Gaze and the Invention of Comics in New York City, 1895." *Comics and the City: Urban Space in Print, Picture and Sequence*. Ed. Jörn Ahrens and Arno Meteling. New York: Continuum. 19–31.

Barker, Jesse. 2014. "Agustín Fernández Mallo's *Nocilla Project*: Seeking Affective Engagement in the World City." *Arizona Journal of Hispanic Cultural Studies* 18: 31–52.

Barnes, David S. 2006. *The Great Stink of Paris and the Nineteenth-Century Struggle against Filth and Germs*. Baltimore: Johns Hopkins University Press.

Barnett, David. 2017. "Nigeria's Comic Book Explosion: Why Lagos Is the New Gotham." *Independent* 1 October. Accessed 20 July 2018. https://www.independent.co.uk/news/long_reads/marvel-black-panther-africa-comic-books-nigeria-lagos-new-gotham-a7973871.html.

Barthes, Roland. 1979. *The Eiffel Tower and Other Mythologies*. Trans. Richard Howard. New York: Hill and Wang.

Beaty, Bart. 2012. *Comics versus Art*. Toronto: University of Toronto Press.

Beaty, Bart. 2007. *Unpopular Culture: Transforming the European Comic Book in the 1990s*. Toronto: University of Toronto Press.

Beaty, Bart. 1997. "Euro-Comics for Beginners: The Compelling Experimentation of Marc-Antoine Mathieu." *Comics Journal* 196: 29–34.

Beaudet, Gérard. 2017. University of Montreal. "URB 1118 et URB 6286 : Histoire de l'urbanisme [Course Syllabus]." http://urbanisme.umontreal.ca/fileadmin/URB/Mon-espace-info/Infos-pratiques/Syllabus_Hiver_2017/2017–01–06_URB1118_6286_BEAUDET_G__H17__S.pdf. Accessed 10 December 2017.

Becker, Stephen. 1959. *Comic Art in America: A Social History of the Funnies, the Political Cartoons, Magazine Humor, Sporting Cartoons and Animated Cartoons.* New York: Simon & Schuster.

Bell, Andrea L., and Yolanda Molina-Gavilán. 2003. "Introduction: Science Fiction in Latin America and Spain." *Cosmos Latinos: An Anthology of Science Fiction from Latin America and Spain.* Ed. Andrea L. Bell and Yolanda Molina-Gavilán. The Wesleyan Early Classics of Science Fiction. Middletown, Connecticut: Wesleyan University Press. 1–19.

Benjamin, Walter. 1985. *Charles Baudelaire: A Lyric Poet in the Era of High Capitalism.* Trans. Harry Zohn. London: Verso.

Bermejo, Victoria, ed. 1987. *Barcelona: 10 visions en historieta.* Barcelona: Editorial Complot.

Bernard, Jean-Pierre Arthur. 2010. "Le Paris de Tardi: Un XIXe siècle éternel?" *Sociétés & Représentations* 29.1: 41–49. https://www.cairn.info/revue-societes-et-representations-2010–1-page-41.htm.

Bernard, Mark, and James Bucky Carter. 2004. "Alan Moore and the Graphic Novel: Confronting the Fourth Dimension." *ImageTexT: Interdisciplinary Comics Studies* 1.2. Accessed 28 July 2017. http://www.english.ufl.edu/imagetext/archives/v1_2/carter/.

Beronä, David A. 2012. "Wordless Comics: The Imaginative Appeal of Peter Kuper's *The System.*" *Critical Approaches to Comics: Theories and Methods.* Ed. Matthew J. Smith and Randy Duncan. New York: Routledge. 17–26.

Beronä, David A. 2008. *Wordless Novels: The Original Graphic Novels.* New York: Abrams.

Beronä, David A. 2001. "Pictures Speak in Comics without Words." *The Language of Comics.* Ed. Robin Varnum and Christina T. Gibbons. Jackson: University Press of Mississippi. 19–39.

Beronä, David A. 1999. "Breaking Taboos: Sexuality in the Work of Will Eisner and the Early Wordless Novels." *International Journal of Comic Art* 1.1: 90–103.

Beyer, Mark. 2016. *Agony.* Intro. Colson Whitehead. New York: New York Review Comics.

Beyer, Mark. 2004. *Amy + Jordan.* New York: Pantheon.

Beyer, Mark. 2000 [1982]. *Dead Stories.* Sudbury, Massachusetts: Water Row Press.

Beyer, Mark. 1999. *We're Depressed.* Sudbury, Massachusetts: Water Row Press.

Beyer, Mark. 1987a. *Agony.* Ed. Art Spiegelman and Françoise Mouly. New York: Pantheon.

Beyer, Mark. 1987b [1980]. "City of Terror." *Read Yourself RAW.* Ed. Art Spiegelman and Françoise Mouly. New York: Pantheon. 40–41.

Beyer, Mark. 1980. *Death.* Self-published.

Beyer, Mark. 1978. *A Disturbing Evening, and Other Stories.* Allentown, Pennsylvania.

Beyer, Mark. 1977. *Tony Target.* Self-published.

Bindman, David. 1997. *Hogarth and His Times: Serious Comedy.* Berkeley: University of California Press.

Blackbeard, Bill. 1995. *R. F. Outcault's The Yellow Kid.* Northampton, Massachusetts: Kitchen Sink Press.

Blackmore, Tim. 1998. "McCay's McChanical Muse: Engineering Comic-Strip Dreams." *Journal of Popular Culture* 32.1: 15–38.

"*Blame!* Volume 1 [Review]." 2005. *Publishers Weekly* 252.34 (August 29): 40.

Blavatsky, Helena Petrovna. 1967. *Practical Occultism and Occultism versus the Occult Arts.* Adyar, Madras, India: Theosophical.

Blavatsky, Helena Petrovna. 1999[1888]. *The Secret Doctrine.* 2 vols. London: Theosophical. Facsimile ed. Pasadena, CA: Theosophical.

Blin-Rolland, Armelle. 2010. "Narrative Techniques in Tardi's *Le Der des ders* and *Voyage au bout de la nuit.*" *European Comic Art* 3.1: 23–36.

Bliss, Jennifer Anderson. 2016. "Visual Postmemory in Tardi's *120, rue de la Gare*." *Mosaic* 49.1 : 73–92.

Bodenhamer, David J., John Corrigan, and Trevor M. Harris, eds. 2015. *Deep Maps and Spatial Narratives*. Bloomington: Indiana University Press.

Bodenhamer, David J., John Corrigan, and Trevor M. Harris, eds. 2010. *The Spatial Humanities: GIS and the Future of Scholarship*. Bloomington: Indiana University Press.

Branwyn, Gareth. 2015. "A Graphic Novel about a Leaf: It's Better than It Sounds." *Boing Boing* 4 November. https://boingboing.net/2015/11/04/a-graphic-novel-about-a-leaf.html.

Bredehoft, Thomas A. 2006. "Comics Architecture, Multidimensionality, and Time: Chris Ware's *Jimmy Corrigan: The Smartest Kid on Earth*." *Modern Fiction Studies* 52.4: 869–90.

Bridgeman, Teresa. 2005. "Figuration and Configuration : Mapping Imaginary Worlds in BD." *The Francophone Bande Dessinée*. Ed. Charles Forsdick, Laurence Grove, and Libbie McQuillan. Amsterdam: Rodopi. 115–36.

Brogniez, Laurence. 2010. "Féminin singulier: Les desseins de moi. Julie Doucet, Dominique Goblet." *Textyles: Revue des lettres belges de langue française* 36–37: 117–38.

Brown, Jeffrey A., and Melissa Loucks. 2014. "A Comic of Her Own: Women Writing, Reading and Embodying through Comics." *ImageTexT: Interdisciplinary Comics Studies* 7.4.http://www .english.ufl.edu/imagetext/archives/v7_4/introduction.shtml.

Burns, Charles, Daniel Clowes, Seth, and Chris Ware. 2014. "Panel: Graphic Novel Forms Today." [Moderated by Hillary Chute at the Comics: Philosophy and Practice Conference on 20 May 2012]. *Critical Inquiry* 40.3: 151–68.

Caballero, Juan. 2015. "The Eternaut: Superpowers and Underdogs." In *The Eternaut* by Héctor Germán Oesterheld and Francisco Solano López. Seattle: Fantagraphics. 353–59.

Cáceres, Germán. 2008. "Paris Mayo del 68: Historias e historietas de una rebelión estudiantil." *Archipiélago* 16.60: 22–26.

Campbell, Eddie. 2004. "Comics on the Main Street of Culture." *ImageTexT: Interdisciplinary Comics Studies* 1.2. Accessed 13 February 2018. http://www.english.ufl.edu/imagetext/archives/ v1_2/campbell.

Canemaker, John. 1995. "The Kid from Hogan's Alley." *New York Times* 17 December. Accessed 1 September 2017. http://www.nytimes.com/1995/12/17/books/the-kid-from-hogan-s-alley.html.

Canyissà, Jordi. 2012. "La literatura en els còmics de Jacques Tardi: Quan la novel·la esdevé partitura i model artístic." *Ítaca: Revista de Filologia* 3: 67–96.

Caro, Robert A. 1974. *The Power Broker: Robert Moses and the Fall of New York*. New York: Knopf.

Carrier, David. 2009. "Caricature." *A Comics Studies Reader*. Ed. Jeet Heer and Kent Worcester. Jackson: University Press of Mississippi. 105–15.

Carrier, David. 2000. *The Aesthetics of Comics*. University Park: Pennsylvania State University Press. 11–25.

Carrier, Mélanie. 2005. Parcourir la cité de Marc-Antoine Mathieu: Lecture d'un artefact fictionnel. Master's thesis. L'Université Laval, French and Quebecois Literature.

Casellas, Antònia. 2009. "Barcelona's Urban Landscape: The Historical Making of a Tourist Product." *Journal of Urban History* 35.6: 815–32.

Castaldi, Simone. 2016. "A Brief History of Comics in Italy and Spain." *The Routledge Companion to Comics*. Ed. Frank Bramlett, Roy T. Cook, and Aaron Meskin. London: Routledge. 79–87.

Castells, Manuel. 2000. *The Rise of the Network Society*. 2nd ed. New York: Blackwell.

Castells, Manuel. 1990. *The Informational City: A Framework for Social Change*. Toronto: University of Toronto Press.

Certeau, Michel de. 1988. *The Practice of Everyday Life*. Berkeley: University of California Press.

Chamberland, Luc, dir. 2016. *Seth's Dominion*. Montreal: National Film Board of Canada.

Chaney, Michael A. 2011. "Animal Subjects of the Graphic Novel." *College Literature* 38.3: 129–49.

Chase, Alisia. 2013. "You Must Look at the Personal Clutter: Diaristic Indulgence, Female Adolescence, and Feminist Autobiography." *Drawing from Life: Memory and Subjectivity in Comic Art*. Ed. Jane Tolmie. Jackson: University Press of Mississippi. 207–40.

Choay, Françoise. 1969. *The Modern City: Planning in the 19th Century*. Trans. M. Hugo and G. R. Collins. New York: George Braziller.

Christin, Pierre, and Olivier Balez. 2014. *Robert Moses: The Master Builder of New York City*. London: Nobrow.

Chute, Hillary. 2014a. *Outside the Box: Interviews with Contemporary Cartoonists*. Chicago: University of Chicago Press.

Chute, Hillary. 2014b. "Panel: Graphic Novel Forms Today: Charles Burns, Daniel Clowes, Seth, Chris Ware." *Critical Inquiry* 40.3: 151–68.

Chute, Hillary. 2008. "Comics as Literature? Reading Graphic Narrative." *PMLA* 123.2: 452–65.

Cioffi, Frank L. 2001. "Disturbing Comics: The Disjunction of Word and Image in the Comics of Andrzej Mleczko, Ben Katchor, R. Crumb, and Art Spiegelman." *The Language of Comics: Word and Image*. Ed. Robin Varnum and Christina T. Gibbons. Jackson: University Press of Mississippi. 97–122.

Classen, Constance, ed. 2005. *The Book of Touch*. Oxford: Berg.

Clough, Rob. 2014. "Review: *War of Streets and Houses*." *Comics Journal* http://www.tcj.com/reviews/war-of-streets-and-houses/.

Cocola, Jim. 2011. "Putting Pablo Neruda's *Alturas de Macchu Picchu* in Its Places." *Envisioning Landscapes, Making Worlds: Geography and the Humanities*. Ed. Stephen Daniels, Dydia DeLyser, J. Nicholas Entrikin, and Douglas Richardson. Abingdon: Routledge. 143–54.Cohn, Jesse. 2009a. "'I Revive, Renew, and Re-establish': Mimetic Catastrophe in Ben Katchor's *The Jew of New York*." *Critique* 50.4: 365–76.

Cohn, Jesse. 2009b. "Mise-en-Page: A Vocabulary for Page Layouts." *Teaching the Graphic Novel*. Ed. Stephen E. Tabachnick. New York: MLA. 44–57.

Comer, Todd A. 2016. "The Hidden Architecture of Disability: Chris Ware's *Building Stories*." *Disability in Comic Books and Graphic Narratives*. Ed. Chris Foss, Jonathan Gray, and Zach Whalen. New York: Palgrave Macmillan. 44–58.

"Comics Reviews [unsigned staff author]." 2014. *Publisher's Weekly* 261.44, 3 November. Accessed 10 December 2017.

Conte Imbert, David. 2011. "El mundo de las ciudades oscuras, de Schuiten y Peeters: Una topografía de la desubicación." *Ángulo Recto: Revista de estudios sobre la ciudad como espacio plural* 3.2: 247–77. http://www.ucm.es/info/angulo/volumen/Volumen03-2/varia08.htm.

Cook, Roy T. 2012. "Why Comics Are Not Films: Metacomics and Medium-Specific Conventions." In *The Art of Comics: A Philosophical Approach*. Ed. Aaron Meskin and Roy T. Cook. Foreword by Warren Ellis. London: Wiley Blackwell. 165–87.

Coppin, Lisa. 2003. "Looking Inside Out: The Vision as Particular Gaze in *From Hell* (Aland Moore & Eddie Campbell)." *Image & Narrative: Online Magazine of the Visual Narrative* 5. Accessed 13 February 2018. http://www.imageandnarrative.be/inarchive/uncanny/lisacoppin.htm.

Córcoles, Raquel, and Marta Rabadán. 2011. *Soy de pueblo: Manual para sobrevivir en la ciudad*. 2nd ed. Barcelona: EDT.

Córcoles Moncusí, Raquel. 2013. *Los capullos no regalan flores* [Dickheads Don't Give You Flowers]. 7th ed. Barcelona: Penguin Random House Grupo Editorial, 2015.

Cormier-Larose, Catherine. 2008. "Julie Doucet: Poésie projetée, petites passoires de peaux." *Spirale* 218: 9–10.

Cortés Navarro, Isabel. 2016. "Cómo ser Moderna de Pueblo." *Cómic digital hoy: Una introducción en presente*. Ed. Pepo Pérez. Barcelona: ACDCómic. 366–75.

Cosgrove, Denis. 2011. "Prologue: Geography within the Humanities." *Envisioning Landscapes, Making Worlds: Geography and the Humanities*. Ed. Stephen Daniels, Dydia DeLyser, J. Nicholas Entrikin, and Douglas Richardson. Abingdon: Routledge. xxii–xxv.

Couperie, Pierre, Maurice C. Horn, Proto Destefanis. Edouard François, Claude Moliterni, and Gérald Gassiot-Talabot. 1968. *A History of the Comic Strip*. Trans. Eileen B. Hennessy. New York: Crown, with Musée des Arts Décoratifs/Palais du Louvre.

Crafton, Donald. 2013. "McCay and Keaton: Colligating, Conjecturing, and Conjuring." *Film History* 25.1–2: 31–44.

Crawford, Philip Charles. 2007. "'Oooh! I Must Be Dreaming!' The Delightfully Strange and Marvelous Worlds of America's Great Fantasist, Winsor McCay." *Knowledge Quest* 35.5: 58–61.

Cronon, William. 1991. *Nature's Metropolis: Chicago and the Great West*. New York: W. W. Norton.

Croonenborghs, Bart. 2015. "Robert Moses: The Master Builder of New York City by Christin and Balez Is a Solid Graphic Introduction to This Enigmatic Architect." *Broken Frontier*, March 13. Accessed 10 December 2017. http://www.brokenfrontier.com/robert-moses-pierre-christin-olivier-balez-nobrow-press-new-york-architecture/.

Crucifix, Benôit. 2017. "From Loose to Boxed Fragments and Back Again: Seriality and Archive in Chris Ware's *Building Stories*." *Journal of Graphic Novels and Comics* 9.1: 3–22.

Crumbaugh, Justin. 2009. *Destination Dictatorship: The Spectacle of Spain's Tourist Boom and the Reinvention of Difference*. Albany: State University of New York Press.

Cuntz, Michael. 2010. "Paris au Pluriel: Depictions of the French Capital in Jacques Tardi's Comic Book Writing." *Comics and the City: Urban Space in Print, Picture and Sequence*. Ed. Jörn Ahrens and Arno Meteling. New York: Continuum. 101–16.

Çelik, Zeynep. 1997. *Urban Forms and Colonial Confrontations: Algiers under French Rule*. Berkeley: University of California Press.

Daley, Matthew. 2012. "Is That All There Is?" *Broken Pencil* (Summer): 56.

Daniels, Stephen, Dydia DeLyser, J. Nicholas Entrikin, and Douglas Richardson, eds. 2011. *Envisioning Landscapes, Making Worlds: Geography and the Humanities*. London: Routledge.

Danner, Alexander, and Dan Mazur. 2014. *Comics a Global History, 1968 to the Present*. London: Thames and Hudson.

Dauber, Jeremy. 2006. "Comic Books, Tragic Stories: Will Eisner's American Jewish History." *AJS Review* 30.2: 277–304.

Davies, Dominic. 2017. "'Comics on the Main Street of Culture': Alan Moore and Eddie Campbell's *From Hell* (1999), Laura Oldfield Ford's *Savage Messiah* (2011) and the Politics of Gentrification." *Journal of Urban Cultural Studies* 4.3: 333–60.

Davis, Rocío G. 2011. "Autographics and the History of the Form: Chronicling Self and Career in Will Eisner's *Life, in Pictures* and Yoshihiro Tatsumi's *A Drifting Life*." *Biography* 34.2: 253–75.

Dear, Michael, Jim Ketchum, Sarah Luria, and Doug Richardson, eds. 2011. *GeoHumanities: Art, History, Text at the Edge of Place*. Abingdon: Routledge.

Debord, Guy. 1995. *The Society of the Spectacle*. Trans. Donald Nicholson-Smith. New York: Zone.

Debord, Guy. 1961. "Perspectives for Conscious Changes in Everyday Life." *Internationale Situationiste* 6: 20–27.

De Domenico, Michela. 2011. "Utopy and Comics Imaginary Cities." Conference Proceedings from My Ideal City: Scenarios for the European Cities of the 3rd Millennium. Edi.Sara Marini. Venezia: Università Iuav di Venezia, May 22–23. 238–46.

De Domenico, Michela. 2012. "Japanese City in Manga." *Ángulo Recto: Revista de Estúdios sobre la Ciudad como Espacio Plural* 4.2: 43–58. http://revistas.ucm.es/index.php/ANRE/article/view/40674.

Degen, Mónica. 2008. *Sensing Cities: Regenerating Public Life in Barcelona and Manchester*. London: Routledge.

De las Heras Bretín, Rut. 2017. "Dibujos en femenino plural." *El País* 18 April: 25.

Delgado Ruiz, Manuel 2007. *Sociedades movedizas: Pasos hacia una antropología de las calles*. Barcelona: Anagrama.

Delisle, Guy. 2011. *Jerusalem: Chronicles from the Holy City*. Montreal: Drawn & Quarterly.

Denéchère, Bruno, and Luc Révillon. 2008. *14–18 dans la bande dessinée: Images de la Grande Guerre de Forton à Tardi*. Turquant, France: Cheminements.

Denson, Shane, Christina Meyer, and Daniel Stein, eds. 2014. *Transnational Perspectives on Graphic Narratives: Comics at the Crossroads*. London: Bloomsbury.

Di Dio, Paula. 2012. "Aventuras éticas y epistemológicas en un viaje sin retorno: *El Eternauta* de H. G. Oesterheld y F. Solano López." *Hispanic Research Journal* 13.2: 131–48.

Diekmann, Stefanie. 2010. "Remembrance of Things to Come: François Schuiten and Benoît Peeters's *Cities of the Fantastic*." *Comics and the City: Urban Space in Print, Picture and Sequence*. Ed. Jörn Ahrens and Arno Meteling. New York: Continuum. 84–100.

Di Liddo, Annalisa. 2009. "Transcending Comics: Crossing the Boundaries of the Medium." *A Comics Studies Reader*. Ed, Jeet Heer and Kent Worcester. Jackson: University Press of Mississippi. 325–39.

Dittmer, Jason, ed. 2014. *Comic Book Geographies*. Stuttgart: Franz Steiner Verlag.

Dittmer, Jason. 2014. "Narrating Urban Assemblages—Chris Ware and *Building Stories*." *Social and Cultural Geography* 15.5: 477–503.

Doane, Alan David. 2016. Review of Seth, *Palookaville, Twenty-Two*. *World Literature Today* (March): 74–75.

Doel, Marcus. 2014. "And So. Some Comic Theory Courtesy of Chris Ware and Gilles Deleuze, amongst Others. Or, an Explication of Why Comics Is Not a Sequential Art." *Comic Book Geographies*. Ed. Jason Dittmer. Stuttgart: Franz Steiner Verlag. 161–80.

Doucet, Isabelle. 2012. "Making a City with Words: Understanding Brussels through Its Urban Heroes and Villains." *City, Culture and Society* 3: 105–16.

Doucet, Julie. 2013. *My New York Diary*. [1993–1998] 1999. 4th paperback ed. Montreal: Drawn & Quarterly.

Doucet, Julie. 2010. "Interview with Julie Doucet!" *Ladygunn*. 8 April 2010. Accessed 1 March 2011.

Doucet, Julie. 2006. Interview by Matthew Woodley. "Plotte Twists." *Montreal Mirror*. 22 June 2006. Accessed 1 March 2011.

Doucet, Julie. 1999. *The Madame Paul Affair*. Montreal: Drawn & Quarterly.

Doucet, Julie. 1998. *Changements d'adresse*. Paris: L'Association.

Doucet, Julie. 1997. *My Most Secret Desire: A Collection of Dream Stories*. Montreal: Drawn & Quarterly.

Doucet, Julie. 1996. *Ciboire de Criss!* Paris: L'Association.

Doucet, Julie. 1993. *Lève ta jambe, mon poisson est mort!* (*Lift Your Leg, My Fish Is Dead!*). Montreal: Drawn & Quarterly.

Doucet, Julie. 1991–1998. *Dirty Plotte*. Montreal: Drawn & Quarterly.

Duncan, Randy. 2012. "Image Functions: Shape and Color as Hermeneutic Images in *Asterios Polyp*." *Critical Approaches to Comics: Theories and Methods*. Ed. Matthew J. Smith and Randy Duncan. New York: Routledge. 43–54.

Eco, Umberto. 1990. "Die Welten der Science Fiction." *Über Spiegel*. Munich: DTV. 214–22.

Eisner, Will. 2008 [1985]. *Comics and Sequential Art*. New York: W. W. Norton.

Eisner, Will. 2006a [1978]. *A Contract with God and Other Tenement Stories*. New York: W. W. Norton.

Eisner, Will. 2006b [1995]. *Dropsie Avenue*. New York: W. W. Norton.

Eisner, Will. 2006c [1988]. *A Life Force*. New York: W. W. Norton.

Eisner, Will. 1996. *Graphic Storytelling and Visual Narrative*. New York: W. W. Norton.

El Refaie, Elisabeth. 2012. *Autobiographical Comics: Life Writing in Pictures*. Jackson: University Press of Mississippi.

Engelmann, Jonas. 2010. "'Picture This': Disease and Autobiographic Narration in the Graphic Novels of David B. and Julie Doucet." *Comics as a Nexus of Cultures: Essays on the Interplay of Media Disciplines and International Perspectives*. Ed. Mark Berninger, Jochen Ecke, and Gideon Haberkorn. Jefferson, NC: McFarland. 45–59.

Evans, Michael. 2009. "War and the City in the New Urban Century." *Quadrant* (1 January). https://quadrant.org.au/magazine/2009/01-02/war-and-the-city-in-the-new-urban-century/.

Feldman, Mark. 2009. "The Urban Studies of Ben Katchor." *Teaching the Graphic Novel*. Ed. Stephen E. Tabachnick. New York: MLA. 129–36.

Ferguson, Christine. 2009a. "The Graphic Novel and the Visualization of the Victorian: Teaching Alan Moore's *The League of Extraordinary Gentlemen* and *From Hell*." *Teaching the Graphic Novel*. Ed. Stephen E. Tabachnick. New York: MLA. 200–207.

Ferguson, Christine. 2009b. "Victoria-Arcana and the Misogynistic Poetics of Resistance in Iain Sinclair's *White Chapell, Scarlet Tracings* and Alan Moore's *From Hell*." *Literature Interpretation Theory* 20: 45–69.

Fernández, Laura Cristina, and Sebastian Gago. 2012. "Historia y mitos políticos: La relectura official de *El Eternauta* en la Argentina democrática." *Anagramas* 10.20: 117–28.

Fernández Recuero, Ángel L. 2015. "Paula Bonet y Raquel Córcoles: 'Siempre hemos sido explicadas desde una voz masculina en la que nosotras pintábamos poco.'" *Jot Down.es*. http://www.jotdown.es/2015/06/paula-bonet-y-raquel-corcoles-siempre-hemos-sido-explicadas-desde-una-voz-masculina-en-la-que-nosotras-pintabamos-poco/.

Ferraro, Julian. 2015. "Comics and the Architecture of Nostalgia: Seth's Dominion City." *Spatial Perspectives: Essays on Literature and Architecture*. Ed. Terri Mullholland and Nicole Sierra. New York: Peter Lang. 27–51.

Figueiredo, Sergio C. 2016. "The Rhetorical Invention of Comics: A Selection of Rodolphe Töpffer's Late Reflections on Composing Image-Text Narratives." *Image-Text: Interdisciplinary Comics Studies* 8.

Fink, Margaret. 2010. "Imaging an Idiosyncratic Belonging: Representing Disability in Chris Ware's 'Building Stories.'" *The Comics of Chris Ware: Drawing Is a Way of Thinking*. Ed. David M. Ball and Martha B. Kuhlman. Jackson: University Press of Mississippi. 191–205.

Fitch, Alex. 2017. "Gotham City and the Gothic Literary and Architectural Traditions." *Studies in Comics* 8.2: 205–25.

Flahn, Juan, dir. 2007. *Chuecatown*. Perf. Pepon Nieto, Pablo Puyol, Concha Velasco, Rosa Maria Sarda. Spain. Prod. Filmax Group, Canónigo Films.

Flinn, Margaret C. 2013. "High Comics Art: The Louvre and the Bande Dessinée." *European Comic Art* 6.2: 69–94.

Forsdick, Charles, Laurence Grove, and Libbie McQuillan, eds. 2005. *The Francophone Bande Dessinée*. Amsterdam: Rodopi.

Foster, David William. 2016. *El Eternauta, Daytripper, and Beyond: Graphic Narrative in Argentina and Brazil*. Austin: University of Texas Press.

Foster, David William. 2011. *São Paolo: Perspectives on the City and Cultural Production*. Gainesville: University Press of Florida.

Fouz-Hernández, Santiago. 2010. "Assimilation and Its Discontents: Representations of Gay Men in Spanish Cinema of the 2000s." *Revista Canadiense de Estudios Hispánicos* 35.1: 81–104.

Frahm, Ole. 2010. "Every Window Tells a Story: Remarks on the Urbanity of Early Comic Strips." *Comics and the City: Urban Space in Print, Picture and Sequence*. New York: Continuum. 32–44.

Francescutti, Pablo. 2015. "Del Eternauta al 'Nestornauta': La transformación de un icono cultural en un símbolo político." *Cuadernos de Información y Comunicación* 20: 27–43.

Fraser, Benjamin. 2018. *Cognitive Disability Aesthetics: Visual Culture: Disability Representations, and the (In)Visibility of Cognitive Difference*. Toronto: University of Toronto Press.

Fraser, Benjamin. 2016. "Comics Art and Urban Cultural Studies Method through Chris Ware's *Building Stories* (2012)." *Journal of Urban Cultural Studies* 3.3: 291–99.

Fraser, Benjamin. 2015. *Toward an Urban Cultural Studies: Henri Lefebvre and the Humanities.* New York: Palgrave.

Fraser, Benjamin. 2014a. "Urban Cultural Studies—A Manifesto [part 1]." *Journal of Urban Cultural Studies* 1.1: 3–17.

Fraser, Benjamin. 2014b. "Urban Cultural Studies—A Manifesto [part 2]." *Journal of Urban Cultural Studies* 1.3: 343–56.

Fraser, Benjamin. 2011. "Ildefons Cerdà's Scalpel: A Lefebvrian Perspective on Nineteenth-Century Urban Planning." *Catalan Review* 25: 181–200.

Fraser, Benjamin, and Claudia Méndez. 2012. "Espacio, tiempo, ciudad: La representación de Buenos Aires en *El Eternauta* (1957–59) de Héctor Germán Oesterheld." *Revista Iberoamericana* 78.238: 57–72.

Freedman, Ariela. 2015. "Chris Ware's Epiphanic Comics." *Partial Answers: Journal of Literature and the History of Ideas* 13.2: 337–58.

Gabilliet, Jean-Paul. 2010. *Of Comics and Men: A Cultural History of American Comic Books.* Trans. Bart Beaty and Nick Nguyen. Jackson: University Press of Mississippi.

Gabilliet, Jean-Paul. 2009. "Comic Art and Bande Dessinée: From the Funnies to Graphic Novel." *The Cambridge History of Canadian Literature.* Ed. Coral Ann Howells and Eva-Marie Kroller. Cambridge: Cambridge University Press. 460–77.

Gallacher, L.-A. 2011. "(Fullmetal) Alchemy: The Monstrosity of Reading Words and Pictures in Shonen Manga." *Cultural Geographies* 18: 457–83.

Galuschak, George. 2006. Review of *Blame! KLIATT Review* (January): 24.

Ganau, Joan. 2008. "Reinventing Memories: The Origin and Development of Barcelona's *Barri Gòtic*, 1880–1950." *Journal of Urban History* 34.5: 795–832.

Gandy, Matthew. 1999. "The Paris Sewers and the Rationalization of Urban Space." *Transactions of the Institute of British Geographers* ns 24: 23–44.

García, Santiago. 2015. *On the Graphic Novel.* Trans. Bruce Campbell. Jackson: University Press of Mississippi.

Gardner, Jared. 2012. "Building Stories: The Missing Manual." Public Books. Web. Accessed 2 August 2017. http://www.publicbooks.org/building-stories-the-missing-manual/.

Gardner, Jared. 2006. "Archives, Collectors, and the New Media Work of Comics." *Modern Fiction Studies* 52.4: 787–806.

Garrido Alarcón, Edmundo. 2011. "Paris como ciudad semántica en dos novelas gráficas de Jacques Tardi." *Ángulo Recto: Revista de Estudios sobre la Ciudad como Espacio Plural* 3.2: 93–117. http://www.ucm.es/info/angulo/volumen/Volumen03-2/articulos06.htm.

Gatewood, Frances, and John Jennings, eds. 2015. *The Blacker the Ink: Constructions of Black Identity in Comics and Sequential Art.* Jackson: University Press of Mississippi.

Gaveler, Chris. 2017. "The Wordless Protagonist of 'Leaf' Doesn't Save the World—Just Improves It." *Popmatters* 14 Aug. https://www.popmatters.com/leaf-daishu-ma-wordless-protagonist-doesnt-save-world-just-improves-it-2495384653.html.

Gehman, Geoff. 1987. "Mark Beyer's Comics Buoyed by the Bizarre Emerging Artists of the Lehigh Valley." *Morning Call* (1 February): F01. Accessed 28 July 2017. https://search.proquest.com/docview/392231210?pq-origsite=summon.

Gerling, David Ross. 2003. "Chuecatown." *World Literature Today* 77.3–4: 143–44.

Gervais, Bertrand. 1989. "Du geste à l'action, du texte à l'image." *Mieux vaut Tardi.* Quebec: Analogon. 7–23.

Ghosal, Torsa. 2015. "Books with Bodies: Narrative Progression in Chris Ware's *Building Stories.*" *StoryWorlds: A Journal of Narrative Studies* 7.1: 75–99.

Giaufret, Anna. 2016a. "Bande dessinée et espace urbain montréalais: Quelques repères." *Espaces réels et imaginaires au Québec et en Acadie: Enjeux culturels, linguistiques et géographiques*. Ed. Dino Gavinelle and Chiara Molinari. Milano: Lingue Culture Mediazioni. 105–26.

Giaufret, Anna. 2016b. "Les jeunes auteurs francophones de bandes dessinées à Montréal: Pratiques, réseaux, représentations." *Alternative Francophone* 1.9: 108–19.

Giorgi, Gabriel. 2002. "Madrid *en Tránsito*: Travelers, Visibility, and Gay Identity." *GLQ: A Journal of Lesbian and Gay Studies* 8.1–2: 57–79.

Glaser, Jennifer. 2007. "An Imaginary Ararat: Jewish Bodies and Jewish Homelands in Ben Katchor's *The Jew of New York*." *Melus* 32.3: 153–73.

Godbey, Matt. 2010. "Chris Ware's 'Building Stories,' Gentrification, and the Lives of/in Houses." In *Comics of Chris Ware*. Ed. David N. Ball and Martha B. Kuhlman. Jackson: University Press of Mississippi. 121–32.

Goodyear, Sarah. 2014. "An Illustrated History of All the Ways Urban Environments Can Control Us." *CityLab*. https://www.citylab.com/design/2014/03/illustrated-history-all-ways-urban-environments-can-control-us/8688/.

Graham, Stephen. 2011. *Cities under Siege: The New Military Urbanism*. London: Verso.

Gravett, Paul. 2013. "Marc-Antoine Mathieu: Prisoner of Dreams." *Paul Gravett Blog*. http://www.paulgravett.com/articles/article/marc_antoine_mathieu. Accessed 28 November 2017.

Gravett, Paul. 2001. "After Maus." *Jewish Quarterly* 48.4: 21–28.

Gregory-Guider, Christopher C. 2005. "Sinclair's *Rodinsky's Room* and the Art of Autobiography." *Literary London: Interdisciplinary Studies in the Representation of London* 3.2. http://www.literarylondon.org/london-journal/september2005/guider.html. Accessed 12 October 2017.

Groß, Florian. 2014. "Lost in Translation: Narratives of Transcultural Displacement in the Wordless Graphic Novel." *Transnational Perspectives on Graphic Narratives: Comics at the Crossroads*. Ed. Shane Denson, Christina Meyer, and Daniel Stein. London: Bloomsbury. 197–210.

Groensteen, Thierry. 2014. "Definitions (2012)." *The French Comics Theory Reader*. Ed. Ann Miller and Bart Beaty. Leuven: Leuven University Press. 93–114.

Groensteen, Thierry. 2013 [2011]. *Comics and Narration*. Trans. Ann Miller. Jackson: University Press of Mississippi.

Groensteen, Thierry. 2009a. "The Impossible Definition." *A Comics Studies Reader*. Ed. Jeet Heer and Kent Worcester. Jackson: University Press of Mississippi. 124–31.

Groensteen, Thierry. 2009b. "Why Are Comics Still in Search of Cultural Legitimization?" *A Comics Studies Reader*. Ed. Jeet Heer and Kent Worcester. Jackson: University Press of Mississippi. 3–11.

Groensteen, Thierry. 2008. "A Few Words about *The System of Comics* and More . . ." *European Comic Art* 1.2: 87–93.

Groensteen, Thierry. 2007 [1999]. *The System of Comics*. Trans. Bart Beaty and Nick Nguyen. Jackson: University Press of Mississippi.

Groensteen, Thierry. 1998. "Töpffer: The Originator of the Modern Comic Strip." *Forging a New Medium: The Comic Strip in the Nineteenth Century*. Ed. Pascal Lefèvre and Charles Dierick. Brussels: VUBPress. 105–14.

Grove, Laurence. 2013. *Comics in French: The European Bande Dessinée in Context*. New York: Berghahn.

Grove, Laurence. 2005. "BD Theory before the Term 'BD' Existed.'" *The Francophone Bande Dessinée*. Ed. Charles Forsdick, Laurence Grove, and Libbie McQuillan. Amsterdam: Rodopi. 39–49.

Grove, Laurence, Mark McKinney, and Ann Miller. 2009. "Introduction: The Nineteenth Century and Beyond." *European Comic Art* 2.2: v–viii.

Grove, Laurence, Mark McKinney, Ann Miller, and Hugo Frey. 2009. "Introduction: Caricature." *European Comic Art* 2.1: v–vii.

Gruber, Phellip William de Paula. 2017. "'Você não precisa mais de mim'—O ser, o pai e a morte em *Daytripper*." Master's thesis, Department of Language Studies, State University of Ponta Grossa.

Guyon, Lionel, François Mutterer, Vincent Lunel. 1985. *Attention travaux! Architectures de bande dessinée*. Paris: Institut Français d'Architecture.

Haddad, Vincent. 2016. "Chris Ware's *Building Stories* as Deleuzian Fabulation, or How and Why to Read Comics Affectively." *ImageTexT: Interdisciplinary Comics Studies* 8.4. Accessed 11 August 2017. imagetext.english.ufl.edu/archives/v8_4/haddad/.

Hadis, Martin. 2015. "The Navigator of Eternity." In *The Eternaut*. By Héctor Germán Oesterheld and Francisco Solano López. Seattle: Fantagraphics. no pag.

Hague, Ian. 2014. *Comics and the Senses: A Multisensory Approach to Comics and Graphic Novels*. New York: Routledge.

Hague, Ian. 2012. "Beyond the Visual: The Roles of the Senses in Contemporary Comics." *Scandinavian Journal of Comic Art* 1.1: 98–110.

Halkin, Hillel. 1999. "Nothing Is Lost." *New Republic* 1 February: 36–37.

Hall, Peter. 2014. *Cities of Tomorrow: An Intellectual History of Urban Planning and Design since 1880*. 4th ed. Malden, MA; Oxford, West Sussex, U: Wiley-Blackwell.

Hannoosh, Michele. 1992. *Baudelaire and Caricature: From the Comic to an Art of Modernity*. University Park: Pennsylvania State University Press.

Harvey, David. 2012. *Rebel Cities*. London: Verso.

Harvey, David. 2009 [1973]. *Social Justice and the City*. Athens: University of Georgia Press.

Harvey, David. 2006. *Paris, Capital of Modernity*. London: Routledge.

Harvey, David. 2003. "City Future in City Past: Balzac's Cartographic Imagination." *After-Images of the City*. Ed. Joan Ramon Resina and Dieter Ingenschay. Ithaca: Cornell University Press. 23–48.

Harvey, David. 2001. *Spaces of Capital: Towards a Critical Geography*. New York: Routledge.

Harvey, David. 2000. *Spaces of Hope*. Berkeley: University of California Press.

Harvey, David. 1998. "What's Green and Makes the Environment Go Round?" *The Cultures of Globalization*. Ed. Fredric Jameson and Masao Miyoshi. Durham: Duke University Press. 327–55.

Harvey, David. 1996. *Justice, Nature and the Geography of Difference*. London: Blackwell.

Harvey, David. 1990. *The Condition of Postmodernity*. Cambridge, MA: Blackwell.

Harvey, David. 1989. *The Urban Experience*. Baltimore: Johns Hopkins University Press.

Harvey, Robert. 1994. *The Art of the Funnies: An Aesthetic History*. Jackson: University Press of Mississippi.

Hatfield, Charles. 2009. "An Art of Tensions." *A Comics Studies Reader*. Ed. Jeet Heer and Kent Worcester. Jackson: University Press of Mississippi. 132–48.

Hatfield, Charles. 2005. *Alternative Comics: An Emerging Literature*. Jackson: University Press of Mississippi.

Haussmann, Georges Eugène. 1854. *Mémoire sur les eaux de Paris, présenté a la commission municipale par m le préfet de la Seine*. Paris: Vinchon.

Hawthorne, Christopher. 2002. "Hard Ware." *Print* 56.4: 22.

Hayes, Summer. 2015. "Leaf." *Booklist Chicago* 112.4: 36.

Haywood Ferreira, Rachel. 2010. "*Más Allá, El Eternauta*, and the Dawn of the Golden Age of Latin American Science Fiction (1953–59)." *Extrapolation* 51.2: 281–303.

Head, Glenn. 2015. *Chicago*. Seattle: Fantagraphics.

Heer, Jeet. 2006. "Little Nemo in Comicsland." *Virginia Quarterly Review* 82.2: 104–21.

Heer, Jeet, and Kent Worchester, eds. 2009. *A Comics Studies Reader*. Jackson: University Press of Mississippi.

Helgesson, Stefan. 2015. "Reading the Cityscape." *Nordic Journal of Architectural Research* 11.1–2: 35–39.

Helgesson, Stefan. 1998. "Reading the Cityscape: Between Theory and Practice: The Place of Private Discourse in the Public Sphere." *Nordish Arkitekturforskning* 1–2: 35–39.

Herbert, Martin. 2008. "Afterword." *Soft City*. Hariton Pushwagner (Terje Brofos). 1969–75. New York: New York Review Comics. 163–66.

Hewitt, Lucy, and Stephen Graham. 2015. "Vertical Cities: Representations of Urban Verticality in 20th-Century Science Fiction Literature." *Urban Studies* 52.5: 923–37.

Hick, Darren Hudson. 2012. "The Language of Comics." *The Art of Comics: Philosophical Approach.* Ed Aaron Meskin and Roy T. Cook. Foreword by Warren Ellis. London: Wiley Blackwell. 125–44.

Hicks, Jeff. 2014. "Residential Differentiation in the Vertical Cities of J. G. Ballard and Robert Silverberg." *Marxism and Urban Culture.* Ed Benjamin Fraser. Lanham, MD: Lexington Books. 137–58.

Hignite, Todd. 2006. *In the Studio: Visits with Contemporary Cartoonists.* New Haven: Yale University Press.

Ho, Elizabeth. 2006. "Postimperial Landscapes: 'Psychogeography' and Englishness in Alan Moore's Graphic Novel *From Hell*: A Melodrama in Sixteen Parts." *Cultural Critique* 63: 99–121.

Hogarth, William. 1955 [1753]. *The Analysis of Beauty.* Ed Joseph Burke. Oxford: Clarendon Press.

Hogarth, William. 1731–32. *A Harlot's Progress.* Engravings.

Holbo, John. 2012. "Redefining Comics." *The Art of Comics: A Philosophical Approach.* Ed. Aaron Meskin and Roy T. Cook. Foreword by Warren Ellis. London: Wiley Blackwell. 3–30.

Holmes, Amanda. 2010. "Modern Heroics: The Flâneur in Adolfo Bioy Casares's *El sueño de los héroes.*" *Circulation and the City: Essays on Urban Culture.* Ed. Alexandra Boutros and Will Straw. Montreal: McGill-Queen's University Press. 240–57.

Hones, Sheila. 2011. "Literary Geography: The Novel as a Spatial Event." *Envisioning Landscapes, Making Worlds: Geography and the Humanities.* Ed. Stephen Daniels, Dydia DeLyser, J. Nicholas Entrikin, and Douglas Richardson. Abingdon: Routledge. 247–55.

Howell, David R. 2015. "The Mystery of Museums in Graphic Novels." *Journal of Graphic Novels and Comics* 6.4: 419–29.

Hughes, Robert. 1992. *Barcelona.* New York: Knopf.

Hungerford, Amy. 2013. "Fiction in Review: Chris Ware." *Yale Review* 101.4: 148–59.

Hunt, Nancy Rose. 2002. "Tintin and the Interruptions of Congolese Comics." *Images and Empires: Visually in Colonial and Postcolonial Africa.* Ed. Paul S. Landau and Deborah D. Kaspin. Berkeley: University of California Press. 86–119.

Huston, Shawn. 2013. "The Conscious Materiality of Chris Ware's *Building Stories.*" *PopMatters.* January 22. Accessed August 2017.

Illas, Edgar. 2012. *Thinking Barcelona: Ideologies of a Global City.* Liverpool: Liverpool University Press.

Inge, M. Thomas. 1990. *Comics as Culture.* Jackson: University Press of Mississippi.

Jacobs, Jane. 199 [1961]. *The Death and Life of Great American Cities.* New York: Vintage.

Jacobs, Jane. 1984. *Cities and the Wealth of Nations: Principles of Economic Life.* New York: Random House.

Jacobs, Jane. 1969. *The Economy of Cities.* New York: Vintage.

Jameson, Fredric. 1991. *Postmodernism, or The Cultural Logic of Late Capitalism.* Durham: Duke University Press.

Jameson, Fredric. 1987. "Science Fiction as a Spatial Genre: Generic Discontinuities and the Problem of Figuration in Vonda McIntyre's *The Exile Waiting.*" *Science Fiction Studies* 14: 44–59.

Jang, Wonho, and Jung Eun Song. 2017. "Webtoon as a New Korean Wave in the Process of Glocalization." *Kritika Kultura* 29: 168–87.

Jenkins, Henry. 2013. "Archival, Ephemeral, and Residual: The Functions of Early Comics in Art Spiegelman's *In the Shadow of No Towers.*" *From Comic Strips to Graphic Novels: Contributions to the Theory and History of Graphic Narrative.* Ed. Daniel Stein and Jan-Nöel Thon. Berlin: De Gruyter. 301–22.

Jenkins, Henry. 2010. "'The Tomorrow That Never Was': Retrofuturism in the Comics of Dean Motter." *Comics and the City: Urban Space in Print, Picture and Sequence.* Ed. Jörn Ahrens and Arno Meteling. London: Continuum. 63–83.

Joan, Pere, and Emilio Manzano. 1987. "Un cocodril a l'Eixample [A Crocodile in the Eixample]. *Barcelona: 10 visions en historieta*. Barcelona: Editorial Complot; Ajuntament de Barcelona; Caixa de Barcelona. 12–15.

Johnson, Derek. 2016. "How Comic Books Travel: Brick-and-Mortar Stores, Digital Networks, and Global Flows." *Locating Emerging Media*. Ed. Germaine R. Halegoua and Ben Aslinger. New York: Routledge. 106–22.

Johnson, Keith Leslie. 2013. "Nihei Tsutomu and the Poetics of Space: Notes toward a Cyberpunk Ecology." *Southeast Review of Asian Studies* 35: 190–203.

Johnson, Robin. 1990. "Comic Books for Grown-ups." *Reference Librarian* 12.27–28: 379–96.

Johnson, Robin. 1986. "Comic-Book Fan Magazine: Watching Pop Turn into Art." *Serials Review* 12.1: 17–26.

Kannenberg, Gene Jr. 2001. "The Comics of Chris Ware: Text, Image and Visual Narrative Strategies." *The Language of Comics: Word and Image*. Ed. Robin Varnum and Christina T. Gibbons. Jackson: University Press of Mississippi. 174–97.

Katchor, Ben. 2017. "An Unexpected Life through Comics: An Interview with Ben Katchor." Interview by Frederick Luis Aldama. *Studies in 20th & 21st Century Literature* 42.1: article 11.

Katchor, Ben. 2016 [1991]. *Cheap Novelties: The Pleasures of Urban Decay*. Montreal: Drawn & Quarterly.

Katchor, Ben. 2013. *Hand-Drying in America: And Other Stories*. Pantheon Books.

Katchor, Ben. 2011. *The Cardboard Valise*. Pantheon Books.

Katchor, Ben. 2002. "Hotel & Farm." *Art Journal* 61.3: 4–5, 28–31, 40–45, 74–77, 88–91.

Katchor, Ben. 2000. *Julius Knipl, Real Estate Photographer: The Beauty Supply District*. Pantheon Books.

Katchor, Ben. 1998. *The Jew of New York*. Pantheon Books.

Katchor, Ben. 1996. *Julius Knipl, Real Estate Photographer*. Little, Brown.

Kelp-Stebbins, Katherine. 2018. "Global Comics: Two Women's Texts and a Critique of Cultural Imperialism." *Feminist Media Histories* 4.3: 135–56.

Kelp-Stebbins, Katherine. 2014. "Graphic Positioning Systems: Global Comics, Radical Literacies." Dissertation, Comparative Literature. University of California, Santa Barbara.

Kent, Conrad. 2002. "From Pleasure Gardens to Places Dures: Continuity and Change in Barcelona's Public Spaces." *Arizona Journal of Hispanic Cultural Studies* 6: 221–44.

Klingenstein, Susanne. 2007. "The Long Roots of Will Eisner's Quarrel with God." *Studies in American Jewish Literature* 26: 81–88.

Knabb, Ken, ed. 2006. *Situationist International Anthology*. Berkeley: Bureau of Public Secrets.

Knight, Stephen. 1977. *Jack the Ripper: The Final Solution*. London: Grafton Books.

Køhlert, Frederik Byrn. 2012. "Female Grotesques: Carnivalesque Subversion in the Comics of Julie Doucet." *Journal of Graphic Novels and Comics* 3.1: 19–38.

Krueger, Rex, and Katherine Shaeffer. 2011. "Introduction: Alan Moore and Adaptation." *ImageTexT: Interdisciplinary Comics Studies* 5.4. Accessed 28 July 2017. http://www.english.ufl.edu/imagetext/archives/v5_4/introduction.shtml.

Kuhlman, Martha B. 2010. "In the Comics Workshop: Chris Ware and the Oubapo." *The Comics of Chris Ware: Drawing Is a Way of Thinking*. Ed. David Ball and Martha Kuhlman. Jackson: University Press of Mississippi. 78–89.

Kunzle, David. 2014. "Review of Groensteen, Thierry, *M. Töpffer invente la bande dessinée*." *European Comic Art* 7.2: 115–20.

Kunzle, David. 2009a. "The Gourary Töpffer Manuscript of *Monsieur Jabot*: A Question of Authenticity." *European Comic Art* 2.2: 173–203.

Kunzle, David. 2009b. "Rodolphe Töpffer's Aesthetic Revolution." *A Comics Studies Reader*. Ed. Jeet Heer and Kent Worcester. Jackson: University Press of Mississippi. 17–24.

Kunzle, David. 2007. *Father of the Comic Strip*: *Rodolphe Töpffer*. Jackson: University Press of Mississippi.

Kunzle, David. 1990. *The History of the Comic Strip: The Nineteenth Century*. Berkeley: University of California Press.

Kunzle, David. 1985. "Goethe and Caricature: From Hogarth to Töpffer." *Journal of the Warburg and Courtauld Institutes* 48: 164–88.

Kunzle, David. 1973. *The Early Comic Strip: Narrative Strips and Picture Stories in the European Broadsheet from c. 1450 to 1825*. Berkeley: University of California Press.

Kuper, Peter. 2014. *The System*. 1996. Oakland: PM Press.

Kuper, Peter. 2008. "Introduction: Speechless." *Wordless Books: The Original Graphic Novels*. By David A. Beronä. New York: Abrams. 7–9.

Labio, Catherine. 2015. "The Architecture of Comics." *Critical Inquiry* 41: 312–43.

Lai, Jimenez. 2012. *Citizens of No Place*: *An Architectural Graphic Novel*. New York: Princeton Architectural Press.

Lambert, Léopold. 2012. "Abject Matter: The Barricade and the Tunnel." *Log* 25: 93–99.

Langdon, David. 2015. "Robert Moses: The Master Builder of New York City/Pierre Christin and Olivier Balez." ArchDaily, 31 August. Accessed 10 December 2017.

Lanier, Chris. 2007. "The 'Woodcut Novel.'" *World Literature Today* 81.2: 15.

Latham, Alan, and Derek McCormack. 2004. "Moving Cities: Rethinking the Materialities of Urban Geographies." *Progress in Human Geography* 28.6: 701–24.

Lazaga, Pedro, dir. 1965. *La ciudad no es para mí*. Pedro Masó, P.C.

Lealess, Jacqueline. 2006. "Making a Spectacle: The Comics of Debbie Drechsler, Phoebe Gloeckner, Diane Dimassa, and Julie Doucet." Master's thesis, Theory, Culture, Politics, Trent University.

Lebas, Frédéric. 2009. "Le manga, mode exploratoire des <<mondes (fictionnels) flottants>>." *Sociétés* 4.106 : 45–56.

Lefebvre, Henri. 2006. *Rhythmanalysis*. Trans. Stuart Elden and Gerald Moore. London: Continuum.

Lefebvre, Henri. 2003 [1970]. *The Urban Revolution*. Trans. Robert Bononno. Minneapolis: University of Minnesota Press.

Lefebvre, Henri. 1996. *The Right to the City. Writings on Cities*. Ed. and trans. E. Kofman and E. Lebas. Oxford: Blackwell. 63–181.

Lefebvre, Henri. 1995. *Introduction to Modernity*. Trans. John Moore. London: Verso.

Lefebvre, Henri. 1991a [1974]. *The Production of Space*. Trans. Donald Nicholson-Smith. Oxford: Blackwell.

Lefebvre, Henri. 1991b [1947]. *Critique of Everyday Life, Vol. 1*. Trans. John Moore. London: Verso.

Lefebvre, Henri. 1988. "Toward a Leftist Cultural Politics: Remarks Occasioned by the Centenary of Marx's Death." Trans. David Reifman.*Marxism and the Interpretation of Culture*. Ed. Lawrence Grossberg and Cary Nelson. Chicago: University of Illinois Press. 75–88.

Lefebvre, Henri. 1976. *The Survival of Capitalism*: *Reproduction of the Relations of Production*. Trans. Frank Bryant. New York: St. Martin's Press.

Lefebvre, Henri. 1969. *The Explosion: Marxism and the French Upheaval*. New York: Monthly Review Press.

Lefèvre, Pascal. 2014. "European Comics." *Comics through Time: A History of Icons, Idols and Ideas*. Vol. 1. Ed. M. Keith Booker. Santa Barbara: Greenwood. 127–31.

Lefèvre, Pascal. 2012. "Mise en Scène and Framing: Visual Storytelling in *Lone Wolf and Cub*." *Critical Approaches to Comics: Theories and Methods*. Ed. Matthew J. Smith and Randy Duncan. New York: Routledge. 71–83.

Lefèvre, Pascal. 2009a. "The Conquest of Space: Evolution of Panel Arrangements and Page Layouts in Early Comics Published in Belgium (1880–1929)." *European Comic Art* 2.2: 227–52.

Lefèvre, Pascal. 2009b. "The Construction of Space in Comics." *A Comics Studies Reader.* Ed. by Jeet Heer and Kent Worcester. Jackson: University Press of Mississippi. 157–62.

Lefèvre, Pascal. 2000. "The Importance of Being 'Published': A Comparative Study of Different Comics Formats." *Comics & Culture: Analytical and Theoretical Approaches to Comics.* Ed. Anne Magnussen and Hans Christian-Christiansen. Copenhagen: University of Copenhagen/ Museum Tusculanem Press. 91–105.

Lefèvre, Pascal, and Christophe Canon. 1996. *Architecture dans le neuvième art/Architectuur in de negende kunst.* Arnhem: NBM-Amstelland Bouw.

Lefèvre, Pascal, and Charles Dierick. 1998. "Introduction." *Forging a New Medium: The Comic Strip in the Nineteenth Century.* Ed. Pascal Lefèvre and Charles Dierick. Brussels: VUB Press. 11–23.

LeGates, Richard T., and Frederic Stout. 2005. "How to Study Cities: Editors' Introduction." *The City Reader.* 3rd ed. London: Routledge. 9–18.

Léger, Marc James. 2006. "Henri Lefebvre and the Moment of the Aesthetic." *Marxism and the History of Art: From William Morris to the New Left.* Ed. Andrew Hemingway. London: Pluto Press. 143–60.

Léger, Marc James, and Cayley Sorochan. 2014. "Psychoprotest: Dérives of the Quebec Maple Spring." *Marxism and Urban Culture.* Ed. Benjamin Fraser. Lanham: Lexington. 89–111.

Lemay, Sylvain. 2007. "*L'Origine* de Marc-Antoine Mathieu, ou le surcroît de l'œuvre." *Poétiques de la bande dessinée.* Ed. Pierre Fresnault-Deruelle and Jacques Samson. Paris: L'Harmattan. 195–205.

Lent, John. 2014. "Foreword." *Transnational Perspectives on Graphic Narratives: Comics at the Cross-roads.* Ed. Shane Denson, Christina Meyer, and Daniel Stein. London: Bloomsbury. xiii–xvi.

Lesage, Sylvain. 2011. "La bande dessinée en son miroir : Images et usages de l'album dans la bande dessinée française." *Érudit* 2.2. Accessed 28 Nov 2017. https://www.erudit.org/en/journals/ memoires/2011-v2-n2-memoires1513107/1001764ar/

Lewis, Joel. 1995. "A Bronx Tale: Will Eisner's 'Dropsie Avenue.'" *Forward* 5 May: 11.

Little, Ben. 2010. "*2000AD*: Understanding the 'British Invasion' of American Comics." *Comics as a Nexus of Cultures: Essays on the Interplay of Media Disciplines and International Perspectives.* Ed. Mark Berninger, Jochen Ecke, and Gideon Haberkorn. Jefferson, NC: McFarland. 140–52.

Liu, Jonathan H. 2011. "*Daytripper* Is Gorgeous and Haunting." *Wired* (31 May). Accessed 5 March 2018. https://www.wired.com/2011/05/daytripper-is-gorgeous-and-haunting/.

Livingstone, David N. 2005. "Science, Text and Space: Thoughts on the Geography of Reading." *Transactions of the Institute of British Geographers* 30: 391–401.

Locke, Simon. 2009. "Considering Comics as Medium, Art, and Culture—the Case of *From Hell.*" *SCAN: Journal of Media Arts Culture* 6.1. http://scan.net.au/scan/journal/display.php?journal _id=127. Accessed 13 February 2018.

Longhurst, Alex. 2000. "Culture and Development: The Impact of 1960s 'desarrollismo.'" *Contemporary Spanish Cultural Studies.* Ed. Barry Jordan and Rikki Morgan-Tamosunas. London: Arnold. 17–28.

Lopes, Dominic McIver. 2009. *A Philosophy of Computer Art.* London: Routledge.

Lopes, Filipe José Seabra Cadete. 2013. "O contributo da arquitectura na identidade da cidade." Master's thesis, Program in Architecture, Universidades Lusíada. http://repositorio.ulusiada .pt/handle/11067/3020.

Loss, Robert. 2013. "'Real Basic Reality, Like AAAAAAAAAARGHHHH!': Notes from Mark Beyer with/without Text." *Comics Journal* (25 April). Accessed 28 July 2017. http://www.tcj .com/real-basic-reality-like-aaaaaaaaaarghhhh-notes-from-mark-beyer-withwithout-text/.

Lukić, Marko, and Tijana Pareanović. 2016. "Strolling through Hell—The Birth of the Aggressive Flâneur." *Journal of Graphic Novels and Comics* 7.4: 322–33.

Lumbala, Hilaire Mbiye. 2009. "Comment la bande dessinée tisse du lien social en Afrique." *Hermés, La Revue* 2.54: 189–90.

Lund, Martin. 2014. "'X Marks the Spot": Urban Dystopia, Slum Voyeurism and Failures of Identity in *District X*.' *Journal of Urban Cultural Studies* 2.1–2: 35–55.

Luria, Sarah. 2011a. "Geotexts." *GeoHumanities: Art, History, Text and the Edge of Place*. Ed. Michael Dear, Jim Ketchum, Sarah Luria, and Doug Richardson. Abingdon: Routledge. 67–70.

Luria, Sarah. 2011b. "Thoreau's Geopoetics." In *GeoHumanities: Art, History, Text and the Edge of Place*. Ed. Michael Dear, Jim Ketchum, Sarah Luria, and Doug Richardson. Abingdon: Routledge. 126–38.

Lus Arana, Luis Miguel (Koldo). 2013. "Le Corbusier leía tebeos: Breves notas sobre las relaciones entre arquitectura y narrativa gráfica." *Ra: Revista de Arquitectura* 15: 47–58.

Lus Arana, Luis Miguel (Koldo). 2006. "La Eclosión del estilo: De la ciudad americana a la utopía Art Nouveau en la obra de Schuiten-Peeters (y Schuiten)." *Urbes* 3: 233–64.

Lutes, Jason. 2008. *Berlin: City of Smoke*. Montreal: Drawn & Quarterly.

Lutes, Jason. 2001. *Berlin: City of Stones*. Montreal: Drawn & Quarterly.

Lutes, Jason. 2018. *Berlin: City of Light*. Montreal: Drawn & Quarterly.

Luther, Diane. 2008. *Neo Tokyo 3: Architecture in Manga and Anime*. Frankfurt: Frankfurt am Main, Dt. Architekturmuseum.

Ma, Daishu. 2015. *Leaf*. Seattle: Fantagraphics.

Macdonald, Sean. 2011. "Two Texts on 'Comics' from China, ca/ 1932: 'In Defense of "Comic Strips"' by Lu Xun and 'Comic Strip Novels' by Mao Dun." Translation and introduction by Sean Macdonald. *ImageTexT: Interdisciplinary Comics Studies* 6.1. http://www.english.ufl.edu/imagetext/archives/v6_1/macdonald/?print.

Macho Stadler, Marta. 2015. "Juegos y rarezas matemáticas: Julius Corentin Acquefacques, prisionero de los sueños." *Pensamiento Matemático* 5.1: 93–100.

MacLeod, Catriona. 2012. "Sex and Death in Quebec: Female AutobioBD and Julie Doucet's *Changements d'adresses*." *European Comic Art* 5.1: 57–70.

Magnussen, Anne. 2009. "Spanish Underground Comics and Society." *Reading the Popular in Contemporary Spanish Texts*. Ed. Shelley Godsland and Nickianne Moody. Newark: University of Delaware Press. 100–20.

Mak, James Charles. 2013. "In Search for an Urban Dystopia—Gotham City," 1–7. https://www.aaschool.ac.uk/Downloads/WritingPrize/2013Shortlist/JamesCMak.pdf.

Makeham, Paul. 2005. "Performing the City." *Theatre Research International* 30.2: 150–60.

Marín i Torné, Marià. 2017. "Gaudí: Poet of Stone, Artistic Hedgehog." *The Barcelona Reader: Cultural Readings of a City*. Ed. Enric Bou and Jaume Subirana. Liverpool: Liverpool University Press. 265–94.

Marrone, Daniel. 2016. "Pictures at a Remove Seth's Drawn Photographs." *ImageTexT* 8.4. Accessed 13 August 2017. http://www.english.ufl.edu/imagetext/archives/v8_4/marrone/.

Marrone, Daniel. 2013. "Between History and Memory: Ambivalent Longing in the Work of Seth." PhD thesis, Birkbeck, University of London.

Marschall, Richard. 1989. *America's Great Comic-Strip Artists*. New York: Abbeville Press.

Martinez, Omar, and Brian Dodge. 2010. "El barrio de La Chueca of Madrid, Spain: An Emerging Epicenter of the Global LGBT Civil Rights Movement." *Journal of Homosexuality* 57.2: 226–48.

Martín Martínez, Antonio. 1998. "Notes on the Birth of the Comics in Spain, 1873–1900." *Forging a New Medium: The Comic Strip in the Nineteenth Century*. Ed. Pascal Lefèvre and Charles Dierick. Brussels: VUB Press. 129–56.

Martínez Castellanos, Rafael. 2002. *Chuecatown*. Barcelona: Odisea.

Marx, Karl. 1977. *Capital*. Vol. 1. Trans. Ben Fowkes, intr. Ernest Mandel. New York: Vintage.

Marx, Karl. 1964. *Economic and Philosophic Manuscripts of 1844*. Trans. Martin Milligan. Ed. and intro. by Dirk J. Struik. New York: International.

Masereel, Frans. 2007 [1919]. *Passionate Journey*. Mineola, NY: Dover.

Masereel, Frans. 2006 [1925]. *The City*. Mineola, NY: Dover.

Mathieu, Marc-Antoine. 2007. *Museum Vaults: Excerpts from the Journal of an Expert*. Trans. Joe Johnson. Paris: NBM, Futuropolis, Musée du Louvre.

Mathieu, Marc-Antoine. 2013. *Julius Corentin Acquefacques, prisonnier des rêves : Le décalage*. Paris: Delcourt.

Mathieu, Marc-Antoine. 2004. *Julius Corentin Acquefacques, prisonnier des rêves : Le début de la fin*. Paris: Delcourt.

Mathieu, Marc-Antoine. 2000. *Dead Memory*. Trans. Helge Dascher. Milwaukie, OR: Dark Horse.

Mathieu, Marc-Antoine. 1995. *Julius Corentin Acquefacques, prisonnier des rêves: La 2.333e dimension*. Paris: Delcourt.

Mathieu, Marc-Antoine. 1993. *Julius Corentin Acquefacques, prisonnier des rêves: Le Processus*. Paris: Delcourt.

Mathieu, Marc-Antoine. 1991. *Julius Corentin Acquefacques, prisonnier des rêves : La Qu . . .* Paris: Delcourt.

Mathieu, Marc-Antoine. 1990. *Julius Corentin Acquefacques, prisonnier des rêves : L'origine*. Paris: Delcourt.

Mauro, Aaron. 2010. "'Mosaic Thresholds': Manifesting the Collection and Production of Comics in the Works of Chris Ware. *ImageTexT: Interdisciplinary Comics Studies* 5.1. Accessed 28 July 2017. http://www.english.ufl.edu/imagetext/archives/v5_1/mauro/.

Mautner, Chris. 2016. Review of *Agony*. *Comics Journal* (21 Mar 2016). Accessed 28 July 2017. http://www.tcj.com/reviews/agony/.

Maynard, Patrick. 2012. "What's So Funny? Comic Content in Depiction." *The Art of Comics: A Philosophical Approach*. Ed. Aaron Meskin and Roy T. Cook. Foreword by Warren Ellis. London: Wiley-Blackwell. 105–24.

McCloud, Scott. 2000. *Reinventing Comics: How Imagination and Technology Are Revolutionizing an Art Form*. New York:. Harper Collins.

McCloud, Scott. 1994. *Understanding Comics: The Invisible Art*. New York: Harper Collins.

McDonough, Tom. 2002. "The Crimes of the Flaneur." *October* 102: 101–22.

McKay, Kelly E. 2015. The Ethics of Occupation: Appropriation and Alignment as Spatial Practices among Mapuche Activists and Student Protesters in Santiago, Chile." diss., University of Minnesota.

McNeill, Donald. 2002. "Barcelona: Urban Identity 1992–2002." *Arizona Journal of Hispanic Cultural Studies* 6: 245–61.

McPhee, Constance C., and Nadine M. Orenstein. 2011. *Infinite Jest: Caricature and Satire from Leonardo to Levine*. New York: Metropolitan Museum of Art.

Mejlænder, Petter. 2008. *Pushwagner*. Oslo: Magikon Forlag.

Mena, Erica. 2015. "About *The Eternaut* and Its Creators." *The Eternaut*. By Héctor Germán Oesterheld and Francisco Solano López. Seattle: Fantagraphics. no pag.

Mendieta, Eduardo. 2008. "The Production of Urban Space in the Age of Transnational Mega-Urbes: Lefebvre's Rhythmanalysis Or Henri Lefebvre: The Philosopher of May '68." *City* 12.2: 148–53.

Menelao, Veronica. 2005. "Sogno di prigioniero: Tre sentieri tra architettura e comunicazione." PhD diss., Dept. of Sociology and Communications, Università di Roma.

Merino, Ana. 2015. "The Impact of Latino Identities and the Humanizing of Multiculturalism in *Love and Rockets.*" Trans. Elizabeth Polli. *Representing Multiculturalism in Comics and Graphic Novels*. Ed. Carolene Ayaka and Ian Hague. New York: Routledge. 34–48.

Merino, Ana. 2001. "Women in Comics: A Space for Recognizing Other Voices." *Comics Journal* 237: no pag.

Merrifield, Andy. 2002. *Metromarxism: A Marxist Tale of the City*. London: Routledge.

Meskin, Aaron, and Roy T. Cook. 2012. "The Art and Philosophy of Comics: An Introduction." *The Art of Comics: A Philosophical Approach*. Ed. Meskin and Cook. Foreword by Warren Ellis. London: Wiley Blackwell. xiv–xli.

Meskin, Aaron, and Roy T. Cook, eds. 2012. *The Art of Comics: A Philosophical Approach.* Foreword by Warren Ellis. London: Wiley Blackwell.

Meyer, Christina. 2012. "Urban America in the Newspaper Comic Strips of the Nineteenth Century: Introducing the Yellow Kid." *ImageText: Interdisciplinary Comics Studies* 6.2.

Miles, Malcolm. 2007. *Cities and Cultures.* London: Routledge.

Miles, Steven, and Malcolm Miles. 2004. *Consuming Cities.* New York: Palgrave Macmillan.

Miller, Ann. 2007. *Reading Bande Dessinée: Critical Approaches to French-Language Comic Strip.* Bristol: Intellect.

Miller, Ann, and Bart Beaty, eds. 2014. *The French Comics Theory Reader.* Leuven: Leuven University Press.

Miller, Ann, and Murray Pratt. 2004. "Transgressive Bodies in the Work of Julie Doucet, Fabrice Neaud and Jean-Christophe Menu: Toward a Theory of the 'AutobioBD.'" *Belphégor* 4.1: no pag. http://etc.dal.ca/belphegor/vo14_no1/articles/04_01_Miller_trnsgr_en_cont.html.

Mills, Josephine. 2015. "Seth: Dominion." Regina: Dunlop Art Gallery. Accessed 13 August 2017. http://e-artexte.ca/27862/1/SethDominion.pdf.

Mira, Alberto. 2004. *De Sodoma a Chueca: Una historia cultural de la homosexualidad en España en el siglo xx.* Madrid: Egales.

Mitchell, David T., and Sharon L. Snyder. 2000. *Narrative Prosthesis: Disability and the Dependencies of Discourse.* Ann Arbor: University of Michigan Press.

Mitchell, Don. 2003. *The Right to the City: Social Justice and the Fight for Public Space.* New York: Guilford Press.

Mitchell, Don. 2000. *Cultural Geography: A Critical Introduction.* Oxford: Blackwell.

Molina, Géraldine. 2007. "Le Paris des Aventures extraordinaires d'Adèle Blanc-Sec de Jacques Tardi : Une 'ville noire'?" *Géographie et Cultures* 61. http://gc.revues.org/2617.

Mollá Liñana, Marta. 2017. "Diseño de una línea de productos de merchandising y su packaging para fomentar la conciencia medioambiental." Grado en Ingenería en Diseño Industrial y Desarrollo de Productos. Valencia: Universitat Politècnica de Valencia.

Molotiu, Andrei. 2012. "Abstract Form: Sequential Dynamism and Iconostasis in Abstract Comics and in Steve Ditko's *Amazing Spider-Man.*" *Critical Approaches to Comics: Theories and Methods.* Ed. Matthew J. Smith and Randy Duncan. New York: Routledge. 84–100.

Montecalvo, Rufus Rey C. 2010. "The Cyberpunk Genre in Japanese Anime and Manga." Requirement for the course History of Modern East Asia. Dept. of History, University of the Philippines Diliman.

Moon, Fábio, and Gabriel Bá. 2011. *Daytripper.* Burbank, CA: DC Comics.

Moore, Alan. 2002. "Alan Moore Interviewed by Eddie Campbell." *Egomania* 2: 1–32.

Moore, Alan, S. Bissette, and J. Totleben. 2011 [1987]. *Saga of the Swamp Thing.* New York: DC Comics.

Moore, Alan, and Eddie Campbell. 2006. *From Hell.* Marietta, GA: Top Shelf.

Moore, Alan, and Eddie Campbell. 1994. *From Hell: The Compleat Scripts.* Brooklandville, MD: Borderline Press.

Moore, Alan, and D. Gibbons. 1995. *Watchmen.* New York: DC Comics.

Moore, Alan, and D. Lloyd. 1990. *V for Vendetta.* New York: DC Comics.

Moore, Alan, and Kevin O'Neill. 1982. *The League of Extraordinary Gentlemen: Black Dossier.* La Jolla, CA: America's Best Comics.

Moore, Alan W. 2004. "Political Economy as Subject and Form in Contemporary Art." *Review of Radical Political Economics* 36.4: 471–86.

Morgan, Harry. 2003. *Principes des littératures dessinées.* Paris: L'An 2.

Morton, Drew. 2010. "Sketching under the Influence? Winsor McCay and the Question of Aesthetic Convergence between Comic Strips and Film." *Animation: An Interdisciplinary Journal* 5.3: 295–312.

Mugavazi, Nyasha. 2017. "How African Comics and Kugali Magazine Are Changing the World." *Comicsverse* 8 September. Accessed 20 July 2018. https://comicsverse.com/african-comics-kugali-magazine/.

Mumford, Lewis. 2005. "What Is a City?" 1937. *The City Reader.* Ed. Richard T. LeGates and Frederic Stout. 3rd ed. London: Routledge. 92–96.

Mumford, Lewis. 1970. *The Culture of Cities.* 1938. New York: Harcourt Brace Jovanovich.

Mumford, Lewis. 1961. *The City in History.* New York: Harcourt, Brace & World.

Mumford, Lewis. 1934. *Technics and Civilization.* New York: Harcourt Brace.

Murray, Dail. 2004. "Introduction." *How the Other Half Lives.* By Jacob A. Riis. New ed. New York: Barnes and Noble. xi–xvi.

Murphy, Susan. 2002. "The Ordinary Street, the Storehouse of Treasures." *Seeking the Centre.* 2001 RLA Conference Proceedings. Ed. Colette Rayment and Mark Levon Byrne. Sydney: RLA Press. 154–68.

Newman, Andy. 2015. "Scram, Boys! It's the Master Builder!" *New York Times,* late ed. (East Coast), 29 March. MB2.

Niedzviecki, Hal. 1999. "My New York Diary [Review]." *Broken Pencil* 11: 63.

Nihei, Tsutomu. 2016 [1998]. *Blame!* Vol. I. New York: Vertical Comics.

Nygaard, Nicole Benestad. 2010. "Pushwagner's *Soft City*: En narrativ of kulturhistorisk tilnærming til tegneserien." Fakultet for humaniora og pedagogikk. Institutt for nordisk og mediefag. Universitetet i Agder.

Oesterheld, Héctor Germán, and Francisco Solano López. 2015. *The Eternaut.* 1957–59. Seattle: Fantagraphics.

Olcayto, Rory. 2012. "Graphic and Novel." *Architects' Journal* (10 December).

Omar Ata, Iasmin. 2017. *Mis(h)adra.* New York: Simon & Schuster.

Op de Beeck, Nathalie. 2006. "Found Objects: (Jem Cohen, Ben Katchor, Walter Benjamin)." *Modern Fiction Studies* 52.4: 807–30.

Otu, John. 2016. "A Critical Study of Emilia Onuegbu's Cartoons." *Chitrolekha International Magazine on Art and Design* 6.1: 90–103.

Page, Joanna. 2016. *Science Fiction in Argentina: Technologies of the Text in a Material Multiverse.* Ann Arbor: University of Michigan Press.

Page, Joanna. 2010. "Intellectuals, Revolution and Popular Culture: A New Reading of *El Eternauta*." *Journal of Latin American Cultural Studies* 19.1: 45–62.

Pallister, James. 2015. "A Comic Look at Moses?" Architectural Review. 12 May. Accessed 11 December 2017. https://www.architectural-review.com/rethink/reviews/a-comic-look-at-moses/8681379.article.

Papieau, Isabelle. 2001. *La banlieue de Paris dans la bande dessinée.* Paris: Harmattan.

Park, Robert. 1967. *On Social Control and Collective Behavior.* Chicago: University of Chicago Press.

Pavlović, Tatjana. 2012. *The Mobile Nation: España Cambia de Piel (1954–64).* Bristol: Intellect.

Peeters, Benoît. 2010. "Between Writing and Image: A Scriptwriter's Way of Working." *European Comic Art* 3.1: 105–15.

Peeters, Benoît. 1998. *Lire la bande dessinée.* Paris: Casterman.

Peeters, Benoît, and Jacques Samson. 2010. *Chris Ware: La bande dessinée réinventée.* Brussels: Les Impressions nouvelles.

Peeters, Benoît, and François Schuiten. 2017 [1983]. *Samaris.* San Diego: IDW.

Peeters, Benoît, and François Schuiten. 1996. *Le Guide des cités.* Brussels: Casterman. (Published in German as *Führer durch die geheimnisvollen Städt.* Stuttgart: Feest Comics 1997).

Pereira, José Miguel Tavares Rodrigues. 2008. "A arquitectura na representaçao da arquitectura." Prova Final de Licenciatura en Arquitectura, Dept. of Architecture, Universidade de Coimbra.

Pérez, Jorge. 2012. "Del cómic a la pantalla: Chuecatown y los irreverentes caminos de una adaptación *queer.*" *Teoría y práctica de la adaptación fílmica.* Ed. Barbara Zecchi. Madrid: Editorial Complutense. 179–204.

Pérez, Pepo. 2016. "A Brand New (Digital) World: A Modo de Introducción." *Cómic digital hoy: Una introducción en presente.* Ed. Pepo Pérez. Barcelona: ACDCómic. ix–xxxvii.

Pérez-Sánchez, Gema. 2007. *Queer Transitions in Contemporary Spanish Culture.* Albany: State University of New York Press.

Perret, Marion D. 2001. "'And Suit the Action to the Word': How a Comics Panel Can Speak Shakespeare." *The Language of Comics: Word and Image.* Ed. Robin Varnum and Christina T. Gibbons. Jackson: University Press of Mississippi. 123–44.

Perry, George, and Alan Aldridge. 1971. *The Penguin Book of Comics.* Harmondsworth, Middlesex: Penguin Books.

Philo, Chris, and Gerry Kearns. 1993. "Culture, History, Capital: A Critical Introduction to the Selling of Places." *Selling Places: The City as Cultural Capital Past and Present.* Ed. Philo and Kearns. Oxford: Pergamon. 1–32.

Picone, Michael D. 2013. "Comic Art in Museums and Museums in Comic Art." *European Comic Art* 6.2: 40–68.

Picone, Michael D. 2009. "Teaching Franco-Belgian *Bande Dessinée.*" *Teaching the Graphic Novel.* Ed. Stephen E. Tabachnick. New York: MLA. 299–323.

Pilcher, Tim, and Brad Brooks. 2005. *The Essential Guide to World Comics.* London: Collins & Brown.

Pinçonnat, Crystel. 2007. "Éloge du déplacement: Paris, cartographies littéraires ou quand la figure fait sens." *Le Manuscrit,* 13–34. hal-01382339.

Platz Cortsen, Rikke. 2014. "Full Page Insight: The Apocalyptic Moment in Comics Written by Alan Moore." *Journal of Graphic Novels and Comics* 5.4: 397–410.

Popova, Maria. 2014. "How New York Became New York: A Love Letter to Jane Jacobs, Tucked inside a Graphic Biography of Robert Moses." Brain Pickings. 18 December Accessed 10 December 2017. https://www.brainpickings.org/2014/12/18/robert-moses-master-builder-new-york-nobrow/.

Postema, Barbara. 2015. "Establishing Relations: Photography in Wordless Comics." *Image & Narrative* 16.2: 84–95.

Postema, Barbara. 2013. *Narrative Structure in Comics: Making Sense of Fragments.* Rochester: RIT Press.

Prince, Michael J. 2017. "The Magic of Patriarchal Oppression in Alan Moore and Eddie Campbell's *From Hell.*" *Journal of Graphic Novels and Comics* 8.3: 252–63.

Prough, Jennifer Sally. 2011. *Straight from the Heart: Gender, Intimacy, and the Cultural Production of Shojo Manga.* Jackson: University Press of Mississippi.

Pushwagner, Hariton (Terje Brofos). 2008. *Soft City.* 1969–75. New York: New York Review Comics.

Pushwagner, Hariton. 2008. *Soft City.* Oslo: No Comprendo Press.

Quayson, Ato. 2007. *Aesthetic Nervousness: Disability and the Crisis of Representation.* New York: Columbia University Press.

Quiring, Björn. 2010. "'A Fiction That We Must Inhabit'—Sense Production in Urban Spaces according to Alan Moore and Eddie Campbell's *From Hell.*" *Comics and the City: Urban Space in Print, Picture and Sequence.* Ed. Jörn Ahrens and Arno Meteling. New York: Continuum. 199–213.

Raban, Jonathan. 1974. *Soft City.* London: Hamish Hamilton.

Raeburn, Daniel. 2004. *Chris Ware.* New Haven: Yale University Press.

Ramalhete Gomes, Miguel. 2007. "The City and the Plan: Schuiten and Peeter's Graphic Meta-utopias." *Spaces of Utopia: An Electronic Journal* 4: 88–105. http://ler.letras.up.pt.

Repetti, Massimo. 2007. "African Wave: Specificity and Cosmopolitanism in African Comics." *African Arts* 40.2: 16–35.

Resina, Joan Ramon. 2008. *Barcelona's Vocation of Modernity: Rise and Decline of an Urban Image.* Stanford: Stanford University Press.

Ribbens, Kees. 2011. "The First World War in *Bande dessinée.*" *European Comic Art* 4.2: 239–44.

Ricard, Sylvain, Bruno Ricard and Christophe Gaultier. 2013. *Beirut 1990: Snapshots of a Civil War.* 2004. Los Angeles: Humanoids, 2013.

Richardson, Douglas. 2011. "Converging Worlds: Geography and the Humanities." *Envisioning Landscapes, Making Worlds: Geography and the Humanities.* Ed. Stephen Daniels, Dydia DeLyser, J. Nicholas Entrikin, and Douglas Richardson. Abingdon: Routledge. xix–xxi.

Richardson, Nathan. 2011. *Constructing Spain: The Reimagination of Space and Place in Fiction and Film, 1953–2003.* Lewisburg: Bucknell University Press.

Richir, Alice. 2011. "La Tour de Peeters et Schuiten: Ruine d'une utopie moderne." *Inter-Lignes* 7: 61–76.

Rid, Thomas. 2009. "Razzia: A Turning Point in Modern Strategy." *Terrorism and Political Violence* 21: 617–35.

Rifkind, Candida. 2015. "The Biotopographies of Seth's *George Sprott 1894–1975.*" *Material Cultures in Canada.* Ed. Thomas Allan and Jennifer Blair. Waterloo: Wilfred Laurier University Press. 225–46.

Riis, Jacob A. 2004. *How the Other Half Lives: Studies among the Tenements of New York.* Intro. Dail Murray. New York: Barnes and Noble.

Robb, Jenny E. 2007. "Winsor McCay, George Randolph Chester, and the Tale of the *Jungle Imps.*" *American Periodicals* 17.2: 245–59.

Robbins, Jill. 2011. *Crossing through Chueca: Lesbian Literary Culture in Queer Madrid.* Minneapolis: University of Minnesota Press.

Robbins, Trina. 2001. *The Great Women Cartoonists.* New York: Watson-Guptill.

Roeder, Katherine. 2014. *Wide Awake in Slumberland: Fantasy, Mass Culture, and Modernism in the Art of Winsor McCay.* Jackson: University Press of Mississippi.

Roeder, Katherine. 2011. "Seeing Inside-Out in the Funny Pages." *American Art* 25.1: 24–27.

Roth, Laurence. 2007. "Drawing Contracts: Will Eisner's Legacy." *Jewish Quarterly Review* 97.3: 463–84.

Rosenzweig, Roy. 1983. *Eight Hours for What We Will: Workers and Leisure in an Industrial City, 1870–1920.* Cambridge: Cambridge University Press.

Rossiter, Caroline. 2009. "Early French Caricature (1795–1830) and English Influence." *European Comic Art* 2.1: 41–64.

Round, Julia. 2010. "'Be Vewy, Vewy Quiet. We're Hunting Wippers: A Barthesian Analysis of the Construction of Fact and Fiction in Alan Moore and Eddie Campbell's *From Hell.*" *The Rise and Reason of Comics and Graphic Literature: Critical Essays on the Form.* Ed. Joyce Goggin and Dan Hassler-Forest. Jefferson, NC: McFarland. 188–201.

Royal, Derek Parker. 2011a. "Jewish Comics; Or, Visualizing Current Jewish Narrative." *Shofar* 29.2: 1–12.

Royal, Derek Parker. 2011b. "Sequential Sketches of Ethnic Identity: Will Eisner's *A Contract with God* as Graphic Cycle." *College Literature* 38.3: 150–67.

Royal, Derek Parker. 2011c. "There Goes the Neighborhood: Cycling Ethnoracial Tensions in Will Eisner's *Dropsie Avenue.*" *Shofar* 29.2: 120–45.

Rubione, Alfredo V. E. 1995. "H. G. Oesterheld: Géneros erráticos y avatares de la ficción." *Jornadas Internacionales de Literatura Argentina/Comparatística: Actas.* Buenos Aires: Facultad de Filosofía y Letras, Universidad de Buenos Aires. 229–34.

Sabin, Roger. 1996. *Comics, Comix & Graphic Novels.* London: Phaidon.

Sadoul, Numa. 2000. *Jacques Tardi: Entretiens avec Numa Sadoul.* Paris: Niffle-Cohen.

Sagan, Hans Nicholas. 2015. "Specters of '68: Protest, Policing, and Urban Space." Diss., University of California, Berkeley.

Sam, Sherman. 2012. "Hariton Pushwagner." *Artforum International* 51.3, 284–85.

Sánchez González, Darío. 2014. "Maricas de etiqueta: Identidad gay en el cine reciente de España y el cono sur." PhD diss., Graduate Program in Spanish, Rutgers, The State University of New Jersey.

Sánchez Soriano, Juan José. 2016. "Iluminando el cuarto oscuro: Tendencias discursivas e imaginario queer en la cinematografía española contemporánea." *Arte y Políticas de Identidad* 15: 171–86.

Santullo, Rodolfo, and Matías Bergara. 2015. *Dengue*. 2012. Los Angeles: Humanoids.

Satrapi, Marjane. 2007. *Persepolis*. 2000–2002. New York: Pantheon.

Sauer, Carl. 1925. "The Morphology of Landscape." *University of California Publications in Geography* 2: 19–54.

Schivelbusch, Wolfgang. 1986. *The Railway Journey: The Industrialization of Time and Space in the Nineteenth Century*. Berkeley: University of California Press.

Schneider, Grace. 2016. *What Happens When Nothing Happens: Boredom and Everyday Life in Contemporary Comics*. Leuven: Leuven University Press.

Scholz, Janek. 2017. "Utopia, Heterotopia, Dystopia—Water in Portuguese and Brazilian Comics." *Brasiliana: Journal for Brazilian Studies* 5.2: 269–80.

Schumacher, Michael. 2010. *Will Eisner: A Dreamer's Life in Comics*. New York: Bloomsbury.

Sécheret, Laurent, and Thomas Schlesser. 2010. "Tardi, un carnaval des monstres." *Sociétés & Représentations* 29.1: 79–98.

Seck, Fatoumata. 2018. "Goorgoorlou, the Neoliberal *Homo Senegalensis*: Comics and Economics in Postcolonial Senegal." *Journal of African Cultural Studies* 30.3: 263–78.

Seneca, Matt. 2010. "Metropoli: Dominion and Panterville." *Death to the Universe* (October). Accessed 20 August 2017. *http://deathtotheuniverse.blogspot.com/*.

Sennett, Richard. 2008. *The Craftsman*. New Haven: Yale University Press.

Sennett, Richard. 1994. *Flesh and Stone: The Body and the City in Western Civilization*. London: W. W. Norton.

Sennett, Richard. 1992. *The Conscience of the Eye: The Design and Social Life of Cities*. New York: W. W. Norton.

Seth (Gregory Gallant). 2015. *Palookaville 22*. Montreal: Drawn & Quarterly.

Seth (Gregory Gallant). 2011. *The Great Northern Brotherhood of Canadian Cartoonists*. Montreal: Drawn & Quarterly.

Seth (Gregory Gallant). 2009. *George Sprott (1894–1975)*. Montreal: Drawn & Quarterly.

Seth (Gregory Gallant). 2005. *Wilmbledon Green: The Greatest Comic Book Collector in the World*. Montreal: Drawn & Quarterly.

Seth (Gregory Gallant). 2004. *Clyde Fans I*. Montreal: Drawn & Quarterly.

Seth (Gregory Gallant). 1996. *It's a Good Life, if You Don't Weaken*. Montreal: Drawn & Quarterly.

Seth (Gregory Gallant). 1991–2017. *Palookaville*. 23 vols. Montreal: Drawn & Quarterly.

Shannon, Edward A. 2010. "Something Black in the American Psyche: Formal Innovation and Freudian Imagery in the Comics of Winsor McCay and Robert Crumb." *Canadian Review of American Studies* 40.2: 187–211.

Sheridan, Martin. 1942. *Comics and Their Creators: Life Stories of American Cartoonists*. Hale, Cushman & Flint.

Sherwin, Skye. 2012. "Artist of the Week 202: Hariton Pushwagner." *Guardian* (August 9). Accessed 14 November 2017. https://www.theguardian.com/artanddesign/2012/aug/09/artist-week-hariton-pushwagner.

Shiel, Mark, and Tony Fitzmaurice, eds. 2001. *Cinema and the City: Film and Urban Societies in a Global Context*. Oxford: Blackwell.

Shields, Rob. 2005. *Lefebvre, Love and Struggle: Spatial Dialectics*. London: Routledge.

Silverberg, David. 2008. "Autobiographic." *Broken Pencil* 39: 11–14.

Simmel, Georg. 2010. "The Metropolis and Mental Life." In *The Blackwell City Reader*. Edited by G. Bridge and S. Watson. Malden, Mass./Oxford & West Sussex, UK: Wiley–Blackwell. 103–10.

Simmel, Georg. 2000. "The Metropolis and Mental Life." *Readings in Social Theory: The Classic Tradition to Post-Modernism*. 3rd ed. Ed. James Farganis. New York: McGraw Hill. 149–57.

Singer, Barnett, and John Langdon. 2004. *Cultural Force: Makers and Defenders of the French Colonial Empire*. Madison: University of Wisconsin Press.

Sistig, Joachim. 2008. "Jacques Tardi – un auteur sous influence." *Frankreichforschung und Französischstudium* 33.130-131: 15–22.

Slessor, Catherine. 2004. "The City as Theatre." *Architectural Review* (March): 68–71.

Smart, Tom. 2016. *Palookaville: Seth and the Art of Graphic Autobiography*. Erin, ON: The Porcupine's Quill.

Smith, Greg M. 2010. "Will Eisner, Vaudevillian of the Cityscape." *Comics and the City: Urban Space in Print, Picture and Sequence*. New York: Continuum. 183–98.

Smith, Matthew J., and Randy Duncan, eds. 2012. *Critical Approaches to Comics: Theories and Methods*. New York: Routledge.

Smith, Neil. 1984. *Uneven Development: Nature, Capital and the Production of Space*. Oxford: Basil Blackwell.

Smolderen, Thierry. 2014a. "Graphic Hybridization, the Crucible of Comics." *The French Comics Theory Reader*. Ed. Ann Miller and Bart Beaty. Leuven: Leuven University Press. 47–61.

Smolderen, Thierry. 2014b. *The Origins of Comics: From William Hogarth to Winsor McCay*. Jackson: University Press of Mississippi.

Smolderen, Thierry. 2003. "Preface." *Stuff and Non-sense*. Arthur Burdett Frost. Seattle: Fantagraphics. 13.

Sobrer, Josep Miquel. 2002. "Against Barcelona? Gaudí, the City, and Nature." *Arizona Journal of Hispanic Cultural Studies* 6: 205–19.

Soja, Edward W. 1996. *Thirdspace: Journeys to Los Angeles and Other Real-and-Imagined Places*. Cambridge, MA: Blackwell.

Soja, Edward W. 1980. "The Socio–Spatial Dialectic." *Annals of the Association of American Geographers* 70(2): 207–25.

Stanek, Lukasz. 2011. *Henri Lefebvre on Space: Architecture, Urban Research, and the Production of Theory*. Minneapolis; London: University of Minnesota Press.

Steimberg, Alejo. 2004. "Les cités obscures de Schuiten et Peeters: analyse d'un dispositif fantastique transmédiatique." *Cuadernos de Filología Francesa* 16: 207–21.

Steiner, Wendy. 2004. "Pictorial Narrativity." In *Narrative across Media: The Language of Storytelling*. Ed. Marie-Louise Ryan. Lincoln and London: University of Nebraska Press. 145–77.

Stephanides, Adam. 2004. "Dead Memory." *Comics Journal* 261: 42–43.

Stone, Aug. 2016. "Joost Swarte: Scratching the Surface." *Comics Journal* (17 Octobert). Accessed 28 July 2017. http://www.tcj.com/joost-swarte-scratching-the-surface/.

Straw, Will, and Alexandra Boutros. 2010. "Introduction." *Circulation and the City: Essays on Urban Culture*. Ed. Alexandra Boutros and Will Straw. Montreal: McGill-Queen's University Press. 3–20.

Subirós, Pep. 1999. "Estrategias culturales y renovación urbana." *Derecho y Opinión* 7: 683–704.

Subirós, Pep. 1992. "The Cultural Olympiad: Objectives, Programme and Development." Barcelona: Centre d'Estudis Olímpics, Universitat Autònoma de Barcelona. Accessed 6 August 2015. http://olympicstudies.uab.es/pdf/wp114_eng.pdf.

Suhr, André. 2010. "Seeing the City through a Frame: Marc-Antoine Mathieu's Acquefaques Comics." *Comics and the City: Urban Space in Print, Picture and Sequence*. Ed. Jörn Ahrens and Arno Meteling. New York: Continuum. 231–46.

Suvin, Darko. 1979. *Metamorphoses of Science Fiction: On the Poetics and History of a Literary Genre*. New Haven: Yale University Press.

Swarte, Joost. 2012a. *Is That All There Is?* Seattle: Fantagraphics.

Swarte, Joost. 2012b. "The Joost Swarte Interview." Interviewers Daniel Peniston and Kim Thompson. *Comics Journal* (5 November). Accessed 28 July 2017. http://www.tcj.com/the-joost-swarte-interview/.

Swarte, Joost. 2010. "[Ann Miller] Interview with Joost Swarte." *European Comic Art* 3.2: 209–15.

Swarte, Joost. 1980. "The Comix Factory." *Read Yourself RAW*. Ed. Art Spiegelman and Françoise Mouly. New York: Pantheon, 1987.

Tardi, Jacques. 2011. *The Extraordinary Adventures of Adèle Blanc-Sec*: Vol. 2. *The Mad Scientist and Mummies on Parade*. Seattle: Fantagraphics.

Tardi, Jacques. 2010. *The Extraordinary Adventures of Adèle Blanc-Sec*: Vol. 1. *Pterror over Paris and The Eiffel Tower Demon*. Seattle: Fantagraphics.

Tensuan, Theresa M. 2006. "Comic Visions and Revisions in the Work of Lynda Barry and Marjane Satrapi." *Modern Fiction Studies* 52.4: 947–64.

Thévenet, Jean-Marc, and Francis Rambert, eds. 2010. *Archi & BD: La ville dessinée*. Paris: Monografik.

Thom, Danielle. 2013. "Impolite Interventions? English Satirical Prints in the Presence of the Academy, c. 1750–1780." *European Comic Art* 6.2: 13–39.

Thon, Jan-Noël, and Lukas R. A. Wilde. 2016. "Introduction: Mediality and Materiality of Contemporary Comics." *Journal of Graphic Novels and Comics* 7.3: 233–41.

Todorov, Tzvetan. 1977. "The Typology of Detective Fiction." *The Poetics of Prose*. Trans. Richard Howard. Ithaca: Cornell University Press. 42–52.

Tomé, Marcel Luiz. 2013. "As inovações estéticas e narrativas nos quadrinhos autorais de Fábio Moon e Gabriel Bá: Un estudo de *Daytripper*." Master's thesis, Program in Communication, City University of São Caetano do Sul.

Torres, El, and Jesús Alonso Iglesias. 2017. *The Ghost of Gaudí*. St. Louis: Lion Forge.

Trabado Cabado, José Manuel. 2017. "Extranjero en tu propia ciudad: Una relectura de *El Eternauta* en la obra de Ricardo Barreiro." *Bulletin of Hispanic Studies* 94.7: 765–87.

Traugott, Mark. 2010. *The Insurgent Barricade*. Berkeley: University of California Press.

Tuan, Yi-Fu. 2013. *Landscapes of Fear*. Minneapolis: University of Minnesota Press.

Uidhir, Christy Mag. 2012. "Comics and Collective Authorship." *The Art of Comics: A Philosophical Approach*. Ed. Aaron Meskin and Roy T. Cook. Foreword by Warren Ellis. London: Wiley-Blackwell. 47–67.

Urban, Florian. 2016. "Robert Moses: The Master Builder of New York City." *Planning Perspectives* 31.4: 659–61.

Uricchio, William. 2010. "The Batman's Gotham City™: Story, Ideology, Performance." *Comics and the City: Urban Space in Print, Picture and Sequence*. Ed. Jörn Ahrens and Arno Meteling. London: Continuum. 119–32.

Van Der Hoorne, Mélanie. 2012. *Bricks and Balloons: Architecture in Comic-Strip Form*. Rotterdam: 010 Publishers.

Varnum, Robin, and Christina T. Gibbons. 2001. "Introduction." *The Language of Comics: Word and Image*. Jackson: University Press of Mississippi. ix–xix.

Vieira, Marina. 2011. "Urban Images in Comic Books: Representation of Metropolis and Gotham in the Late 1930s." *International Journal of the Image* 1.1: 45–56.

Villaamil, Fernando. 2004. *La transformación de la identidad gay en España*. Madrid: Catarata.

Vollmar, Rob. 2012. "*Daytripper* by Fábio Moon and Gabriel Bá." *World Literature Today* 86.2: 68–69.

Vollmar, Rob. 2011. "The Extraordinary Adventures of Adele Blanc-Sec. Vol 1 by Jacques Tardi" [Book Review]. *World Literature Today*. https://www.worldliteraturetoday.org/2011/july/extraordinary-adventures-adele-blanc-sec-vol-1-jacques-tardi.

Vonnegut, Kurt Jr. 1970. "The Mysterious Madame Blavatsky." *McCall's* (March): 142–44.

Ware, Chris. 2012a. *Building Stories*. New York: Pantheon.

Ware, Chris. 2012b. "Foreword." *Is That All There Is?* By Joost Swarte. Seattle: Fantagraphics. 3–6.

Ware, Chris. 2008. "Introduction." *Soft City*. Hariton Pushwagner (Terje Brofos). 1969–1975. New York: New York Review Comics. 5–6.

Wark, McKenzie. 2011. *The Beach beneath the Street: The Everyday Life and Glorious Times of the Situationist International*. London: Verso.

Wartenberg, Thomas E. 2012. "Wordy Pictures: Theorizing the Relationship between Image and Text in Comics." *The Art of Comics: A Philosophical Approach*. Ed. Aaron Meskin and Roy T. Cook. Foreword by Warren Ellis. London: Wiley-Blackwell. 87–104.

Watson, Sasha. 2009. "A Morsel of the Infinite: The Art of Marc-Antoine Mathieu." *Arthur Magazine*. Accessed 28 November 2017. https://arthurmag.com/2009/02/19/a-morsel-of -the-infinite-the-art-of-marc-antoine-mathieu/.

Waugh, Coulton. 1974 [1947]. *The Comics*. New York: Luna Press.

Weizman, Eyal. 2012. "Archaeology of the Present: Organized Crime through the Study of Urban Built Environments." *Journal of International Affairs* 66.1: 163–68.

Weizman, Eyal. 2006. "Introduction to The War of Streets and Houses by Thomas Bugeaud." *Cabinet Magazine* 22: no pag.

Weldon, Glen. 2016. *The Caped Crusade: Batman and the Rise of Nerd Culture*. New York: Simon & Schuster.

Weschler, Lawrence. 1993. "A Wanderer in the Perfect City." *New Yorker* 9 August: 58–67.

Widiss, Benjamin. 2013. "Comics as Non-Sequential Art: Chris Ware's Joseph Cornell." *Drawing from Life: Memory and Subjectivity in Comic Art*. Ed. Jane Tolmie. Jackson: University Press of Mississippi. 86–111.

Williams, Raymond. 2007. "The Future of Cultural Studies." *Politics of Modernism: Against the New Conformists*. London: Verso. 151–62.

Wirth, Louis. 1938. "Urbanism as Way of Life." *American Journal of Sociology* 44.1: 1–24.

Witek, Joseph. 2012. "Comics Modes: Caricature and Illustration in the Crumb Family's *Dirty Laundry*." *Critical Approaches to Comics: Theories and Methods*. Ed. Matthew J. Smith and Randy Duncan. New York: Routledge. 27–42.

Witek, Joseph, ed. 2007. *Art Spiegelman: Conversations*. Jackson: University Press of Mississippi.

Wolfreys, Julian. 2004. "London Khorographic." *ImageTexT: Interdisciplinary Comics Studies* 1.2. Accessed 28 July 2017. http://www.english.ufl.edu/imagetext/archives/v1_2/wolfreys.

Wolk, Douglas. 2017. "Dystopias, Fantasies, Memoirs." *New York Times Book Review* (1 January): 18–19.

Wolk, Douglas. 2012. "Dreams of Youth." *New York Times Book Review* (15 April): 24.

Wolk, Douglas. 2007. *Reading Comics: How Graphic Novels Work and What They Mean*. Cambridge, MA: Da Capo Press.

Worden, Daniel. 2010. "On Modernism's Ruins: The Architecture of 'Building Stories' and *Lost Buildings*." *The Comics of Chris Ware: Drawing Is a Way of Thinking*. Ed. David N. Ball and Martha B. Kuhlman. Jackson: University Press of Mississippi. 107–20.

Wright, Leslee Rene. 2006. "Re-Imagining Genre: Comics, Literature, and Textual Form." PhD diss., English, University of Nebraska.

Wrobel, Jasmin. 2017. "Narrating Other Perspectives, Re-Drawing History: The Protagonization of Afro-Brazilians in the Work of Graphic Novelist Marcelo d'Salete." *Literature and Ethics in Contemporary Brazil*. Ed. Vinicius Mariano De Carvalho and Nicola Gavioli. London: Routledge. 106–23.

Xiao, Tie. 2013. "Masereel, Lu, and the Development of the Woodcut Picture Book (連環畫) in China." *CLCWeb: Comparative Literature and Culture* 15.2 (2013): no pag. https://doi. org/10.7771/1481–4374.2230.

Yanke, Rebeca. 2016. "Intoxicadas por el 'boom' del 'detox.'" *El Mundo* 25 April: 27.

Yanow, Sophie. 2017. *What Is a Glacier?* Philadelphia; Washington,: Retrofit; Big Planet.

Yanow, Sophie. 2014. *War of Streets and Houses*. Minneapolis: Uncivilized Books.

Yegulalp, Serdar. 2016. "Tsutomu Nihei's 'Blame!': Sisyphus in the Labyrinth." *Ganriki*. Accessed 11 February 2018. https://www.ganriki.org/article/blame/.

York, Chris. 2013. "'Architectural Scripts': Gotham and the Museum in Batman Comics, 1946–1963." *International Journal of Comics Art* 15.2: 702–12.

Zaleski, Jeff. "Amy and Jordan." *Publishers Weekly* (22 March 2004): 64.

Ziegler, Kevin. 2013. "Drawing on the Margins of History: English-Language Graphic Narratives in Canada." PhD diss., English, University of Waterloo.

Zukin, Sharon. 1995. *The Cultures of Cities*. Malden, MA: Oxford.

INDEX

ABOUT THE AUTHOR

Benjamin Fraser is professor of Hispanic studies and head of the department of Spanish and Portuguese in the College of Humanities at the University of Arizona. He has held faculty positions at Christopher Newport University, the College of Charleston, and East Carolina University, where he was department chair from 2014 to 2018. Fraser is the founding and executive editor of the *Journal of Urban Cultural Studies,* editor-in-chief of *Hispania* (2018–2021), senior editor of the *Arizona Journal of Hispanic Cultural Studies,* and founding co-editor of the Hispanic Urban Studies book series. He has published sixteen books and some eighty essays on themes of urban life, disability, literary and cultural studies, film and visual studies, and transportation and mobility. His comics scholarship has appeared in *European Comic Art* (2018), *Romance Studies* (2018), *Journal of Spanish Cultural Studies* (2018), *Transmodernity: Journal of Peripheral Cultural Production of the Luso-Hispanic World* (2018), *International Journal of Comic Art* (2016), *Revista Iberoamericana* (2012), the edited book *Entre la ética y la estética*: *Estudios en homenaje a Joan Gilabert* (2017), and the single-authored monographs *Disability Studies and Spanish Culture* (Liverpool University Press, 2013), *Cognitive Disability Aesthetics* (University of Toronto Press, 2018), and *The Art of Pere Joan*: *Space, Landscape and Comics Form* (University of Texas Press, 2019).